PARTY POLICY AND GOVERNMENT COALITIONS

Also by M. J. Laver

PLAYING POLITICS
THE POLITICS OF PRIVATE DESIRES
THE CRIME GAME
SOCIAL CHANGE AND PUBLIC POLICY
INVITATION TO POLITICS
MULTIPARTY GOVERNMENT (*with N. Schofield*)

Also by Ian Budge

SCOTTISH POLITICAL BEHAVIOUR (*with D. W. Urwin*)
AGREEMENT AND THE STABILITY OF DEMOCRACY
POLITICAL STRATIFICATION AND DEMOCRACY
   (*with J. A. Brand*)
BELFAST: APPROACH TO CRISIS (*with C. O'Leary*)
PARTY IDENTIFICATION AND BEYOND (*editor with I. Crewe
   and D. J. Farlie*)
VOTING AND PARTY COMPETITION (*with D. J. Farlie*)
EXPLAINING AND PREDICTING ELECTIONS
   (*with D. J. Farlie*)
THE NEW BRITISH POLITICAL SYSTEM
   (*editor with D. Mackay*)
IDEOLOGY, STRATEGY AND PARTY MOVEMENT (*editor with
   D. Robertson and D. J. Hearl*)
PARTIES AND DEMOCRACY (*with H. Keman*)

Party Policy and Government Coalitions

Edited by

M. J. Laver
Professor of Political Science and Sociology
University College of Galway

and

Ian Budge
Professor of Government
University of Essex

M

St. Martin's Press

First published in Great Britain 1992 by
THE MACMILLAN PRESS LTD
Houndmills, Basingstoke, Hampshire RG21 2XS
and London
Companies and representatives
throughout the world

A catalogue record for this book is available
from the British Library.

ISBN 0–333–55617–8

Printed in Great Britain by
Antony Rowe Ltd
Chippenham, Wiltshire

First published in the United States of America 1992 by
Scholarly and Reference Division,
ST. MARTIN'S PRESS, INC.,
175 Fifth Avenue,
New York, N.Y. 10010

ISBN 0–312–07979–6

Library of Congress Cataloging-in-Publication Data
Party policy and government coalitions / edited by M. J. Laver and Ian
Budge.
p.   cm.
Includes bibliographical references (p.   ) and index.
ISBN 0–312–07979–6
1. Political parties—Europe.   2. Coalition governments—Europe.
I. Laver, Michael, 1949–   .   II. Budge, Ian.
JN94. A979P377   1992   92–3447
324.2'094—dc20   CIP

Contents

List of Tables

vii

List of Figures

List of Figures

Notes on the Contributors

Judith Bara is Senior Lecturer and Head of Department, Ealing College, England. Associated with the Manifesto Research Group from its foundation, Dr Bara's particular interests are the politics of Israel, on which she has written both from a comparative and historical point of view.

Torbjorn Bergman is Assistant Professor of Political Science, University of Umea, Sweden. Dr Bergman has recently returned from working on coalition theory at the University of Minnesota and is currently undertaking a study of Swedish politics from that perspective.

Ian Budge is Professor of Government, University of Essex, Colchester, England. Director of the Manifesto Research Group since 1979, Professor Budge has studied many aspects of comparative democratic politics, from voting in elections to party behaviour in government. He has tried to link this research with central questions of democratic theory, and is currently relating the programmatic emphases of political parties to government action in order to check key assertions of the mandate theory of party democracy.

Karl Dittrich is Associate Professor of Politics, University of Limburg, Maastricht, The Netherlands. Dr Dittrich is Dean of Faculty at the new University of Limburg and has conducted several studies of Dutch party politics, covering elections, modes of competition and now coalition behaviour.

Derek John Hearl is Associate, West European Politics Centre, University of Exeter, England. Within comparative politics, Dr Hearl's special interests are the politics of the Low Countries, with special emphasis on Belgium and Luxembourg and European Liberal Parties.

Hans-Dieter Klingemann is a founder member of the Manifesto Research Group, Professor of Politics at the Free University of Berlin and a Director of Research at the Science Centre, Berlin. Well-known for his work on comparative electoral behaviour he is now engaged, from the Science Centre, in fostering systematic research on the new patterns of democratic voting and party competition emerging in Eastern Europe.

xvi

M.J. Laver is Professor of Politics, University College, Galway, Ireland. A leading rational choice theorist and analyst, Professor Laver has written many books and articles on political parties and their activities in elections and governments. He has also authored a book popularising rational choice analyses entitled *Playing Politics*.

Jorn Leipart has just moved from the Norwegian Social Science Archive at Bergen to Oslo, where he is now an independent political consultant.

Alfio Mastropaolo is Professor of Political Science, University of Palermo, Italy. Professor Mastropaolo is primarily a political theorist in the Weberian tradition, with a strong interest in politics as a profession. He is joint editor of *Teoria Politica*, a leading Italian journal of theoretical issues in politics.

François Petry is Assistant Professor of Public Administration, University of Manitoba, Canada. Dr Petry has worked on both sides of the Atlantic. As a Frenchman now resident in Canada he is well versed in the politics of both countries. His extensive research has been concerned with applying and checking rational choice models in the context of actual politics and administration.

Tove-Lise Schou is Associate Professor of Politics, University of Copenhagen, Denmark. Dr Schou has worked on the mapping of Danish parties' ideological positions as well as on governmental politics in Denmark. She has also authored a study of cabinet decision-making there.

Martin Slater has had a varied career in universities, business and administration. He is currently working as a business consultant in Milan.

Kaare Strom is Associate Professor of Political Science, University of California at San Diego, USA. Of Norwegian origin, Dr Strom has worked most of his life in the United States, but has retained his interest in Western European politics. He is the author of a book and articles on minority governments which have been important in redirecting coalition research towards a concern with this important phenomenon.

Pieter Tops is Associate Professor of Administration, University of Nymegan, The Netherlands. Dr Tops is primarily a specialist in local government coalitions in the Netherlands, so it has been a natural extension of his research to analyse the formation of national coalition governments as well.

Andrea Volkens is a collaborator of Klingemann at the Science Centre, Berlin, and has been particularly concerned with the archival side of the Manifesto Research Group's work. She has extended the collection and coding of documents to several new countries and has played a large part in collecting party and election documents for the new democracies of Eastern Europe.

Introduction

This book deals with a topic which is absolutely central to the business of representative government – the link between the policies which political parties put before voters at election time and the policies which governments promote once the election is over and done with. It is one of a series of books dealing with this relationship, each based on a large cross-national research project conducted by the Party Manifesto Research Group of the European Consortium For Political Research (ECPR), under the direction of Ian Budge.

From the point of view both of describing and of justifying representative democracy, the relationship between party and government policy is obviously crucial. If a party says one thing to the voters and then goes into a government which does something quite different, then its supporters have been disfranchised (at least as far as getting their preferred policies enacted) just as effectively as if they never had a vote in the first place.

There are, of course, all sorts of reasons why parties may not be able to redeem the policy pledges that they make to the electorate. Even when a party wins a majority of seats in the legislature and is able to form a government on its own, there may be valid reasons why it cannot do what it said it would do. Unexpected events may supervene: a crisis in the financial markets or in foreign affairs for example; one policy may have unanticipated and negative consequences for another; and so on. (These are the subject of another study in our series: Klingemann, Hofferbert, Budge and Petry (eds) forthcoming.)

In this book, however, we concentrate on the situation which is far more often the outcome of an election in Western Europe – the situation in which no single party controls an overall majority of seats so that some form of coalition bargaining is necessary before a government can be formed. The result of this bargaining at the legislative level may either be a 'minority' executive, in which the government parties do not control a legislative majority (Strom, 1984), or a multi-party coalition government that does control a majority.

Our central focus, therefore, is on how the electoral programmes of political parties relate to the policies of coalition governments. For all the merits of coalitions, it is clear that the need for prospective partners to agree on joint policies before they take office must reduce the possibility that any single party will get all the points in its election programmes incorporated into the government programme. When parties with different ideological outlooks, and often quite incompatible policies, go into coalitions together, then the government's policy programme cannot possibly reflect all of the promises that the government parties made to the electorate.

The main task that we have set ourselves is thus to explore the extent to which government policy in coalition systems does in fact tend to diverge from the policies of government members. Related to this are the questions of whether any particular party or party 'family' is more successful in getting its policies adopted than others; and of whether coalitions are more likely to be formed between parties that are closer in terms of policy.

Existing studies of the role of party policy in the politics of coalition fall into one of three basic traditions. First there is the 'case studies' approach. This focuses on an individual political system, and we might think of it rather crudely as the 'coalitions in Belgium (or Norway or Italy) tradition'. This is not by any means to decry 'case studies' but we must be clear about their purpose; a case study of coalition politics in Belgium, for example, is more concerned with politics in Belgium than with the politics of coalitions. Collecting such studies together, as has been done recently by Bogdanor (1983) and Pridham (1986), provides us with much invaluable raw material. But it leaves the onus on the reader to isolate general patterns of coalitional politics that might be important in a range of different systems.

Collections of case studies provide useful starting points for the second general approach to the study of coalitions, which we might think of as the 'comparative European politics' tradition. This approach is concerned above all with describing and interpreting general features of the process of coalition government in Western Europe. It takes 'coalition' as a key concept in comparative politics and tests general propositions about coalitional politics using comparative data from a wide range of Western European and related systems. The work of Browne and Franklin (1973) on coalition payoffs, of Budge and Keman (1990) on the formation and functioning of governments in general, including coalitions, and of Strom (1984, 1990) on minority governments, are good examples of this approach.

The third tradition in the study of European coalition government operates from a very different perspective, that of game theory. Since coalitional behaviour, whatever else it may be, is a complex strategic interaction between small numbers of highly-motivated rational actors, it is clear that game theory should have a lot to say on the matter. This type of approach tends to be formal and deductive in style, driven entirely by the specific content of its assumptions and the unfolding of its logic. In recent years it has developed an extensive and elaborate account of coalitional behaviour that does indeed deal with our primary concern, the relationship between coalition and party policy. The work of McKelvey, Ordeshook and Winer (1978), Schofield (1986), Austen-Smith and Banks (1988) provides good examples of this approach.

The argument in this book is set firmly within the 'comparative European politics' tradition. There has not, until now, been a comprehensive cross national study of the role of party policy in the coalitional process. We must first, therefore, assemble a range of basic raw material about this. For these reasons, a series of country studies (chapters 3–13 inclusive) lie at the heart of our book. Each country study, however, is based upon the same theoretical foundations, and presents the same set of qualitative and quantitative information for each system. Those interested in coalitional politics in general can draw upon some excellent collections of case studies (Brown and Dreijmanis, 1982; Bogdanor, 1983; Pridham, 1986). What we do, in contrast, is concentrate our attention on the role of policy in the politics of coalition inside each system.

This book, however, is much more than a collection of country chapters. We base our exploration of policy effects in particular countries on a developing body of theory about coalition politics. Our argument begins, therefore, with a discussion of this. Chapter I reviews the treatment of policy in a number of theories of coalition government. We argue that taking policy seriously has more fundamental consequences for the rest of coalition theory than many authors have realised. We also move our theoretical framework closer to the real world of coalition politics, by examining the structures and constraints that influence government formation in almost every European political system.

In Chapter 2 we deal with problems of operationalisation. Such problems are particularly acute, since time series data on party and coalition policy in Europe has not been available before. This means that a number of ideas that have been breezily bandied around by those who have written on the politics of coalition must now be defined more precisely. As is often the case, some of those ideas turn out to be under-specified, needing further theoretical refinement before they can be taken out and applied in the real world.

Having set up the theoretical terms of reference, we move on in Chapters 3 to 13 to the eleven country studies, each addressing itself to the same concerns. These chapters deal with the role of policy in the coalition politics of Ireland, Norway, Sweden, West Germany, Luxembourg, Belgium, the Netherlands, Denmark, Israel, Italy and France. Each chapter was written on the basis of the authors's participation in an extended series of workshops, during which the strategy to be pursued at each stage of the analysis was discussed at length. In a real sense, therefore, this book is not an edited collection at all, but rather a work co-authored by fifteen or so people. While much of the analysis was conducted centrally, all results for all countries were circulated to each member of the group and these results informed each author's interpretation of their own particular area.

At the outset of each country chapter we answer a series of specific qualitative questions about the role of party policy in coalition bargaining. Such questions deal with how far bargaining is subject to specific constitutional or political constraints; how far actors seem to be motivated by policy considerations; how often policy disputes between members cause coalition governments to fall; and so on. Each chapter then proceeds to a systematic quantitative analysis of post-war party election programmes and government policy declarations. This is carried out in two main ways. First, party and government policy positions are described in terms of a single left–right policy dimension identified as being relevant in all systems. Second, a richer and more complex set of twenty policy dimensions is used, which allows much more information about party and coalition policy to be taken into account. Both the one-dimensional and the twenty-dimensional analyses are conducted in the same terms in each chapter, allowing a genuinely comparative evaluation to be made of the various policy-based interpretations of coalition functioning with which we are concerned. Some of the country investigators go on to generate specific representations of party and coalition politics which take account of the specific structures and idiosyncracies of the political systems examined. But the empirical analysis common to all country chapters is the core of our argument.

Chapter 14 relates the policy packages promoted by coalition governments to the policies of the member parties in an attempt to answer the general question with which we began this discussion. The apparent disjunction between coalition and party policy raises fundamental questions for coalition theory, which are tackled, within a synthesis of our main results, at the end of the chapter.

M. J. LAVER
IAN BUDGE

1 Coalition Theory, Government Policy and Party Policy
Ian Budge and M. J. Laver

In this chapter we consider how conventional coalition theory has handled the link between party and coalition policy and discuss ways in which the analysis of party manifestos and government declarations might throw light on the issues that have been raised. We also consider the extent to which this link might be attenuated by the range of structural constraints and influences affecting coalition bargaining in any given system. Since Laver and Schofield have recently provided a comprehensive review of coalition theory as it applies to all aspects of government formation and maintenance, we concentrate here only upon those aspects that have a direct bearing upon the interaction of party and coalition policy (Laver and Schofield, 1990).

Fundamental to any theoretical account of coalition politics is a set of assumptions about the motivations of the relevant actors. Early theories were concerned almost exclusively with the 'intrinsic' rewards going to those politicians who got into office, rewards such as power, prestige, a place in the limelight and so on. More recent theories have been based upon the assumption that politicians are motivated in their coalition bargaining solely by a desire to affect public policy outputs.

As Budge and Laver have argued, however, getting into office may be valued either as an end in itself or as a means to affect policy; in the same way, policy outputs may be valued either as ends in themselves or as a means to increase the chance of maximising votes at subsequent elections (Budge and Laver, 1986). More 'instrumental' motivations for affecting public policy or getting into office have until recently been treated hardly at all by coalition theorists, though Austen-Smith and Banks (1988) modelled the interaction of vote maximisation at election time and policy bargaining during government formation. Most existing coalition theory, however, is concerned exclusively with the assumed 'intrinsic' motivations of politicians either to get into office or to affect public policy.

'POLICY BLIND' THEORIES OF COALITION GOVERNMENT

The theoretical tradition that emphasises office-seeking motivations can be traced back to Riker's influential 'theory of political coalitions' (1962), although it clearly pre-dates this. The intrinsic rewards of office are typically conceived of as the set of cabinet portfolios, a fixed prize to be divided by the winners of the coalition game. For this reason, Riker's famous 'minimal winning' proposition suggests that coalitions will comprise no more than the minimum number of actors necessary to achieve office. Any 'surplus' actors, according to Riker, would consume some of the spoils of office without having contributed to winning them.

The minimal winning proposition has by now been tested many times, most recently by Laver and Schofield (1985), who found it to make accurate predictions in about 35 percent of all governments analysed (see also Browne, 1973; Taylor and Laver, 1973; de Swaan, 1973; de Swaan, and Mokken, 1980; Franklin and Mackie, 1984). This is not a bad success rate for an extremely simple theory employed cross-nationally in complex bargaining environments. The theory performs much better than picking possible coalitions out of a hat, considering the very many coalitions that are arithmetically possible after an election in a typical European party system. This notwithstanding, much remains to be explained.

POLICY-BASED THEORIES OF COALITION GOVERNMENT

Moving beyond the assumption that politicians are concerned exclusively with getting into office, coalition theorists now usually assume that they are also motivated by policy. Initially, 'policy-seeking' models of coalitional behaviour comprised sets of proposed additions to minimal winning theory, but were not models that were driven, from the bottom up, by policy-seeking motivations. Typically, they considered only coalitions that are minimal winning, and predicted that those with the smallest ideological distance between parties would be preferred. Well-known early examples of this approach can be found in the work of Leiserson (1966), Axelrod (1970) and de Swaan (1973). De Swaan offers the most succinct statement of the essential thrust of theories which combine statements about party policy with a minimal winning criterion based on an assumed office-seeking motivation: 'an actor strives to bring about a winning coalition in which he is included and which he expects to adopt a policy that is as close as possible . . . *to his own most preferred policy*' (1973, emphasis added).

Policy-based theories of coalition government have moved considerably beyond this approach, however, and sophisticated models of coalition bargaining over policy have been developed within a game-theoretic tradition that has become a major academic industry (Plott, 1967; Kramer, 1973; McKelvey, 1976; Cohen, 1979; Cohen and Matthews, 1980; McKelvey, 1976; Mckelvey, 1979; McKelvey and Schofield, 1987; Schofield, 1983; Schofield, 1986; Calvert, 1985; Baron and Ferejohn, 1987; Austen-Smith and Banks, 1988). Good overviews of the entire field have been provided by Krehbiel (1988) and by Miller, Grofman and Feld (1989). These approaches are based on the idea that both party and coalition policy can be described in terms of a number of 'dimensions' of policy. The best known of these is, of course, the familiar 'left–right' dimension that deals with general economic strategy, but many other policy dimensions are potentially salient for party competition. These include social policy, foreign policy, policy on church–state relations, and so on. Taken together, the collection of policy dimensions that are salient for a given party system make up a 'policy space' within which party competition takes place. The policy position of any actor, be it party or government, can be defined in terms of a set of co-ordinates in this space. Distances between parties can be measured in the same terms. The description of party competition in terms of policy spaces has become one of the standard tools of contemporary political science.

The conclusions of the game theorists who have analysed coalition bargaining within this spatial framework have been striking. When only one policy dimension is important, the party controlling the median legislator on that dimension is effectively a policy dictator. Parties to the left of it will be unwilling to tolerate a policy move in a rightwards direction. Parties to the right of it will be unwilling to tolerate a move leftwards. Obviously, the party controlling the median legislator can form a legislative majority together with either the parties of the left or the parties of the right. If that party forms a government on its own and enacts its ideal policy position, therefore, it cannot be defeated in the legislature. Any move to substitute a more left wing government will be blocked from the right. Any move to substitute a more right wing government will be blocked from the left. In the language of game theory, the policy position preferred by the party controlling the median legislator is thus the 'core' of the bargaining game when only one dimension of policy is important.

However, when more than one dimension of policy is salient and particularly when the number of salient policy dimensions is three or more, game theoretic models predict that coalition bargaining over policy will become very unstable. The argument is best encapsulated by McKelvey

(1979) in his famous 'chaos' theorem. In a nutshell this states that, in a multidimensional policy space, any policy position (including by implication the policy position of any government) is such that there is at least one alternative preferred by a majority of the legislature. Thus any government is at any stage liable to be defeated by an alternative majority legislative coalition that prefers a specific alternative policy package.

Various reasons have been advanced to explain why the chaos predicted by the theories does not, in practice, materialise. One of the earliest and most influential was Shepsle's 'structure induced equilibrium' approach, which suggested that the fact that real world parties must operate within specific legislative structures – in the US context the legislative committee system – imposed a set of constraints upon bargaining which negated the effects of the chaos theorem (Shepsle and Weingast, 1981). More recently, Laver (1989) has suggested that coalition bargaining and electoral strategy may often dictate policy moves in quite different directions, thereby 'damping' the inherent instability of party competition in multidimensional issue spaces. Finally, current work suggests that the allocation of policy portfolios to cabinet ministers who have considerable autonomy to set the policy in their own jurisdictions (Budge and Keman, 1990, Chapters 4 and 5) may also cut down dramatically on the range of credible alternative coalitions, and thereby greatly reduce instability (Austen-Smith and Banks, 1990; Laver and Shepsle, 1990).

Game theorists therefore have had a lot to say about the role of policy in coalition bargaining. Most of the models developed so far, however, have had one major failing; they have continued, explicitly or implicitly, to use the majority winning criterion. This is their most telling empirical weakness. This criterion cannot conceivably explain the formation of minority administrations, which in practice comprise about one-third of all European governments (Herman and Pope,1973; Laver and Schofield, 1985; Strom, 1984; Strom, 1990). Moreover, it does not emerge from the bargaining assumptions of the models themselves, but is imposed on them as an (assumed) universal institutional constraint (Bergman, 1989). As this constraint is itself empirically variable (c.f. the final section of this chapter, below), some alternative theoretical conception more closely related to bargaining assumptions must clearly be found. We develop this in the notion of 'government viability' below.

MINORITY GOVERNMENT, VIABLE GOVERNMENT AND PARTY POLICY

The failure of many game theoretic models of government formation to address the issue of minority government, results from not taking full account of the constitutional relationship between legislature and executive typically found in most West European countries. Parliamentary government is based on the principle that the executive continues in office so long as it does not lose the confidence of the legislature – a matter that is settled unambiguously by the legislative device of the vote of confidence, or no confidence, in the executive (Budge and Herman, 1978). Two types of coalition are therefore important. There is the legislative coalition which sustains the government in office. And there is the executive coalition – the collection of parties which between them make up the cabinet. The majority winning criterion may be appropriate for assessing the effectiveness of a legislative coalition. But it is not appropriate for assessing the membership of an executive coalition.

Votes of confidence will, of course, generally be won by majority governments, defined as executives whose member parties between them control a legislative majority. If policy is what is important to political parties when they bargain over the formation and maintenance of a government, however, it is not all inevitable that votes of confidence will be lost by minority governments, defined as executives whose member parties between them do not control a legislative majority.

What is obviously crucial for the formation and survival of minority governments is the set of divisions between the opposition parties. And one of the most clear-cut bases of such division has to do with party policy. We have already seen that, if a single dimension of policy is all that is important for party competition, the party controlling the median legislator is in a very powerful position, being at the core of the bargaining game. It can only be evicted if parties to the left of it combine with parties to the right, but a group of parties such as this could not agree upon an alternative policy position that all preferred to the position of the core party. Parties to the left would not prefer a policy to the right of the core party. Parties to the right would not prefer a position to the left of it. Even if the core party controlled far less than a majority of seats, there is no majority legislative coalition that prefers an alternative. In our terms, a minority government comprising only the core party would be 'viable'. Note that it is only viable provided that policy is important to the parties. Indeed, minority government in general becomes much less easy to interpret if policy is not important, since in this case an opposition that has the votes to evict the government, and the incentive to do so, for some reason refrains. Taking policy seriously shows us the range of circumstances in which the opposition, collectively, does not in fact have an incentive to evict the government.

Elaborating this argument, Budge and Laver have suggested that the majority winning criterion be replaced with the 'government viability criterion', when analysing the formation and maintenance of governments in parliamentary government systems. They define the viability criterion as follows: 'A protocoalition V will form a viable government if there is no alternative coalition A which is supported by parties controlling more legislative votes than those supporting V, and which all parties supporting A prefer to form rather than V' (Budge and Laver, 1986, p. 488).

Though it is in the end a matter of terminology, we prefer the idea of a 'viable' government to that of a 'winning' government. The latter carries the connotation that parties which form a government win the game in some absolute sense while all others 'lose' it completely. In short, the notion of winning implies that the game is constant sum rather than variable sum and this is exactly the implication we are trying to get away from. Once policy is taken into account there are no absolute winners and losers and the notion of government viability expresses this clearly. This point can be made more explicit by introducing the notion of 'policy viability', which can be specified as follows: 'an incumbent government is "policy viable" if its policy position is such that there is no alternative executive coalition that can put forward a credible policy position that is preferred to the incumbent government by a majority of legislators.' (The notion of 'policy viability' owes much to conversations with Kaare Strom.)

Thus the policy package of a coalition becomes just as important a piece of information as its party composition. This is one of the key ideas upon which our analysis is based. This approach covers the possibility of minority governments, as well as bare-majority and surplus majority governments. All can be 'policy-viable' if they meet the prescribed conditions.

We note that the game theoretic results we referred to above imply (where they do not make further assumptions) that only governments containing the party with a policy position at the core of the bargaining game will be policy viable. In such a case there will only be policy viable governments – majority or minority – in party systems where only one dimension of policy is important, since only in one dimensional systems is it certain that a core exists at all (in almost all other systems it is more or less certain that a core does not exist).

While our notion of policy viability and the core of the bargaining game are very similar in situations where no further assumptions can be made about the bargaining environment, most coalition bargaining, as we shall see, is in fact circumscribed by a range of constraints. Game theorists can treat these constraints as defining a new game, with a new core. As we have seen, the imposition of such constraints can be used to identify situations in which large numbers of dimensions are salient but in which a core – and hence a potential policy viable government – exists (Austen-Smith and Banks, 1990; Laver and Shepsle, 1990).

We regard the notion of policy viability as a useful one, since it enables us to assess the ability of any given government to survive. What is required is to specify all potential alternative governments, given the constraints on the situation, and to test whether any of these is preferred to the incumbent government by a legislative majority. Institutional constraints typically restrict the list of potential alternative governments. Adding and deleting governments from this list provides a useful *ad hoc* exploratory technique for assessing the impact of particular constraints upon the viability of any government.

A specific one-dimensional example gives more content to the notion of government viability in the context of the ideas that we have discussed in this chapter. Table 1.1 shows the set of all arithmetically possible coalitions in a four party minority situation in which only one dimension of ideology is salient. There are four single party 'coalitions' comprising each of the parties on its own; there are six two party coalitions; four three party coalitions; and the 'grand' coalition of all parties.

Table 1.1   Government viability in a hypothetical party system

Party Seats	A 20	B 20	C 40	D 20
Coalitions				
1	*			
2		*		
3			*	
4				*
5	*	*		
6	*		*	
7	*			*
8		*	*	
9		*		*
10			*	*
11	*	*	*	
12	*	*		*
13	*		*	*
14		*	*	*
15	*	*	*	*

If we ignore policy entirely for a moment, and assume that parties are motivated solely by the desire to get into office, then it seems likely that one of four minimal winning coalitions – *AC, BC, CD, ABD* – will form. No minority government will be viable.

If we assume, in addition, that some constraint prevents parties *A* and *B* from going into government together – perhaps because of a bitter personal feud between party leaders – then all governments including both *A* and *B* must be excluded from consideration. Note that this means that there is now no 'available' winning coalition that excludes party *C*. Since party *C* cannot be excluded from office, it can form a viable minority government on its own.

Now assume that there are no such constraints on government formation, but that policy is important to politicians. Continue to assume that the parties comprising the executive must control a majority in the legislature, perhaps because they also value office payoffs. In these circumstances, one of two minimal connected winning coalitions – *BC* and *CD* – seems likely form. Any other coalition that controls a majority is bound to have greater ideological diversity. Party *C* can be excluded from office, but only by a coalition that is ideologically more diverse. If policy is not the only consideration in the minds of politicians, a minority government of *C* alone may not be viable. But coalitions *BC* and *CD* are clearly viable.

If we assume that parties are motivated only by policy considerations, however, we see that the single party minority government of *C* alone is indeed likely to be viable. This is because parties *A, B* and *C* can successfully oppose any rightwards move away from *C's* ideal policy position, while parties *C* and *D* can successfully oppose any leftwards move away from *C's* ideal point. The policy position *C* is the core of this one-dimensional coalition game; party *C* is thus an essential member of any viable coalition. If it forms a government on its own, it will not be defeated in the legislature.

Both this example and the preceding theoretical example show that 'winning' is altogether too simple a concept to capture the complexities of government formation. What is ultimately important is the ability of an actual or proposed government to survive, given the need to maintain the confidence of the legislature, a requirement captured much more clearly by the concept of government viability. When policy is important, furthermore, we must take account of the absolutely critical point that opposition parties have preferences between alternative government, this means that minority governments may be quite viable, given certain constellations of party weights and policy positions. This is without doubt the most important implication of taking policy seriously in coalition theory. Certainly, from this perspective, there seems no justification at all for retaining the majority winning criterion in policy-based theories of coalition government.

The example in Table 1.1 also showed us that the balance of power in government formation can be dramatically shifted through the impact of a single 'constraint' on coalition bargaining – in this case a feud between two party leaders – that restricts the universe of possible coalitions. It is not possible, of course, to generalise much about feuds between party leaders. But a number of other types of bargaining constraint do have general properties, and it is to these that we now turn.

CONSTRAINTS AND INFLUENCES ON COALITION BARGAINING
(Kaare Strom contributed many ideas to this section)

The real world of politics is a world of constraints. Many factors – related to institutions and constitutions, to international politics and to many other things besides – can constrain or influence the decisions of politicians about participating in a coalition, quite apart from policy preferences or the desire to get into office. It is clear, to take just one example, that most West European Communist parties have been excluded from government for most of the post-war period, despite the fact that there is quite close agreement between them and certain other parties on many aspects of policy (Budge, Robertson and Hearl, 1987). Theories based only on assumptions about office seeking and policy pursuit cannot provide an account of a phenomenon such as this. This is because very little systematic empirical work has been done to assess the impact of the various structural constraints and influences that in practice bear upon the formation of governments in Western Europe.

The problem, of course, is that many of the constraints and influences that we need to consider, relate specifically to a particular political system. There is thus a real danger that constraints on bargaining might be dealt with in an *ad hoc* manner, as "explanations" of why particular theories do not apply in particular circumstances. The challenge that faces us is that on the one hand to take realistically into account the impact of external constraints and influences in assessing the role of policy in government formation; but on the other, to avoid explaining away failed theoretical predictions by perpetual recourse to *ad hoc* bargaining constraints. To ignore such constraints would be to stick our heads in the sand. But to conjure up a constraint to explain every deviant case would render coalition theory completely unscientific.

One partial solution is to insist that any constraints and influences that are considered must be specified *a priori*, before coming to the assessment of particular cases. Thus, each country chapter will operationalise the structure influences and constraints that have a bearing on coalition bargaining before undertaking a systematic analysis of coalition theories within the particular national context. Hopefully, this prior listing will prevent us from deriving unique combinations of special factors which may seem to 'explain' every deviation from our models of policy-bargaining, but in reality, of course, assume everything away, leaving us nothing to explain with the theory itself.

Here we begin the process of specifying constraints and influences on bargaining, by discussing some of the more obvious factors that appear to operate in a range of political systems. We do this to provide guidelines for the discussion of local constraints and influences at the outset of each country chapter.

Perhaps the clearest example of a constraint in Western Europe can be found in the effective prohibition of Communist participation in government in the period after early 1948 – the time of the Soviet takeover of Czechoslovakia. Communist parties were effectively treated as pariahs, a situation that resulted from fears on the part of others about whether the Communists would abide by the results of electoral procedures if they moved into positions of power; from perceptions of them as agents of a hostile power; and from US diplomatic and other pressure against their participation in European governments, at a time when almost all European countries depended on the United States for trade, aid and defence. The country authors in the previous volume in this series found, on analysing party policy positions, that the positions of Communist Parties were often not very far from those of other left-wing parties (Budge, Robertson and Hearl, 1987). No matter how much agreement existed between Communists and other parties on immediate policy, however, no matter how pliable the Communists might have been in conceding cabinet positions to other parties, they were ruled out of coalition-making from the start by what amounted to a set of firm side-constraints upon the range of possible coalitions. Coalitions containing the Communists were not in the list of feasible possibilities.

A similar process seems to have been at work in relation to neo-Nazi or neo-Fascist parties such as the Italian MSI. Once more, the official policy positions of such parties are often no more right wing than ideological near neighbours, but the emotive associations of Fascism or Nazism have effectively turned these parties into pariahs as far as participation in government is concerned. Especially in the immediate post-war period they were ruled out of coalition bargaining because of the violent internal reactions which their participation in government would have provoked.

Another striking example of a strong side constraint on coalition bargaining is institutionalised in systems of 'consociational' democracy. Such systems may impose a requirement that all governments involve the participation of two or more social groups. The most obvious example of this is in Belgium and deals with the representation in government of the two language communities, the Flemings and the Walloons. Articles of the Belgian constitution stipulate that the cabinet comprises an equal number of French speaking and Dutch speaking members and that legislation on issues related to the language question requires a majority vote within each linguistic group. These constraints rule out many possible coalitions and made it impossible, for a time, to form a government without the Christian Socials (Rudd, 1986). In the Belgian case, therefore, many of the arithmetically possible coalitions are not merely unlikely, they are unconstitutional. Any theoretical account that ignores this is doomed to failure.

While there are relatively few rigid side constraints, the number of institutional factors that might influence the government formation process is immense. It is obviously impossible to provide an exhaustive list of these. In order to give an idea of how such factors can affect the bargaining process, therefore, we can do no more than offer a few examples.

First, it is clear that electoral systems can have a major impact on coalition bargaining. Certain electoral systems, for example, create strong incentives for politicians to form pre-electoral coalitions. This is particularly important when the electoral law distorts representation in the legislature in favour of large parties. It also arises when the electoral system involves voters transferring support from one party to another, an explicit feature of the Irish and Maltese single transferable vote systems and an implicit feature of the French second ballot and the British first-past-the-post system.

A good example of pre-electoral coalitions can be found in Ireland in 1973. Fine Gael and Labour agreed a fourteen-point electoral programme and contested the election as a prospective coalition government. Each encouraged its supporters to give lower preference votes to the other. The two parties gained seats in the election and controlled a legislative majority between them. Without any further real negotiation, they formed a coalition government that lasted four years.

A second set of major structural influences on bargaining has to do with the constitutional provisions that regulate the formation of governments. For example, a number of West European constitutions require an incoming government to survive an investiture vote; many others do not. An investiture requirement forces an incoming government to survive on the basis of its programme and cabinet taken as a whole, and thus provides a much sterner test, making it more difficult for minority governments to form. In the absence of an investiture requirement (for example in Denmark), minority governments are more likely to be viable, since the entire government package does not need the agreement of a majority of the legislature.

A third set of influences on bargaining has to do with the status of the incumbent government. The outgoing government often remains in office during negotiations for the formation of the new government, acting as a 'caretaker', that is, running the essential affairs of the state but not taking any controversial policy decisions. The caretaker government is the status quo and continues in office until it is replaced. The party or parties in the caretaker government thus have less to lose than the other parties if coalition bargaining fails.

A fourth, and crucial, institutional feature of government formation concerns the role played by the head of state. In some states, West Germany for example, the President is nothing more than a figurehead, who has no real role in the appointment, let alone the selection, of the government. In other countries, such as the Netherlands, the head of state plays a much more active role. Typically, this role involves the identification of a particular senior politician as *formateur* – government former – a situation which gives the designated politician a key role in the bargaining process. A process that allows a specific coalition nucleus to be designated by the head of state produces quite a different bargaining environment to the 'freestyle' bargaining between elites that obtains when the head of state remains aloof.

This list of possible constraints influences on coalition bargaining could be extended. Our examples suffice however in demonstrating that there are many factors other than the immediate motivations of politicians which shape government coalitions. Budge and Keman (1990, Chapter 2) have gone a long way towards developing a full comparative, institutional explanation of government formation and functioning, using many of these factors. From the point of view of a purely policy based study of coalitions, however, structural constraints and external influences on bargaining remain essentially external to our theoretical concerns, serving to delimit their scope but not to provide a comprehensive element in our explanation. Inevitably, our treatment of them must remain rather informal, but each country chapter does discuss the constraints and influences that circumscribe bargaining in the relevant system, so that at least some sense can be made of the deviant cases.

THE EMPIRICAL TASKS AHEAD

The vast majority of those currently writing on the politics of coalition in Western Europe consider that party policy is an important factor in government formation and functioning. This implies that parties have an eye to the policy outputs of the eventual government when they bargain over coalition formation. It further implies that the coalition which forms, other things being equal, will be more, rather than less, ideologically compact. Despite these theoretical concerns, empirical data permitting a spatial representation of the relationship between coalition and party policy in Western Europe has never, to our knowledge, been collected. In the chapters that follow we explore the empirical implications of the theoretical assumptions discussed above.

The first process investigated is government formation. When only one dimension of policy is important, most policy based theories, as we have seen, give a special status to the party controlling the median legislator on this dimension, the person whose ideal policy point is at the core of the bargaining game. We will therefore be examining the extent to which the median party on the left–right policy scale (which characterises every European system) seems in practice to be in a particularly powerful position.

When more than one dimension of policy is important, it is unlikely that any single party will be in such a dominant position. In such cases, we model the process of government building as one of the progressive coalescence between parties that are close to each other in the policy space, borrowing from a model developed by Grofman (Grofman, 1982). At any stage in the government building process, this model assumes that the next fusion of parties or protocoalitions will be between the two elements that are currently closest together in the policy space. Unlike Grofman, we will not necessarily expect a majority coalition to form. Rather, we see the coalescence of parties as a process that continues until the criterion of government viability for the particular system in question has been reached.

The second major phenomenon we investigate is the relationship between coalition policy and the policy of coalition members. Party policy should affect coalition bargaining because policy-motivated politicians will have an eye on the eventual policies of the government that forms. This assumes that government policy is in some sense related to government membership, an assumption that also, of course, underlies the entire theory of representative parliamentary democracy. Our second empirical task, therefore, is to determine whether government membership does make a difference to government policy, in the sense of bringing it closer to the election promises of constituent members. If we find that it does not, then it becomes difficult to see how politicians bargaining over government formation take policy into consideration at all.

Before beginning the analysis, however, we need to develop some working specifications of the concepts and models that we will be using; and this is the task to which we now turn.

2 Measuring Policy Distances and Modelling Coalition Formation

M. J. Laver and Ian Budge

In the previous chapter we looked at various theories of government formation that deal with the role of party policy. Before we can evaluate any of these theories, we must develop a set of working definitions of each of the concepts involved. The most important empirical task is to describe party policy and government policy in terms that enable one to be compared to another. Having developed such a description, we can move on to our second main task, which is to develop an empirical model that can be used to evaluate the approaches outlined above.

The most straightforward approach to describing policy positions is to work with simple dichotomies, classifying pairs of parties as 'agreeing' or 'disagreeing' with one another over a particular policy. There is a lot to be said for this method, used by Luebbert (1986) and by Budge and Keman (1990) in their analyses of the politics of coalition in Western Europe. It is straightforward and intuitively appealing, allowing formal analysis to correspond rather closely to the language of real political debate – which of course tends to be couched in terms of basic agreement and disagreement.

However, the theories discussed in the previous chapter depend upon more complex information about the extent of agreement or disagreement between pairs of parties on particular issues. Such theories typically describe pairs of parties being 'closer' or 'further apart' from each other in policy terms, making use of the key concept of 'policy distance' between actors. Policy distances can only be measured in terms of some basic set of reference points, defined in terms of a particular set of dimensions of policy. The important dimensions of policy in any political system span what is usually referred to as a 'policy space'. The use of policy spaces is by now a very conventional way of describing party policy. Most "rational choice" theories of electoral behaviour and coalition bargaining make use of some form of spatial representation of party competition. (For non-spatial alternatives see Budge and Farlie, 1983; Budge and Keman, 1990).

15

ESTIMATING EMPIRICAL POLICY SPACES: ANALYSING PARTY
PROGRAMMES

Most empirical investigations into the role of policy in coalition bargaining
have worked with a one-dimensional policy space. Almost invariably the
dimension that defines this space has been conceived as a 'left–right socio-
economic' dimension, in which left and right correspond closely to the
colloquial political usage of these terms. Typically party policy positions on
this dimension have been estimated using either the investigator's own
judgement or the judgements of specialists. The obvious possibility of bias
in these judgements has been investigated by Laver and Hunt (1992), and
found not to be as serious a problem in practice as might have been
expected. There are, however, other drawbacks with relying on expert
judgements for estimating policy positions. First, in any given system, there
are almost certainly other important dimensions of policy which affect party
competition. Second, since party policy positions are liable to change over
time, and since no published set of expert judgements tracks changes over
time, no dynamic model of party politics or government formation can be
tested using these data.

The content analysis of party programmes offers an alternative which
does take time into account. This task has been performed by the Manifesto
Research Group; their reported findings, while showing the confrontation
between left and right to be the most widespread underlying theme in
party programmes, reveals the importance of many other significant policy
dimensions (Budge, Robertson and Hearl, 1987, chapter 18). Some of these
dimensions are relevant to all parties, others were relevant only to specific
parties. Party programmes are published for each election, so that changes
in policy position can be tracked over time.

Estimating policy positions using the content analysis of policy declarations, furthermore, provides the major added bonus of being able to
locate other actors, and notably coalition governments, in the policy space.
The policy position of each government that forms can thereby be characterised in identical terms to the policy position of each party. This allows us
to model the link between party and coalition policy empirically, and to
operationalise most of the concepts discussed in the previous chapter.
Accordingly, we base our policy spaces upon content analyses of party
programmes and government policy declarations. These are described in
detail elsewhere (Budge, Robertson and Hearl, 1987, chapter 2 and ap-
pendices A and B), so we provide only a brief summary below.

Selecting countries, parties, governments and policy documents

The selection of countries is obviously the single most critical decision to be made. It is especially important given Franklin and Mackie's finding that the use of different country sets explains why some theories are evaluated more favourably by some researchers than by others (Franklin and Mackie, 1984). In the present case, however, the choice of countries was determined largely by the availability of investigators, who needed to be familiar both with their national politics and fluent in the necessary languages. We should have been happy to have investigated every European coalition system, but no country expert came forward for Austria, Finland, Iceland, or Switzerland. Spain, Portugal and Greece, with their limited experience of democracy in the post-war period, did not provide a sufficiently extended time-period for study. Israel was included because its multi-party system and its experience of coalition government are familiar in the West European context. The list of countries can be found in Table 2.1, which also shows the countries studied by other empirical researchers in this tradition.

For each country studied, all but the most 'insignificant' parties were examined, subject to the availability of their policy programmes. The set of 'significant' parties was selected broadly on Sartori's (1976, pp. 121–3) criteria of 'coalition potential' and 'blackmail potential'. All parties gaining more than five per cent of the vote at any post-war election were included, together with all which were potentially pivotal in coalition bargaining. (More detailed discussion of the choice of parties can be found in Budge, Robertson and Hearl, 1987).

In selecting documents to represent each party's policy position at each election, we looked first for election programmes, taking the US party platform or the British party manifesto as exemplars and searching for 'manifesto-equivalents' in other countries. The advantage of using an official party manifesto is that it is a unique and authoritative statement of policy endorsed by the party as a whole at a certain point in time. A disadvantage (more for analysing party competition in a mass electorate than for analysing coalition bargaining between elites) is that few people may actually read the original. However we have argued elsewhere that through media reports and setting terms of reference for television and in the newspapers, the party manifesto does exert an important general influence over the nature of political debate (Budge, Robertson and Hearl, 1987). We thus take it to represent the best single measure of a party's policy position at the time of an election (See Budge, Robertson and Hearl, 1987, for a much more detailed discussion of the choice of party policy documents).

Table 2.1 West European countries included in empirical analysis of coalitional politics

Country	Browne and Franklin Laver 1973	Taylor and Laver 1973	de Swaan 1973	Herman and Pope 1973	Dodd 1976	Budge and Herman 1978	Strom 1984	Schofield 1985	Luebbert 1986	Budge et al. 1987	Laver and Schofield 1990	Budge and Keman 1990
Austria	Yes	Yes	No	Yes	Yes	Yes	No	Yes	No	Yes	Yes	Yes
Belgium	Yes	Yes	No	Yes	Yes	Yes	Yes	Yes	No	Yes	Yes	Yes
Denmark	Yes	Yes	Yes	Yes	Yes	Yes	Yes	Yes	Yes	Yes	Yes	Yes
Finland	Yes	Yes	Yes	Yes	Yes	Yes	Yes	Yes	Yes	No	Yes	Yes
France	No	No	*	Yes	Yes	*	No	No	No	Yes	Yes	Yes
Germany	Yes	Yes	†	No	Yes	Yes	No	Yes	No	Yes	No	No
Greece	No	No	No	No	No	No	Yes	No	No	No	Yes	Yes
Iceland	Yes	Yes	No	Yes	Yes	Yes	Yes	Yes	No	No	Yes	Yes
Ireland	Yes	Yes	No	Yes	Yes	Yes	Yes	Yes	No	Yes	Yes	Yes
Israel	Yes	No	Yes	No	No	Yes	Yes	No	Yes	Yes	No	Yes
Italy	Yes	Yes	Yes	Yes	Yes	Yes	Yes	Yes	Yes	Yes	Yes	Yes
Luxembourg	Yes	Yes	No	No	Yes	Yes	No	Yes	No	Yes	Yes	Yes
Netherlands	Yes	Yes	Yes	Yes	Yes	Yes	Yes	Yes	Yes	‡	Yes	Yes
Norway	No	No	No	No	No	Yes	Yes	Yes	Yes	No	No	No
Portugal	No	No	No	No	No	No	Yes	No	No	No	No	No
Spain	No	No	No	No	No	No	Yes	No	No	No	No	No
Sweden	Yes	Yes	Yes	Yes	Yes	Yes	Yes	Yes	Yes	Yes	Yes	Yes
No of countries	13	12	9	11	13	14	13	12	7	11	13	14

* Fourth Republic only
† Weimar Republic only
‡ Norway added to analysis of party programmes later – Strom and Liepart, 1989.

The empirical research reported in this book adds the content analysis of government policy positions to the content analysis of party manifestos. These were chosen as the most authoritative statements of policy on behalf of each coalition government in the selected countries for the post-war period. The documents take various forms. They may be the King's, Queen's or President's speech delivered on behalf of the Government at the opening of a Parliamentary session and containing the agreed government programme. Sometimes a similar role is fulfilled by the Prime Minister's speech to Parliament at the beginning of the investiture debate. More rarely, parties entering a coalition issue an agreed programme, either before or after they officially constitute the government. We have in all cases selected the document issued as close as possible in time to the formation of the government which seemed to give the most authoritative statement of policy on behalf of the whole coalition. Specific details on the selection and coding of documents are given in each country chapter.

In the empirical analyses that form the backbone of this book, the fundamental unit of analysis that we use is a 'government'. A new government forms after the incumbent government resigns or is defeated, or after an election has been held for whatever reason. Each new government typically, though not invariably, issues a new policy declaration and we have coded all such declarations, thereby triggering a new case in our analysis every time there is a change of government

While several new governments may form between two elections, a new party manifesto is issued only at election time. In order to be able to compare party and coalition policy, we are forced to make the assumption that party policy positions remain fixed from one election to the next. In reality, of course, they may change and this is without doubt a limitation on our approach. Nonetheless, it is possible to interpolate party policy between two election positions, as some of the authors of the country chapters have done informally. Furthermore, it is quite common for an election to follow the fall of a government (indeed this almost happens invariably in some systems) so that the problem is not as serious in practice as it might seem in theory. We can thus track movements of party policy from election to election, so that our estimates of party policy positions are never too far out of date – a significant advance on earlier empirical work.

The content analysis of policy documents

Having selected the most suitable document to reflect party and government policy positions, the document was coded on the basis of a set of fifty-four categories of policy summarised in Table 2.2. This coding scheme and the coding techniques that were applied are described extensively by Budge, Robertson and Hearl (1987).

Table 2.2   Category headings and domains used in the comparative coding of party election programmes

---

Domain 1   External Relations
101   Foreign special relationships: positive
102   Foreign special relationships: negative
103   Decolonisation
104   Military: positive
105   Military: negative
106   Peace
107   Internationalism: positive
108   European Community: positive
109   Internationalism: negative
110   European Community: negative

Domain 2   Freedom and Democracy
201   Freedom and domestic human rights
202   Democracy
203   Constitutionalism: positive
204   Constitutionalism: negative

Domain 3   Government
301   Decentralization: positive
302   Decentralization: negative
303   Government efficiency
304   Government corruption
305   Government effectiveness and authority

Domain 4   Economy
401   Enterprise
402   Incentives
403   Regulation of capitalism
404   Economic planning
405   Corporatism
406   Protectionism: positive
407   Protectionism: negative
408   Economic goals
409   Keynesian
410   Productivity
411   Technology and infrastructure
412   Controlled economy
413   Nationalisation
414   Economic orthodoxy and efficiency

Domain 5   Welfare and Quality of Life
501   Environmental protection
502   Art, sport, leisure and media
503   Social justice
504   Social services expansion: positive
505   Social services expansion: negative
506   Education pro-expansion
507   Education anti-expansion

Domain 6   Fabric of Society
601   Defence of national way of life: positive
602   Defence of national way of life: negative
603   Traditional morality: positive
604   Traditional morality: negative
605   Law and order
606   National effort, social harmony
607   Communalism, pluralism, pillarisation: positive
608   Communalism, pluralism, pillarisation: negative

Domain 7   Social Groups
701   Labour groups: positive
702   Labour groups: negative
703   Agriculture and farmers
704   Other economic groups
705   Underprivileged minority groups
706   Non-economic demographic groups

Briefly, the set of coding categories was developed as a result of extensive comparative experimentation and discussion within the research group. Each sentence in the policy document was then coded into one of the policy categories in Table 2.2 or into an 'uncoded category'.[1] The relative emphasis of the document on each policy category was estimated as the proportion of all policy references devoted to the category in question.

Although the coding procedure is straightforward, one basic characteristic decisively affects our results. This is the treatment of policy references as general emphases on an area of policy rather than as policy positions adopted within that area. This approach rests on a saliency theory of party competition (Robertson, 1976, chapter 3; Budge and Farlie, 1983, chapter 2) which characterises party competition in terms of the stress by each party on issues of advantage to it, rather than in terms of a direct confrontation between parties on each particular issue. In strictly practical terms, the saliency approach allows us to code almost all the policy documents, since the number of policy references on which parties take up clearly defined positions is on average less than ten per cent (Budge, Robertson and Hearl, 1987). Many of the coding categories, furthermore, ('nationalisation' for example, or 'labour groups: positive') do indeed have a strong positional content. This enables us, when we reduce the data to more manageable proportions, to construct ideological dimensions with clear 'positional' interpretations. The major check on the validity of our coding procedure is the extent to which it generates results that make sense within countries. The individual chapters assess this in more detail, but their overall results suggest that the estimates of party and government policy generated by the coding scheme are quite plausible.

Deriving empirical policy spaces from content analyses of policy documents

Having coded each of the policy documents, the next stage in the analysis is to estimate the location of the ideal policy point of each party and government. In the original analyses of party manifestoes reported by Budge, Robertson and Hearl (1987), the underlying dimensions of each policy space were identified using the technique of factor analysis. This explored the extent to which manifesto emphases on particular policy themes could be found to co-vary systematically with one another. Each party was located on each dimension in the space by calculating a 'factor score' on that dimension. The essential thrust of the analyses, however, was to identify key policy dimensions.

In the present study, however, we are not concerned with policy dimensions in and for themselves. Rather, we are concerned with policy distances between parties. Above all we want to be sure, as far as possible, that any changes that we observe in the policy distance between a pair of actors derive from real shifts in their policy emphases. These considerations suggest the use of techniques which stick very closely to our original data.

The most direct way to do this is to operate directly with the original set of 54 coding categories, without reducing their dimensionality in any way; this would generate what amounts to a 54 – dimensional policy space. Even if we eliminate a number of very sparsely populated coding categories, we will be dealing with a high-dimensional space. Such spaces are unfamiliar to empirical researchers, who generally work with one – or at most two or three – dimensions of party policy. But there is no reason to confine ourselves to these, and policy distances between pairs of actors can easily be calculated in spaces of much higher dimensionality, spaces which effectively take many more aspects of party and government policy into account. Given our desire to stick as close as possible to published party policy programmes in their entirety, this is one approach that we will follow.

A major disadvantage with high dimensional policy spaces, however, is that they are difficult to visualise. They thus sacrifice much of the heuristic appeal of the spatial analogy. Low dimensional spatial representations of policy positions are useful for providing intuitively appealing representations of complicated information. This is not a matter of 'mere' presentation, since it is important that new data can be checked to see that it makes sense by country specialists who are accustomed to representing party politics in terms of a small number of policy dimensions. It is also desirable to set our work in context by generating policy spaces which relate broadly to those postulated by earlier empirical theorists. For all these reasons we also work, in the discussions that follow, with a policy space based on a single left–right dimension. We describe below a robust method for estimating policy positions on such a dimension using our data.

Estimating high dimensional policy spaces

A perfect coding scheme for the analysis of policy statements in election and government programmes would use one, and only one, coding category for each independent element of policy. If more than one coding category is available for the same element of policy, then the coder is driven to make an often rather arbitrary decision about which category to use. This could mean that a set of very similar programme references could be classified very differently by the same coder; and it could mean that the same reference could be coded differently by different coders. Policy differences would thereby be created as an artefact of the coding procedure. On the basis of an earlier critical evaluation in light of results (Budge, Robertson and Hearl, 1987, chapter 18) it is clear that the original 54 category coding scheme does not fully meet these requirements and needs to be modified in certain areas. The most effective way to do this is to group those coding categories that appear to be closely related to one another, theoretically or empirically, in order to avoid the creation of artificial policy differences between parties where none really exist. Rather than work directly with the 54-dimensional policy space generated by our 'raw' analyses, therefore, we first collapsed categories that seemed to be closely related to each other.

The rationale behind the grouping of coding categories was based largely on the lessons learned from the original analysis. Certain theoretical distinctions between categories persistently forced coders into awkward decisions, so these were combined. In addition, we did a large number of exploratory factor analyses to search for combinations of variables that persistently loaded together over a wide range of systems. These were also grouped together; Table. 2.3 summarises our amalgamation of the original

Table 2.3   Combination of 54 policy-coding categories into 20

New category	Old categories	
State intervention	403	Regulation of capitalism
	404	Economic planning
	406	Protectionism: positive
	412	Controlled economy
	413	Nationalisation
Quality of life	501	Environmental protection
	502	Art, sport, leisure and media
Peace and co-operation	103	Decolonisation
	105	Military: negative
	106	Peace
	107	Internationalism: positive
Anti-establishment views	204	Constitutionalism: negative
	304	Government corruption
	602	Defence of national way of life: negative
	604	Traditional morality: negative
Capitalist economics	401	Free enterprise
	402	Incentives
	407	Protectionism: negative
	414	Economic orthodoxy and efficiency
	505	Social services expansion: negative
Social conservatism	203	Constitutionalism: positive
	305	Government effectiveness and authority
	601	National way of life: positive
	603	Traditional morality: positive
	605	Law and order
	606	National effort, social harmony
Productivity and technology	410	Productivity
	411	Technology and infrastructure

Coding categories retained intact

104	Military: positive
108	European Community: positive
110	European Community: negative
201	Freedom and domestic human rights
202	Democracy
301	Decentralisation: positive
303	Government efficiency
503	Social justice
504	Social services expansion: positive
506	Education: positive
701	Labour groups: positive
703	Agriculture and farmers
705	Underprivileged minorities

54 category coding scheme into one with 20 policy categories; certain coding categories were excluded from subsequent analysis because they were very little referred to or because of their inherent theoretical ambiguity.

A consequence of the combinations was that seven much more comprehensive coding categories were created. These were 'State intervention', 'Quality of life', 'Peace and cooperation', 'Anti-establishment views', 'Capitalist economics', 'Social conservatism', and 'Productivity and technology'. In addition, thirteen coding categories were retained intact from our earlier analysis; these categories could not sensibly be grouped with others, yet they were too important in too many systems to be excluded. These thirteen 'old' categories plus the seven 'new' variables leave us with 20 policy dimensions that form the basis of the high dimensional spaces with which we shall work in subsequent analyses of party and coalition policy.

Estimating one dimensional policy spaces

We argued above in favour of staying as close to the original data as possible when we generate spatial representations of party competition. We also stressed the benefits of comparing our study with others that use only one or two dimensions – and of allowing the face validity of our data to be assessed by country specialists. We have therefore developed a robust method for estimating policy positions in a one dimensional policy space.

This estimation process is based solely on the intrinsic plausibility and coherence of the sets of issues that define the underlying policy dimension. The actual policy positions of the actors are not considered until after the dimension has been defined. This is done to avoid the potential for circular argument that would arise if a particular dimension was selected because it generated policy positions that looked plausible in light of what we know about the subsequent coalition behaviour of the actors concerned. Different spatial representations of party positions on the new policy dimensions were tested on data from Britain, not a coalition system included in the later analysis. This was in order to allow us to remain 'blind' to party positions in the coalition systems, so as to remove any possibility that a particular dimensional analysis could be selected, consciously or unconsciously, simply because it generated a particular set of results.

Given the prevalence of the left–right dimension in all other spatial representations of European party systems and, indeed, in our original content analyses of election programmes, we set out to find an operational definition for a left–right scale common to all systems in the analysis. While *a priori* theoretical coherence was the prime consideration, we used a series of exploratory factor analyses to identify potential combinations of variables on an empirical basis. If two variables loaded together consistently in these exploratory factor analyses, we thought hard about combining them, but we did so only if the combination made theoretical sense. Throughout this process we kept as close as possible to the original data, whenever a combination of variables was indicated, by adding together their raw scores. This means that our final estimates of party policy positions can still be thought of in terms of proportions of manifesto references devoted to a particular set of coding categories.

The precise method for deriving the estimates of party policy positions on a 'common' left–right scale involved a number of stages. First, the 20 grouped variables that formed the basis of our high dimensional representation was used as input to exploratory principal components analyses conducted on a country-specific basis. Systematic comparisons of the rotated factor loadings for each of the eleven countries in the study showed that four of these categories loaded together consistently. These categories, furthermore, can be seen clearly to deal with more 'left' or more 'right-wing' policy concerns. These 'marker variables' are 'State intervention', and 'Peace and co-operation', loading on the left, and 'Capitalist economics' and 'Social conservatism', loading on the right. The other themes that we might have expected, *a priori*, to find at the left hand end of the scale, 'Quality of life' and 'Anti-establishment views', did not load together consistently. 'Quality of life' loaded against 'Peace and co-operation' in Belgium, Britain, Austria and Luxembourg, while 'Anti-establishment views' loaded with 'Social conservatism' in Ireland and Sweden, and against 'Peace and co-operation' in Britain.

We then inspected the loadings of the other variables, relative to the left- and right-wing 'marker' variables. We found empirical as well as intuitive grounds for incorporating 'Democracy', 'Social service expansion: positive', 'Education: positive', and 'Labour: positive' at the left hand end of the scale. Furthermore, we found grounds to incorporate 'Military: positive' and 'Freedom' at the right hand end of the scale. Possible additional candidates for incorporation in the left–right scale are 'EEC: negative' and 'Social justice' on the left and 'Agriculture and farmers' on the right. There was some ambiguity in the loadings of each of these, however, and there is no reason for – indeed much to be said against – adding ambiguous categories to the left–right scale. Results are summarised in Table 2.4.

As a result of this first stage, therefore, a common left–right scale was computed for each country. The right-hand end of the scale was constructed by adding together the frequency counts for references to 'Capitalist eco-

Table 2.4 The relation of various policy variables to the potential left–right scale

Variables loading consistently with marker variables at one end or the other of left–right scale:

Country	Left	Right
Austria	202	*201* 703
Belgium	108 *202 506 701*	110
Britain	110 *504 506 701*	*104* 303
Denmark	110 202 503 *504 506*	*104 201*
France	110 *701* 705	703
Ireland	303 503 *504 506 701 703*	
Italy	110 *202* 303 *504 506 701 703*	503
Luxembourg	110 *701*	*104* 108 303 504 703
Netherlands	*202* 301 *504 506 701*	108 301 703
Sweden	*202* 503 *701*	301

Variable numbers are those used in Table 2.2. Italicised variables load consistently in several countries.

nomics', 'Social conservatism', 'Freedom and domestic human rights' and 'Military: positive'. The left hand end of the scale was constructed by adding together the frequency counts for 'State intervention', 'Peace and co-operation', 'Democracy', 'Social service: positive', 'Education: positive' and 'Labour groups: positive'. The final left–right scale was computed as the total proportion of the manifesto devoted to right wing references minus the total proportion devoted to left-wing references.

In the second stage of the investigation, an attempt was made to identify any other policy dimensions that might consistently appear in conjunction with the left–right scale. The computed left–right scale was treated as a single variable and used as input to a second set of exploratory factor analyses together with the remaining unclassified variables. This analysis was intended to identify potential variables or clusters of variables that were consistently orthogonal to the left–right scale, in order to consider them as candidates for treatment as independent policy dimensions.

Taking the set as whole, one possible combination of coding categories suggested itself; this is a grouping of 'Quality of life', 'Decentralisation' and 'Underprivileged minorities'. This can be considered a 'New Politics' or a 'Green' dimension on intuitive grounds, and the variables load together consistently in the second stage factor analyses. A similar dimension appeared in many countries in our original analysis of party manifestos, and this 'New politics' dimension can be considered as the most plausible candidate for adoption as a second general dimension in each of the coun-

Table 2.5 The relationship of the other policy variables to the left–right scale

| | Variables loading left–right scale | | Variables orthogonal to left–right scale | | |
	Left	Right			
Austria	503 705		*110+301+703*	108 vs 303	*Qual+301*
Belgium		303	*(301+Anti) vs 705*	*(Qual +301) vs 703*	Prod+110
Britain	503	303	*(Qual+Prod) vs 703*	108+301	*Qual+705 +110*
Denmark*	503		*Prod+703*	Qual+Anti+ 303	*301+705*
France	Qual+Anti 705				
Ireland*	503	Anti	*110+301+ 705*	*Qual+301 +303*	Prod+108
Italy	110 303 703	503	*Anti+705*	*Qual+301*	Prod vs 108
Luxembourg	110	703	*Prod+108 +303*	*Qual+301 +705*	
Netherlands	705 Qual	703	*Anti+110*	Prod+305 vs 503	108 vs 301
Sweden	503	303	*Qual+301+ 705*	Prod+103	Anti+110

* The following variables also load orthogonally to the left–right scale: Denmark, variable 108; and Ireland, variable 703.
Note: variable numbers are taken from Table 2.2. Variables that load consistently in several countries are highlighted.

tries considered. References to it comprise much less of the total manifesto than references to the variables comprising the left–right scale, however, while its interpretation is potentially ambiguous in certain countries. For this reason, country authors have used the 'New politics' dimension only when they felt that it was appropriate (Table 2.5).

As we indicated above, the face validity of the 'common' left–right scale was tested informally on the British case, and is illustrated in Figure 2.1, which shows the positions of the Conservative, Labour and Liberal parties over time. As it happens, the scale seems to work rather well. Not only does it always distinctly separate the two main parties, but party movements seem to correspond with historical factors that intuitively 'should' be reflected in party policy. The 'end of ideology' or 'Butskellite' convergence of the two main parties in the late 1950s shows up, as does the continued rightward

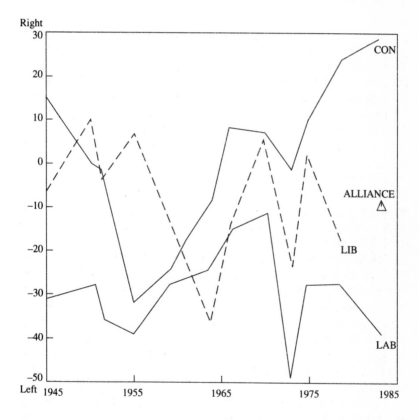

Figure 2.1   Movement of British parties on final left–right scale, 1945–85

drift of Labour under Wilson. The 'Three Day Week' crisis election of February 1974 appears as a clear deviation. The rightward shift of the Conservatives under Thatcher and the rather later shift of Labour to the left also emerge quite clearly. All in all, the scale paints an eminently sensible picture of the policy positions of Labour and the Conservatives, though it probably does rather exaggerate the impact of the events of February 1974 on Labour policy. All of this, with the possible exception of the scores for the Liberals in the 1950s and 1964, suggests that the scale is performing well and we therefore felt confident in adopting it for use in the coalition systems discussed in the chapters that follow.

MODELLING COALITION FORMATION IN HIGH-DIMENSIONAL POLICY SPACES

Having estimated party and government policy positions in our 20 dimensional policy spaces, we are in a position to calculate the 'policy distances' between actors and then to test theories of government formation based on the notion of policy distance minimisation. As we have argued previously, game theoretic models will not be of much help to us in this context – since they predict the absence of a core and generic instability in policy spaces of high dimensionality. In the country chapters that follow, however, the authors structure their discussion of government formation in a multi-dimensional policy space round a more inductive model, adapted from one originally proposed by Grofman (1982).

Grofman's model assumes that coalitions are built in a series of stages, in which parties first combine into protocoalitions, and that protocoalitions then combine into larger coalitions until some threshold is reached which makes the coalition large enough to take office. Grofman recognizes that in theory the formation threshold need not be a legislative majority, but in practice applies the majority winning criterion in his model. However, as the discussion in the previous chapter should indicate, this may not be appropriate when policy is important in government formation, since governments could be viable if they control less than a majority. We therefore adopt a more conservative position and, except in countries where a majority is required, assume only that the government that forms will be one of the series of protocoalitions predicted by the model, whether or not this has a majority.

Grofman suggests that each stage of the formation process is driven by the desire of the actors to form coalitions with the minimum ideological diversity: 'At Stage 1 each actor looks to form a protocoalition of himself and the actor nearest to him in N-space' (Grofman, 1982, p.78). If no winning coalition is formed, then the process moves on to Stage 2, in which 'each protocoalition seeks to merge with exactly one other protocoalition' (ibid, p.78) and the process continues until a winning coalition is formed.

By a happy coincidence, the data presentation technique of cluster analysis effectively operationalises this model. If we see coalitions as 'clusters' of parties, then cluster analysis takes a set of points (the policy positions of parties in this case) and combines the two closest points into a cluster (a coalition in this case). The process continues until there is a single cluster of all points (a grand coalition).

The information used by cluster analysis is the matrix of policy distances between all pairs of parties in the system. While Grofman tests a similar model on two-dimensional policy spaces derived for Norway, Denmark and Germany, the technique we propose works just as well with policy distances in policy spaces of high dimensionality. There is thus no need to reduce our full 20-dimensional space and thereby lose information. The use of cluster analysis to test policy distance models of coalition formation thus allows us to stay close to our original data.

As with any technique, particular operational decisions must be made before we can apply cluster analysis to the specific problem at hand. These decisions can have a significant effect on our results and, what is more, force us to consider theoretical matters that are underspecified in the theories as they currently stand.

The first operational decision to be made relates to which of the two alternative clustering strategies should be adopted. The first is based on hierarchical and the other on non-hierarchical assumptions about how the process of clustering is most appropriately modelled. A second key decision relates to how we should model the policy position of a coalition of several parties with different policy positions. A third decision relates to the most appropriate way to measure the distances between parties and protocoalitions in our 20-dimensional policy space.

Hierarchical or non-hierarchical clustering strategies?

One of two fundamentally different approaches can be used to model the clustering of any spatially distributed set of points. The first is hierarchical, the second is not. (A more extended discussion of some of the issues raised in this and the next section can be found in Laver and Schofield (1990). Hierarchical strategies assume that, at each stage in the process of clustering (coalition formation), the two 'closest' points (parties) are combined into a new cluster (protocoalition), a process that is iterated until all points lie within a single cluster (the grand coalition). Clusters (protocoalitions), once formed, are treated as indivisible units in subsequent stages in the analysis. This approach models a process of coalition formation that is very close to the one described by Grofman whose analysis provides that 'once a protocoalition has formed, it is assumed to act as a single actor . . .' (1982, p.78). This is the theory: its validity is an entirely empirical matter, upon which light can only be thrown by detailed discussions of the history of coalition formation in particular cases. We would be looking, in order to reject the assumption that coalition formation is a hierarchical process, for evidence that a protocoalition which had bargained as a unit at one stage in the process had subsequently split up. Since such evidence is in principle available, the assumption of hierarchical clustering can be tested, though to the best of our knowledge neither Grofman nor anyone else has yet done so in any systematic manner. The country chapters below do, however, explicitly consider this issue.

If we accept the hierarchical clustering assumption, with its implication that protocoalitions cannot break up once they have formed, then we can represent the process of coalition formation by a tree diagram, or 'dendrogram'. In the hypothetical example shown in Figure 2.2, parties D and E fuse first, followed by parties A and B. Party C then joins protocoalition AB. Finally protocoalitions ABC and DE fuse to form the grand coalition. (It is particularly important to note that this dendrogram carries no implication whatsoever that parties A, B, C, D and E are in any sense arranged upon a one-dimensional policy scale.) If we assume that it is necessary for government coalitions to control a majority of seats in the legislature, then this dendrogram contains a unique prediction of the outcome. The predicted coalition will be the first cluster to appear in the dendrogram that controls a majority of legislative seats. In this example the predicted coalition will be ABC. It is worth noting that, since a party cannot leave a coalition once it has joined it, a process of hierarchical clustering is quite likely to produce surplus majority coalitions, as it does in this case.

On the assumption that we are looking for viable rather than for majority coalitions, the dendrogram plots a path of coalition formation from a set of individual parties to a grand coalition. In this case we can say no more than that the coalition which forms will be found somewhere along this path. In the example given in Figure 2.2, this leaves open the possibility of the following coalitions: $A, B, C, D, E, AB, ABC, DE, ABCDE$. It rules out many more, including coalitions that include D but not E, for example, or those that include B but not A.

Party and percentage of seats

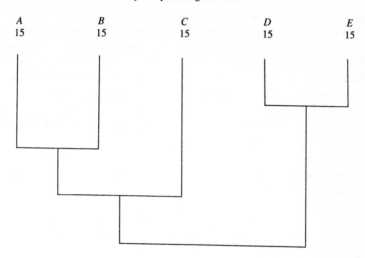

Figure 2.2 A hypothetical hierarchical clustering of parties into coalitions

The alternative to this whole approach is to assume that coalitions form as a result of a process of non-hierarchical clustering. Non-hierarchical clustering algorithms look for the optimum partition of the points (parties) into a given number of subsets (protocoalitions) given the distances between all pairs of points. They are more general than hierarchical algorithms since there is nothing sacred about the clusters (protocoalitions) which form *en route* to a particular solution. These can easily be broken up and the members relocated if, further down the line, a new protocoalition requires some but not all of the members of an old one.

One way of using non-hierarchical clustering techniques to model policy-driven coalition building in an *m*-party system is to look first at the set of *m* single-party coalitions. In the next stage, two parties are fused by looking for a partition of the parties into *m*-1 coalitions and so on until, after *m*-1 stages, the grand coalition is reached. Figure 2.3 shows a hypothetical example of this process for the same party system as that in Figure 2.2. As with the process of hierarchical clustering, the first multi-party coalition to form is *DE*. At the next stage, however, *DE* is broken up as coalitions *AB* and *CD* form. (This could be because, while *C* and *D* are quite close to each other, the hierarchical clustering algorithm forces *D* to remain in an indis-soluble coalition with *E*, at a combined policy point further from *C* than that

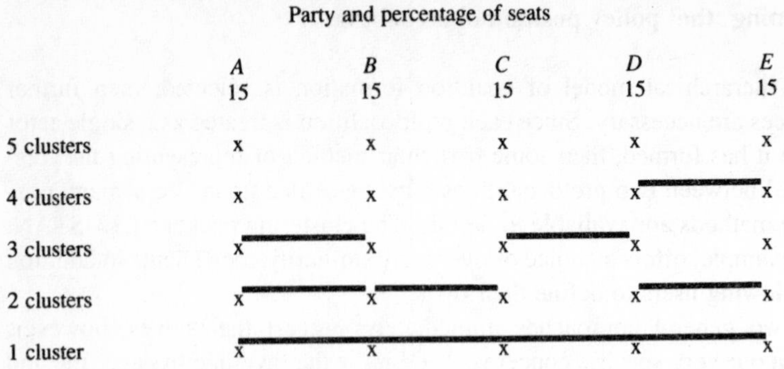

Party and percentage of seats

	A 15	B 15	C 15	D 15	E 15
5 clusters	x	x	x	x	x
4 clusters	x	x	x	x———x	
3 clusters	x———x		x———x		x
2 clusters	x———x		———x	x———x	
1 cluster	x———————————————x				

Figure 2.3   A hypothetical non-hierarchical clustering of parties into coalitions

of *D* alone. *C* could join *D* easily, but finds it much harder to join *DE*.) Protocoalitions are broken up once more at the next stage, as the two most compact sets of parties are *ABC* and *DE*. Finally, the grand coalition forms.

Once more, if coalitions must for some reason control a majority, then the first coalition to pass this winning post is the unique prediction of the model. In this case the prediction is *CD*. Once more, there is no reason for predicted coalitions to be minimal winning. Though *CD* is minimal winning in this case, the partition of the parties into three coalitions could just as easily, with different policy distances, have been *A*, *B*, *CDE*, and the prediction would then have been the surplus majority coalition *CDE*. Once more, when we abandon the notion of a majority winning post and concentrate on policy-viable governments, then the model predicts a set of possible coalitions – though relaxing the assumption of hierarchical formation increases the number of coalitions in this prediction set. In this example, it includes *A*, *B*, *C*, *D*, *E*, *AB*, *DE*, *CD*, *ABC*, *ABCDE*.

Choosing between hierarchical and non-hierarchical clustering techniques involves making a quite fundamental assumption about the coalition formation process. Nobody, presumably, would want to argue that coalition formation is a rigidly hierarchical process based on the progressive construction of indissoluble protocoalitions. Nonetheless it is possible to model coalition formation, as Grofman does, as a process in which the eventual coalition is built up in stages as a series of protocoalitions (even if these are allowed to be dissoluble in extremis). This contrasts with a model in which a period of 'at large' bargaining is followed by a series of attempts to move directly to the final coalition, a model in which any deal is ultimately possible, whatever has gone before.

Defining 'the' policy position of a coalition

If a hierarchical model of coalition formation is selected, then further choices are necessary. Since each protocoalition is treated as a single actor once it has formed, then some particular method of representing the 'distance' between two protocoalitions must be settled upon. Very many possible methods are available to do this. The clustering package CLUSTAN, for example, offers a choice of over forty similarity coefficients in addition to allowing users to define their own.

Two general approaches immediately suggest themselves, however, given our very specific concerns. The first is the 'average linkage' method which, as its name suggests, works with the 'average distance' between pairs of clusters. (The 'average distance' between two clusters defined as the mean distance between all pairs of points, such that the two points are one in each of the two clusters.) The average linkage method thus works by looking, at each stage, for the two clusters with the smallest average distance between them and combining these.

The second approach works on the distance between cluster centroids or between some other set of points that can be taken to represent, in some sense, the 'centre' of the cluster. The 'centroid linkage' algorithm computes the distance between the centroids of all pairs of clusters, at each stage combining the pair of clusters with the shortest distance between centroids.

The average linkage algorithm thus takes into consideration the ideal policy points of each member of the protocoalition when considering which protocoalitions should be fused. This retains a notion that the individual members of the protocoalition, though irrevocably fused together as a single actor, continue to evaluate actions on the basis of their own individual policy objectives. Put rather crudely, the average linkage algorithm views each protocoalition as a single body with several distinct brains. The centroid linkage algorithm in contrast, assumes that policy compromises are struck at each stage of the proceedings and that the members of a protocoalition then go on to behave as if protocoalition policy is their own preferred policy. In this case, not only do the actors' bodies fuse into a single body but their brains fuse into a single brain located at the centroid of their individual brains. The latter is the solution adopted, for example, by Grofman (1982), though he also weights party policy positions before calculating the centroid. The distinction between average linkage and centroid linkage highlights the fact that hierarchical coalition formation algorithms, though they do assume that indivisible protocoalitions form along the road, do not necessarily need to assume that the members evaluate events with a single mind. The more conservative approach is to assume that they do not think as one and that the average linkage coalition formation method, failing a strong argument to the contrary, is the more appropriate. There is no real need, in short, to assume that all protocoalitions are best represented during the formation process by their policy centroids, even if we assume that they are indivisible bargaining units. Accordingly, each of the country chapters that follows reports the results of a hierarchical cluster analysis using the average linkage method, though some authors may refer to centroid-linkage results when they feel that these are appropriate.[2]

Choosing a metric with which to measure policy distance

One major operational issue that remains to be resolved is how to calculate the policy distance between two points on the basis of their positions on 20 policy dimensions. This matter is not as straightforward as it might seem. We are accustomed, in physical space, to think of the distance between two points in Euclidean terms, as the length of the straight line that joins them. Most formal analyses of the behaviour of actors in policy spaces also use a Euclidean notion of difference. For the purpose of analysing coalition bargaining, however, choice of a metric for calculating the distance between two points is far from obvious.

The selection of a distance metric must be based upon assumptions about the way in which the actors perceive the policy space. Imagine, for example, the situation in Figure 2.4. Party *A* prefers to spend 100*m* on Policy *X* and nothing on unrelated Policy *Y*. Party *B* prefers to spend nothing on *X* and 100*m* on *Y*. If the two parties must agree on a budget, an interpretation based on Euclidean policy distances would predict an outcome spending 50*m* on each policy, or 75 on *X* and 25 on *Y* or, indeed, any other combination of policies on the straight line between *A* and *B* in the policy space. Each of these outcomes is preferred by both parties to an outcome involving, say, spending nothing on both policies. At the 50*m*/50*m* point, for example, each party is conceding 50*m* on each policy. But why should this compromise be seen as 'better' than conceding 100*m* on one policy and nothing on the other?

An alternative way of measuring distances, more plausible in this context, is the city block metric. In this case, the distance between two points is the sum of the distances between them on each dimension. As might be expected from its name, 'diagonal' movement across the block is not permitted when using the city block metric. The (0, 0) and the (100, 100) points are the same distance from each party as is the (50, 50) point. All three points, after all, involve each party in making 100 million of concessions on valued policies. There is no reason to suppose that the (50, 50) compromise represents a more palatable package of 100m concessions than the (0,0) or the (100,100) compromise. This is because the two policy

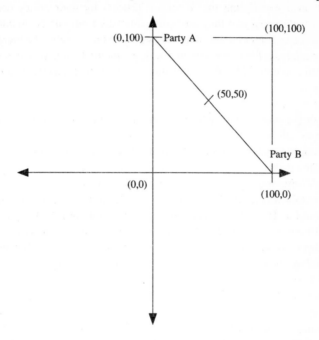

Figure 2.4   City-block and Euclidean policy bargaining

dimensions might well be quite independent of one another, in the sense that nothing would be lost in representing them on separate pieces of paper (and, indeed, by storing these pieces of paper in separate bank vaults on separate planets). The right-angle linking them is a graphical convenience, indicating independence, and we should not be seduced into taking any notice of it when calculating policy distances. There seem to us to be overwhelming *a priori* reasons, therefore, for using a city block metric when expressing distances in policy space. Conversely, we can see no *a priori* theoretical argument, based on assumptions about the perceptions of politicians, for using a Euclidean metric to measure policy distances.

Euclidean and city block metrics, however, are only two out of a variety of ways in which distances can be expressed. It might be argued, for example, that parties, in their competitive, argumentative environment, might be much more sensitive to the differences separating them than to the points that they agree on. This might indicate use of an 'infinity' metric, which measures the distance between the two parties as the distance between them on the dimension on which they are furthest apart – and ignores all other dimensions.

In order to explore the empirical implications of our choice of metric more fully, we made a complete investigation of the Belgian case, using a range of different metrics. For each of the elections investigated, distances between party policy positions in the full 20-dimensional space were expressed in terms of six different metrics. The cluster analysis was repeated six times, using the six different distance matrices that were thus created. Most of the time, the choice of metric did not in fact make a difference to the results of the cluster analysis. Significantly, when the choice of metric did make a difference, it was the city block metric that stood apart from the others.

While the results of our empirical exploration suggest that the choice of metric may not make a huge amount of difference to our cluster analyses, we opted for the city block metric on *a priori* theoretical grounds. The choice of metric does sometimes make a difference and, when it does, we feel that the city block metric provides the most realistic view of policy bargaining.

THE COUNTRY STUDIES

This chapter has been concerned with establishing a common empirical framework for the country chapters which follow. Whether based on the richness and complexity of the full 20-dimensional coding scheme or on the simplicity and intuitive appeal of the one-dimensional left–right scale, the common techniques of empirical analysis used in each chapter enable like to be compared with like – as far as this is ever possible in cross-national analysis.

To this end, each of the chapters concludes with an assessment of the usefulness of a number of policy-based theories of coalitional behaviour. While there are considerable problems associated with the rigorous cross-national testing of coalition theories, these theories do set out to help us interpret the politics of coalition in real political systems, and should be evaluated in the same terms. Individual country authors often consider theories that they regard as being particularly appropriate to the system concerned, but all country authors at least evaluate a common set of theories, derived from those discussed in the previous chapter.

The common set of theories includes some that are relevant only to a one-dimensional representation, and some relevant only to multidimensional representations. The one-dimensional theories evaluated include the one-dimensional 'core' model, which predicts that the government will always include the party with the median legislator on the left–right scale, whether or not it controls a legislative majority, and two versions of Axelrod's MCW (Minimal Connected Winning) theory. The first is the prediction that minimal connected winning coalitions will form (as defined in the previous chapter); the second relaxes the majority winning requirement, given our interest in policy payoffs, and predicts merely that the coalitions that form will be connected in the main left–right dimension. The multidimensional approaches considered always include the inductive clustering model, which predicts that the coalition which forms will be found at some point on the cluster-analytic coalition-formation tree, as defined above, whether or not this controls a legislative majority. In addition, a 'predominant party' approach is evaluated, derived from the analysis of the role of core parties in multidimensional issue spaces; this predicts that the coalition which forms will include the party that controls the median legislator on more salient policy dimensions than any other. (This latter approach is not strictly derived from the analysis of the core in multidimensional policy spaces – rather it represents an informal attempt, within this general style of argument, to identify the potential role of 'strong' parties). The results of all these evaluations are synthesised in the final chapter of the book.

The country chapters that follow, of course, are much more than a set of comparable quantitative analyses. As we argue in the introduction, their fundamental concern is with the role of policy in coalition bargaining. As a consequence, they deal with a wide range of qualitative phenomena. These include constraints on coalition bargaining, the motivations of the actors, significance of policy in the bargaining process – all the factors already discussed in Chapter 1. It is in no sense our intention to downgrade these issues by applying an invariant analysis. Thus, when a country author presents a coalition tree, a matrix of 20-dimensional city-block distances, or a set of party positions on a left–right scale, these should not be treated as sacrosanct. Obviously, local circumstances will vary widely and must be taken into account. What the common approach elaborated here sets out to provide, therefore, is a solid empirical foundation upon which the systematic analysis of a particular case can be built. Since we are concerned with policy, this foundation comprises a common body of information about policy: the positions of parties on twenty policy areas; their positions on a single left–right dimension; and the route towards the formation of a coalition that would be followed if all other things were equal. They never are equal, of course, which is the whole point of a country by country approach. But neither are they ever completely different, which is the reason for using a common empirical foundation as our starting point.

NOTES

1   Strictly speaking, the basic unit of analysis was the quasi-sentence rather than the sentence. The quasi-sentence is a statement which, grammatically and substantively, can stand alone as a vehicle of meaning. It is used as the basic unit of counting manifesto references because of the tendency in some languages to write complex 'periods' in which a range of different policy statements are embedded.
2   The data analyses that follow were conducted using the C-LAB subset of clustering routines within the M-LAB interactive mathematical modelling package.

3 Coalition and Party Policy in Ireland
M. J. Laver

The most striking feature of coalition politics in Ireland is the domination of the Irish party system by Fianna Fail. Measured by its share of the popular vote, Fianna Fail is Europe's second most popular party (Coakley, 1987). In the period 1948–87 it won an average of 46 per cent of the vote and 49 per cent of all seats in the legislature. Only the Swedish Social Democrats got a (very slightly) higher share of the popular vote, while only the British Conservative Party got a higher proportion of the seats. Because of the proportionality of the single transferable vote (STV) electoral system that is used in Ireland, however, the fact that Fianna Fail has got rather less than half of the vote has also meant that it has often got just under half of the seats. When the opposition has been divided, such election results have left the way clear for a Fianna Fail minority government. When two or more of the opposition parties have been able to agree, a single party Fianna Fail government has been replaced by a coalition. Until 1989, therefore, the politics of coalition in Ireland were characterised by the alternation of a single party Fianna Fail government with a coalition of its main opponents (Farrell, 1987; Laver, 1986).

The traditional coalition of Fianna Fail's main opponents broke up irrevocably in 1987, however. In the election that followed the fall of the coalition, Fianna Fail did well enough to form a viable minority government, but called another election in 1989 in search of an overall parliamentary majority. In fact, Fianna Fail lost seats, while its opponents gained. Desperate to remain in office in the context of an economy that was at last booming, Fianna Fail leaders finally compromised and, in an historic reversal of party strategy, agreed to share cabinet seats with another party, the Progressive Democrats (Laver and Arkins, 1990).

Before this, and for all of the period covered by this study, however, Ireland was a system in which the only real question to be answered by coalition bargaining was whether the members of the only alternative government to Fianna Fail could make the policy compromises necessary before they could take office.

THE IRISH PARTY SYSTEM

The Irish party system assumed substantially its present form around the time of the 1932 election, although traditional rivalries between Fianna Fail and Fine Gael can be traced back to the Irish civil war. The political groupings that were to become Fianna Fail opposed the signing of the treaty with Britain which partitioned Ireland into Northern and Southern Ireland, while the factions that were to become Fine Gael approved of it. Labour, in contrast, stood back from these vital issues surrounding the formation of the state and failed, as a result, to build a solid electoral base in the new party system. To this day, the image of Fianna Fail as the more nationalist and anti-British party remains while Labour continues to form the basis of the smallest left in Europe. Since 1932, Fianna Fail has never won less than 42 per cent and never won more than 52 per cent of the popular vote. (See Table A.1 in the appendix to this chapter). The level of Fine Gael support dipped to 20 per cent in 1948 and rose to 39 per cent in November 1982.

The contemporary era in Irish politics began in 1957, and this particular study takes up the story at this point. Fringe parties were in decline and Fianna Fail began an unbroken 16-year stint as the sole party of government. The government's famous Programme for National Recovery was published in 1958, marking the end of an inward looking and protectionist economic policy and the emergence of a more open and outward looking approach to economic development. The party system for most of the time since 1957 comprised three main parties though a fourth party, the Workers' Party grew steadily during the latter part of the period and became a force in government formation after successes in the 1987 and 1989 elections. A fifth party, the Progressive Democrats, emerged suddenly in 1986 (Lyne, 1987).

A list of the governments that formed in the 1957–89 period can be found in Table A.2 of the appendix to this chapter. From 1957 to 1973, Fianna Fail governed alone, though often in a minority position. In 1973, however, the Labour Party decided that it had had enough of opposition and forged a fourteen-point Joint Electoral Programme with Fine Gael. (For an extended discussion of the coalition issue within the Labour Party see Gallagher (1982). The two parties contested and won the 1973 election on this programme. This coalition went on to fight and lose the 1977 election on another joint programme and Fianna Fail won the largest parliamentary majority in the history of the state. In 1981, however, Fianna Fail was defeated once more by a Fine Gael/Labour coalition. The election result was extremely close and the coalition formed a minority government. This government was short-lived, being defeated on its first budget in early 1982 and losing the subsequent election to Fianna Fail, who formed another minority administration. This government was also short lived, losing power in the election of November 1982 to a Fine Gael/Labour coalition that had a working majority and held office until Labour withdrew its support in 1987.

As a result of its disastrous losses in the opinion polls during the lifetime of the 1982–87 coalition, the Labour Party set up a Commission on Electoral Strategy. This considered several options and eventually recommended that the party stay out of coalition for the foreseeable future, a strategy that subsequently became official party policy. In the 1987 election, therefore, Fianna Fail was not challenged by an agreed alternative government. Fianna Fail gained enough seats to form a viable minority administration. Encouraged by favourable opinion polls ratings and irritated by government defeats on specific issues, Fianna Fail called an election in 1989. In the event they lost substantial ground and had to form the coalition administration already mentioned with the tiny Progressive Democrat Party, which gained two cabinet posts as a result. Michael Gallagher (1985) and Peter Mair (1987a) give excellent detailed accounts of the Irish party system. Brian Farrell (1987; 1990) and Peter Mair (1990) give accounts of government formation after the 1987 and 1989 elections.

THE ROLE OF POLICY IN COALITION BARGAINING

In comparison with other European systems, Ireland can probably be characterised as one in which politicians are motivated more by the desire to get into office than by a desire to affect public policy. About 40 specialists in Irish politics were asked by Laver and Hunt to rate the extent to which politicians valued cabinet portfolios as rewards of office or as means to affect policy. A similar exercise was performed for 17 other European systems. Of these, only in Greece and Italy were politicians rated as being more interested in office rather than policy (Laver and Hunt, 1992). The lack of a strong left–right dimension (see below) and the role of traditional loyalties in determining patterns of party support have meant that intense ideological competition has rarely been presented as the basic motivation of Irish politicians. At the same time, the pervasive nature of clientelism in Irish politics means that the benefits of office are highly valued by politicians hoping for re-election.

Obviously these are gross over-simplifications. Many within the Labour Party feel that the party has certain fundamental ideological goals that should never be compromised by the desire to get into office. While a

number of Labour TDs are rural representatives who use clientelistic practices as much as anyone else, much of the Labour party organization is
urban. The party has a radical Militant Tendency and party conferences
debate matters of policy intently. Fianna Fail policy on Northern Ireland, in
particular, and on nationalism, in general, is dear to the hearts of many party
politicians and activists. Fianna Fail is without doubt the most nationalist of
the constitutional political parties in Ireland, the ideological home for many
who have very strong views on the matter.

Perhaps the most reasonable way to present the role of policy in Irish
politics, therefore, is to see it as an influence on politicians rather than as the
driving force behind party competition. As elsewhere, rank-and-file party
members tend to have stronger views while senior party politicians and
strategists tend to make policy compromises in order to maximise electoral
chances. Policy influences coalition behaviour in Ireland in three main
ways. It has an effect on the party composition of coalitions, on the allocation
of particular portfolios and of course on the content of the joint programme
of government.

Of these, the allocation of particular ministries to particular parties is
the only one that tends to be left to bargaining after the election. Taking
charge of particular portfolios is one of the most effective ways in which
parties can control policy once they get into office. There has been a clear
tendency for Labour to take a disproportionate number of the 'spending'
ministries when it has gone into coalition with Fine Gael, reflecting
Labour's much greater concern to protect policy programmes involving
public spending.

While the allocation of cabinet portfolios takes place after the election,
most other aspects of coalition bargaining tend to be dealt with beforehand.
This is because the STV electoral system makes it sensible for parties to
form coalitions before rather than after elections (see below). In each of the
five elections between 1973 and November 1982, the Irish electorate faced
a clear choice between a Fine Gael/Labour coalition and a Fianna Fail
single party government. The 'normal' sequence of coalition bargaining
was thus turned on its head. The composition of the coalition was agreed
before the election and, if the prospective coalition won the election, then
the presumption was it would form a government.

In 1973 and 1977, this process was taken one stage further and the
prospective Fine Gael/Labour coalition fought the election on the basis of
an agreed policy programme. This meant that there was no need to bargain
over policy after the election. In the three elections held in 1981 and 1982,
in contrast, bargaining over coalition policy was left until later. There was
a general agreement that the parties would go into government together if

they won, but a Joint Programme of Government was negotiated after the election, and required ratification by a Labour delegate conference.

Policy bargaining between the parties, whether it takes place before or after the election, is encapsulated in a joint programme. Whether this is a joint electoral programme or a joint programme of government, it is publicised at the end of the negotiations and forms a reasonably unambiguous statement of the policy compromises that have been reached. The document has no official status but it is widely referred to by the press. Particular proposals in the joint programme tend to be seen as the 'property' of particular parties. The implementation of these becomes a yardstick against which the success of the party in question is subsequently measured in the continuing competition between parties that goes on after the formation of coalition.

A notable feature of joint policy programmes in Ireland is that issues on which the potential coalition partners are diametrically opposed tend to be ignored; they are statements of points agreed between the parties. Such agreement may be forged on the basis of policies that are shared anyway, or on the basis of policy compromises negotiated between them during the formation phase; but they are points of agreement nonetheless. Joint programmes do not, for obvious reasons, draw attention to outstanding points of difference. It is certainly feasible, furthermore, for coalition partners to avoid covering the full universe of policies when they publish a joint programme. Leaving something out of the joint programme, indeed, is a typical response to a deadlock in coalition negotiations. The programme is thus unambiguous as far as it deals with points of agreement but it is ambiguous in relation to what is left out.

STRUCTURAL INFLUENCES AND CONSTRAINTS ON COALITION BARGAINING

The main constraints and influences on coalition bargaining in Ireland are summarised in Table 3.1. Almost none of these are imposed from outside the system. The only one that might theoretically have an impact concerns the attitude of the British government towards Sinn Fein. If Sinn Fein were ever to be in the position to enter a coalition administration in the Republic it might well be felt that the British might intervene in some way to prevent this happening. The prospect of such a thoroughly hostile presence in government just south of the border with Northern Ireland would certainly be very unwelcome to the British, but it is a prospect that is so remote that it is not worth considering further.

Table 3.1   Constraints and influences upon coalition bargaining in Ireland

1. British attitude to Sinn Fein participation in government. (Not an imminent possibility.)
2. Section 31 of Broadcasting Act prohibits broadcasting of interviews with Sinn Fein.
3. Refusal of Fianna Fail to enter coalitions with other parties throughout the entire period before 1989.
4. Refusal of the Labour Party to enter coalitions with other parties before 1973 and after 1987.
5. STV electoral system encourages coalition formation before, rather than after, elections.
6. President has no power to nominate Prime Minister, leading to 'freestyle' bargaining between parties.
7. Doctrine of collective cabinet responsibility forces coalition partners defeated in cabinet decisions to defend coalition policy.

There are several constraints on coalition bargaining in Ireland imposed from within the system itself. Only one is a formal legal matter; Section 31 of the Broadcasting Act prohibits RTE, the state broadcasting authority, from broadcasting interviews with members of Sinn Fein, among other proscribed associations. This obviously has a major impact on the reporting of election campaigns. It is a provision that has not yet had any practical impact on government formation process, given the small level of support for Sinn Fein and the fact that it has not won a seat in recent times.

Other constraints in Ireland are more behavioural. The most important of these has already been discussed in the introduction and relates to the refusal of Fianna Fail, prior to 1989, to share power with any other party. The tradition that Fianna Fail does not go into coalition cabinets is rooted deep in the party's consciousness and was treated as an axiom by almost everyone when various governmental possibilities were discussed. The abandoning of the policy in 1989 proved quite traumatic for the party, with grassroots protests from a number of regions, but particularly the west of Ireland. For the period of this study, this constraint obviously has a fundamental impact on the structure of coalition negotiations since, given the pattern of most election results, it eliminated most potential majority coalitions. After the 1987 election, for example, there were sixteen possible winning coalitions in Ireland including the grand coalition. Of these, fifteen included Fianna Fail and were thus ruled out by the party's refusal to share power. In 1973, 1981 and November 1982, the Fianna Fail constraint effectively meant that only a coalition of Fine Gael and Labour could form.

Before 1973 and since 1987 the Labour party, too, has ruled out participation in coalition governments, preferring to offer 'undiluted' Labour policies to the electorate. This has meant that Labour was available for coalition only between 1973 and 1987, and eliminated the remaining available winning coalition in 1987. This matter is effectively out of the hands of the party leadership since a change of strategy requires the approval of a Labour delegate conference.

In addition to the constraints on bargaining that eliminate particular coalitions from consideration, a number of structural factors are influential. The first has to do with the STV electoral system, which provides significant rewards, constituting the balance between victory and defeat, for parties that can agree to transfer votes from one to the other. This provides a very strong inducement for parties considering coalition to move the coalition formation phase forward to the period before an election. In effect, STV makes pre-electoral coalitions the norm in Ireland.

The second major structural influence on coalition bargaining in Ireland concerns the part played by the President, who is unusual in the European context in having almost no role in the process of forming a government. He appoints the incoming Prime Minister on the nomination of the Dail. If the Dail is deadlocked, however, the President appears to have no role in resolving the problem, though he is not obliged to call a new election (Coakley,1987; Farrell, 1987). The behaviour of the President in the situation that arose in the potential deadlock over government formation in 1987, however, suggests that he would indeed have called an election rather than taken any other step. This means – in contrast with the situation in the Netherlands or Belgium for example – that the President does not take the initiative, even in specifying the starting point of the coalition formation process. The outcome of coalition bargaining is the result of free negotiations between the parties (within the constraints listed above).

The third major structural influence on government formation is a product of the doctrine of collective cabinet responsibility, laid down in Article 28.4.2 of the Irish constitution. The doctrine means that 'the government must present a united front to the public – that all its members must publicly support its policies and decisions' (Casey, 1987, p.148). This doctrine has a major impact on policy bargaining within coalitions since it gives the whip hand to the party that controls the majority of cabinet seats. If a particular policy divides the coalition partners, then the majority party can ultimately win the day in cabinet. The losing party must then defend this decision in public. Particularly since Labour ministers have tended to control spending departments when in coalition with Fine Gael, this has been a serious problem for Labour ministers who have had to announce and then defend unpopular spending cuts, despite having argued strongly against them in cabinet (Laver, 1986).

Overall, Irish politics is remarkable in the extent to which the composition of recent governments has been more or less fixed by various constraints and influences on bargaining. Certainly, to ignore constraints when considering the role of policy in coalition formation in Ireland would be to miss most of the point of what is going on. What is clear is that, until 1989, the party composition of the coalition that could displace Fianna Fail was pretty much fixed. The impact of party policy, therefore, was in determining how difficult it was for Fianna Fail's opponents to go into government together.

POLICY COMPETITION IN IRISH POLITICS

Party and coalition policy have typically been relegated to a secondary position in accounts of the Irish political system. This is largely because of the weakness of the left and the similarity of the two main parties on the economic policy positions that have differentiated parties in most of the rest of Europe. Party politics in Ireland is more often discussed in terms of traditional partisan loyalties, of personality conflicts, and of clientelism and brokerage at the local level.

Certainly, dimensional analyses of the content of Irish party manifestos have not generated a clear left–right dimension unless they are forced to do so, though Mair (1987b) does detect evidence of an emerging left–right dimension in recent years. Indeed, Mair's recent work explicitly uses a left–right dimension when analysing government formation in Ireland (1990). Using the expert survey referred to above, Laver and Hunt (1992) found that a left–right dimension, operationalised in terms of party policy on the public ownership of business, was seen as very important by most of the Irish parties.

All of these suggests that the traditional left–right dimension may be more important in Ireland than many traditional accounts suggest. The scores of the parties on the standard left–right dimension are presented in Table 3.2. Party positions at each election since 1957 confirm the main points made above. Differences between Fianna Fail and Fine Gael are both erratic and unpredictable; there have been dramatic swings in position and one of these two parties has not always been to the left or right, of the other. There is no obvious pattern of left–right policy competition between Fianna Fail and Fine Gael. On the other hand, the policy position of the Labour

Table 3.2   Left–right scores of parties and coalitions in Ireland, 1957–87

| Year | Party | | | |
	Fianna Fail	Fine Gael	Labour	Fine Gael–Labour coalition
1957	30	78	−32	
1961	33	9	−34	
1965	−1	−8	−16	
1969	34	−7	−17	
1973	57	n/a	n/a	−19*
1977	−4	n/a	n/a	−16*
1981	−1	7	−9	−14
1982(F)	−5	−9	−15	
1982(N)	−23	+5	−17	−15

* In 1973 and 1977 Fine Gael and Labour issued a joint electoral programme, the coding of which is reported here. In 1977 the coalition was defeated, however, so the 1977 'coalition' programme did not become a government programme.
Party with the median legislator is italicised.

Party is always to the left of the other two parties, which suggests that the common left–right dimension does give us an insight into one element in the situation.

DOCUMENTS CODED

This matter has effectively already been discussed in the section on the role of policy in coalition bargaining. In 1973, the Fine Gael and Labour issued a 14-point joint electoral programme. They did not issue a new coalition policy statement after winning the election and taking office so the joint electoral programme is used in this analysis. In 1977, Fine Gael and Labour issued another joint electoral programme, this time as the outgoing government. This document is used in the analysis of party positions but, since the coalition lost the election, did not form the basis of a government programme. In 1981 and November 1982 the coalition parties, having each fought the election on their own distinctive programme, negotiated a Joint Programme of Government before taking office. These were each published and widely discussed in the media and were approved by a Labour delegate conference. It is these documents that we have taken and analysed as the outcome of coalition bargaining.

THE 'LEFT–RIGHT' ONE DIMENSIONAL ANALYSIS

Government formation

The positions of the main Irish parties on the common left–right dimension over the period 1957–87 are given in Table 3.2. This also identifies the party controlling the median legislator on this dimension and presents quite a striking picture of the role of policy in the politics of coalition in Ireland. With only two exceptions, the party or electoral coalition controlling the median legislator did indeed succeed in forcing its way into government. This is of course not surprising in the case of single party majority governments such as those of Fianna Fail in 1957, 1965, 1969 and 1977, or of the majority Fine Gael–Labour electoral coalition in 1973. It does, however, account for the remarkable stability of the minority Fianna Fail administration of 1961–65, since the party was in a core position at this time. In more recent years, furthermore, we see a fascinating pattern. In 1981, the core party was Fianna Fail but it was kept out of office by a Fine Gael–Labour coalition. In February 1982 the core party was Fine Gael but it was kept out of office by a minority Fianna Fail government. Each government was short-lived. In November 1982 in contrast, the core party was Labour, which went into a stable coalition with Fine Gael on what were perceived at the time to be rather favourable terms.

In other words, the standard one-dimensional left–right analysis shows that the extreme instability of the 1981–82 era, with three elections within eighteen months, was associated with governments which excluded the core party. Furthermore, this period of instability ended with the formation of a government that included the core party. Overall, therefore, the one dimensional analysis clearly offers some tantalising insight into the more salient features of recent government formation in Ireland.

The detailed codings for the 1987 manifestos are not yet available, but are likely to make Fianna Fail the core party.

Government policy and policy payoffs

It should be remembered that we are dealing in the Irish case only with two situations in which parties issued separate election manifestos, then bargained to produce a joint programme of government, then went into government together. This happened in 1981 and in November 1982. In the case of the 1973 coalition government, a joint programme was agreed before the election and no subsequent policy bargaining appears to have taken place prior to the formation of the government. We thus do not have 'independent' party policy positions against which to measure government policy. Another untypical case arose in 1977, when there was bargaining between the parties to produce a joint election programme that did not become the government programme because the coalition was defeated at the election.

In the two clear cases in which we can compare party and coalition policy we see from Table 3.2 that, considering only the standard left–right dimension, Labour appears to have done well out of the deal. In 1981, government policy actually appears to the left of Labour policy and is obviously much closer to that of Labour than to that of Fine Gael. In November 1982 government policy is between that of Labour and Fine Gael, but once more much closer to that of Labour. If we compare the Fine Gael–Labour joint electoral programmes of 1973 and 1977 with both Fine Gael and Labour policy before and after this era, we once more see that 'coalition' policy seems much closer to Labour than to that of Fine Gael. These differences are summarised in Table 3.3, which shows that, for the two cases in which we can draw firm conclusions, Labour did best out of the coalition policy package and Fine Gael actually did worse than Fianna Fail, the opposition party.

The evidence supports the interpretation that Labour had a stronger influence than Fine Gael on, and hence derived higher initial 'policy payoffs' from, the official joint policy programmes of Fine Gael–Labour coalitions. (The actual policy outputs of the governments in question, with which Labour activists, in particular were much less satisfied, may well of course have been quite different but we have no systematic evidence on this.) A possible explanation for the apparent success of Labour in getting its policies into the Joint Programmes of Government can be found in the need to get the Programme agreed by a special Labour delegate conference before the party was allowed under its rules to enter a coalition.

Table 3.3 Distance between coalition and party policy on standard left–right dimension, Ireland, 1981–82

| | *Distance between coalition and party policy* | |
	1981	*1982 (November)*
Fine Gael	21	20
Labour	5	2
Fianna Fail	13	8

THE TWENTY-DIMENSIONAL ANALYSIS

Coalition formation

If we deal with the full set of twenty policy categories we can calculate policy distances between parties directly and model coalition formation as a process of clustering (see Chapter 2 above). The twenty-dimensional city block distances between parties and the results of the cluster analyses are given in Figure A.1 in the Appendix to this chapter. What is striking is the confirmation of Mair's earlier finding, based on a one-dimensional analysis, that the Fine Gael–Labour coalition can be anticipated several years before it actually formed (Mair, 1987b). This conclusion is based on a process of policy convergence, between the two parties, that began in 1961 and continued until the issuing of the fourteen point joint electoral programme in 1973, the year of electoral victory for the coalition. This is a particularly significant point given the prevalence in much popular writing of the notion that Fine Gael and Labour were in some senses an ideological odd couple who were forced into each other's arms by no more than the need to get rid of Fianna Fail. They may have come together from very different directions and for very different reasons and there may have remained a number of very visible policy differences between them but, taking the policy packages as a whole, the steady convergence between Fine Gael and Labour in the run up to 1973 is quite striking. A Fine Gael–Labour coalition is indicated on policy grounds by every cluster analysis since 1961, though Fianna Fail's electoral success and the failure of the future coalition partners to come to an electoral arrangement before 1973 kept Fianna Fail in office. Between 1973 and November 1982, not only was a Fine Gael–Labour coalition predicted, but one formed whenever possible. We find, therefore, that the twenty-dimensional analysis not only predicts what happened, but also shows the emerging policy basis of the Fine Gael–Labour coalition some time before this was officially recognised at a tactical level by the parties themselves.

Coalition payoffs

The city block distances between party and coalition policy, measured in the full twenty dimensional policy space, are given in Table 3.4. Coalition policy was closer to the policies of the coalition members than it was to that of Fianna Fail in 1981 – thereby providing at least some policy payoff to the parties for going into government. Of the two coalition partners, Labour did

Table 3.4 Twenty-dimensional city-block distances between party and coalition policy, Ireland, 1981–82

	Fine Gael–Labour coalition	
	1981	1982 (November)
Fianna Fail	81	95
Fine Gael	70	93
Labour	57	90

better than Fine Gael, reproducing the pattern suggested by the one-dimensional analysis.

The situation in November 1982 was much less clear-cut, a result largely of the tendency of the Joint Programme of Government to emphasise issues that did not figure in any of the party manifestos. This left all of the parties more or less equidistant from the position of government policy, with no obvious benefits to the government parties in general or to Labour in particular. The straightforward pattern suggested by the one-dimensional analysis is not reproduced in twenty dimensions, almost certainly as a result of the evasiveness of the Joint Programme of Government.

DISAGGREGATED TWENTY-DIMENSIONAL ANALYSIS

As well as looking at the aggregate distances between parties in the twenty dimensional policy space, it is possible to look at each of the dimensions individually to see whether a particular party occupied a predominant position over the range of policy dimensions. It would be amazing, of course, if a single party were found to control the median legislator on every one of the twenty dimensions that have been analysed. But the more a given party does occupy such a position, the stronger its bargaining position ought to be. Table 3.5 shows which party controlled the median legislator on each of the twenty dimensions for the three elections in the time period in which any of the three main parties could in theory have controlled the median legislator.[1] We see that Fine Gael was in a very central policy position in 1981. It controlled the median legislator on eleven of the seventeen dimensions for which there was a single median party. (On the other three, two or more parties had the same position.) Measuring the salience of each dimension as the mean proportion of the sentences in all party manifestos devoted to it, the bottom section of Table 3.5 shows that Fine Gael sat on the median of the most salient dimensions. It was clearly the predominant party, in these terms, and it did go into government.

It is not clear, however, how much this predominant position translated into an influence over government policy. The second column of Table 3.5 for each year (in parenthesis) shows which of the three parties had the closest policy position to that of the government. Fine Gael did the worst of the three parties on this score, while Labour did best of all. The Joint Programme of Government was actually closer to Fianna Fail policy on

Table 3.5 Parties controlling median legislator on 20 dimensions, Ireland, 1981–82 (and party closest to government policy)

Policy dimension	Party occupying median position on dimension in				
	1981		March 1982	November 1982	
State intervention	FG	(Lab)	*	FG	(Lab)
Quality of life	FG	(FG)	Lab	FF	(FG)
Peace and co-operation	FF	(FF)	Lab	Lab	(Lab)
Anti establishment views	*		FG	Lab	(FF)
Capitalist economy	Lab	(Lab)	FG	Lab	(FF)
Social conservatism	Lab	(FF)	*	Lab	(Lab)
Productivity	FG	(Lab)	FF	FG	(Lab)
Military: positive	Lab	(Lab)	*	*	*
EEC: positive	FF	*	*	FF	(FG)
EEC: negative	*	*	*	*	*
Freedom and human rights	FG	(FF)	*	*	*
Democracy	FG	(FG)	*	*	*
Decentralisation	FG	(FF)	*	*	*
Government efficiency	FG	(Lab)	*	*	*
Social justice	FG	(FF)	*	Lab	(FF)
Social services: positive	FF	(Lab)	FG	FG	(FF)
Education: positive	FG	(Lab)	*	*	*
Labour groups: positive	FG	(Lab)	*	*	*
Agriculture and farmers	FG	(Lab)	*	*	*
Underprivileged minorities	*	*	*	*	*
Number of dimensions in which:					
FG in core position (salience)	11		3	3	
FG closest to govt policy	2			2	
FF in core position (salience)	3		2	2	
FF closest to govt policy	5			4	
Labour in core position (salience)	3		2	5	
Labour closest in govt policy	9			4	

* No party occupies median position

more dimensions than it was to Fine Gael policy. We know from Table 3.4 that, taking account of the magnitude of the policy distances, Fine Gael did better than Fianna Fail overall, but not much. The predominant position in the policy space occupied by Fine Gael thus seems to have done it little good in policy bargaining (perhaps because it was more concerned with getting into office for its own sake).

In February 1982, there were few policy dimensions on which parties expressed positions, so that no pattern is clear; no judgement has been made as to which party was closest to government position. By November 1982, however, Labour had clearly emerged in quite a central position. Certainly Labour and Fine Gael between them dominated the policy space and went into government with each other. Once more, however, controlling the median legislator on a particular policy dimensions does not seem to have translated into having a strong influence over published policy intentions on that dimension. Indeed, in November 1982, it is almost always the case that the party in the median position on a given dimension was not the closest to government policy on it.

Overall, the disaggregated twenty dimensional analysis, while seeming to point to the key positions held by certain actors, does not explain who gets what in policy terms. This underlines a point that has emerged several times in this discussion, that parties' policies seem to be more helpful in interpreting the party composition of the government, than in helping us to understand its policy programme.

CONCLUSION

Most of this analysis has been forced to concentrate on a very brief period in Irish political history. This is because of the long dominance of Fianna Fail up to 1973, followed by the sustained electoral pact between Fine Gael and Labour. While this pact was successful and resulted in a Fine Gael–Labour coalition, we are not able to distinguish unambiguously between the policy positions of the two coalition partners because they did not issue separate policy documents. For the period 1981–82, however, with three elections in a very short period, there was an intensive spate of 'conventional' coalition politics in Ireland, a situation that resumed in 1989. For this brief period, the policy-based analysis is in many ways more impressive than the crude success rates summarised in Table 3.6. It is not so much that the theories considered make incorrect predictions about which government forms; by and large they do not. Rather it is that they tend to predict too

Table 3.6   Success rates of policy-based coalition theories in Ireland

Theory A:	Coalition will be at node on cluster tree.		
Theory B:	Coalition will contain predominant party.		
Theory C:	Coalition will be based on one dimensional clustering.		

	1981	March 1982	November 1982
Number of possible coalitions (2^n-1)	7	7	7
Number of possible coalitions, given constraints	3	3	3
Number of coalitions predicted by theory A	5	5	5
Does theory A predict correctly?	yes	yes	yes
Number of coalitions predicted by theory B	4	0	4
Does theory B predict correctly?	yes	n/a	yes
Number of coalitions predicted by theory C	5	5	5
Does theory C predict correctly?	yes	yes	no

many of the arithmetically possible coalitions. This is a product, in part, of the small number of parties in contention in Ireland, and of the constraints on coalition bargaining discussed above.

In particular, the refusal of the largest party, Fianna Fail, to share power with any other for most of this period has had a major impact. On occasion, as in 1987, these constraints have meant that no majority government was viable. In this context, the policy-based analysis provides a language for talking about the politics of coalition, rather than a set of definitive predictions.

Finally, there seems to be little evidence of systematic policy payoffs in the Joint programmes of Government, though there does seem to be clear evidence of a policy convergence between Fine Gael and Labour that predated their actual coalition. Policy, in short, does seem to be related to coalition formation in Ireland, but it seems to be only very scantily related to coalition payoffs.

APPENDIX A

Table A.1   Votes cast and seats won in Irish elections 1957–82

| Date | Percentage of votes | | | | Number of seats | | | | |
	FF	FG	Lab	Other	FF	FG	Lab	Other	Total
				(Government parties italicised)					
1957	*48*	27	9	16	78	40	12	17	147
1961	*44*	32	12	13	70	47	16	11	144
1965	*48*	34	15	3	72	47	22	3	144
1969	*46*	34	17	3	75	50	18	1	144
1973	46	*35*	*14*	5	69	54	19	2	144
1977	*51*	31	12	7	84	43	17	4	148
1981	45	*37*	*10*	8	78	65	15	8	166
1982(Feb)	*47*	37	9	6	81	63	15	7	166
1982(Nov)	45	*39*	*9*	6	75	70	16	5	166
1987	*44*	27	6	11	81	51	12	22	166
1989	*44*	29	10	17	77	55	15	19	166

FF   Fianna Fail
FG   Fine Gael
Lab   Labour
Other   Small parties and independents

Table A.2   Governments formed in Ireland, 1957–88

Taoiseach		Dates	Party Composition	% of Dail seats
1957	deValera (to 1959) Lemass (from 1959)	March 1957–Nov 1961	Fianna Fail	53.1
1961	Lemass	Nov 1961–May 1965	Fianna Fail	48.6
1965	Lemass (to 1966) Lynch (from 1966)	May 1965–July 1969	Fianna Fail	50.0
1969	Lynch	July 1969–March 1973	Fianna Fail	52.1
1973	Cosgrave	March 1973–June 1977	Fine Gael–Labour	50.7
1977	Lynch (to 1979) Haughey (from1979)	June 1977–June 1981	Fianna Fail	56.8
1981	FitzGerald	June 1981–March 1982	Fine Gael–Labour	48.2
1982	Haughey	March 1982–Dec 1982	Fianna Fail	48.8
1982	FitzGerald	Dec 1982–Jan 1987	Fine Gael–Labour	51.8
1987	FitzGerald	Jan 1987–March 1987	Fine Gael	41.8
1987	Haughey	March 1987–July 1989	Fianna Fail	48.8
1989	Haughey	July 1989–	Fianna Fail–PD	50.0

Table A.3   Twenty-dimensional distance matrices, Ireland

1957				1961				1965		
FG	72			FG	113			FG	93	
LAB	84	148		LAB	120	83		LAB	95	84
	FF	FG			FF	FG			FF	FG

1969				1981			
FG	83			FG	43		
LAB	90	55		LAB	59	40	
	FF	FG			FF	FG	

1982				1982			
FF				FF			
FG	53			FG	82		
LAB	75	48		LAB	75	39	
	FF	FG			FF	FG	

Figure A.1   Cluster diagrams

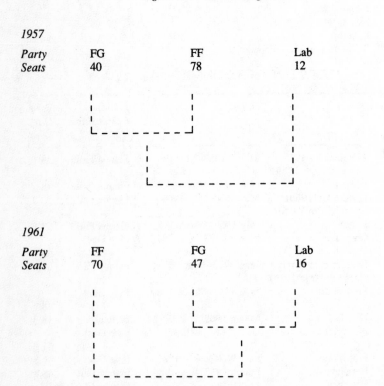

1957

Party	FG	FF	Lab
Seats	40	78	12

1961

Party	FF	FG	Lab
Seats	70	47	16

1965

Party	FF	FG	Lab
Seats	72	47	22

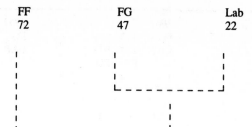

1969

Party	FF	FG	Lab
Seats	75	50	18

1981

Party	FF	FG	Lab
Seats	78	65	15

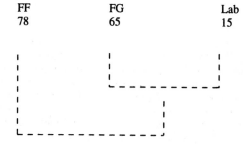

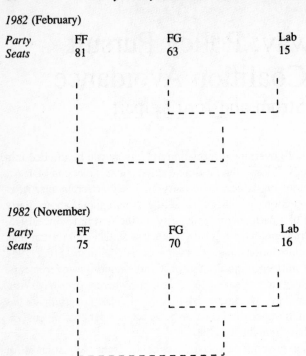

1982 (February)

Party	FF	FG	Lab
Seats	81	63	15

1982 (November)

Party	FF	FG	Lab
Seats	75	70	16

NOTE

1   In 1957, 1965, 1969 and 1977 Fianna Fail was a majority party which formed the government and obviously controlled the median legislator on all dimensions. In 1973 the electoral coalition of Fine Gael and Labour, with a single policy document, was in the same position. In 1961, minor parties, on which we have no data, were most likely pivotal on many dimensions, given the very fragmented result. In 1981 and February 1982, minor parties were also arithmetically in a key position but the three main parties held the ring, at least as far as actual participation in government is concerned. Accordingly, these two cases have been treated 'as if' any coalition involving two of the three main parties was at least arithmetically viable.

4 Norway: Policy Pursuit and Coalition Avoidance

Kaare Strom and Jorn Leipart

The post-war era of government formation in Norway can be divided into two distinct periods. Prior to the Storting (parliamentary) election of 1961, Norway had a series of stable, single-party, majority governments. After this watershed election, which deprived the Norwegian Labour Party (Arbeiderpartiet) of a parliamentary majority for the first time since 1945, Norwegian governments have typically been less stable, more often than not minority administrations, and in several cases coalitions. Since 1961 Norway has had thirteen minority and only three majority governments. Seven of these governments have been coalitions, whereas nine have consisted of only one party. While the basis of Norwegian governments has changed substantially over the post-war period, other patterns of government formation have remained stable:

(1) All Norwegian governments have been either exclusively socialist or exclusively non-socialist. Peacetime coalitions between socialist and non-socialist parties have never existed.

(2) The Labour Party has eschewed coalitions not only with non-socialist parties, but also with any of the smaller parties to its left. In several elections, the Labour Party has indeed made a campaign issue out of its resistance to coalition politics. Thus, a socialist government has meant a cabinet of Labour alone. Since 1961 a socialist government has therefore also meant a minority government.

(3) Non-socialist governments, on the other hand, have tended to be coalitions (see Rommetvedt, 1984). In all but one case, non-socialist governments have included at least three parties. The exception is the first Willoch government (1981–83), a purely Conservative administration. This government nevertheless enjoyed fairly consistent parliamentary support from the Christian People's and Centre parties.

Thus, Norway in the post-war period has witnessed two-bloc competition within a multiparty system. More precisely, a dominant party has alternated in power with a bloc of challengers.

THE NORWEGIAN PARTY SYSTEM

The shift from majority to minority goverments in 1960s was produced by changes in the Norwegian party system. In the 1950s Norway had a stable five-party system pitting the dominant Labour Party [A or DNA] against an uncohesive bloc of four non-socialist parties: the Conservatives (Hoyre [H]), the Liberals (Venstre [V]), the agrarian Centre Party (Senterpartiet [SP] – before 1959 known as the Farmers' Party, Bondepartiet) and the Christian People's Party (Kristelig Folkeparti [KRF]). After the onset of the cold war, the Communist Party (Norges Kommunistiske Parti [NKP]) faded into oblivion, losing its parliamentary representation in 1961.

The 1960s and 1970s brought two new parliamentary parties: the Socialist Left Party (Sosialistisk Folkeparti [SF]), later to become part of Sosialistisk Venstreparti [SV], and the Progress Party (Fremskrittspartiet [FRP] on the far right). The Liberals declined precipitously and, acrimoniously, split into two parties in 1972. The majority of the members of the parliamentary party left to form the pro-EEC Liberal People's Party (Det Liberale Folkeparti [DLF]). The anti-EEC rump retained the name and the party organisation. Both of these parties have since disappeared from parliamentary politics (for surveys of the Norwegian party system, see Urwin, 1987; Valen, 1981; Valen and Urwin, 1985). Effectively, therefore, the post-war development of the Norwegian party system can be broken down into three periods:

(1) Social Democratic predominance: 1945–61. From the end of the Second World War until 1961, the Labour Party enjoyed a predominant position in Norwegian party politics (Sartori, 1976). Four consecutive elections yielded an outright parliamentary majority and single-party Labour governments. The undisputed social democratic leader throughout this period was Einar Gerhardsen, who held the premiership for almost 17 years between 1945 and 1965.

(2) Stable two-bloc competition: 1961–73. The emergence of the Socialist People's Party caused some erosion of support on Labour's left, and on the right the non-socialist parties strengthened their position. However, until the early 1970s electoral volatility remained low, and the party system deviated only slightly from its previous five-party format. The socialist and non-socialist blocs were extremely evenly balanced, and minority Labour governments alternated with bourgeois coalitions (see Groennings, 1961; Rommetvedt, 1984).

(3) Polarisation and fractionalisation: 1973–85. The referendum on whether or not to join the European Community in 1972 caused a political earthquake. More party system change followed than at any time since the 1920s. The outcome was a substantially weakened Labour Party,

significant new parties on the extreme left and right, a Conservative resurgence, and eventually an atrophy of the non-socialist centre (Bjorklund and Hagtvet, 1981; Kuhnle, Strom, and Svasand, 1986; Sainsbury, 1985; Valen, 1981). In 1981, after eight years of Labour minority governments, the Conservatives formed their first single-party (minority) government since the 1920s. This government, subsequently expanded to include the Christian People's and Centre parties, was eventually replaced by another Labour government in 1986.

The longer-term party system trend has been toward fragmentation, volatility, and some polarisation (Heidar, 1988; Pedersen, 1984). However, the two major parties, and particularly the Conservatives, have weathered the crises reasonably well. Table B.1 in the Appendix, which presents the results of post-war Storting elections, demonstrates the destabilisation of the party system. As noted above, Norwegian governments (listed in Table B.2) have also been destabilised in the process.

PARTY OBJECTIVES: POLICY, OFFICE AND VOTES

Two important characteristics distinguish Norwegian parties from those in many other democracies. First, Norwegian political parties are un-commonly cohesive, with a high organisational capacity for concerted pursuit of their objectives. Secondly, they place a high value on policy objectives. By comparative European standards, Norwegian parties are intrinsic policy-seekers. These two characteristics are interrelated. The high degree of policy orientation found in Norwegian political parties is predicated on a high organisational potential for unitary action.

Organisational capacity and cohesiveness

All the major Norwegian parties have extensive mass organisations with high ratios of members to voters, providing cheap and reliable labour. In the early 1980s, these ratios ranged from .07 for the Socialist Left Party to .34 for the Centre Party. The national mean, at .17, was the highest in Scandinavia (Eliassen and Pedersen, 1985; Svasand, 1985. See also Heidar, 1983; Urwin, 1987). Over the post-war period, these figures have remained rather constant, though the Conservatives have experienced a decline and the Christian People's Party an increase in membership density.

Whereas membership organisations provide Norwegian parties with a plentiful supply of labour, public subsidies are a more important source of party finance. Public financing was first introduced in1970 and has grown substantially. All parties polling at least 2.5 per cent of the national vote qualify for public funds in the subsequent parliamentary term. About half of these funds go to the national party organisations, with the rest split between country and municipal organisations (see Svasand, 1985; Urwin, 1987). In addition to direct subsidies, Norwegian parties are indirectly subsidised through the provision of free media time by Norwegian public broadcasting.

The organisational capacity of Norwegian parties is enhanced by a tradition of long and secure tenure for party leaders, exemplified by Einar Gerhardsen (Labour), Carl J Hambro (Conservatives), Bent Roiseland (Liberals), Lars Korvald (Christian People's Party), and Johan J. Jakobsen (Centre Party). Organised factions are rarely found in Norwegian parties and expressly prohibited in the Labour Party. Whereas different tendencies can be identified in several parties, they tend to be fluid and informal. It is therefore eminently reasonably to model Norwegian parties as unitary actors with a considerable capacity for strategic behaviour.

Policy orientation

Norwegian parties have never had much of an opportunity to develop clientelistic orientations. Norway emerged from Danish rule in 1814 as a 'civil servant state' (Seip, 1963; Sejersted, 1984a; Steen, 1958). An autonomous and professional civil service prevented any extensive spoils ever developing during the formative period of the new state. The number of political appointments at the national and lower levels of government has always remained very low (Olsen, 1983; Roness, 1979). Hence, Norwegian parties have lacked incentives to develop an intrinsic office-orientation. The available spoils have simply not been worth it.

Of course, concern with policy is compatible with instrumental office-seeking. Norwegian parties have tended to emerge from distinct social groups (e.g. workers, farmers) and to retain strong commitments to these groups and their interest organisations. This has predisposed them toward the pursuit of policy objectives, often through control of particular governmental offices. Depending on the control they give over the policy making process, different ministerial portfolios are sought by different parties. Such differences in portfolio preferences are clearly manifested in coalitions of the non-socialist parties. In all five coalitions in which the party has participated, the Conservative Party has held the ministries of Defence and Industry. In all but one case, it has also controlled Justice and Foreign Affairs. The Centre Party and the Christian People's Party have each participated in six coalitions, all but one of which included the considerably larger Conservatives. Despite being junior partners, the Christian People's Party has captured the portfolios of Social Services and Church and Education four times each. The Centre Party has controlled its preferred trio of Agriculture, Fisheries, and Transportation four times. Finally, the Liberals have held Finance and Municipal Affairs in three of their four coalitions.

The strong orientation of Norwegian parties toward policy, rather than office for its own sake, helps explain their exceptional willingness to forego the benefits of office, especially since incumbency may entail electoral costs. Except for 1977, incumbents have lost votes in every Norwegian election since 1961, and the balance between the socialist and non-socialist blocs has remained very close throughout this period. These circumstances have given Norwegian parties a keen sense of the importance of marginal votes, and enhanced electoral competition (Strom, 1986).

POLICY AND PORTFOLIOS IN INTERPARTY NEGOTIATIONS

How are these party objectives reflected in negotiations over government formation? In only six cases have there been serious interparty negotiations during post-war cabinet crises. Four of these (1963, 1965, 1972 and 1983) led to the formation of coalition governments. In two other cases (1971 and 1981) negotiations broke down and single-party minority governments formed. Because of the small number of cases, it is difficult to generalise about the importance of policy and office payoffs in coalition bargaining. A further problem is caused by the fact that policy negotiations between the non-socialist parties have often taken place before elections. Notably, this was the case in 1977 and 1985. Hence, a focus on post-election negotiations may exaggerate the importance of portfolio concerns to Norwegian parties.

Schofield and Laver (1985: 163) classify Norway as a country in which the distribution of cabinet portfolios corresponds closely with Gamson's (1961) prediction that each party's share of the portfolios will be proportional to the number of legislative seats it controls. They interpret this result to mean that the coalition bargaining game in Norway focuses on policy choices along a single dimension. While this may be a reasonable characterisation of Norwegian party politics, evidence on interparty negotiations during cabinet crises suggests that different crises have occasioned different concerns and procedures.

The cabinet crisis preceding the formation of the first non-socialist coalition in 1963 was hectic and historic. The four non-socialist parties that participated in these negotiations realised that their government would be short-lived. In 1965 and 1972, however, negotiations seem to have been dominated by office payoff considerations. The 1965 non-socialist coalition had a precedent in the short-lived Lyng cabinet, and the Lyng declaration was considered a joint commitment even two years later (Lyng, 1973). Informally, the leaders of the non-socialist parties had also met regularly prior to the election. In his authoritative memoirs, Lyng (1976, p. 12) admitted that the negotiation process was one of 'hard and protracted bargaining over political portfolios'. However, the most contentious portfolio clearly represented a profound policy conflict and a clear case of instrumental office-seeking. This was the ministry of Church and Education, over which the Christian People's Party and the Liberals fought bitterly.

The unsuccessful bourgeois efforts to form a coalition in 1971 were, like those ten years later, dominated by policy conflicts, in this case the upcoming decision on EC membership. The negotiations of 1972 were conducted in the aftermath of the traumatic referendum on this decision which had caused the resignation of the previous Labour government. The cabinet crisis was exacerbated by deep rifts within several parties, as well as between pro- and anti-EEC parties. This is the cabinet formation in which the assumption of parties as unitary actors is least plausible. The outgoing Labour Party, as well as the Liberals and the Christian People's Party (both of which were involved in the negotiations), were most severely divided. Only the Christian People's Party managed to unite pro- and anti-EEC forces in support of government participation. Negotiations were again dominated by portfolio concerns but foreign policy orientations were ever present as a background to the discussions (Korvald and Heradstveit, 1982).

On the other hand, policy issues were in the forefront of the negotiations of 1981 and 1983. In 1981, the attempt to form a non-socialist majority government stranded on the abortion issue, which split the Conservative Party and separated it from its would-be-partners (see Rimehaug, 1983; Sejersted, 1984b). The renewed negotiations between these three parties in 1983 were again dominated by policy issues, such as tax relief, de-bureaucratisation, industrial subsidies, regional development, and public sector growth. After these policy issues had been settled, the negotiations moved on to portfolio allocation.

Fiscal policies, regional development, and the government's position *vis-à-vis* the European Community were focal point of the 1989 negotiations. Again, portfolio allocation seems to have taken place after the main policy divergences had been straightened out. Yet portfolio concerns were certainly prominent, and an expansion of the cabinet had to be undertaken in order to satisfy the demands of the centrist parties.

On the whole, explicit or implicit policy compromises appeared to have been the crucial concern in Norwegian government formation. When negotiations have broken down, as in 1971 and 1981, it has been over policy rather than portfolios. Normally, policy discussions also precede portfolio distribution in the formation process. This is not always obvious because policy compromises are frequently reached before the formal process of government formation begins. On the other hand, there is no doubt that negotiations about office payoffs have dominated during several cabinet crises. Though portfolio distributions may be of secondary importance to the parties, they are nonetheless vigorously contested. Finally, it is difficult to discern any significant differences between parties in their relative valuation of office and policy.

FORMING NORWEGIAN GOVERNMENTS

The process by which Norwegian governments are formed is informal and permissive. The Norwegian constitution, which dates back to 1814, has never been amended to reflect the introduction of parliamentary government more than a hundred years ago. Consequently, the written constitution contains no guide-lines or restrictions concerning government formation. Below we shall consider the implications of this constitutional peculiarity, together with Norwegian conventions and constraints bearing on the process by which governments are formed.

Formal procedures and actors

Formally, the constitution grants the king the freedom to select his council at will. In practice, however, the king has exerted no personal influence on government formation since 1928. The king normally follows the advice of the outgoing prime minister in designating a *formateur*. In especially difficult situations, he may consult with the parliamentary party leaders or the President of the Storting, who may act as *informateur*. The latter situation has occurred only once since the Second World War, in 1971, when Per Broten's four-party non-socialist government broke up. The (Conservative) President Bernt Ingvaldsen was initially given the task of exploring the prospects for continued non-socialist coalition government. It was always obvious that, even if successful, the deeply conservative Ingvaldsen would not be the new prime minister. As government formation has generally not been too complicated, it has rarely been very protracted.

Government viability

Parliamentary government in Norway is not highly codified (Rasch, 1983; 1987), so it is difficult to determine what constitutes a viable government. When the first Norwegian minority government was formed in 1908, it occasioned some trauma (see Bjornberg, 1939; Stavang, 1971). However, fears of dire consequences quickly subsided and the experience was soon repeated. Norway had nothing but minority governments between 1919 and 1940. Many of these were radically undersized; between January 1928 and March 1935, Norway experienced a succession of six governments supported by less than 25 per cent of the national legislature. Size is definitely not the decisive variable.

Since 1945, the government has generally come out of the majority bloc (socialist or non-socialist) in the Storting. However, this pattern was broken in 1963 and again in 1986. None of the five major traditional parties (excluding the Socialist Left and the Progress Party) has been considered illegitimate in government. Indeed, all have participated in government since 1972 and all but the Liberals have held the premiership at least once, since 1945.

Thus the norms concerning cabinet viability in Norway must be considered permissive. There clearly is no majority size requirement, since minority governments have been so common and widely accepted. But although many governments have lacked parliamentary majorities, there has been a tendency for them to represent the majority bloc in the Storting. Socialist majorities in the Storting have occasioned socialist cabinets, and bourgeois governments have been in place when the non-socialist parties have held the legislative majority. However, even this regularity did not hold in 1963, 1972, and 1986.

STRUCTURAL INFLUENCES AND CONSTRAINTS ON GOVERNMENT FORMATION

Exogenous constraints

Exogenous constraints have operated in Norway to exclude certain parties from government. One such case occurred in 1972, when the government was precluded from including parties favouring EEC membership, including Labour and the Conservatives. This was because the principal item on the foreign-policy agenda of the new government would be negotiations on a trade agreement with the EEC, and the pro-EEC parties had already rejected this option. Another straightforward case is the general exclusion of the Communists from government between 1949 and 1961, when the party finally lost its parliamentary representation. Though the issue never had to be confronted directly, Communist participation at that time would have seemed to undermine Norway's NATO commitments. Presumably this would have been strenuously opposed by the United States.

Endogenous constraints

Norwegian parties have rarely issued negative formal statements on the desirability of other specified parties as coalition partners. Prescriptive constraints, on the other hand, have been particularly significant when non-socialist governments have been in office. In both cases where such coalitions have faced elections (1969 and 1985), they have pledged to continue their coalition if they retained their legislative majority. Similarly, in 1977 the three major non-socialist parties (Conservatives, Centre Party, and Christian People's Party) committed themselves in advance to form a coalition government in the event they got a parliamentary majority. Occasionally, a self-imposed constraint has committed the centrist bourgeois parties to joint action. The only unambiguous case, however, is that of 1983, when the Centre Party made their coalition with the Conservatives conditional on the inclusion of the Christian People's Party in government.

The most important case of a proscriptive endogenous constraint concerns the Labour Party. In the 1930s, the party decided to eschew formal govermental collaboration with any other party, a policy which turned out to be very successful. This has remained a Labour tradition and the party has never even entered into coalition negotiations. Although the possibility was aired in 1961 and 1973, it was not accepted, so this constraint has clearly remained up to the present time. The Labour Party's tactics resemble those of Fianna Fail in Ireland up until 1989, and are similarly designed to bolster its claim to be the sole effective party of government.

Arguably, the Progress Party, between 1973 and 1977, was considered unfit for any coalition. In recent years the Conservatives have equivocated on the issue. Because of the lack of any explicit and binding formulation, we discount any endogenous constraint concerning the Progress Party.

Structural influences on coalition bargaining

Beyond these more or less straightforward constraints, relatively few structural features of Norwegian politics act to reduce the probability of otherwise viable government solutions. This lack of coalitional restrictions stems partly from the constitutional freedom alluded to above. Since parliamentary government has never been recognised in the constitution, there is no formal investiture. Incumbent governments must submit to a vote of confidence only by their own volition or at the insistence of the opposition. Both are rare events. Consequently, ambiguities may exist concerning the parliamentary basis of governments (see Stavang, 1971). Such ambiguity in turn facilitates the formation and maintenance of minority governments that are tolerated, if not supported, by parties in opposition (Strom, 1986). Nor are incumbents expected to resign at election time or at the time of accession of a new head of state. This favours continuity in government.

The electoral system, however, does constitute an important structural influence on Norwegian coalition bargaining. Norway has had a Proportional Representation system, since 1953 based on a modified Sainte-Lague formula with 1.4 as the first divisor. However, the Norwegian version of PR is tainted with considerable malapportionment, and until 1989 there was no provision for supplementary seats. Consequently, the actual disproportionality in representation has consistently been the highest in Scandinavia and one of the highest of all PR countries (see Sarlvik, 1983; Strom, 1985; Valen, 1985). This disproportionality has given the non-socialist parties, and particularly the smaller ones, strong incentives to form electoral coalitions in the form of joint lists, which have been very common in the post-war period. In two elections (1945 and 1985) the even more attractive option of withdrawal in favour of preferred partners has been available. These forms of pre-electoral coalition building have clearly facilitated non-socialist government coalitions as well.

The Norwegian constitution requires qualified parliamentary majorities for constitutional amendments (eg. reforms of the electoral system) and for membership in supranational organisations entailing concessions of sovereignty (eg. the EEC). Yet such considerations have never seriously entered the process of government formation. A more unusual feature of the Norwegian constitution is that there is no provision for the early dissolution of the Storting. Norway is the only country in Western Europe without recourse to this parliamentary 'safety valve'. While it is difficult to identify any particular consequence of this constitutional anomaly, it clearly influences the process of government formation in more general ways. The impossi-

Table 4.1 Constraints and structural influences upon coalition bargaining in Norway

Type	Substance	Operative Period	Effect
(1)	Communists excluded from government	1949–57	In practice, none
(2)	No pro-EEC party in government	1972	Exclusion of A, H, DLF
(3)	If majority retained, continuation of Borten government	1969	Dictated government solution
(4)	If three-party non-Socialist (H,KRF,SP), coalition of these parties	1977	No such majority, but disfavoured coalition of any of these parties with Labour
(5)	Center Party coalition contingent upon participation of Christian People's Party	1981	Reduced set of non-socialist solutions
(6)	If majority retained, continuation of Willoch	1985	Favoured this coalition even without majority government
(7)	Labour Party refuses to consider coalition with any other party	all years	After 1960 favours minority single-party government when left as a whole has legislative majority
(8)	*Apparentement* in electoral system	1945, 1985	Predisposed non-socialist parties toward coalition
(9)	Disproportionality of electoral system	all years	Predisposes smaller non-socialist parties toward coalition
(10)	Doctrine of collective responsibility	all years	Favours policy-compact governments
(11)	No need for government to resign at election time	all years	Favours incumbents
(12)	No provision for early dissolution of Parliament	all years	Decreases uncertainty in coalition bargaining; favours minority governments

bility of early dissolution reduces uncertainty concerning cabinet durability and future elections. In this sense, it eliminates one source of incumbency advantage and probably also induces toleration of numerically weak cabinets in difficult parliamentary circumstances. The constraints and structural influences we have identified are summarised in Table 4.1.

POLICY DIMENSIONS IN NORWEGIAN POLITICS

The Norwegian policy space has most commonly been investigated through surveys and ecological analyses of voting behaviour. Six social cleavage dimensions have thus been identified as significant bases for the modern Norwegian party system (Rokkan, 1970; Valen, 1981; Valen and Urwin, 1985):

(1) a territorial cleavage between the central area around Oslo and two peripheries: the Southwest and the North (see Rokkan, 1970; Aarebrot, 1982);
(2) a socio-cultural cleavage manifested in the development of two competing national languages, bokmal (urban) and nynorsk (rural and southwestern);
(3) a religious cleavage between fundamentalists inside and outside the Lutheran state church on the one hand and the liberal Lutheran leadership and secular groups on the other;
(4) a moral cleavage concerning the production and use of alcohol. In the 1920s alone, the prohibition issue caused three Norwegian governments to fall;
(5) a class cleavage between workers and employers;
(6) and finally, an urban-rural cleavage between, on the one hand, those tied to farming and fisheries and on the other those within the secondary and tertiary sectors of the economy.

These cleavage dimensions have been politicised successively and form a cumulative pattern of party conflict. Over time, the class cleavage between workers and employers has come to dominate and several of the other lines of conflict have merged to form a secondary centre–periphery dimension in Norwegian politics. When party manifestos have been scrutinised for evidence on party system dimensionality, the results have been consistent with the patterns from survey data.The left–right dimension, corresponding to the class cleavage, has consistently emerged as the most significant. Occasionally, two different versions of the left–right dimension, one urban and one rural, have been identified. A moral–religious axis has been prevalent in party programmes (see Bilstad, 1986; Gronmo, 1975a and 1975b; Pettersen,1973 and 1979; Strom and Leipart,1989; Valen and Gronmo, 1972).

THE POLICY DOCUMENTS

Norwegian parties and governments issue a number of different statements of policy. The most authoritative of these are action programmes (*handlingsprogram*) for the parties and government declarations for governments. In addition to these programmes, non-socialist coalitions have on occasion committed themselves to joint legislative programmes for particular parliamentary terms (e.g., 1985–89). Our quantitative analysis focuses on the contents of the most important documents: Norwegian party manifestos and government declarations. The Norwegian party programmes have been described elsewhere (Strom and Leipart, 1989). The governmental documents analyzed are generally declarations made at the time of cabinet formation.

However, two problems should be noted. First, some Norwegian governments have presented no declaration upon taking office. This is due to the fact that Norwegian governments do not resign and hence are not formally reconstituted in many situations where this would be customary in many other parliamentary democracies. In such cases, we have relied on the first throne speech of governments which did not present a separate declaration. There are problems of equivalence since throne speeches are different in form and function from government declarations. Second, even some governments which did issue ordinary declarations present problems in the analysis. The reason is that many government declarations have been (mercifully) short. In the unidimensional analysis, these taciturn administrations stand out as being among the most conservative Labour governments. Their scores are presumably a result of stressing continuity with previous Labour administrations.

ONE-DIMENSIONAL ANALYSIS

In our factor analysis of Norwegian party manifestos (Strom and Leipart, 1989) a left–right dimension predictably emerged as most salient. Out of four factors extracted and interpreted in that analysis, two were in fact related to the left–right socio-economic policy dimension. As a first step in the analysis here, we have imposed the cross-national left–right dimension on Norwegian parties and governments. In addition, we have constructed a modified left–right dimension in order to capture more accurately the contents of the left–right axis in Norwegian politics. The standard and modified left–right dimensions yield results that correspond closely to previous studies, as demonstrated in Table 4.2 which presents the left–right positions of Norwegian governments and parliamentary parties in the post-war period. The salience of this dimension for Norwegian politics is evidently high, as items in the scale collectively account for approximately 45 per cent of all quasi-sentences in Norwegian government declarations and a similar proportion of party programmes. The salience of the left–right dimension was lowest for the Nordli and Borten governments (all under 40 per cent) and highest for Gerhardsen II and Willoch I (both over 60 per cent). Not surprisingly, the party most concerned with left–right issues is the Progress Party (60–79 per cent), whereas the Centre Party devotes the least attention to such issues.

Norwegian parties exhibit fairly stable and intuitively reasonable left–right positions. The various parties' relative policy positions are strikingly consistent with conventional placements. In fact, party positions on the standard left–right dimension are consistent with conventional placements in 180 out of 195 pairwise comparisons (92.3 per cent). With the modified Norwegian dimension, this record improves to 185 out of 195, or 94.9 per cent. The most important qualification concerns the Christian People's Party, which, contrary to conventional placement, is located to the right of the Conservatives on either scale in six elections. The fact that this party is involved in at least two-thirds of all 'incorrect' pairwise rankings on either scale suggests that there may be a component of traditionalism in the right-wing categories of the common scale. These elements would likely be captured by a separate moral–religious dimension in a country-specific analysis. For alternative placements see Figures B.1–B.5 in the chapter Appendix. No other party occupies a consistently 'wrong' position in the policy space. The modified Norwegian left–right dimension clearly reduces the incidence of 'incorrect' placements.

The temporal pattern is also interesting. Most deviations from conventional placement occur in the early part of the post-war period. The greater consistency in recent elections may reflect the fact that party programmes have become more elaborate and standardized, and that parties devote greater resources to their preparation. If we focus on changes in the entire party system over time, the analysis clearly reflects the radical drift of Norwegian parties and governments in the 1960s and early 1970s, as well as the reversal of this trend between 1973 and 1981.

Table 4.2 Left–right position of parties and governments in Norway

Electoral Period	Party or Government									
	NKP/SF/SV	A	V	SP	KRF	H	FRP	GOVT 1	GOVT 2	GOVT 3
1945	—	—	—	—	—	—	—	-7.3 (3.6)	—	—
1949	-36.4 (-32.7)	-37.2 (-26.3)	-0.9 (7.4)	16.7 (20.4)	20.9 (29.5)	18.9 (23.1)	—	-25.9 (3.7)	9.1 (9.1)	—
1953	-18.0 (-16.2)	-31.2 (-23.1)	-22.1 (-14.7)	13.4 (18.2)	19.1 (27.2)	18.0 (25.0)	—	-20.8 (8.3)	-17.4 (-8.7)	—
1957	-44.9 (-42.1)	-32.7 (-18.9)	-1.6 (2.7)	12.2 (15.1)	10.5 (16.2)	13.2 (17.8)	—	-33.3 (-19.3)	—	—
1961	-41.0 (-34.3)	-27.4 (-19.2)	-18.3 (-8.8)	-5.8 (0.4)	8.2 (17.6)	5.6 (11.4)	—	-31.8 (27.3)	-2.4 (6.4)	—
1965	-49.5 (-41.6)	-40.0 (-28.6)	-34.3 (-20.7)	-15.1 (-12.0)	-3.4 (-4.8)	-4.3 (3.6)	—	-16.2 (11.0)	—	—
1969	-49.2 (-41.6)	-35.1 (-20.5)	-31.2 (-18.5)	-17.8 (-6.9)	-19.0 (-9.1)	-1.4 (7.6)	—	-24.2 (-11.0)	-34.0 (-26.4)	-21.2 (-10.3)

Table 4.2 (cont'd)

Electoral Period	NKP/ SF/SV	A	V	Party or Government SP	KRF	H	FRP	GOVT 1	GOVT 2	GOVT 3
1973	-42.0 (-35.8)	-36.9 (-25.0)	-30.7 (-15.8)	-14.4 (-3.4)	-5.0 (5.9)	-17.9 (-4.7)	70.2 (72.3)	-45.1 (-39.2)	-8.3 (8.3)	—
1977	-37.3 (-30.8)	-32.1 (-19.5)	-22.3 (-11.4)	-19.0 (-4.7)	-5.5 (10.3)	-10.1 (3.7)	22.1 (30.3)	-20.9 (-13.2)	-17.1 (-8.6)	—
1981	-39.7 (-27.2)	-23.1 (-12.1)	-22.6 (-11.0)	-14.9 (-5.8)	-7.9 (8.2)	8.1 (17.5)	32.4 (38.8)	-3.3 (9.8)	1.1 (12.1)	—
1985	-36.3 (-28.4)	-25.9 (-16.6)	-22.0 (-14.1)	-12.9 (-6.7)	-12.0 (1.2)	-8.0 (1.2)	34.4 (40.5)	-14.0 (-2.3)	-6.1 (4.0)	—
1989	-35.1 (-30.1)	-35.9 (-25.6)	-20.5 (-12.5)	-19.7 (-13.1)	-21.4 (-7.4)	7.0 (0.9)	24.1 (30.3)	9.1 (12.4)	—	—

Notes:
Governments counted chronologically.
High scores indicate right-wing positions.
Standard left–right dimension, modifed Norwegian version in parentheses.

Government formation

The governments formed up to and including Gerhardsen IV are of limited
theoretical interest, since a majority Labour government is so obviously the
dominant solution. In the following, therefore, we discuss the formation of
post-1961 governments, all in minority situations, on the basis of our
common unidimensional representation of Norwegian political space (noting
differences between this and the country-specific scale where appropriate).
As Table 4.2 shows, the first two governments after 1961, Gerhardsen V
(1961–63) and VI (1963–65), were marginally policy-viable along the left–
right dimension, since Labour and the non-socialist opposition each controlled
seventy-four seats in the 150-member assembly. The two members of the
Socialist People's Party found themselves on the opposite side of the
Labour Party from the bourgeois parties. Therefore, these governments are
compatible with the predictions of pure policy-based theory. The
unidimensional analysis also shows Labour to be closer to the Liberals than
to any other party. Although the 'Lib-Lab' coalition never has materialised
in Norwegian politics,it was not a far-fetched prediction in 1961, when both
Gerhardsen and some Liberals seemed to favour a rapprochement. But the
Liberals were pressed hard by the other non-socialist parties to maintain a
common front against the social democrats.

The four-party coalition that formed under Borten is in the prediction set
of the one-dimensional analysis. Given the proximity of the Liberals to the
Labour Party, a coalition of these two parties would have been more policy
compact. However, once the Liberals had joined the other bourgeois parties
in the short-lived Lyng government of 1963, their hands were essentially
tied for 1965. The principal importance of the Lyng administration was that
it signalled the ability and willingness of the bourgeois parties to provide an
alternative to Labour. Liberal withdrawal from this coalition after the electoral
triumph of 1965 would have caused intense hostility from the other non-
socialist parties and, probably, most Liberal voters.

The continuation of Borten's government, in 1969, was even more
predetermined, given the non-socialist parliamentary majority. The governing
parties had precommitted themselves to continuation in office in the event
that they retained their majority (which they did by the slightest of margins).
After the break-up of this coalition, the one-dimensional analysis predicts
another coalition of Labour and the Liberals. Bratteli's first government
(1971) was in fact not policy-viable and therefore not predictable on (left–
right) policy grounds. It owed its existence to the special circumstances
surrounding the approaching EEC referendum. Korvald's post-referendum

cabinet is in the prediction set, once the foreign-policy constraint is introduced and majority size is not required. This coalition is again connected along the left–right dimension.

Labour's string of minority governments between 1973 and 1981 were all policy-viable in unidimensional space, since Labour again controlled the median legislator along this dimension. However, in 1981 they lost this privileged position. In fact, a policy-viable Labour-based government would then have had to include both the Liberals and the Centre Party. Another policy-viable option would have been a majority coalition of the three major non-socialist parties. Neither materialised. Instead, the Conservatives formed a minority government which was not policy-viable, with the requisite external support from the Centre Party and the Christian People's Party. This coalition was formalised at cabinet level in 1983, and remained in office after 1985. The parties in the Willoch government had imposed this solution on themselves contingent on a continued majority. While the three parties failed to retain their majority, they remained policy-viable and indeed continued to govern together until they were defeated in May 1986, on a bill to raise gasoline taxes. In unidimensional space, moreover, this coalition is the most compact viable solution in the 1985–89 Storting. Brundtland's second government was born of a rather difficult parliamentary situation. It was not policy-viable and, therefore, not predictable. On our (left–right) policy criteria the minimum viable coalition for Labour would have included the Centre Party, and this is in fact the legislative coalition on which Brundtland has relied most heavily. Despite its narrow legislative support, Syse's government is again clearly policy-viable in a unidimensional space.

Government policy positions

The one-dimensional analysis shows most Norwegian governments to have been moderately placed on the common left–right dimension, a result consistent with a received wisdom which portrays no post-war government as extremist. Movements in policy from government to government are also quite plausible. Transitions between socialist and non-socialist governments in all but one case (1986) are accompanied by substantial shifts in the expected leftwards and rightwards directions. The results are presented in greater detail in Table 4.2.

When Gerhardsen took over the reins in 1955, he turned the Labour government decisively to the left until, by 1961, it was more radical than the party. Predictably, Lyng made a sharp turn to the right. However, Borten's two governments occupied virtually identical positions about half-way between their immediate predecessors. In 1971, Bratteli swung the government out to the approximate position of Gerhardsen V, whereas Korvald's centrist cabinet reclaimed the position of the two previous non-socialist governments. Then, in 1973, Bratteli presented the most leftist government declaration in post-war Norway so far. In fact, Bratteli's programme was to the left even of the Socialist Left. While Bratteli personally represented the moderate wing of the Labour Party, there is no doubt that he was severely challenged by the Socialist Left and the left wing of his own party at this time, which pushed him to extremes in policy terms. In 1976, however, his successor Odvar Nordli presented a much more moderate declaration and subsequent Labour government declarations have been to the right of party manifestos. Recall, however, that all these governments have lacked majority support in the legislature.

Willoch's first two governments presented predictably conservative declarations, with the expanded and more centrist second administration slightly to the right of its predecessor. In 1985, however, the Willoch government moved decisively to the left, perhaps in response to its electoral decline. When Willoch was replaced by Brundtland in 1986, the unexpected result was a more conservative government declaration. This declaration is again far to the right of the Labour Party and on the surface defies explanation. Finally, Syse's position is well to the right of any of the coalition parties, but left of the Progress Party. Generally speaking, however, the left–right positions of the various governments are consistent with accepted interpretations of Norwegian Party politics. This is particularly true of the non-socialist cabinets.

Party payoffs

Policy payoffs to the various parties as a result of these government declarations, measured in terms of the distance between government and party policy positions along the left–right dimension, are summarised in Table 4.3. This Table also gives the allocation of cabinet portfolios between government members, and shows these to have been distributed in close correspondence to each party's contribution to the government legislative seat total (Browne and Franklin, 1973; Gamson, 1961). In recent years most clearly in the current Syse government, small parties have gained more than their strict seat contribution.

Table 4.3 shows that the mean policy distance between government and opposition parties is about twice as large as between governments and

Table 4.3 Policy payoffs for unidimensional space, Norway (Distances between party and government positions)

| Government | Party | | | | | | | Absolute Distance (All Parties(x)) |
	NKP/ SF/SV	A	V	SP	KRF	H	FRP	
Gerhardsen II	11(29)	11(30)[1]	-25(4)	-43(17)	-47(33)	-45(19)	—	30(22)
Torp I	46(42)	46(35)[1]	10(2)	-8(11)	-12(20)	-10(14)	—	22(21)
Torp II	-3(25)	10(31)[1]	1(23)	-34(10)	-40(19)	-39(17)	—	21(21)
Gerhardsen III	1(8)	14(14)[1]	5(6)	-31(27)	-37(36)	-35(34)	—	21(21)
Gerhardsen IV	12(23)	-1(0)[1]	-32(22)	-46(34)	-44(36)	-47(37)	—	30(25)
Gerhardsen V	9(7)	-4(8)[1]	-14(18)	-26(28)	-40(45)	-37(39)	—	22(24)
Lyng	39(41)	25(26)	16{15}[.2]	3(6)[.27]	-11(11)[.2]	-8(5)[.33]	—	17(17)
Borten I	33(24)	24(18)	18(10)[.2]	-1(1)[.2]	-13(16)[.2]	-12(15)[.4]	—	17(14)
Borten II	25(31)	11(10)	7(8)[.2]	-6(4)[.2]	-5(2)[.2]	-23(19)[.4]	—	13(12)
Bratteli I	15(15)	1(6)[1]	-3(8)	-16(20)	-15(17)	-33(34)	—	14(17)
Korvald	28(31)	14(10)	10(8)[.33]	-3(3)[.41]	-2(1)[.27]	-20(18)	—	13(12)
Bratteli II	-3(3)	-8(14)[1]	-14(23)	-30(33)	-40(45)	-27(35)	-115(111)	34(38)
Nordli I	34(44)	29(33)[1]	22(24)	6(12)	-3(2)	10(13)	-79(81)	26(30)
Nordli II	16(18)	11(6)[1]	1(2)	-2(9)	-15(24)	-11(17)	-43(43)	14(17)
Brundtland I	20(22)	15(11)[1]	5(3)	2(4)	-12(19)	-7(12)	-39(39)	14(16)
Willoch I	36(37)	20(22)	19(21)	12(16)	5(2)	-11(8)[1]	-36(29)	20(19)
Willoch II	41(39)	24(24)	24(23)	16(18)[.17]	9(4)[.22]	-7(5)[.61]	-31(27)	22(20)
Willoch III	22(26)	12(14)	8(12)	-1(4)[.22]	-2(1)[.22]	-6(1)[.56]	-48(43)	14(14)
Brundtland II	30(32)	20(21)[1]	16(18)	7(11)	6(3)	2(3)	-41(45)	17(19)
Syse	44(43)	45(38)	30(26)	29(25)[.26]	30(20)[.26]	16(11)[.48]	-15(-18)	30(26)

Table 4.3 (cont'd)

| Government | Party | | | | | | | Absolute Distance (All Parties(x)) |
	NKP/ SF/SV	A	V	SP	KRF	H	FRP	
(x) Mean absolute distance	23(27)	17(19)	14(14)	16(15)	19(18)	20(18)	50(48)	23(23)**
(x) When in government	—	14(17)	13(10)	8(9)	10(8)	12(9)	—	11(11)**
(x) When in opposition	23(27)	22(20)	14(15)	20(18)	24(23)	25(22)	50(48)	25(25)**

Mean absolute distance (Standard dimension):	All governments	Minority situation*
Governing parties	11.2	10.3
Opposition	24.8	24.0

Note: Figures represent standard left–right dimension, modified Norwegian version in parentheses. Figures in brackets represent proportions of cabinet portfolios. Positive scores indicate that the government was to the right of the party, negative scores the opposite. Italicised figures represent parties in government.

* Nordli I and Brundtland I excluded (see text).
** These represent the averages of the row means; since the N's differ these values are not equal to the grand mean of the table entries.

governing parties. For minority situations the difference is even larger. In other words, government membership confers a relative policy payoff. Note also that Labour has gained less in policy terms from being in office than most of the bourgeois parties. Furthermore, the Liberals, at the left end of the non-socialist spectrum and often close to Labour in policy space, have reaped little or no policy benefit from participation in bourgeois coalitions. Indeed the Liberals typically do better under Labour governments! The other non-socialist parties, on the other hand, have done substantially better in government than in opposition.

Non-socialist coalitions exhibit the best fit to the policy positions of the governing parties. Both Lyng and Borten I (using the Norwegian country-specific dimension only), for example, located themselves in the median position within their coalitions, and Borten II was very close to such a position. In 1961 (country-specific dimension only) and 1965, again, the government's position was closest to the prime minister's party. In Borten II, the prime minister's party was the second closest to the government. Under Korvald, the government was again closest to the prime minister's party (the Christian People' Party). Thus declarations issued by coalition governments conform better to game-theoretic expectations than those delivered by single-party governments. The reason may be that the former have been seen as more authoritative policy statements by their authors. Whereas Labour's single-party governments may have perceived the party manifesto as their principal statement of policy, bourgeois coalitions have been forced to draw up a separate document. Consequently, the declarations made by non-socialist coalitions may have been more carefully drafted and negotiated.

In a finding consistent with popular wisdom, the Conservatives found themselves at some distance from the centre of gravity of the Borten governments. On the other hand, the party received more than a proportional share of ministerial portfolios. This suggests that the Conservatives may have sacrificed policy for office payoffs in these cabinets. The same may have been the case for the more recent non-socialist coalitions under Willoch. All of Willoch's three governments placed themselves to the left of the Conservative party, as one would expect given their need for centrist parliamentary support. The two coalitions both placed themselves within the policy range covered by the participating parties, though not as close to the position of the Conservative Party as one might have expected.

THE TWENTY-DIMENSIONAL ANALYSIS

Government formation

The twenty-dimensional distances presented in Table B.3 in the Appendix to this chapter form the empirical basis for the application of the cluster analytic model of coalition formation in the Norwegian context. Norwegian coalition bargaining tends to be straightforward, committed and structured, with well defined sets of participants, so that hierarchical bargaining models best capture the spirit of Norwegian government formation. The results of the cluster analysis are presented in Figure B.1 in the chapter appendix.

Taking the 1981 election as an example, we can see that if the model is constrained to yield majority predictions, then it predicts for 1981 a coalition of Labour, the Christian People' party, and the Centre Party as the minimum of winning with the smallest aggregate policy distance. However, as has been argued above, there is no need to constrain governments either to be 'winning' or 'minimal'. Were this coalition to be expanded, Figure B.1 indicates that a proto-coalition of the Socialist Left and the Liberals would be added next, and then finally another proto-coalition of the Conservatives and the Progress Party. If the minimum winning coalition is broken up, we see that it in turn decomposes into Labour on the one hand and a proto-coalition of the two non-socialist centre parties on the other. Though Figure B.1 does not yield a very realistic set of predictions for 1981, it does illustrate the isolation of the Conservatives, which in the event led to the formation of a minority government with low viability.

The interested reader can scrutinise the other cluster diagrams in Figure B.1 for their predictions. For most years, the cluster models overestimate the likelihood of coalitions between Labour and the centrist non-socialist parties. The Labour–Liberal coalition, in particular, is the minimum winning coalition with the smallest aggregate policy distance in all three elections in 1960s. Labour's predicted coalition partners, if a majority were sought, would be the entire non-socialist bloc (minus the Progress Party in 1973 and the Socialist Left in 1977). Although not unreasonable in the abstract, no such coalitions have been sought by Labour for reasons connected with the constraints and structural influences listed in Table 4.1. For the 1985–89 electoral period, the cluster analysis predicts an incongruous alliance between Labour, the Socialist Left, and the Christian People's Party. The prediction for 1989 is the same with the centre party substituted for the KRF. The overall adequacy of the cluster analysis of government formation is sum-

Table 4.4 Policy payoffs in 20–dimensional space, Norway (City block distances between party and government positions)

Government	NKPl/SF/SV	A	V	Party SP	XRF	H	FRP	All Parties (x)
Gerhardsen II	76	65	80	91	101	83	—	83
Torp I	112	112	101	117	111	115	—	111
Torp II	77	71	88	89	94	84	—	84
Gerhardsen III	75	63	69	78	84	68	—	73
Gerhardsen IV	79	46	63	72	67	63	—	65
Gerhardsen V	67	50	61	64	68	60	—	62
Lyng	74	45	55	47	45	51	—	53
Borten I	60	52	36	45	52	38	—	47
Borten II	77	41	52	41	43	60	—	52
Bratteli I	82	63	56	65	64	89	—	70
Korvald	70	52	45	41	40	66	—	52
Bratteli II	44	42	45	61	72	66	176	73
Nordli I	96	99	103	104	109	108	158	111
Nordli II	40	31	32	39	49	48	88	47
Brundtland I	66	71	73	75	71	77	92	75

Table 4.4 (cont'd)

Government	NKP/ SF/SV	A	V	Party SP	XRF	H	FRP	All Parties (x)
Willoch I	68	49	51	51	52	34	68	53
Willoch II	71	54	47	46	40	49	83	56
Willoch III	54	48	49	43	33	45	81	50
Brundtland II	60	40	57	64	42	67	87	60
Syse	76	72	75	56	54	44	63	63
(x) Mean Absolute Distance	71	58	62	64	65	66	100	69**
(x) When In Government	—	63	47	46	44	46	—	49**
(x) When In Opposition	71	52	66	75	76	76	100	74**

Note: Italicised figures represent governing parties.

	All governments	Minority situations*
Mean Distance: Governing parties:	51.0	45.4
Opposition parties:	73.2	62.9

* Nordli I and Brundtland I excluded (see text).
** These represent the averages of the row means; since the N's differ these values are not equal to the grand mean of the table entries.

marised in Table 4.6 below, where it is assessed in the context of other predictive models.

Party payoffs

Table 4.4 reports the distances between government and party positions in the full twenty-dimensional space and thus gives an alternative appreciation of policy payoffs going to parties both inside and outside the government. Note the great distances between all parties and governments which presented only perfunctory declarations (Torp I, Nordli I, Brundtland I). This is precisely what we should expect, since many dimensions which are salient in party programmes must necessarily be neglected in such truncated statements of policy. It is also reassuring that the more substantive declarations yield smaller distances and more plausible results.

Note that government declarations were on the whole considerably closer to the policy positions of governing than to non-governing parties. The mean twenty-dimensional distance is about 51 points (on a scale from 0 to 200) for governing parties and about 71 points for opposition parties. The same relationship holds up if we confine the analysis to minority situations (excluding the very brief Nordli I and Brundtland I declarations). In this case, the means are approximately 45 and 63 points, respectively. In 16 out of 20 cases, the party closest to the government position has in fact been in the government. Three out of the four exceptions are accounted for by the very brief government declarations mentioned. The fourth and final exception is Bratteli I, where Labour ran second to the Liberals in proximity. Recall that Bratteli's government was the first post-war socialist government in a situation with a non-socialist parliamentary majority. A placement close to the centrist parties may therefore have been a strategic necessity.

As in the unidimensional analysis, the tendency to benefit in policy terms from being in office is strongest for the non-socialist parties. In fact, as in the single dimension, the Christian People's Party derived the greatest differential policy benefit from government participation. The Liberals have had more to gain from being in office in the larger policy space than on the left–right dimension. This is perfectly reasonable, since many of the issues most salient to the Liberals do not fit the left–right scale. Paradoxically, Labour has done better in opposition than in government, but again this result is largely due to such anomalous cases as Torp I, Nordli I, and Brundtland I, which have been discussed above. Overall, the results in Table 4.4 reinforce qualitative impressions of the importance of policy pursuit in Norwegian coalition bargaining.

Over time the aggregate distances between governments and the parliamentary parties have diminished. This trend is especially evident between Labour governments and centrist parties like the Liberals and the Christian People' Party. As Labour has become accustomed to minority situations and the need for legislative bargaining, perhaps its government declarations have begun to anticipate bargaining situations.

DISAGGREGATED TWENTY-DIMENSIONAL ANALYSIS

Table 4.5 identifies the party controlling the median legislator on each of the twenty policy dimensions for every election since 1961 (as the majority party, Labour obviously controlled the median position on all dimensions before 1961). Of course, these dimensions are not all equally important. We can measure their relative salience as the mean proportion of the coded sentences they represent in Norwegian party programmes. Several dimensions stand out as being especially salient. One is Quality of life, which particularly since the 1970s has come to occupy a major portion of party programmes – in recent elections more than one-eighth of all sentences. Other salient dimensions are Productivity, Peace and cooperation, Social services, Education and, somewhat less consistently, State intervention and Capitalist economy. On the other hand, Military (positive), EEC (positive and negative), and Government efficiency are very low-salience dimensions in Norwegian party politics.

Table 4.5 demonstrates that the distribution of parties along these various dimensions is far from random. The dominant position of the Labour Party is especially noteworthy. Since the party lost its parliamentary majority, it has nevertheless continued to occupy the median position along a great many policy dimensions. Never has the Labour Party controlled fewer than eight dimensions, or less than three more than any of its competitors. This persistent pattern of dominance may justify continued reference to Labour as a predominant party in Norwegian politics (see Sartori, 1976). The spatial domination of Labour is particularly evident in comparison to its main rival, the Conservatives, who have only once controlled more than two policy dimensions at one time. The strong growth of the Conservative Party from 1973 to the early 1980s did not pay off in terms of control of important policy dimensions (Kuhnle, Strom, and Svasand, 1986), and the Conservatives have remained much more dependent on coalition partners than Labour. Paradoxically, only with the electoral set-back of 1985 have the Conservatives measurably improved their bargaining power.

Table 4.5 Parties controlling median legislator on 20 dimensions, Norway 1961–89

Dimension	Year							
	1961	1965	1969	1973	1977	1981	1985	1989
State intervention	SF	V	V	SV	SV	KRF	H	FRP
Quality of life	A	A	A	A	A	SP	A	A
Peace and cooperation	A	V	A	A	A	KRF	KRF	SV
Anti-establishment	–	–	–	–	–	–	H	–
Capitalist economy	A	V	KRF	SV	A	KRF	SP	A
Social conservatism	A	V	A	SV	A	A	H	H
Productivity	A	H	H	H	A	KRF	A	A
Military (+)	A	A	A	A	A	A	A	KRF
EEC (+)	A	A	H	A	A	A	A	A
EEC (–)	–	–	–	–	–	–	–	–
Freedom/human rights	SF	V	A	KRF	A	SP	A	SP/KRF
Democracy	A	A	SP	SP	H	H	FRP	SV
Decentralisation (+)	A	KRF	A	A	A	A	A	A
Government efficiency	A	V	A	SV	A	A	A	A
Social justice	A	A	SP	A	A	A	KRF	A
Social services (+)	A	A	A	A	A	A	KRF	A
Education (+)	A	A	SP	A	A	KRF	SV	A

Table 4.5 (cont'd)

	Year							
Dimension	1961	1965	1969	1973	1977	1981	1985	1989
Labor groups (+)	A	H	A	A	A	SP	SP	—
Agriculture & farmers	H	A	A	A	A	A	H	A
Underprivileged minorities	SP	A	A	A	A	A	A	A
	A:14(69)	A:9(43)	A:11(44)	A:11(56)	A:16(77)	A:9(32)	A:8(36)	A:11(69)
	SF:2(6)	V:6(24)	SP:3(15)	SV:4(15)	SV:1(7)	KRF:5(34)	H:4(11)	SV:2(8)
	H:1(8)	H:2(15)	H:2(12)	H:1(9)	H:1(2)	SP:3(16)	KRF:3(20)	KRF:2(3)
	SP:1(1)	KRF:1(5)	V:1(9)	SP:1(4)		H:1(2)	SP:2(9)	H:1(5)
		KRF:1(4)	KRF:1(1)			SV:1(6)	FRP:1(3)	SP:1(1)
							FRP:1(2)	

Note: Figures in bottom section represent the number of dimensions on which each party controlled the median legislator. For each party, the aggregate salience of these dimensions is parenthesized. In 1989 SP and FRF had exactly the same emphasis in 'Freedom and Human Rights' and collectively controlled the median legislator on this dimension. Both parties have been counted as pivotal.

However, Labour dominance has not been unqualified. The party has several times failed to control a number of important policy dimensions, especially those related to the larger left–right dimension. Here, Labour has had to share control, not with the Conservatives, but with centrist non-socialist parties such as the Liberals and the Christian People's Party. Note that although Labour led the Christians in the number of policy dimensions controlled in 1981, those dimensions controlled by the latter were actually somewhat more salient in total, since they included key areas of economic policy (State intervention, Capitalist economy, productivity). Over time, Labour control has weakened, particularly in the domain of economic policy. Yet the Labour Party has quite consistently controlled the median legislator on important policy dimensions such as Quality of life and Social services.

CONCLUSIONS

Our analysis of party and government policy in Norway has in many ways supported the conclusions drawn by previous historical and survey-based work. The placement of parties is consistent with conventional wisdom, as is that of governments, especially those formed by the non-socialist parties. However, formal theories of government formation have not worked too well in the Norwegian context (though see Grofman, 1982, for a partial exception). In this context we have managed to go beyond previous results. We have confirmed the importance of policy concerns to parties and hence their influence over government formation, while specifying the constraints and structural influences whch also shape this process.

Table 4.6 summarizes the success of various policy-based coalition theories in the Norwegian context. Models A, B, and C are compatible with the theoretical arguments presented in this book. Theories A and C presume a process of proto-coalition formation akin to that developed by Grofman (1982), with the relaxed assumption that governments need to be policy-viable but not 'winning' (majoritarian). Theory B develops the argument developed here about the bargaining power of predominant parties. The predominant party is operationally defined as the party that occupies the position of the median legislator on the set of dimensions with the largest aggregate salience (this is the Christian People's Party in 1981 and the Labour Party in every other case). Finally, theory D represents a more traditional policy-based theory developed by Axelrod (1970), specifying that government coalitions should be minimum connected winning coalitions in unidimensional space. For theories C and D, which assume unidimensional space, the common left–right dimension has been applied.

Table 4.6 Success rates of policy-based coalition theories in Norway, 1961–89

Year	Number of coalitions arithmetically possible	Feasible under constraint	Theory A predictions		Theory B predictions		Theory C predictions		Theory D predictions	
			Set	Correct	Set	Correct	Set	Correct	Set	Correct
1961	63	63	9	Yes	32	Yes	5	Yes	2	No
1963	63	63	9	No	32	No	5	No	2	No
1963	63	63	9	Yes	32	Yes	5	Yes	2	No
1965	63	63	9	No	32	No	3	No	2	Yes
1969	31	1	0	No	0	No	1	Yes	1	Yes
1971	31	31	9	Yes	16	Yes	4	No	2	No
1972	127	15	9	No	8	Yes	0	No	0	No
1973	255	255	12	Yes	128	Yes	5	Yes	2	No
1976	255	255	12	Yes	128	Yes	5	Yes	2	No
1977	63	63	6	Yes	32	Yes	5	Yes	2	No
1981	63	63	6	Yes	32	Yes	5	Yes	2	No
1981	127	111	9	Yes	64	No	4	No	2	No

Table 4.6 (cont'd)

Year	Number of coalitions arithmetically possible	Feasible under constraint	Theory A predictions		Theory B predictions		Theory C predictions		Theory D predictions	
			Set	Correct	Set	Correct	Set	Correct	Set	Correct
1983	127	111	9	No	64	Yes	4	No	2	Yes
1985	63	63	11	No	32	No	3	Yes	2	No
1986	63	63	11	Yes	32	Yes	3	No	2	No
1989	63	63	11	No	32	No	5	Yes	2	No
Predictive accuracy (No. Correct/No. Cases)			.56 (9/16)		.63 (10/16)		.56 (9/16)		.19 (3/16)	
Predictive efficiency			.064 (9/141)		.014 (10/696)		.145 (9/62)		.103 (3/29)	

Notes:
Theory A: Coalition will be at node on 20-dimension cluster tree and policy-viable in at least one dimension.
Theory B: Coalition will include 20-dimension predominant party.
Theory C: Coalition will be policy-viable based on 1-dimension clustering.
Theory D: Coalition will be 1-dimension minimum connected winning.
1-dimension analysis based on standard left–right dimension.

It is immediately evident that theory D performs more poorly than any of the others. This is caused by its insistence on the government having a majority. The three viability-based theories correctly predict at least half the Norwegian governments since 1961; theory D only three. However, the apparent superiority of the former is partly due to a number of 'easy' predictions of single-party Labour governments. Note also that different theories yield prediction sets of very different size. None yield unique predictions, but for the 1973–77 electoral period, theory D is compatible with only two solutions, theory B with no fewer than 128! It we take these differences into account and consider efficiency as well at accuracy, the unidimensional theories, including theory D, look stronger. Theory C appears to have the best all-round performance.

None of the theories considered perform superbly in the Norwegian context. However, all predictions they generate are improvements over randomness. Since a total of 1346 solutions are possible under the constraints identified in the 16 government formation situations (Borten II excluded), a random prediction would have only slightly better than a 1 per cent chance of success. Even theory B does better than that, and theory C does more than twelve times as well. Consider also the fact that Norway has always been a difficult case for coalition theory, and that the baseline of expected success is therefore low. Our analysis thus indicates that the standard left–right dimension gives a lot of mileage in the analysis of Norwegian party behaviour. Where our predictions most seriously break down is in their failure to capture the depth of the socialist versus non-socialist division in Norwegian party politics. Coalitions between Labour and centrist bourgeois parties (especially the Liberals) are consistently predicted by our models, but have never materialised in the post-war period.

Structural influences and strategic party behaviour explain a large part of this discrepancy. The disproportionality of the Norwegian electoral system has forced the smaller centrist parties into electoral alliances and these have continued into government coalitions. Also, given the predominant position of Labour, the non-socialist parties have recognised the necessity of presenting a united front if they are to have any hopes of office themselves. Moreover, these parties, and especially the Conservatives, have made clear their willingness to punish those who break ranks. Curiously, Labour has reinforced the tendency by consistently refusing to go into coalition. The party has always been reluctant to contradict its own arguments about the ineffectiveness of coalition governments, so as to cultivate an image of itself as the 'natural party of government' (as has typically been the case with Fianna Fail in Ireland).

Some interesting results also emerge from the analysis of coalition payoffs. While it appears highly advantageous in policy terms to secure the prime ministership, some other portfolios, e.g. Foreign Affairs and Foreign Aid, may be trade-offs for policy concessions. The regularity with which particular parties have sought and obtained particular portfolios consistent with their policy profiles, suggests that much office-seeking is instrumental. (Cf. Budge and Keman, 1990, Chapter 4 for detailed analyses.)

So far as coalition policy goes, governments seem to converge on the median participating party, even when the parties with greatest legislative weight are at the policy extremes of the coalition. These results again confirm the utility of the simple left–right scale for the analysis of Norwegian party politics and highlight the importance of policy bargaining.

APPENDIX B

Table B.1 Norwegian election results 1945–89 (Percentage of popular vote, Number of parliamentary seats in parentheses)

Party		Election year										
	1945	1949	1953	1957	1961	1965	1969	1973	1977	1981	1985	1989
Communists* (NKP)	11.9(11)	5.8(0)	5.1(3)	3.4(1)	2.9(0)	1.4(0)	1.0(0)	–	0.4(0)	0.3(0)	0.2(0)	0.7(0)
Socialist Left (SV)								11.2(16)	4.2(2)	4.9(4)	5.5(6)	10.1(17)
Socialist People's Party (SP)					2.4(2)	6.0(2)	3.5(0)					
Labour Party (A)	41.0(76)	45.7(85)	46.7(77)	48.3(78)	46.8(74)	43.1(68)	46.5(74)	35.3(62)	42.3(76)	37.2(66)	40.8(71)	34.3(63)
Liberals (V)	13.8(20)	13.1(21)	10.0(15)	9.7(15)	8.8(14)	10.4(18)	9.4(13)	3.5(2)	3.2(2)	3.9(2)	3.1(0)	3.2(0)
Liberal People's Party (DLP)								3.4(1)	1.0(0)	0.5(0)	0.5(0)	–
Center Party (SP)	8.0(10)	7.9(12)	9.1(14)	9.3(15)	9.4(16)	9.9(18)	10.5(20)	11.0(21)	8.6(12)	6.7(11)	6.6(12)	6.5(11)

Table B.1 (cont'd)

Party	1945	1949	1953	1957	1961	1965	1969	1973	1977	1981	1985	1989
					Election year							
Christian People's Party (KRP)	7.9(8)	8.6(8)	10.5(14)	10.2(12)	9.6(15)	8.1(13)	9.4(14)	12.3(20)	12.4(22)	9.4(15)	8.3(16)	8.5(14)
Conservatives (H)	17.0(25)	18.3(23)	18.6(27)	18.9(29)	20.0(29)	21.1(31)	19.6(29)	17.4(29)	24.8(41)	31.7(53)	30.4(50)	22.2(37)
Progress Party (FRP)								5.0(4)	1.9(0)	4.5(4)	3.7(2)	13.0(22)
Total	(150)	(150)	(150)	(150)	(150)	(150)	(150)	(155)	(155)	(155)	(157)	(165)†

Note: Party names are current. Several parties have previously contested elections under different labels. Party affiliations as at the beginning of the legislative period. During the 1969–1973 period, a total of ten representatives changed party affiliations.
*) Communist results for 1989 represent the 'County Lists for the Environment and Solidarity', an electoral coalition including the NKP and the Red Electoral Allaince (RV).
†) The total figure for the 1989 includes an independent, Anders Aume, representing *Folkeaksjonen Fremtid for Finnmark* ('The Popular Movement for Finnmark's Future').
Sources: Heidar (1983), Torp (1986) and previous editions; for 1989: *Statistisk Ukehefte* no.48, 1989.

Table B.2 Norwegian governments 1945–88

Government	Tenure	Parties*	Parliamentary basis (%)
Gerhardsen I	Nov 45 – Oct 49	A	50.7
Gerhardsen II	Oct 49 – Nov 51	A	56.7
Torp I	Nov 51 – Oct 53	A	56.7
Torp II	Oct 53 – Jan 55	A	51.3
Gerhardsen III	Jan 55 – Oct 57	A	51.3
Gerhardsen IV	Oct 57 – Sep 61	A	52.0
Gerhardsen V	Sep 61 – Aug 63	A	49.3
Lyng	Aug 63 – Sep 63	H, SP,V, KRF	49.3
Gerhardsen VI	Sep 63 – Oct 65	A	49.3
Borten I	Oct 65 – Sep 69	SP, H, V, KRF	53.4
Borten II	Sep 69 – Mar 71	SP, H, V, KRF	50.6
Bratteli I	Mar 71 – Oct 72	A	49.3
Korvald	Oct 72 – Oct 73	KRF, SP, V	25.3
Bratteli II	Oct 73 – Jan 76	A	40.0
Nordli I	Jan 76 – Sep 77	A	40.0
Nordli II	Sep 77 – Feb 81	A	49.0
Brundtland I	Feb 81 – Oct 81	A	49.0
Willoch I	Oct 81 – Jun 83	H	34.2
Willoch II	Jun 83 – Sep 85	H, KRF, SP	51.6
Willoch III	Sep 85 – May 86	H, KRF, SP	49.7
Brundtland II	May 86 – Oct 89	A	45.2
Syse	Oct 89 –	H, KRF, SP	37.6

Sources: Nordby (1985), Torp (1986) and previous editions

Party Abbreviations:

A	Det Norske Arbeiderparti (Labour Party)
H	Hoyre (Conservatives)
KRF	Kristelig Folkeparti (Christian People's Party)
SP	Senterpartiet (Center Party). Until 1959: Bondepartiet (Farmer's Party)
V	Venstre (Liberals)

* Party of Prime Minister listed first.

Table B.3 Twenty-dimensional policy distances between Norwegian parties in election years, 1945–89

1945						1949					
A	72					A	72				
V	84	48				V	66	52			
SP	83	81	77			SP	77	81	39		
KRF	76	68	66	57		KRF	83	81	55	62	
H	83	69	57	78	63	H	73	73	37	30	58
	NKP	A	V	SP	KRF		NKP	A	V	SP	KRF

1953						1957					
A	80					A	70				
V	71	41				V	77	51			
SP	92	78	59			SP	98	62	37		
KRF	83	69	60	71		KRF	89	67	46	51	
H	86	66	53	36	59	H	93	61	34	31	50
	NKP	A	V	SP	KRF		NKP	A	V	SP	KRF

1961						1965					
A	43					A	37				
V	39	38				V	46	33			
SP	77	42	50			SP	68	61	42		
KRF	79	54	60	40		KRF	68	55	48	56	
H	83	44	56	38	60	H	74	61	40	42	64
	SF	A	V	SP	KRF		SF	A	V	SP	KRF

1969					
A	58				
V	67	39			
SP	78	48	35		
KRF	83	47	46	33	
H	96	62	49	38	49
	SF	A	V	SP	KRF

1973							
A	49						
V	45	42					
SP	66	45	39				
KRF	69	52	40	31			
DLF	67	40	44	25	38		
H	68	53	43	36	41	29	
FRP	159	160	158	153	156	146	151
	SV	A	V	SP	KRF	DLF	H

1977						
A	23					
V	41	28				
SP	46	31	17			
KRF	56	43	37	28		
H	56	41	45	34	44	
FRP	88	81	83	74	78	52
	SF	A	V	SP	KRF	H

1981						
A	41					
V	39	38				
SP	53	34	40			
KRF	55	42	44	26		
H	84	53	57	49	57	
FRP	112	95	91	101	99	58
	SF	A	V	SP	KRF	H

1985						
A	32					
V	38	34				
SP	53	51	33			
KRF	33	37	41	42		
H	56	48	50	43	51	
FRP	91	87	89	86	80	59
	SF	A	V	SP	KRF	H

1989						
A	35					
V	37	42				
SP	42	34	53			
KRF	48	41	53	42		
H	68	48	67	46	55	
FRP	92	82	87	79	78	54
	SF	A	V	SP	KRF	H

Figure B.1   Cluster diagrams of Norwegian coalition formation, 1945–89

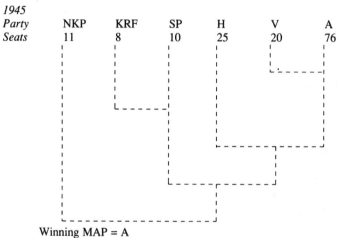

1945

Party	NKP	KRF	SP	H	V	A
Seats	11	8	10	25	20	76

Winning MAP = A
Actual Government = A

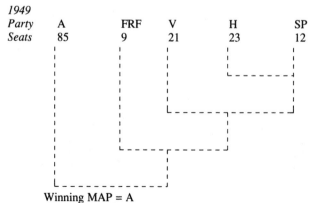

1949

Party	A	FRF	V	H	SP
Seats	85	9	21	23	12

Winning MAP = A
Actual Government = A

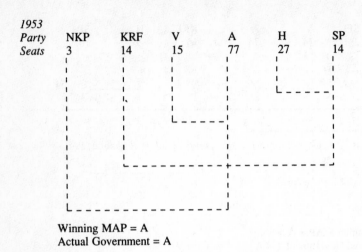

1953
Party
Seats

Winning MAP = A
Actual Government = A

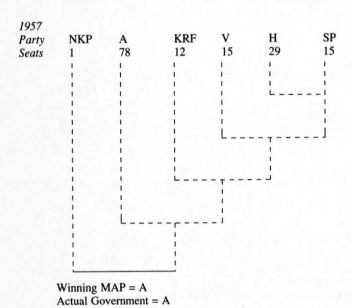

1957
Party
Seats

Winning MAP = A
Actual Government = A

1961

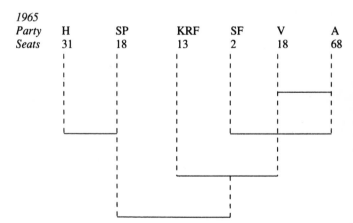

Party SF V A KRF H SP
Seats 2 14 74 15 26 16

Winning MAP = A + V
Actual Government 1 = A
Actual Government 2 = H + SP + V + KRF
Actual Government 3 = A

1965

Party H SP KRF SF V A
Seats 31 18 13 2 18 68

Winning Map = A + V
Actual Government = SP + H + V + KRF

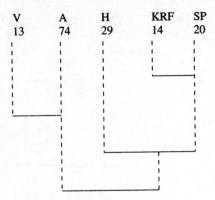

1969
Party
Seats

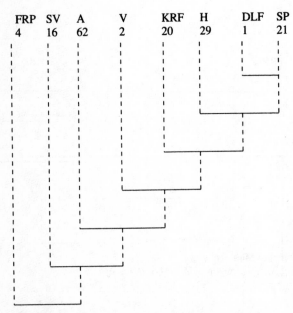

Winning MAP = A + V
Actual Government 1 = SP + H + V + KRF
Actual Government 2 = A
Actual Government 3 = KRF + SP + V

1973
Party
Seats

Winning MAP = SP + DLF + H + KRF + V + A
Actual Government = A

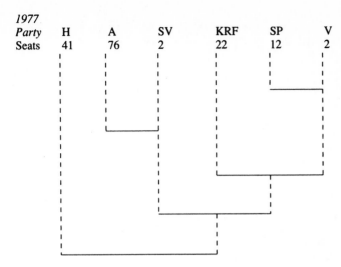

1977
Party H A SV KRF SP V
Seats 41 76 2 22 12 2

Winning MAP = A + SV
Actual Government = A

1981
Party FRP H V SV A KRF SP
Seats 4 53 2 4 66 15 11

Winning MAP = SP + KRF + A
Actual Government 1 = H
Actual Government 2 = H + KRF + SP

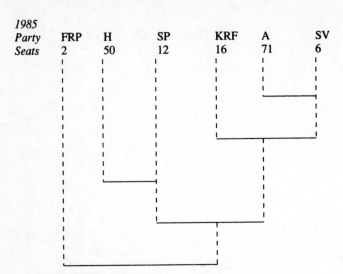

1985
Party
Seats

Winning MAP = SV + A + KRF
Actual Government 1 = H + KRF + SP
Actual Government 2 = A

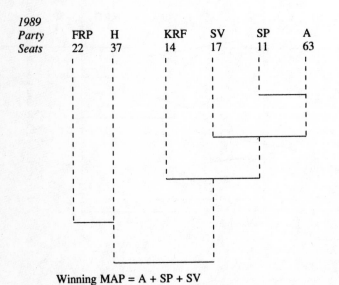

1989
Party
Seats

Winning MAP = A + SP + SV
Actual Government = H + KRF + SP

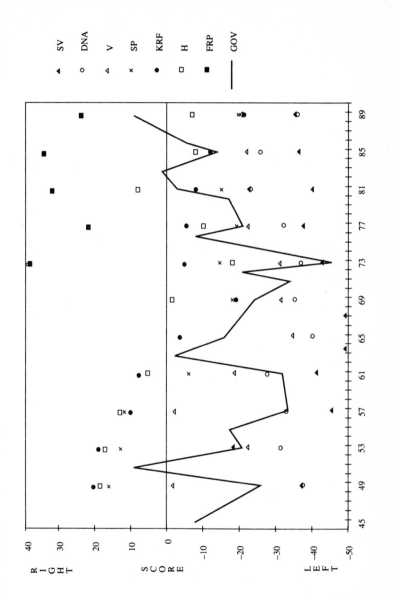

Figure B.2   Party and government positions in Norway on standard left–right dimension

106

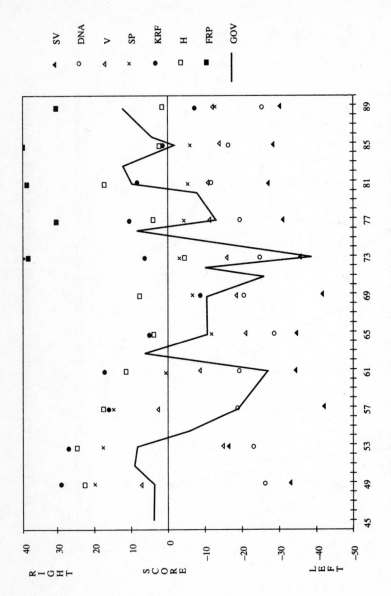

Figure B.3   Party and government positions in Norway on national left–right dimension

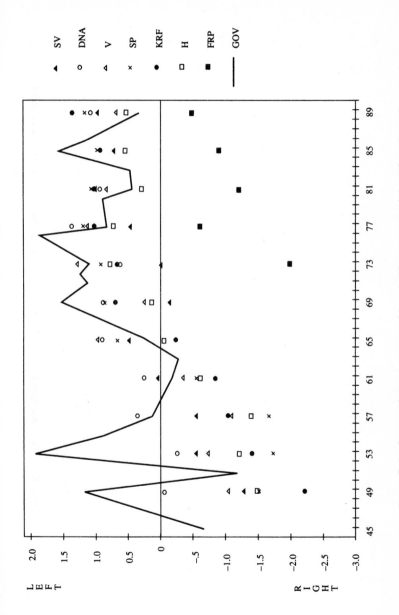

Figure B.4 Party and government positions in Norway on social welfare dimension

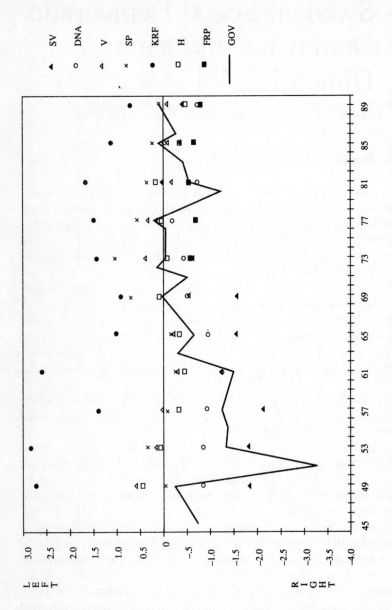

Figure B.5 Party and government positions in Norway on traditional religion dimension

5 Sweden: Social Democratic Dominance in One Dimension

Kaare Strom and Torbjorn Bergman

Introduction: The Swedish Party System

Five parties and two 'blocs' have dominated Swedish politics in the post-war era. The two blocs (socialist and bourgeois) are defined by party positions on a popularly perceived left–right dimension, and in this respect the Swedish party system follows a general Scandinavian pattern. Berglund *et al.* (1981) have argued that this Scandinavian model fits the Swedish case so well that the model 'might have been generated on Swedish data alone'. 'The Conservative, Liberal, and Agrarian or Centre parties form one cluster, the Labour (Social Democratic) and Communist parties another. This kind of configuration suggests the predominance of a socialist–nonsocialist cleavage throughout Scandinavia. Party Programmes lend support to this notion as does electoral behaviour. Class is still the major determinant of voting behaviour' (Berglund, Pesonen, and Gislason, 1982, p. 80).

The socialist bloc in Swedish politics consists of the Social Democratic Party (Sveriges Socialdemokratiska Arbetareparti [S or SAP] and a small Communist Party (Vansterpartiet Kommunisterna [VPK]). The non-socialist bloc is composed of the Centre Party (Centerpartiet [CP]), the liberal People's Party (Folkpartiet [FP]) and the Moderate Unity Party (Moderata Samlingspartiet [M]). The Centre Party was until 1957 known as the Agrarians, and the Moderates called themselves Conservatives (or literally: 'The Right') until 1969.

Note that the terms 'non-socialist' (icke-socialistisk) and 'bourgeois' (borgerlig) in Swedish politics are used synonymously in reference to the three non-socialist parties. The latter term is embraced without embarrassment by the non-socialist parties themselves. Note also that class voting has remained very high by West-European standards. Although the 1960s witnessed some decline, class voting has remained virtually unchanged since 1970. Thus, the Alford index for the 1985 election was 34, only two points lower than the score from 1970 (Holmberg and Gilljam, 1987; see also Arter, 1984; Lipset, 1981).

Only occasionally have parties other than the five traditional ones knocked on the gates of the parliamentary party system. Contrary to the experience of other Scandinavian polities, no 'new left' party has arisen to displace the Communists. Despite the highest taxation levels in the Western world, no tax revolt party has emerged. Right-wing extremism has found exceptionally infertile ground (see Lindstrom, 1985). In 1964 a locally constituted party-association (Medborgerlig Samling), which argued for more extensive non-socialist cooperation, gained representation in the Riksdag, the Swedish Parliament. However, this group was created by politicians clearly affiliated with the existing non-socialist parties and was soon subsumed by these parties (Birgersson *et al.* 1984, pp. 247–51; Hadenius, 1985). In 1985 the chairman of the Christian Democrats (Kristdemokratiska Samhallspartiet [KDS]) was elected through an electoral alliance with the Centre Party but that co-operation only lasted one term. In 1988, however, the Green Party (Miljopartiet de Grona) gained parliamentary representation. For the most part, however, the Swedish party system is noted for its stability, bloc politics, and class basis. Thus the party system meets one of the general assumptions in coalition theory; a stable set of unitary actors is involved in government formation. (see Axelrod, 1970; von Beyme, 1985; and Laver, 1986, for a discussion of this assumption).

PARTY, SUPPORT AND BEHAVIOUR

Until September, 1988, therefore, membership in the Swedish parliament had for more than forty years been reserved for the five established parties. Electoral support for the two socialist parties has been relatively stable over the entire post-war period. The exception is the fall in the 'normal' vote for the Social Democratic Party from a level of approximately 46–47 per cent in the early 1970s to around 43–44 per cent. Its position as the largest party has, however, never been remotely endangered (election results are presented in Table C.1 in the appendix to this chapter). Fluctuations in parliamentary seats and voting patterns have been greater for the bourgeois parties and especially for the People's Party. From a post-war peak of 24.4 per cent of the vote in 1952, the Liberals declined to a meagre 5.9 per cent in 1982 and then rebounded dramatically to 14.2 per cent in 1985 (see Lindstrom and Worlund, 1988). The two other non-socialist parties have experienced similar surges and declines, with the Centre Party reaching its peak in the mid-1970s, and the Moderates theirs, in the early 1980s. Note that, in contrast to neighbouring Norway, no party has consistently led the non-socialist bloc. The People's Party was in this position in the 1950s, the Centre Party in the 1970s and, finally, the Moderates have been the largest bourgeois party of the 1980s.

The Social Democratic Party has had a massive hold on Swedish cabinet portfolios; with the exception of the years between 1976 and 1982, it has been represented in every cabinet since World War II. The Social Democrats are thus a prototypical predominant party (Sartori, 1976). Few, if any, European parties can match their longevity in government, mean electoral support, or plurality over the second largest party. In total, the party has participated in 18 out of 22 post-war cabinets (see Table C.2). However, out of 15 single-party Social Democratic governments, only two (Erlander X and Palme I) collectively accounting for no more than two cabinet years, have had an unambiguous parliamentary majority.

Thus, the Swedish governmental record is dominated by one-party minority Social Democratic government. However, out of six coalition cabinets (three of these including the Social Democrats), only one (Falldin III) has done without a parliamentary majority.

POLICY PURSUIT AND PORTFOLIOS IN INTERPARTY NEGOTIATIONS

In Swedish coalition bargaining, questions of portfolio distribution have been of less importance than policy disagreements. This is especially true for government resignations. It has been policy disagreement and expectations of future electoral payoffs, not portfolio allocations, that have caused Swedish coalition cabinets to resign. The coalition cabinets between the Social Democrats and the Centre (the Agrarian) Party are historical examples of the predominance of policy over portfolio concerns in Swedish coalition formation. These cabinets were formed by the Social Democrats and the Centre Party between 1951 and 1957. The rationale behind this has been described as follows: 'To the Social Democrats, it was important to have a stable parliamentary base for continued reform. . . . The Agrarians saw the coalition as an opportunity to ensure that conditions for farmers did not worsen. There was also a need to underline the party's position in the political centre compared with the other more "bourgeois" parties' (Hadenius, 1985:76).

This so-called 'red–green' coalition is considered to have been relatively stable, and its tenure marked a period of relative consensus in Swedish politics (Birgersson *et al.*, 1984, pp. 199–212; Hadenius, 1985). The coalition broke up over a Social Democratic proposal to create public and mandatory pension funds. It deserves, however, to be pointed out that the split into two blocs should not be interpreted as a division that prohibits all cooperation between parties in different blocs. While the split has been evident on major issues along the left–right dimension and in government formation, there does exist a considerable amount of 'interbloc' cooperation and consensus in the day to day work in the Riksdag (Arter, 1984; Sarlvik, 1983). Similarly, the existence of a strong left–right voting pattern in the Riksdag does not, on the evidence of call analyses, rule out inter-bloc voting in the Riksdag (Arter, 1984; Berglund and Lindstrom, 1978, Clausen and Holmberg, 1977).

The next coalition formed in 1976 when the three bourgeois parties gained a parliamentary majority and formed a coalition. But even though the three parties were united in their opposition to some Social Democratic proposals they differed substantially on many issues (Pesonen and Thomas, 1983). In spite of these differences, they held no meetings prior to the election in order to discuss how these questions were to be settled in the event of an electoral victory (Bergstrom, 1987), leaving policy disputes to be settled by bargaining after the election (Bergstrom, 1987). The most difficult policy decision for the coalition concerned nuclear power. The Centre Party had argued that Swedish nuclear power plants could be dismantled within ten years, and this had proved to be a 'vote winner' for the party. However, the other non-socialist parties, as well as the Social Democrats, were determined to continue the nuclear power programme. Hence, the Centre Party was in a minority on this issue both within the coalition and in parliament (Birgersson *et al.*, 1984 pp. 287–96). Following inter-party bargaining the bourgeois cabinet declared that a new nuclear power plant could be brought into operation only if the power companies could guarantee safe keeping of the nuclear waste. This was seen as a concession from the new Prime Minister (Falldin), the chairman of the Centre Party, designed to ensure the formation of a non-socialist government after more than four decades in opposition. The nuclear power compromise cleared the way for the formation of the bourgeois cabinet but proved to be a time bomb, leading within two years to the government's resignation (Birgersson *et al.*, 1984, pp. 295; Sarlvik 1983b p. 127).

The 1979 election resulted in another bourgeois majority but this time the coalition formation process was more straightforward since the parties were not split on any issue as big as nuclear power. Indeed, Pesonen and Thomas (1983, p. 93) go so far as to argue that the lack of any issue as divisive as nuclear power meant that portfolio distribution 'caused the main problem during these negotiations'. Later, however, the coalition again ran into trouble, this time because of a policy dispute between the Moderates and the other two parties in the coalition. The crucial issue was a revision of the tax-system. The coalition parties at first seemed prepared to offer a joint tax-cut proposal. The socialist opposition protested, claiming that the People's Party and the Centre Party were giving in to the Moderates. Suddenly, in 1981, an agreement was reached between the two centrist parties and the Social Democrats (Hadenius, 1981, pp. 242–95). The Moderates resigned from the government after this and a Centre–People's Party coalition was left to soldier on as a minority government from May 1981 until the elections in 1982 (Birgersson *et al.*, 1981; Sarlvik, 1983).

Why this sudden rapprochement between two out of three coalition parties and the major opposition party? One reason was that the Social Democrats saw a chance both to change the tax proposal and to splinter the coalition. The two other parties wanted a broad majority to ensure that the tax bill would survive even if the Social Democrats won the next election. At the same time they could make an electorally useful distinction between themselves and the Moderates. In that case, the 1982 elections must have come as a rude surprise. In these elections, both governing parties suffered significant losses. The non-socialist parties lost their overall majority and the Social Democrats formed a minority government, which was returned to power in 1985 and 1988 (Lewing, 1984).

As regards bargaining over cabinet portfolios, the Swedish case is consistent with the robust cross-national correlations found for parliamentary democracies between the distribution of cabinet seats and each party's numerical basis in the parliament – the so called parity norm (Gamson, 1961; Browne and Franklin, 1973 and 1986; Bueno de Mesquita, 1979; Budge, 1985; Schofield and Laver, 1985; Budge and Keman, 1990).

For example, when the three non-socialist parties gained a Riksdag majority in 1976, they collectively controlled 180 out of 349 parliamentary seats. The Centre Party held 48 per cent, the Moderates 31 per cent, and the People's Party 22 per cent of the seats within the bourgeois bloc. During the process of coalition bargaining, the Moderates took the position that each party should receive a proportional share of the portfolios. The People's Party, on the other hand, wanted a clear emphasis on centrist co-operation (ie, dominance of the People's Party and the Centre Party) and advocated an allocation of the cabinet seats which would give the People's Party one seat more than the Moderates. In the end it was the largest party, the Centre Party, that had to settle for one seat less than a strictly proportional allocation would have yielded. The Prime Ministership was counted as two 'ordinary' ministerial posts, a solution that was also used in the case of the next three party coalition formed in 1979 (Bergstrom, 1987, p. 216). Thus, the Centre Party captured eight (40 per cent) of the twenty cabinet portfolios, including Foreign Affairs, Social Welfare and Agriculture. The Moderates received six cabinet portfolios (30 per cent) and the People's Party five (25 per cent).

The distribution of ministerial positions has also been linked to the parties' policy preferences. As content analyses of election manifestos have shown, all the Swedish parties, except the Moderates, have had Social Service concerns at the top of their policy agenda (see Holmstedt and Schou, 1987). The People's Party and the Social Democrats rate Education as number two, while no other party has had Education among its top four. It is thus no coincidence that the People's Party has held the Ministry of Education in every cabinet in which it has participated. The Centre (former Agrarian) Party has been a member of all post-war coalitions and has invariably headed the Department of Agriculture; its manifestos throughout the post-war period have emphasised the role of Agriculture far more than other parties. The Moderate Party's manifestos emphasise Economic Orthodoxy, Enterprise, and Freedom; this is reflected in the party's consistent tenure of the Ministries of Trade and Economic Affairs in both of the coalitions in which it has participated.

CONSTRAINTS AND STRUCTURAL INFLUENCES ON COALITION FORMATION

Exogenous constraints on bargaining have not significantly influenced any government formation in Sweden. Thus, the constraints we deal with are all endogenous feature of the party system. They are behavioural constraints (especially precommitments) which affect the motivations and behaviour of the bargaining actors. In this chapter we consider only constraints that unambiguously violate a central assumption of coalition theories, that all 'winning' combinations of parties represent feasible coalitions (Laver, 1986). Endogenous constraints and structural influences on coalition bargaining in Sweden are summarised in Table 5.1.

Endogenous constraints

Overall, coalition formation in Sweden is a rather regulated and orderly process, which suggests a hierarchical model of bargaining in the cluster analyses below. Once coalitions have formed they tend to persist informally

Table 5.1   Constraints and structural influences upon coalition bargaining in Sweden

Substance	Operative period	Effect
(1) Centre Party explicitly refuses to join coalition with other non-socialist parties	1957	Precluded non-socialist majority coalition
(2) If three-party non-socialist majority (M, CP, FP), the three parties committed themselves to a non-socialist cabinet solution.	1973–1985	Dictated government solution in 1976 and 1979, reduced set of options in the other years
(3) Bicameral legislature where First Chamber supported the Social Democrats	1945–1970	Favored Social Democrats
(4) National 4 per cent threshold of electoral system	1970–	Stablises set of actors (parties), reduces uncertainty, favours pre-electoral alliances
(5) Doctrine of collective cabinet responsibility	All years	Favours policy-compact governments
(6) Constitutional provisions which in practice drastically reduce the likelihood of early elections	1975–	Decreases uncertainty in coalition bargaining; favours minority governments
(7) The Speaker of the *Riksdag* (a party nominee, thus far always a Social Democrat) nominates candidates for Prime Minister	1975–	In practice: none so far
(8) Prime ministerial nominees elected unless an absolute parliamentary majority votes against them	1975–	Favours minority governments
(9) Cabinets survive votes of confidence unless an absolute parliamentary majority votes against them	1975–	Favours minority governments
(10) Decentralised and consensual parliamentary procedure	All years	Favours minority governments

beyond the date of cabinet resignation, since Swedish parties avoid being seen as 'unreliable bed-fellows'. A good example of this is the behaviour of the Centre Party after the dissolution of the coalition with the Social Democrats in 1957. The King invited the four largest parties to consultations after which he rather surprisingly gave the Liberal and Conservative leaders the task of trying to form a government. The Centre Party was unwilling to move directly from one coalition to another. Thus, the attempt at a bourgeois coalition failed and the Social Democrats subsequently accepted an invitation to form a minority government (Birgersson *et al.*, 1984, pp. 221–22; Hadenius, 1985, pp. 92–3).

During the 1960s the Moderate Party was relatively isolated by its extreme position on the left–right dimension. In the late 1960s and early 1970s, the three parties changed leadership, the Conservative Party changed its name to the Moderate Party (1969), and the likelihood of a non-socialist coalition increased (Birgersson *et al.*, 1984, p. 283). By the election of 1973, the three bourgeois parties were ready to make an unambiguous and explicit commitment: the three parties declared their desire to form a coalition government (Keesing's Contemporary Archives, October 22–28, 1973, p. 26157).

The situation was equally clear in the election campaign of 1976, 1979 and 1982; a non-socialist majority would lead to a non-socialist government (Birgersson *et al.*, 1984; Pesonen and Thomas, 1983). This commitment by the bourgeois parties to a non-socialist cabinet in the case of a bourgeois majority has since 1973 been sufficiently strong to qualify as an endogenous constraint. Note, that they have been open to the formation of non-socialist cabinets in constellations other than a three-party coalition, especially in inter-election periods. Nonetheless, this constraint precluded all interbloc coalitions under bourgeois majorities.

Structural influences on coalition bargaining

The formal–legal framework very much conditions coalition bargaining in Sweden, especially in terms of (1) administrative institutions; (2) electoral laws; (3) parliamentary structures; and (4) parliamentary procedures concerning government formation (summarised in Table 5.1).

The administrative structure
The formal separation of power between the cabinet as a collectivity; individual ministries and their heads; and state agencies and civil servants, has consequences for coalition formation and the pursuit of policy and portfolios. The Swedish constitution formally rejects the idea of direct

ministerial control of the agencies charged with policy implementation. With the exception of some issues concerning the ministries of Defence and Foreign Affairs, government decisions are supposed to express the views of the government as a whole (Nyman, 1982, pp. 188–89). Hence, administrative state agencies fall under the authority of the government as a total entity and not under the ministries or, for that matter, their heads.

This does not imply that department ministers are without means to enforce their will; they have substantial control over routine matters as well as over the budgetary process. Besides, they have substantial formal and informal agenda control in preparing collective decisions for the government. Yet, the specific utility of a ministerial portfolio may be more restricted in Sweden than in systems where ministers exercise more formal and direct control over the implementing agencies. As in Ireland the tradition of collective cabinet responsibility may force coalition partners and individual ministers to defend coalition policies with which they disagree, thus creating a disincentive to join a coalition unless there is some assurance that its policies will be acceptable. This disincentive may at least in part explain the frequency of minority governments and the central position of policy in the politics of government formation.

The electoral laws serve to limit the number of relevant actors in the government formation process. At the same time they provide an incentive to pre-electoral alliances. Thus, the only national representation the Christian Democrats have had came in 1985 through a pre-electoral alliance with the Centre Party. The alliance was not a success and it lasted only for one election, but the Chairman of the Christian Democrats did get to serve in the Riksdag for one term. It is also commonly believed that quite a few of the Social Democratic supporters vote tactically to ensure the continued representation of the Communist Party in the Riksdag. According to the 1985 election survey, every fourth voter who switched from the Social Democrats to the Communists referred to their decision as a 'tactical' one (Holmberg and Gilljam, 1987, p. 114).

Electoral laws
The impact of electoral laws on government formation can be substantial, albeit indirect. One effect stems from the exclusion of parties that fail to gain either 4 per cent of the vote nationally or 12 per cent in one constituency (Halverson, 1980, p. 46). In some elections this threshold has endangered the parliamentary representation of the Communist Party. If the Communist Party were to fall below the 4 per cent threshold, this would not only change the set of actors in the parliamentary arena, but also severely challenge the predominance of the Social Democratic Party. Electoral laws shape the

framework in which government formation takes place in at least one additional way. Elections must be held every three years, regardless of whether an early election has been held during that legislative term. This constitutional provision effectively decreases the likelihood of premature elections. In both 1978 and 1981 premature elections were discussed as possible solutions to the cabinet crises, but in the end this option was ruled out. One of the main reasons was that an early election would have to be followed by another within a year (Birgersson *et al.*, 1984, p. 297, 304–5; Sarlvik, 1983b, pp. 130–2). Consequently, minority cabinets with a weak legislative basis were formed and tolerated until the end of the regular parliamentary term. This restriction on the scheduling of elections promotes governmental solutions that might otherwise have been avoided, such as minority cabinets.

Parliamentary structure

The structure of the Riksdag also influences government formation. One reason for Social Democratic dominance up through the 1970s lay in the structure of the old parliament, and of its First Chamber in particular (Lewin, 1984, p. 276). The members of the First Chamber were elected indirectly by County Councils. Since only one eighth of the First Chamber was elected at one time (every year), this produced a time lag between changes in electoral support and the distribution of seats in the First Chamber (Halvarson, 1980, p. 6).

The Social Democratic Party held a majority of the seats in the First Chamber until the chamber was abolished after the election of 1970 (Birgersson, 1984). Even though the parliamentary basis for cabinets lay in the Second (lower) Chamber, a cabinet without support in the First (upper) chamber would have found it difficult to survive. The bargaining power of the Social Democrats was, thus, significantly enhanced by their strength in the First Chamber.

One feature of the Riksdag which continues to affect the government formation process is the high degree of influence the opposition enjoys over policy decisions, exercised via the committee system. The Riksdag has sixteen standing committees, all authorised to take legislative initiatives of their own, these have full time staffs that provide administrative assistance (Arter, 1985; Nyman, 1982). The standing committees are specialised in areas that roughly correspond to the jurisdictions of the governmental ministries, and committee chairs are distributed roughly proportionally among the parties in the legislature. Internal parliamentary structures and norms thus provide opportunities for the opposition to exercise policy influence, thereby reducing inducements to participate in government. This can contribute to the high frequency of minority governments (Strom, 1984 and 1986). (This is not dissimilar to the situation in Denmark: see the next chapter.)

Procedures for government formation
One innovation of the new constitution of 1975 was the introduction of explicit rules for government formation. The old constitution of 1809 contained no such rules, as parliamentary democracy had developed much later, and the process of government formation was governed by conventions which gave the King substantial discretion in deciding whom to ask to form a new government (Pesonen and Thomas, 1983, pp. 89–91). The constitutional reforms of 1975 radically curtailed the political functions of the monarch, who is still head of state but with duties that are almost exclusively ceremonial. The Monarch no longer presents the government declaration at the opening of the Riksdag, attends cabinet meetings, signs government decisions, or plays any role in the process of government formation (Arter, 1984).

When a government resigns after losing an election, it is now the task of the Speaker of the Riksdag to initiate deliberations and to propose a new Prime Minister (Birgersson *et al.*, 1984, pp. 279–80). If this designated prime minister is rejected by parliament, the Speaker has another opportunity to propose a candidate. If the Riksdag rejects the Speaker's proposals four times, the process is terminated and elections must be held. It has been assumed that 'the threat of extra elections will force the parties to reach an agreement on the formation of a government, at any rate before the fourth vote takes place' (Pesonen and Thomas, 1983). So far the Speaker's role in government formation has not been controversial. The potential for conflict exists, however, since the Speaker is an elected member of the Riksdag who, unlike his opposite number in some other countries, does not relinquish his party affiliation. Since the new constitution of 1970, even under the non-socialist majorities of 1976 and 1979, a Social Democrat has always been elected Speaker (Birgersson *et al.*, 1984).

A third distinctive feature of the Swedish system is that the Speaker's candidate as Prime Minister is elected unless a majority of the members of the parliament votes against him. Thus, abstentions are in practice counted as part of the government's parliamentary basis (Holmberg and Stjernquist, 1983). There is no requirement that a new government must enjoy the positive support of a parliamentary majority, only that it must be tolerated by a majority (Pesonen and Thomas, 1983, pp. 89–90; Sarlvik, 1983b, p. 139). This permissive rule helped the People's Party form a minority government in 1978. The Moderates and the Communist Party voted against this solution but the abstentions of the Centre Party and the Social Democrats enabled the prime ministerial candidate of the People's Party, to form a cabinet on the basis of only 39 per cent of the 349 legislators. (Bergersson *et al.*, 1984, pp. 297–8; Petersson, 1979).

The use of confidence votes is also regulated in the new constitution, which requires an absolute parliamentary majority to bring down a government, thus giving incumbents the benefit of abstentions. This procedure has never been used, though the Social Democrats tried to show discontent with the coalition government formed in 1979. However, they fell short of a majority (175 votes) and the bourgeois coalition remained in power (Bergstrom, 1987; Bergersson *et al.*, pp. 303–34).

The high frequency of minority governments, as well as the low frequency of coalition governments, are substantially explained by the structural features we have discussed. The electoral threshold prevents a high degree of fractionalisation and contributes to a stable set of unitary actors in the Riksdag. The voting procedures on the Speaker's prime ministerial candidate prior to government formation are tailored to facilitate government formation. The structures and practices of the Riksdag facilitate oppositional influence over government policy and, thereby, the formation of minority governments. At the same time mandatory elections every three years effectively exclude one of the standard ways out of a governmental deadlock, and have in practice favoured minority governments.

POLICY DOCUMENTS

In the following sections we analyse the relation between the policy positions of the five main Swedish parties and those of the 22 governments formed between 1945 and 1986 (Table C.2 in the chapter appendix). Party policy data in this study have been generated from the contents of election manifestos and leaflets used in national election campaigns between 1944 and 1982, most collected by Holmstedt. The government data are derived from the annual editions of Riksdagens Protokoll (The Protocols of the Riksdag) between 1946 and 1988.

The significance of these documents in Swedish politics has been investigated in a survey of the top officials in 1976 and 1982 (Bergstrom, 1987). The cabinet ministers and their top political secretaries had mixed estimates of the impact of election manifestos on their actions in government. Especially in the case of the 1976 coalition the election manifestos were de-emphasised by the cabinet elite. However, the same respondents attributed a great deal of importance to government declarations. Policy positions mentioned in the government declaration were seen as strong commitments, leaving little or no discretion for further bargaining or renegotiations. These findings show that Swedish party elites see their policies as being constrained, though not determined, by the commitments that they make in electoral campaigns and government declarations. These commitments and their impact on government formation are analysed below.

DIMENSIONS OF POLICY COMPETITION

Compared even to her Scandinavian neighbours, party politics in Sweden is much more strictly dominated by the class cleavage. Cross-cutting cleavages based on language, religion, or region are much less significant than those found elsewhere in the Nordic region (Holmberg, 1981). Consequently, left–right issues have been high on the agenda of all parties and governments. Swedish cabinets have devoted an average 56 per cent of the quasi-sentences in their government declarations to the cross-national left–right scale used in this book; the parties allocated on average 55 per cent of their election manifestos to this theme. The Moderate Party has stressed it the most (63 per cent of all coded policy statements); but all five parties on average allocated at least half of their manifestos to issues on the left–right dimension.

Although very important, the left–right axis is not the only dimension in Swedish politics; an urban–rural (in other words, agrarian–industrial) conflict has also exerted sustained influence. The rural segment of society has had its main parliamentary representative in the Centre Party and the party still has an agricultural–rural core of voters (Berglund and Lindstrom, 1978; Holmberg, 1981; Petersson, 1977). Overall, however, the left–right dimension is the most important in any analysis of the politics of government formation in Sweden. Other dimensions exist but none is as salient.

ONE-DIMENSIONAL ANALYSIS

Party positions

A conventional ordinal ranking of parties on the left–right dimension is, from left to right: The Communist Party, the Social Democratic Party, the Centre Party, the People's Party, and the Moderate Party (Berglund and Lindstrom, 1978). Our results corroborate this alignment. In pairwise comparisons of left–right orderings of the parties in the 15 post-war elections for which data are available, party positions are consistent with this conventional ordering in 132 (88 per cent) of 150 cases. The fit is perfect for four elections (1948, 1952, 1958 and 1982) and otherwise very close.

There are, however, as Table 5.2 indicate, some very interesting exceptions to the conventional ordering of the parties. Most of these involve the People's Party. In fact, there are only five incorrect pairwise orderings not involving the People's Party. In the 1970s the Centre Party and the People's Party shifted positions and both appear twice as the non-socialist party furthest to the left. This corroborates survey results to the effect that voters had difficulty in ordering these two parties on the left–right scale since they are seen as occupying more or less the same ground between the Social Democrats and the Moderates (Holmberg, 1981; Petersson, 1977, pp. 138–9; see also Castles and Mair, 1984, p. 82).

The extreme left-wing positions of the People's Party in 1964 and 1968 are more unexpected. In both elections the party placed itself to the left of the Social Democrats, in 1968 even to the left of the Communists.

A mundane explanation exists for the deviant scores for the People's Party in 1964 and 1968. These were the only two elections for which the People's Party position is not based on the contents of its regular election manifesto. Because these documents were unavailable, Holmstedt had to rely on a magazine for young voters for 1964 and a shorter campaign leaflet for 1968 (Holmstedt and Schou, 1987). It is perfectly conceivable that these publications varied systematically in their contents from the party manifestos.

While the magnitude of this swing should be interpreted cautiously its direction is quite plausible. The party's pronounced shift towards the Left in the 1960s may have been a response to a string of electoral frustrations. The People's Party was the largest opposition party, and the leading alternative to the Social Democrats, for most of the two decades between 1948 and 1968 without ever being able to form a government. Over time this led the People's Party more and more to address policy issues of concern to the Social Democrats. In a way the liberal opposition came to be based on criticism of the failure of Social Democrats to achieve their objectives, instead of a critique of these objectives per se (see Ruin, 1986).

The two polar parties in the Swedish system, the Communist and Moderate Parties, have been remarkably consistent in their positions. The isolation of the Moderates on the right was particularly evident in the 1960s. Later, the wide gap between the People's Party and the Moderate Party diminished. By 1976, the two parties held almost identical positions on the left–right scale and both had moved closer to the centre. It was in this decade that the non-socialist parties twice gained a majority in parliament.

Table 5.2   Left–right positions of Swedish parties and governments

Year	Government	VPK	S	CP	FP	M	S	S+CP	CP+FP+M	CP+FP	FP
			Party					*Cabinet Composition*			
1944	1	10	*–38*	24	9	28	–32				
1946	2						18				
1948	3	–44	–33	–5	23	56	25				
1951	4							32			
1952	5	–41	–28	1	16	41		–5			
1956	6	–46	–44	2	*–17*	54		–23			
1957	7						–2				
1958	8	–42	–25	12	22	56	–6				
1960	9	*–40*	–61	6	9	35	–24				
1964	10	–50	*–34*	–14	–49	60	–29				
1968	11	–47	*–43*	–12	–60	26	–29				
1969	12						–35				
1970	13	*–41*	*–41*	–15	–33	11	–39				
1973	14	–43	*–8*	–24	–11	20	–41				
1976	15	–38	*–11*	–18	–2	2			–8		
1978	16										–1
1979	17	–47	*–15*	–8	*–15*	23			4		
1981	18									–16	
1982	19	–40	*–18*	–14	5	25	–10				
1985	20	–37	*–21*	–1	13	60	–11				
1986	21						–13				
1988	22	–37	*–24*	–5	–8	37	–9				

Note: Governments counted chronologically. Positive scores indicate a right-wing and negative scores indicate a left-wing position. Italicised figures represent party controlling the median legislator. Note that there occasionally are two median legislators in even-numbered parliaments or when two parties have identical positions. The Left–Right score for the Green Party in 1988 was –18.

Abbreviations:
  VPK = The Communist party
     S = The Social Democratic Party
   CP = The Centre Party
   FP = The People's Party
    M = The Moderate Party

The severe policy differences that prevented the bourgeois parties from forming a joint opposition in the 1960s had by then diminished.

Government formation

Taken together with the bargaining constraints identified above, Table 5.2 gives a good explanation of the predominance of the Social Democratic Party in government formation. The predominant Social Democrats have successfully exploited a bipolar opposition, divided between the Communists on the left and the three non-socialist parties on the right. The policy distance on the left–right dimension between the Communist Party and the bourgeois parties has made coalitions between them highly unlikely. At the same time the Communists have been kept out of government by the Social Democrats. In 10 out of 15 electoral periods the Communists have been the party closest to the Social Democrats, in unidimensional space, but the latter have had good electoral reasons to eschew this particular coalition.

We see that the party that controlled the median legislator on the left–right dimension in Swedish politics has normally also controlled the cabinet. In 18 out of 22 governments formed between 1944 and 1988 (82.7 per cent), the median legislator's party has been a member of the cabinet. The Social Democrats have controlled the median legislator on the left–right dimension in all but three instances in the post-war period. In most instances, the party has formed single-party minority governments and only in the era of the 'red-green' coalition (1951–7) have the Social Democrats been in a government coalition. In 1960, the Communist Party came to be in control of the median legislator since the Social Democrats presented the most leftist program of any party in the postwar period. However, the distance between the Communist Party and the non-socialist parties was too wide to make a Communist–Bourgeois coalition a realistic alternative. Specifically, the absolute distance to the Moderates was seventy-one, and to the parties of the middle approximately fifty.

Only rarely have other parties been able to challenge the Social Democrats' hold on the median legislator. After the 1956 election the People's Party was pivotal, but the party was unable to transform its bargaining power into cabinet portfolios. Instead, the established Social Democratic–Centre party coalition prevented the People's Party from exploiting its position. One reason may be the unwillingness, discussed above, of Swedish parties to make short-term switches in coalition partners. Another is that, even though one of the non-socialist parties controlled the median legislator, the Moderate Party was isolated in an extreme right-wing position and the prospects for successful non-socialist coalition were therefore bleak.

In contrast, the non-socialist parties were able to form a coalition in 1976, when left–right policy distances between them were small. The distance between the two most extreme non-socialist parties was one quarter the equivalent distance eight years earlier. The situation was similar in 1979, when the distance between the non-socialist parties was a bit higher but the Centre Party was in a pivotal position. The three parties were connected in unidimensional space and had made a campaign commitment to form a non-socialist cabinet.

Government policy positions and payoffs

Overall, the policy positions of Swedish governments have tended to be somewhat to the right of those of the governing parties, especially in the first half of the post-war period (see Table 5.2). Only one Social Democratic government (Palme III) (1973–76) took a position to the left of the party programme. In many cases other parties, and particularly the two centrist parties, have been considerably closer to the government. This was particularly the case in the 1940s and 1950s.

From the mid-1950s, Swedish cabinets tended to move further and further to the left until, in 1973, the government was to the left of the governing Social Democratic Party (see Table 5.3). Perhaps this move towards the left reflected the success of the Social Democratic Sweden of the 1960s. Table 5.2 also shows how the Social Democrats managed to shift government policies more and more to the left during the subsequent coalition with the Centre Party. What had started out as a coalition that stressed 'Economic Orthodoxy and Efficiency' became one that emphasised positive views towards 'Social Services' and 'International Co-operation'. However, in 1957, when the coalition had broken up and the public pension funds issue dominated the political agenda, the new Social Democratic government moved to the right, followed in 1958 by the social Democratic Party.

Perhaps the reasons behind this movement were similar to those of the two-party bourgeois coalition in 1981 after the withdrawal of the Moderates. These shifts can be understood as concessions to former coalition partners by government under siege. In both instances the parties remaining in government were heavily pressured on a specific issue (pension funds in one case and taxes in the other) by the party leaving the government. In response, the parties that stayed on in government were not inclined to emphasise other policies that separated them from their former coalition partners. Instead they tried to find new grounds for parliamentary co-operation.

Table 5.3　Policy payoffs in left–right unidimensional space, Sweden (Distances between party and government positions)

Government	Year	Party VPK	S	CP	FP	M	Absolute Distance all parties (X)
1 Hansson	1945	–42	6	–56	–41	–60	41
2 Erlander I	1946	8	56	–6	9	–10	18
3 Erlander II	1948	69	58	30	2	–31	38
4 Erlander III	1951	76	65	37	9	–24	42
5 Erlander IV	1952	36	23	–6	–21	–46	26
6 Erlander V	1956	23	21	–25	–6	–77	30
7 Erlander VI	1957	44	42	–4	15	–56	32
8 Erlander VII	1958	36	19	–18	–28	–62	33
9 Erlander VIII	1960	16	37	–30	–33	–59	35
10 Erlander IX	1964	21	5	–15	20	–89	30
11 Erlander X	1968	18	14	–17	31	–55	27
12 Palme I	1969	12	8	–23	25	–61	26
13 Palme II	1970	2	2	–24	–6	–50	17
14 Palme III	1973	2	–33	–17	–30	–61	29
15 Falldin I	1976	30	3	10	–6	–10	12
16 Ullsten	1978	37	10	17	1	–3	14
17 Falldin II	1979	51	19	12	19	–19	24
18 Falldin III	1981	63	31	24	31	–7	31
19 Palme IV	1982	30	8	4	–15	–35	18
20 Palme V	1985	26	10	–10	–24	–71	28
21 Carlsson I	1986	24	8	–12	–26	–73	29
22 Carlsson II	1988	28	15	–4	–1	–46	19
X Mean Absolute Distance		32	22	18	18	46	27*
X When in Government		–	24	19	14	14	18*
X When in Opposition		32	16	18	19	49	27*

Note: Positive scores indicates that the government was more right-wing than the party's position. Negative scores indicates that the government was more left-wing than the party.
The score for the Green Party in 1988 was 9.
Italicised figures represent governing parties.
* This score represents the average of the row means.

The election of 1976 represents a decisive break in this leftward trend. The non-socialist parties formed a coalition on a relatively centrist platform. This is also the year in which the aggregate distance between all parties and the government was least. Although far more rightist than previous Social Democratic cabinets, Falldin I fell very close to the manifesto position of the Social Democratic party. Overall, the non-socialist coalitions have been better matched to the programs of their participating parties. In both three-party coalitions (Falldin I and II) the government position was almost exactly in the center of the policy range covered by the three coalition partners. Ullsten's single-party government (1978) had a position almost identical to that of his People's Party. Moreover, in two of the three 'red-green' coalitions, the government position fell between those of the participating parties.

As in the case of the Social Democratic–Centre Party coalition in the 1950s, the bourgeois coalition changed policy positions, this time towards the right. For example, the proportion of positive references towards 'Social Services' declined from 12 per cent for Falldin I in 1976 to 2 per cent for the Centre Party–People's Party coalition formed in 1981 (Falldin III).

TWENTY-DIMENSIONAL ANALYSIS

The importance of the left–right dimension for Swedish politics, including the politics of coalition formation, is evident from the previous section. In this section, we analyse the full twenty-dimensional policy space to assess the importance of other policy dimensions in Swedish coalition politics. As an example, Table 5.4 presents the matrix of twenty-dimensional city-block distances for the 1988 election.

Party positions

Table 5.4 shows how the Communists, Social Democrats and Green Party, on the one hand, and the Moderates on the other, tended to cluster together. The different policy priorities of, for example, the Communist and Moderate parties clearly transcend the traditional left–right dimension. As Table C.3 shows, this difference has been persistent. At no election in the post-war period have the two parties been closely connected in multi-dimensional space. This distance between the Communists and the Moderates has been about 100 (on a scale upwardly bounded by the value 200) in all but three elections. However, the two parties have been the most widely separated

Table 5.4   Twenty-dimensional party distance matrix, Sweden, 1988

	M	FP	CP	G	S	VPK
M	0					
FP	67	0				
CP	87	72	0			
G	103	68	60	0		
S	106	83	67	68	0	
VPK	102	60	78	50	73	0
	M	FP	CP	G	S	VPK

Note: Policy distance varies between the hypothetical bounds of 0 and 200.

Abbreviations:

   VPK = The Communist Party
     S = The Social Democratic Party
     G = The Green Party
   CP = Centre Party
   FP = The People's Party
    M = The Moderate Party

pair in 'only' half of the post-war elections. In the early post-war period other parties were also widely dispersed in policy space. Later, the multi-dimensional distances between the other Swedish parties decreased (they came to stress more similar themes), while the difference between the Communists and the Moderates has remained more or less constant.

The post-war period can be divided into four distinct periods. In the period from 1944 to 1956, competition between Social Democrats and the People's Party led these parties to converge closely in twenty-dimensional space. In the 1956–68 period the socialist parties clustered in twenty-dimensional space, while in the 1970s the Social Democrats moved closer to the centrist parties than to the Communists. For the 1980s, the picture is more mixed, but it is interesting to note that the newcomer in the Riksdag, the Green Party, has positioned itself relatively close to the Social Democrats, the centrist parties, and especially the Communist Party, in multi-dimensional space.

In no fewer than 10 out of 15 elections the Social Democratic Party has been one of the two parties most closely connected in twenty-dimensional policy space. No other party can match this record, which suggests that the policy predominance of the Social Democrats in Swedish politics goes beyond the left–right dimension. Similarly, the relative isolation of the Moderate Party in the 1960s, in relation to its potential coalition partners (and especially the People's Party), went above and beyond the left–right dimension. By the beginning of the next decade this had changed and the Moderates increasingly addressed the same issues as the other parties until by 1976 they approached not only the two centrist parties but also the Social Democrats.

Another noteworthy result, in Table C.3, is the tendency for inter-party distances to decline over time. In 1952, five out of ten such distances were above 100 points. For the four elections since 1973 combined, there have been only three distances in excess of 100 (always Communists and Moderates). Lately, however, the trend has been the reversed and in 1988 the Moderates once again deviate quite significantly from their potential coalition partners: the People's and Centre parties.

Government formation

The strength of the underlying left–right dimension is illustrated once more when we turn our attention to party and cabinet distances. Three out of the six coalitions did not form between the two parties most closely connected in twenty-dimensions. The exceptions are the first two 'red-green' coalition cabinets and the 1981 coalition between the People's Party and the Centre Party. The latter came very close to being the most compact in twenty-dimensional space; in fact the distance between the People's Party and the Social Democrats for the same election is the only smaller policy distance in the entire post-war period.

We can take as an example the cluster analytic government formation model for 1979, which can be examined in Figure C.1 the election preceding the 1981 coalition, based on twenty-dimensional distances. Note how the Social Democrats, the Centre Party, and the People's Party cluster together in the first two steps of the twenty dimensional prediction, something that we would have expected from the one-dimensional analysis (recall Table 5.3). However, this coalition was effectively prevented by the pre-election commitment discussed above.

Figure C.1 provides similar cluster diagrams for all elections between 1948 and 1988. The cluster analysis is based on a hierarchical clustering procedure, as we consider this the most faithful reflection of the Swedish bargaining environment (see above). For each election, we have indicated the 'winning' (majority) coalition representing the Minimum Aggregate Policy distance (MAP) according to this clustering procedure. This coalition represents a prediction similar to a twenty-dimensional version of Grofman's (1982) dynamic theory of protocoalitional formation, operationalised in our city-block policy space.

As argued in Chapter 1, the majority requirement is neither theoretically compelling nor empirically plausible, especially in cases such as Sweden. If a majority requirement is imposed the predictions in Figures C.1 are more often wrong than right. The governments formed in 1951, 1952, 1968 and 1969 are the only ones correctly predicted. The Social Democratic–Centre Party coalition is thus predicted by the twenty-dimensional clustering. Similarly, the break-up of this coalition about a year after the 1956 election can be interpreted as evidence in favour of the validity of the twenty-dimensional clustering since by then the two parties had moved apart. Note, however, that the cluster analysis predicts a unique majority outcome in each situation, which necessarily leaves it more error-prone than theories compatible with many different cabinet solutions. Furthermore, the repeated and erroneous cluster analysis predictions of coalitions between the Social Democrats and the Communists (three cases) or between the Social Democrats and the People's Party (five cases) are not at all implausible.

For other elections, the twenty-dimensional analysis fits less well. For example, in 1976, the cluster analysis predicts a coalition between the Social Democrats and the Moderates. It might be that these two parties stressed similar policies when their manifestos are considered in their entirety. However, the salience of policies on the left–right dimensions always has made this coalition highly unlikely. Together with the bourgeois pre-electoral commitments discussed above, this has effectively eliminated such an outcome from consideration.

Government policy positions and payoffs

As in the unidimensional analysis, the policy positions of Swedish governments have not been particularly close to those of their component parties in twenty-dimensional policy space. Again, the discrepancies were particularly great in the early post-war period. However, even in more recent years, the distances between party and government policy positions have remained significantly greater in twenty-dimensional policy space than on the left–right axis. The smallest distances overall are between Fälldin I and the Moderates (1976), between Hansson and the Social Democrats (1945), and between Ullsten and the People's Party (1978). The results also reveal that Social Democratic governments often have taken positions at a substantial distance from their party's manifesto. Moreover, in no fewer than 18 out of 22 cabinets the party in government has been further from the government position than one of the opposition parties! Thus, the Social Democrats have been close to the positions of many non-socialist govern-

Table 5.5 Policy payoffs in twenty-dimensional space, Sweden (distances between party and government positions)

Government	Year	VPK	S	Party CP	FP	M	All Parties (X)
1 Hansson	1945	82	*48*	93	97	89	82
2 Erlander I	1946	70	*86*	57	84	52	70
3 Erlander II	1948	88	*105*	94	58	74	84
4 Erlander III	1951	102	*125*	*123*	92	88	106
5 Erlander IV	1952	84	*67*	*64*	67	83	73
6 Erlander V	1956	77	*79*	*108*	89	105	92
7 Erlander VI	1957	80	*70*	77	61	76	73
8 Erlander VII	1958	79	*61*	58	51	77	65
9 Erlander VIII	1960	44	*91*	89	69	97	78
10 Erlander IX	1964	91	*68*	72	60	105	79
11 Erlander X	1968	77	*76*	60	68	84	73
12 Palme I	1969	83	*76*	73	83	91	81
13 Palme II	1970	119	*75*	85	81	107	93
14 Palme III	1973	61	*69*	77	76	97	76
15 Falldin I	1976	87	44	*62*	*62*	*46*	60
16 Ullsten	1978	79	60	67	*52*	65	65
17 Falldin II	1979	91	49	*55*	*55*	*70*	64
18 Falldin III	1981	97	57	*75*	*77*	*76*	76
19 Palme IV	1982	80	*67*	63	71	80	72
20 Palme V	1985	88	*37*	66	71	104	73
21 Carlsson I	1986	74	*46*	69	78	96	73
22 Carlsson II	1988	61	*92*	72	46	76	69
X Mean		82	70	75	70	84	76*
X Mean When in Government		–	74	81	62	58	69*
X Mean When in Opposition		82	52	73	72	86	73*

Note: Maximum hypothetical distance is a score of 200.
Italicised figures represent governing parties.
The score for the Green Party in 1988 was 74.
* This score represents the average of the row means.

ments, and the policy positions of the People's Party have been well represented by Social Democratic governments. Table 5.5 provides the details.

Note again that the aggregate distance between the government and all parties reached its lowest point in 1976 with the first non-socialist coalition. We can also observe that the moderate declarations of the various bourgeois coalitions gives the paradoxical result that the Social Democrats have received greater policy 'payoffs' (in programmatic terms) in opposition than when they have controlled the government. This peculiar result holds even for the Centre Party. In the late 1940s the right-wing Swedish parties received unpredictably good payoffs from Social Democratic governments. Later, around 1960 and in 1973, the government position was much closer to the parties of the left; recall that the 1960 Social Democratic manifesto was their most leftist post-war programme (and Palme's 1973 government programme was the most left-wing of its kind).

Overall, the superior predictions of the one dimensional analysis suggest that the underlying left–right dimension dominates the twenty policy dimensions when it comes to government formation and payoffs. Because of the dominance of the left–right axis, it is apparently more important for Swedish parties to control the median legislator on this dimension than to be strategically well-positioned in twenty-dimensional policy space.

DISAGGREGATED TWENTY-DIMENSIONAL ANALYSIS

We have just argued that knowing which parties form a policy-compact winning coalition in twenty-dimensional policy space is less likely to help us predict bargaining outcomes than knowing the median legislator on the left–right dimension. However, if we consider which party controls the median legislator on each policy dimension taken one at a time, then the result of the multi-dimensional analysis improves. Table 5.6 identifies the party that controls the median legislator on each of the twenty dimensions for each electoral period. Overall, the Social Democratic Party has control of more dimensions that all other parties combined. The two centrist bourgeois parties follow in distant second and third places. Trailing even these parties are the parties at the opposite poles of the left–right dimension, the Communists and the Moderates. The weak position of the latter party is particular noteworthy. Only in 1973 and 1976, has this party been pivotal on more than one dimension at a time. Indeed, between 1952 and 1973, the Moderates were never pivotal on a single dimension. These results again confirm the importance of the basic left–right ordering for coalition bargaining in Sweden.

The elections in which Social Democratic dominance has been broken do indeed coincide with the emergence of bourgeois coalitions. In 1952 Social Democratic dominance was replaced by a situation in which the non-socialist parties were pivotal on the same number of dimensions. These dimensions were also slightly more salient than those controlled by the Social Democrats. In 1956, the salience of the dimensions on which non-socialist parties were pivotal clearly exceeded those of the Social Demo-

Table 5.6 Parties controlling the median legislator over 20 dimensions, 1944–88

Dimension	1944	1948	1952	1956	1958	1960	1964	1968	1970	1973	1976	1979	1982	1985	1988
State Intervention	S/FP	S	FP/S	FP	S	S	S	S	S	S	M	CP	S	–	–
Quality of Life													S	S	S
Peace and Co-operation	S/FP +CP	S	CP/S	FP	S	S	S	S	S	S	FP	CP	S	FP	M
Anti-Establishment										CP					
Capitalist Economy	S	S	CP/S	CP	S	S	S	–	S	CP/S	S	S	S	S	S
Social															
Conservatism	VPK/S	VPK	–	–	S	VPK	S	S	–	S	S	S	S	VPK	
Productivity	–	S	S	S	VPK	S	S	S	CP	M	FP	S	S	CP	S
Military (+)	S	–	CP	–	–	S	–	S	–	–	–	–	–	FP	
EEC (+)	–	S	–	–	–	S	–	S	–	–	–	–	–	–	S
EEC (–)		S													
Freedom & Human Rights	S	S	S	S	–	–	CP	–	–	CP	CP	FP	S	–	–
Democracy	S	S	M	S	–	–	–	S	VPK	S	S	CP	S	M	–
Decentralization (+)	–	–	–	S	–	S	–	–	–	S	M/VPK	MFP	–	FP	–
Government Efficiency	–	FP	–	–	–	–	S	–	–	CP	CP	–	–	M	
Social Justice	S/M	S	–	S	S	S	S	–	VPK	S	CP	–	–	CP	–
Social Services (+)	S/FP	VPK	FP	S	S	CP	CP	S	S	CP	CP	S	S	CP	CP
Education (+)	S	M	CP	S	VPK	FP	CP	S	S	CP	S	FP	CP	CP	CP
Labour Groups (+)	–	–	–	–	–	–	–	S	S	–	S	FP	–	S+VPK	S
Agriculture & Farming	S	S	S	S	S	–	–	–	S	–	–	–	–	–	–
Underprivileged Minorities	–	S	S	S	S	–	–	–	S	–	–	S	–	–	–

Table 5.6 (cont'd)

Dimension	Year															Total
	1944	1948	1952	1956	1958	1960	1964	1968	1970	1973	1976	1979	1982	1985	1988	
Median Legislator in:																
VPK:	1	2	–	–	2	2	–	–	2	1	–	–	–	2	–	12
S:	11	9	7	6	7	6	7	9	9	6	5	5	9	3	5	104
CP:	1	–	4	2	–	1	3	–	1	5	3	3	1	4	1	29
FP:	3	1	2	3	–	1	1	–	–	–	2	5	–	3	1	22
M:	1	1	1	–	–	–	–	–	–	3	3	–	–	1	1	11
Sum:	17	13	14	11	9	10	11	9	12	15	13	13	10	13	8	178
Saliance of dimensions on which party has median legislator:																
VPK:	6	13	–	–	9	22	–	–	18	5	–	–	–	9	–	
S:	58	56	48	31	58	16	35	54	53	33	31	28	57	37	41	
CP:	5	–	34	21	–	16	21	–	3	28	10	15	10	19	6	
FP:	16	5	12	25	–	5	3	–	–	–	10	33	–	12	11	
M:	2	5	3	–	–	–	–	–	–	15	24	–	–	1	9	

Note:
The number of dimensions varies from election to election because in some cases no median legislator could be found. These are cases where the aggregate proportion of parliamentary seats for the parties with positions on this specific dimension is less than a majority. In 1968 the Social Democratic Party gained a parliamentary majority. This automatically gave the party a pivotal position on any dimension to which it made reference. Conversely, for dimensions to which the Social Democrats did not make reference, there can be no pivotal party. Note that when two parties control median legislators (because there occasionally are two median legislators in even-numbered parliaments), both are counted as pivotal and salience is calculated for both parties. Note also that parties bound together with the '+' sign are parties with exactly the same position on the relevant dimension.

crats, indicating the shift in Swedish politics that subsequently led to the breakup of the 'red–green' coalition. In the elections following this breakup, the Social Democrats re-established their dominant position, and until 1973 they generally had the median legislator on most dimensions. With the help of the Communists (in 1960), they enjoyed the same dominance on the most salient dimensions. In 1973, however, the Social Democratic 'hegemony' was broken and a more balanced situation established. In the following two elections the balance tilted in favour of the non-socialist parties, and the Social Democrats had to leave office for the first time in forty years. When the Social Democrats returned to power in 1982, they did so on the basis of an overwhelming control of the most salient twenty dimensions.

CONCLUSIONS

This chapter has provided evidence of the importance of policy concerns for government formation in Sweden. In particular, we have found strong evidence of the significance of left–right conflict in Swedish party politics. The cross-national left–right scale provides a very interpretable and plausible ordering of Swedish political parties. Further evidence on this matter comes from tests of the predictive power of various policy-based coalition theories, presented in Table 5.7.

At first glance, Table 5.7 gives the unexpected impression that the predictions based on twenty-dimensional policy spaces (Hypotheses A and B) are borne out to a much greater extent than those of the unidimensional ones (Hypotheses C and D). Both of the former hypotheses correctly predict at least three-fourths of the cases, whereas the predictive accuracy especially of Hypothesis D is quite modest. However, a significant part of this superiority is caused by the fact that the hypotheses based on 20-dimensional policy spaces are compatible with a larger set of outcomes in each case. When predictive efficiency (ie, the ratio of correct predictions to all predictions) is considered, the unidimensional hypotheses perform better on the whole. A random prediction in a random case would have an approximate probability of .034 of being correct, and all hypotheses exceed this baseline. The most efficient hypothesis perform four times better than chance.

Both the multi-dimensional and the unidimensional results suggest that policy viability is a much more plausible requirement than the majority-winning criterion. This is illustrated by the evident superiority of hypothesis C over hypothesis D. Furthermore, even more than in the previous analysis, we are struck by the congruity between the results based on one-dimensional

Table 5.7   Success rates of policy-based coalition theories in Sweden, 1944–88

| | Number of coalitions | | Theory A Predictions | | Theory B Predictions | | Theory C Predictions | | Theory D Predictions | |
Year	Arithmetically possible	Feasible under constraints	Set	Correct	Set	Correct	Set	Correct	Set	Correct
1944	31	31	9	Yes	16	Yes	2	Yes	2	Yes
1948	31	31	8	Yes	16	Yes	5	Yes	2	No
1951	31	31	8	Yes	16	Yes	5	No	2	Yes
1952	31	31	8	Yes	16	Yes	3	No	2	Yes
1956	31	31	7	No	16	Yes	4	No	2	No
1957	31	19	6	Yes	13	Yes	3	No	2	No
1958	31	31	4	Yes	16	Yes	4	Yes	2	No
1960	31	31	8	Yes	16	No	3	No	2	No
1964	31	31	7	Yes	16	Yes	4	Yes	2	No
1968	31	31	4	Yes	16	Yes	5	Yes	2	No
1969	31	31	4	Yes	16	Yes	5	Yes	2	No
1970	31	31	7	Yes	16	Yes	6	Yes	2	No
1973	31	31	8	Yes	16	Yes	5	Yes	2	No
1976	31	1	0	No	0	No	0	No	0	No
1978	31	31	8	Yes	16	No	4	No	2	No
1979	31	1	0	No	1	Yes	0	No	1	Yes
1981	31	31	7	No	16	Yes	6	No	3	No
1982	31	31	6	Yes	16	Yes	5	Yes	2	No
1985	31	31	9	Yes	16	Yes	4	Yes	2	No
1988	63	63	8	Yes	32	Yes	5	Yes	2	No

Predictive Success
(No. Correct/No. Cases)   .80(16/20)   .85(17/20)   .55(11/20)   .20(4/20)

Predictive Efficiency
(No. Correct/No. Predictions)   .127(16/126) .056(17/302) .141(11/78) .105(4/38)

Notes: Theory A: Coalition will be at node on 20-dimensional cluster tree and policy-viable in at least one dimension.

Theory B: Coalition will include 20-dimensional predominant party.

Theory C: Coalition will be policy-viable based on one-dimensional clustering.

Theory D: Coalition will be one-dimensional minimum connected winning.

One-dimensional analysis based on standard left–right dimension.

and 20-dimensional policy spaces. This is probably due to the strong effect of the left–right ordering even within a more multi-dimensional representation of Swedish politics. The contrast with neighbouring Norway, where cross-cutting dimensions are more evident, is instructive here.

All of this brings us to the conclusion that the Swedish case is one in which (1) the most important and salient policy disagreements usually occur along the left–right dimension; (2) interparty competition takes place mainly, though not exclusively, in this one-dimensional space; and (3) a predominant Social Democratic party is faced with a bipolar opposition. If we add to this (4) the size of the Social Democratic party, which gives it an excellent bargaining position; (5) wide policy disagreements among the non-socialist parties; and (6) institutional rules and procedures which facilitate the formation of minority governments, then we have a good account of why Swedish governments so frequently have been Social Democratic minority governments.

However, Social Democratic dominance has not been as secure as the governmental record might suggest. Party competition is fierce and our analysis of twenty policy dimensions in Swedish politics has shown that when the predominant Social Democratic party has lost its hold on the most salient dimension, it has also lost, or come very close to losing, its control over the cabinet. Nor has the dominance of the cabinet carried over completely to government policy. Almost constantly in a minority position, most Social Democratic cabinets have not advocated policies as left-wing as the party has promoted in election campaigns. Their reluctance to rely exclusively on Communist support is a strong reason for this. Our results indicates that the Social democratic cabinets instead have tried to create a situation favourable to co-operation with the non-socialist parties, notably the Centre and People's parties. The critical importance of having the median legislator in unidimensional space is easily recognised, and the Social Democrats have routinely held this position. The apparent generalisation of this insight to twenty-dimensional space is intriguing and, we suggest, provides valuable confirmation of the validity of our data and methods of analysis. The one-dimensional and twenty-dimensional constructions of the Swedish policy space are complementary, rather than competing, representations of the party system. In an analysis combining these two representations we can trace shifts in favour of the non-socialist parties that occurred in Swedish politics in the mid-1950s and again in the 1970s. In the former case the shift came after the coalition had been formed, whereas in the latter case the shift preceded (and predicted) the non-socialist coalition. Thus, it appears that changes in coalitional arrangements sometimes follow shifts in party positions and at other times precede them.

APPENDIX C

Table C.1 Swedish election results, 1944–88 (percentage of popular vote, number of parliamentary seats in parentheses)

Party	1944	1948	1952	1956	1958	1960	1964	1968	1970	1973	1976	1979	1982	1985	1988
Communist (VPK)	10.3 (15)	6.3 (8)	4.3 (5)	5.0 (6)	3.4 (5)	4.5 (5)	5.2 (8)	3.0 (3)	4.8 (17)	5.3 (19)	4.8 (17)	5.6 (20)	5.6 (20)	5.4 (19)	5.8 (21)
Social Democrats (S)	46.7 (115)	46.1 (112)	46.1 (110)	44.6 (106)	46.2 (111)	47.8 (114)	47.3 (113)	50.1 (125)	45.3 (163)	43.6 (156)	42.7 (152)	43.2 (154)	45.6 (166)	44.7 (159)	43.2 (156)
Centre Party (CP)	13.6 (35)	12.4 (30)	10.7 (26)	9.4 (19)	12.7 (32)	13.6 (34)	13.4 (36)	15.7 (39)	19.9 (71)	25.1 (90)	24.1 (86)	18.1 (64)	15.5 (56)	12.4 (44)	11.3 (42)
People's Party (FP)	12.9 (26)	22.8 (57)	24.4 (58)	23.8 (58)	18.2 (38)	17.5 (40)	17.1 (43)	14.3 (34)	16.2 (58)	9.4 (34)	11.1 (39)	10.6 (38)	5.9 (21)	14.2 (51)	12.2 (44)
Moderates (M)	15.9 (39)	12.3 (23)	14.4 (31)	17.1 (42)	19.5 (45)	16.5 (39)	13.7 (33)	12.9 (32)	11.5 (41)	14.3 (51)	15.6 (55)	20.3 (73)	23.6 (86)	21.3 (76)	18.3 (66)
Others	.6	.1	.1	.1	.0	.1	3.3	4.1	2.2	2.3	1.7	2.2	3.8	2.0	3.6
Green Party															5.5 (20)

Table C.1 (cont'd)

Party	1944	1948	1952	1956	1958	1960	1964	1968	1970	1973	1976	1979	1982	1985	1988
'Bloc' Seats															
Socialist	56.5	52.5	50.0	48.5	50.2	51.3	51.9	54.9	51.4	50.0	48.4	49.9	53.3	51.0	50.7
	(130)	(120)	(115)	(112)	(116)	(119)	(121)	(128)	(180)	(175)	(169)	(174)	(186)	(178)	(177)
Non-Socialist	43.5	47.8	50.0	51.5	49.8	48.7	48.1	45.1	48.6	50.0	51.6	50.1	46.7	49.0	43.6
	(100)	(110)	(115)	(119)	(115)	(113)	(112)	(105)	(170)	(175)	(180)	(175)	(163)	(171)	(152)
Green Party															5.5
															(20)
Total	230	230	230	231	231	232	233	233	350	350	349	349	349	349	349

Note: The table refers to the Second (Lower) Chamber (1944–70) and to the unicameral Riksdag from 1970. In the distribution of seats and votes in 1964, 1968 and 1985, groups which in practice, either through an electoral alliance or by fusion after the election, belonged to one of the parties of the non-socialist bloc are counted as such.

Sources: Birgersson, *et al.* (1984, pp. 344–347), Fran Riksdag & Departement (1988), Lindstrom, (1986).

Party Policy and Government Coalitions

Table C.2   Swedish governments 1945–88

Government	Tenure		Parties	Seats(%)
1 Hansson	Jul 1945	– Oct 1946	S	50.0
2 Erlander I	Oct 1945	– Sep 1948	S	50.0
3 Erlander II	Sep 1948	– Oct 1951	S	48.7
4 Erlander III	Oct 1951	– Sep 1952	S, CP	61.7
5 Erlander IV	Sep 1952	– Sep 1956	S, CP	59.1
6 Erlander V	Sep 1956	– Oct 1957	S, CP	54.1
7 Erlander VI	Oct 1957	– Jun 1958	S	45.9
8 Erlander VII	Jun 1958	– Sep 1960	S	48.1
9 Erlander VIII	Sep 1960	– Sep 1964	S	49.1
10 Erlander IX	Sep 1964	– Sep 1968	S	48.5
11 Erlander X	Sep 1968	– Oct 1969	S	53.6
12 Palme I	Oct 1969	– Sep 1970	S	53.6
13 Palme II	Sep 1970	– Sep 1973	S	46.6
14 Palme III	Sep 1973	– Oct 1976	S	44.6
15 Falldin I	Oct 1976	– Oct 1978	CP, FP, M	51.6
16 Ullsten	Oct 1978	– Oct 1979	FP	11.2
17 Falldin II	Oct 1979	– May 1981	CP, FP, M	50.1
18 Falldin III	May 1981	– Oct 1982	CP, FP	29.2
19 Palme IV	Oct 1982	– Sep 1985	S	47.6
20 Palme V	Sep 1985	– Feb 1986	S	45.6
21 Carlsson I	Mar 1986	– Sep 1988	S	45.6
22 Carlsson II	Sep 1988	–	S	43.2

Sources: Strom (1986); Keesing's Contemporary Archives.
Note: The percentage of parliamentary seats refers to the directly elected lower (Second) Chamber of the parliament up through 1970 (Palme I). A new government has been recorded at (1) every general and direct election, (2) every change of prime minister, and (3) every change in party composition.

Table C.3 Twenty-dimensional distances between parties in election years, Sweden 1944–88

1944

	M	FP	CP	S
FP	54			
CP	68	84		
S	82	73	96	
VPK	64	67	63	66

1948

	M	FP	CP	S
FP	78			
CP	121	83		
S	137	89	50	
VPK	129	79	94	76
S	106	83	67	68

1952

	M	FP	CP	S
FP	66			
CP	94	70		
S	104	66	58	
VPK	102	108	122	102

1964

	M	FP	CP	S
FP	130			
CP	112	92		
S	111	62	56	
VPK	112	84	99	67

1968

	M	FP	CP	S
FP	99			
CP	70	89		
S	91	70	69	
VPK	86	87	86	43

1970

	M	FP	CP	S
FP	72			
CP	78	52		
S	105	43	59	
VPK	134	84	106	73

1982

	M	FP	CP	S
FP	67			
CP	78	75		
S	84	51	54	
VPK	112	75	86	44

1985

	M	FP	CP	S
FP	66			
CP	98	65		
S	113	54	55	
VPK	129	85	98	74

1988

	M	FP	CP	G	S
FP	67				
CP	87	72			
G	103	68	60		
S	106	83	67	68	
VPK	102	60	78	50	73

Table C.3 (cont'd)

1956

	M	FP	CP	S
FP	99			
CP	129	76		
S	115	46	82	
VPK	125	66	102	58

1958

	M	FP	CP	S
FP	75			
CP	82	65		
S	106	87	58	
VPK	136	91	92	48

1960

	M	FP	CP	S
FP	70			
CP	67	57		
S	114	92	93	
VPK	93	71	96	79

1973

	M	FP	CP	S
FP	73			
CP	73	44		
S	60	65	55	
VPK	95	50	58	77

1976

	M	FP	CP	S
FP	67			
CP	76	61		
S	58	75	86	
VPK	112	69	88	80

1979

	M	FP	CP	S
FP	60			
CP	65	43		
S	77	41	52	
VPK	106	62	87	57

Note : Maximum hypothetical variance is a score of 200.

Figure C.1   Cluster diagrams of Swedish coalition formation, 1944–88

1944

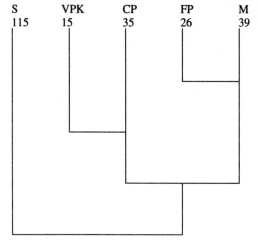

Party	S	VPK	CP	FP	M
Seats	115	15	35	26	39

Winning MAP = S
Actual Govt 1 = S
Actual Govt 2 = S

1948

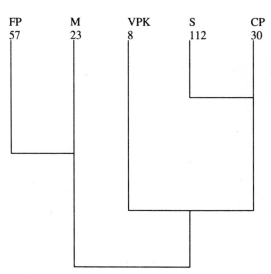

Party	FP	M	VPK	S	CP
Seats	57	23	8	112	30

Winning MAP = CP + S
Actual Govt 1 = S
Actual Govt 2 + CP + S

1952

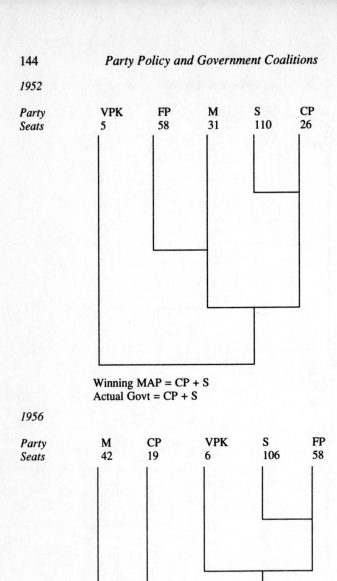

Party	VPK	FP	M	S	CP
Seats	5	58	31	110	26

Winning MAP = CP + S
Actual Govt = CP + S

1956

Party	M	CP	VPK	S	FP
Seats	42	19	6	106	58

Winning MAP = FP + S
Actual Govt 1 = CP + S
Actual Govt 2 = S

1958

Party	M	CP	FP	VPK	S
Seats	45	32	38	5	111

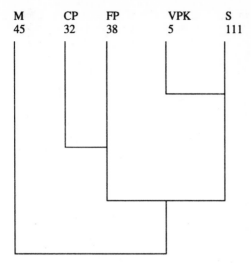

Winning MAP = S + VPK
Actual Govt = S

1960

Party	VPK	S	M	CP	FP
Seats	5	114	39	34	40

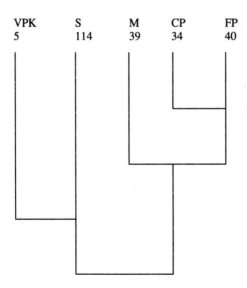

Winning MAP = S + VPK
Actual Govt = S

1964

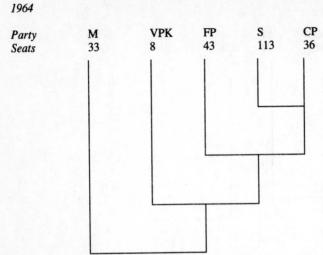

Winning MAP = CP + S
Actual Govt = S

1968

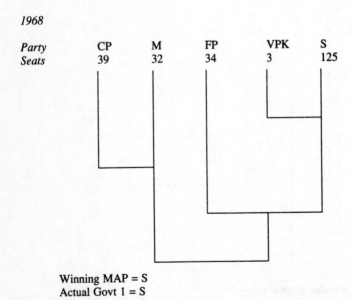

Winning MAP = S
Actual Govt 1 = S
Actual Govt 2 = S

1970

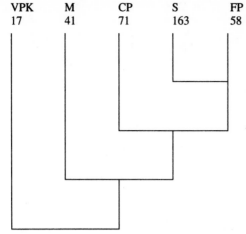

Party	VPK	M	CP	S	FP
Seats	17	41	71	163	58

Winning MAP = FP + S
Actual Govt = S

1973

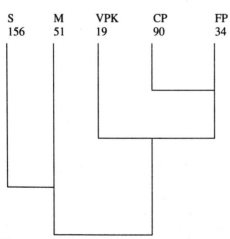

Party	S	M	VPK	CP	FP
Seats	156	51	19	90	34

Winning MAP = M + S
Actual Govt = S

1976

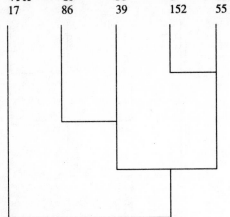

Party	VPK	CP	FP	S	M
Seats	17	86	39	152	55

Winning MAP = M + S
Actual Govt 1 = CP + FP + M
Actual Govt 2 = FP

1979

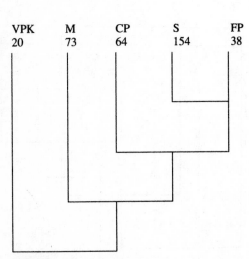

Party	VPK	M	CP	S	FP
Seats	20	73	64	154	38

Winning MAP = FP + S
Actual Govt 1 = CP + FP + M
Actual Govt 2 = CP + FP

1982

Party	M	CP	FP	VPK	S
Seats	86	56	21	20	166

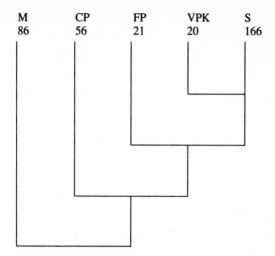

Winning MAP = S + VPK
Actual Govt = S

1985

Party	M	VPK	CP	S	FP
Seats	76	19	44	159	51

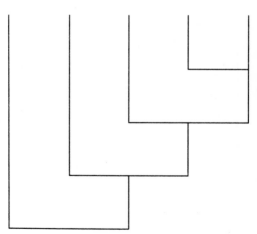

Winning MAP = FP + S
Actual Govt 1 = S
Actual Govt 2 = S

1988

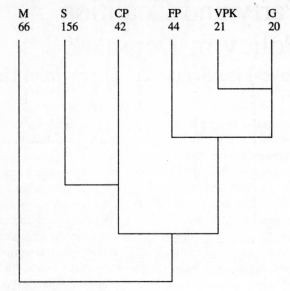

Party	M	S	CP	FP	VPK	G
Seats	66	156	42	44	21	20

Winning MAP = CP + S
Actual Govt = S

6 Party and Coalition Policy in Denmark

Tove-Lise Schou and Derek John Hearl

The most notable feature of Danish politics from our point of view, is the great frequency of minority governments. Since 1945 there have been only two governments with clear majorities in the Folketing – a coalition of Social Democrats, Radical Liberals and the small Justice Party that lasted from 1957 to 1960; and a coalition of Radical and Agrarian Liberals and Conservatives that lasted from 1968 to 71. We can add to these the *de facto* majority coalition from 1960–64 of Social Democrats and Radical Liberals, which had the support of one of the two Members for Greenland. These governments – all, significantly, from a 15-year period covering mainly the 1960s – are the only ones with a majority of legislative seats. All other post-war governments (excluding the 1945 government of national unity imme-diately after Liberation) have been minority administrations, often with a mere 30–40 per cent of legislative votes.

The immediate reason for minority government is to be found in the relative strength of the Danish Social Democrats compared to other Danish parties. For much of the post-war period, the Social Democrats were a natural focus for government formation. However, with no more than 37 or 38 per cent of the vote, they were too weak to provide a majority govern-ment. Opposition fragmentation and Social Democratic strength thus pro-duced eleven single-party governments with minority status, leaving eight coalitions, only three of which have had parliamentary majorities.

Obviously, minority governments in Denmark could not have survived without considerable tolerance from the legislature, which brings us to an important distinguishing feature of Danish politics, the power and importance of the Folketing. This is often exerted through authoritative all-party committees such as the Committees on Foreign Affairs (Udenrigs Politiske Naevn) and on European Community Affairs (Markedsudvalg). The latter has a de facto right to lay down ministerial mandates for EC negotiations. The Government thus gives up considerable power in relation to Parliament but also gives up responsibility for issues which in other systems would attract hostile votes of no confidence.

The tendency for governments to win legislative agreement for their policy extends beyond the institutional sphere. Faced with the economic

crisis of the late 1970s and early 1980s, Social Democratic minority governments made formal agreements on policy with the non-governmental
parties. These agreements covered packages of issues, including unemploy-
ment, housing, finance, incomes policy and defence. Interventions on wage
settlements in 1975, 1977 and 1979 were also undertaken with broad
agreement in the Folketing. There has been more divergence in the 1980s,
but the Radical Liberals agreed to support the non-socialist 'Four-leaf
clover' government in a package of austerity measures, that had been
implicitly tolerated by the Social Democrats. The latter also joined the
bourgeois parties of government in supporting the NATO alliance against
the other parties of the Left in the 1987 and 1988 elections.

Increasing fragmentation of the party system has been caused by the
sudden entry of three new parties at the 1973 election (Progress Party,
Christian People's Party and Centre Democrats); none of these has subsequently disappeared. This has been associated with a steady decrease in
the duration of governments over the post-war period. During the 1950s
governments lasted on average 41 months; during the 1960s they lasted 32
months; during the 1970s, 18 months; and during the 1980s, 20 months.
There is no indication, however, that this has undermined the close working
relationships between parties and Parliament, praised by Poul Schluter,
leader of the bourgeois 'Four-leaf clover' government, who remarked in a
New Year's television address: 'It is fruitful: it is Danish!'

THE DANISH PARTIES AND THE PARTY SYSTEM

The respective strengths of the eleven parties which have had a reasonably
stable existence in the post-war period can be gauged from Table D.2 in the
Appendix to this chapter, which gives the party shares of legislative seats,
over the post-war period.

The Danish party system of the early post-war period can be seen as a
more or less standard 'Scandinavian' party system, in which a large Social
Democratic party and small Communist party confronted a fragmented
bourgeois opposition divided between Liberals, Agrarians and Conservatives.
Partly owing to the greater differentiation of the Danish economy, and the
prosperity of agriculture, the bourgeois parties always remained stronger
and the Left weaker than in Norway and Sweden. A splintering of the
established parties then compounded the situation and intensified the need
for parliamentary agreement among the various groupings. Seen in this
light, we do not necessarily need to depend on a multi-dimensional interpretation in order to explain the Danish party system. Fragmentation may

simply reflect a more finely differentiated array of positions in Denmark, but positions defined on a left–right spectrum that is basically the same as is found in the other Scandinavian politics (Holmstedt and Schou, 1987).

Most of the parties thus take up ideological positions which are familiar in other national contexts, and which resemble those already discussed for Norway and Sweden. There are, of course, shades of difference which reflect the 'niche economy' of Denmark, with its prosperous export-oriented agriculture of efficient small farmers and its many small factories and firms and highly specialised products. Consequently, the Social Democrats are less concerned with economic intervention so long as the economy produces a sufficient surplus to sustain the welfare state. Paradoxically, the Agrarian Liberals, otherwise more conservative, are more interventionist, as they want state subsidies for their rural voters. Agricultural policy has been largely taken over by the EC, however, so the Agrarians supported the tax-cutting exercises of the Conservatives, who pursued fairly orthodox monetary policies in the 1980s. The Radical Liberals are very like their counterparts in Norway and Sweden – supporters of progressive causes such as feminism. Unlike the other Scandinavian liberals, however, they have kept their distance from the Conservatives – partly because of foreign policy differences – and have tended to give critical support from the outside to both Social Democratic and bourgeois coalitions.

The main differences in Danish politics occur with the protest parties of Left and Right. Of these, the 'New Left' socialist groupings are familiar elsewhere in Scandinavia: their basic aim is to pull the Social Democrats further towards a position of opposition to what they see as capitalist foreign entanglements, and towards a more radical restructuring of economy and society internally.

The most spectacularly different of the Danish parties in the Progress Party. This has a populist ideology which has few parallels elsewhere in Western Europe (the Anders Lange party in Norway was never as successful). It straddles established ideologies since, in order to cut taxes, it has urged scrapping both welfare and defence. (It made a famous proposal to replace the armed forces with a recorded telephone message repeating 'We surrender'.) As the Social Democrats supported both welfare and defence they became the chief target of the Progress Party, which in the process started to emphasise welfare cuts more heavily. As it also changed its tone in order to win more standing in parliament, it offered the bourgeois 'Four-leaf clover' coalition external support in the mid 1980s, and adopted an orthodox anti-tax position not far from that of the Conservatives.

The positions of the other two parties which emerged in 1973 are more conventional, the Christian People's Party has much in common with other

Christian Democrat parties throughout Europe: and the Centre Democrats finding parallels in other break-away Socialist groups.

THE MOTIVATIONS OF POLITICIANS; OFFICE OR POLICY?

Our description of Danish party politics bears a strong resemblance to the earlier theoretical accounts (see Chapter 1 above) of how policy-pursuing politicians would behave. It is quite clear that Danish governments, even in the rare cases when they command a clear majority, are executive managers for a parliamentary policy coalition: when they cease to pursue policies which are acceptable to that majority, the government falls. When politicians lose important legislative votes they resign on points of principle rather than clinging to office.

The facts of minority government, heavy dependence on the legislature, and short governmental terms in office clearly mark out a role for Danish parties as policy pursuers rather than officer-seekers. This is reinforced by the fact that membership or chairmanship of the central Parliamentary committees carries as much weight and prestige as cabinet office; and possibly more power. It is, of course, true that parties in government can push the detailed implementation of policy in their own direction, especially where they have been able to build a legislative coalition round their characteristic policies. Danish parties, like those elsewhere, consistently hold ministries which are important for their own policy concerns (Budge and Keman, 1990, Chapter 4). At most, however, this is a policy-instrumental reason for holding office. And there are many examples of parties, such as the Progress Party, which show a consistent disregard for office and no disposition whatsoever to bargain policy points away in return for participation.

STRUCTURAL INFLUENCES AND CONSTRAINTS

The main constraints on coalition formation in Denmark, summarised in Table 6.1 are endogenous and behavioural. The most obvious example concerns ostracisation of the Progress Party by all the 'established' parties. Given the personal 'edge' the latter used when attacking existing groups, this is not surprising. Its founder, Mogens Glistrup, boasted about his success in avoiding taxes, and was eventually tried and sent to prison on this count in the mid-1980s. There is thus more than a whiff of anti-democratic and anti-system sentiment hanging about the Progress Party which makes

Table 6.1   Constraints and influences upon coalition formation in Denmark

Substance	*Effect*
1. Exclusion of Communists, Socialist People's Party, Progress Party, Left Socialists from government	Shifts influence to parties of moderate Left and Right, and especially to Centre.
2. (1968) Electoral alliance of Radical and Agrarian Liberals and Conservatives pledges to form government if elected.	Makes bourgeois coalition government inevitable once majority obtained, regardless of policy relationships.
3. Monarch selects Prime Ministerial candidate on advice of party leaders leaders.	Favours established Parliamentary and initial legislative agreements necessary for government.
4. PM can dissolve Parliament and call early election.	Ambiguous effects on duration of some governments. Gives government power in relation to small marginal parties.
5. PR electoral system with low (2 per cent) threshold encourages entry of new small parties to Parliament	Increases fragmentation and difficulties of forming majority coalitions – encourages minority governments.
6. Cabinet survives vote of confidence unless an absolute majority votes against them.	Favours minority government.

this boycott understandable. The party's declining strength and Glistrup's disappearance from the scene gave it more acceptability in the 1980s, and its legislative support was actually solicited by the 'Four-leaf clover' government in 1984. However, no *quid pro quo* is offered in terms of a seat at the Cabinet table; the veto on formal government participation still seems to be enforced by other parties.

The same ban on government participation applied, more implicitly, to the parties of the extreme left (Communist, Socialist People's Party and the Left Socialists). This is in part explained by their vehement opposition to NATO and the European Community, which would cause complications with these bodies were they to enter government. However, their isolation seems due less to external than to internal pressures; the changes they want to see are so massive and far-reaching.

The other factors affecting government formation in Denmark are better seen as structural influences rather than as firm constraints on the range of coalitions that can form. The arrangement whereby the monarch, in consultation with party leaders, can designate a prospective prime minister and give him a mandate to form a government gives a clear potential bonus to the larger and more established parties. This is compounded by the ability of the prime minister to call premature elections, which gives a potent threat that can prolong the life of some minority governments in a situation where smaller parties are afraid of losing heavily at election time, even of disappearing from Parliament. The very low entry threshold in the Danish proportional representation electoral system gives new parties the potential to enter Parliament, and generates a fragmented legislature in which majority governments are much more difficult to assemble. By creating a divided 'opposition', however, this factor also makes it easier for minority governments to survive. A further institutional factor that may well encourage minority government is the provision that an absolute majority is required before a government is defeated. Abstentions on confidence votes, therefore, are the same as votes for the government.

GENERAL POLICY DIMENSIONS OF PARTY COMPETITION

Holmsted and Schou's (1987) factor-analysis of Danish electoral programmes found two policy dimensions of policy that were substantially independent of each other. The first was the orthodox left–right confrontation. The left pole was defined by opposition to Conservative economics, support for labour groups, a concern for increased democracy and a pacifist, pro-disarmament stance. The second dimension was overwhelmingly concerned with welfare policies. The left pole of this dimension was defined by support for expanding social welfare provision. The right pole of the second dimension was defined by support for free enterprise and economic orthodoxy. Holmsted and Schou thus identified two separate left–right dimensions; one contrasted a concern for labour and peace with right-wing economics; one contrasted a concern for social welfare with right-wing economics.

Party scores for each election on our 'standard' left–right dimension, which in effect combines the two divisions found in our original analysis, can be found in Table 6.2.

Party positions correspond quite closely with the received wisdom about Danish politics. Looking at the overall array of scores, we see that the smaller left-wing parties consistently maintain their leftward positions, tending to the extreme in most cases. The Social Democrats themselves seem anchored in the left centre with moves in the late 1950s and in 1971 to quite extreme positions. The Radical Liberals stay mainly in the left-centre, and the gap between the positions of the centre-left parties and

Table 6.2 Party and government scores on the left–right dimensions in Denmark, 1945–84

Year	DKP	SFP	VS	SD	RV	RF	VEN	KPF	FP	KrfP	CD	Prime Minister	Government score
1945	-21			-22	-15*	6	_16_	0				Kristensen	0
1947	-10			_-10_	-2*	25	3	19				Hedtoft I	0
1950	-26			-9	0*	10	_20_	_38_				Eriksen	18
1953:1	-15			_-7_	-5*	19	5	5				Hedtoft II	-7
1953:2	-27			_-6_	-5*	23	14	16				Hansen I	-7
1957	-41			_-28_	_0*_	_15_	32	38				Hansen II	4
1960	-43	-68		_-31*_	-12	-6	22	59				Kampman	-18
1964	-25	-29		_-19*_	-13	15	6	18				Krag II	-18
1966	-43	-25		_-3*_	-15		12	35				Krag III	-5
1968	-50	-31	-44	-11*	_-12_	9	_8_	_14_				Baunsgaard	-10
1971	-31	-28	-12	_-35_	2*	26	7	39		21		Krag IV	-21
1973	-30	-18	-7	1	-12	_10*_	_37_	38	12	39	73	Hartling	10
1975	-30	-22	-16	_-9_	18	-2	11*	8*	25	25	14	Jorgensen I	8
1977	-23	-28	-22	_-12*_	-12*	7	20	22	8	31	29	Jorgensen II	25
1978	-23	-28	-22	_-12*_	-12*	7	_20_	22	8	31	29	Jorgensen III	-4
1979	-51	-43	-26	_-11*_	-11*	18	51	36	45	32	50	Jorgensen IV	1
1981	-37	-37	-25	_-5_	-1*	8	23	51	36	15	42	Jorgensen V	15
1982	-37	-37	-25	-5	-1*	8	_23_	_51_	36	_15*_	_42_	Schluter	23
Mean	-31	-32	-22	-13	-6.3	11.9	18.1	26.9	22.3	27.7	39.5	Mean absolute distance	

Note: Government parties italicised, median party marked with asterisk.

those of the Agrarian Liberals (Venstre) and Conservatives (KRF), who maintain a steady right-wing posture, highlights the 'two bloc' nature of Danish politics. This may well explain why the Radical Liberals have not linked up with the centre-right to form an alternative to the Social Democrats, as they have in Sweden and Norway. Overall, we feel confident that the common left–right scale applies well in Denmark, and this forms the basis of our subsequent one-dimensional analysis.

DOCUMENTS CODED

The selection of party policy documents on which our analyses are based has already been described and a list of named documents given (Budge, Robertson and Hearl, eds, 1987, pp. 179–186). Basically our procedure was to analyse an election manifesto when parties had issued one; otherwise we took the statement most resembling a manifesto – the main election leaflet or newspaper statement. The new documents introduced into our current analysis are statements of government positions. Since we were aiming at getting a full, authoritative representation of government policy which in a coalition government would also have been agreed by all the partners, we selected the prime minister's declaration of government policy made at the outset of the investiture debate. This has the merit of being made by the most senior and responsible figure of the government under very formal and binding circumstances. It is made, moreover, under the scrutiny of coalition partners and/or of parliamentary supporters and opponents of the government. Unfortunately, not all governments made a declaration. The seventeen governments for which we do have declarations, however, constitute all of the long-lived governments in Denmark, and most of the short-lived ones too.

PARTY AND GOVERNMENT RELATIONSHIPS ON THE LEFT–RIGHT CONTINUUM

Government formation

Table 6.2 also highlights the party controlling the median legislator on the left–right dimension after each election and the members of each government. The scores highlight the central position of the Social Democrats. Notwithstanding this, the Social Democrats were the median party on the scale only for about half of the time under consideration. For most of the rest of the time the Radical Liberals (RV), a party that only rarely went into government, was the median party. Certainly, on the basis of these data, the most important question to be answered is why an executive coalition between the RV and the Social Democrats has not been much more common in Denmark, given their closeness on the left–right scale. Part of the answer is that there was an effective Parliamentary and (sometimes governmental) coalition between them over the period 1953 and 1968, the period of the Social Democrats' greatest success. The Radical Liberals also supported the minority Jorgensen governments of the 1970s, but so, of course, did the more extreme right-wing Venstre and Conservatives (the Venstre even went into a coalition with the Social Democrats from 1978–9). The general proximity between Venstre and Conservatives, which increased in the 1970s, clearly provides a basis for co-operation.

The new parties which broke into the system in 1973, (excluding the Left-Socialists) have all taken consistently Rightist positions as time went on, providing a good basis of support for the Agrarian-Conservative bloc; the Christians and the Centre Democrats in fact formed part of the Four Leaf Clover coalitions from 1982 to 1988, while the Progress Party supported some of these from the outside.

The clearest general conclusion we can draw from Table 6.2 is that, over the post-war period as a whole, the median legislator has been found among parties with left-wing positions in the overwhelming majority of cases, and that this has been associated with a party of the left (not necessarily the one with the median legislator) holding office. Whether there is really a relationship between these two 'macro' phenomena is not something one can confirm in only one country, so it is a point taken up for cross-national evaluation in the concluding chapter.

Government policy

In contrast to the non-correspondence between patterns of government formation and movements in party policies, policy payoffs (interpreted as the distance between party policy and government policy) correspond much more closely. The relationship between party and government policy seems to be affected both by the balance of forces in the legislature and by the party composition of the cabinet. The right wing Eriksen cabinet in 1950, for example, shifts government policy to the right. Policy shifts back leftwards with the Social Democratic cabinet in 1953. The introduction of a right-wing cabinet partner in the form of RF shifts policy to the right in 1957, while the dropping of the RF in 1960 shifts government policy back to the left. The 1968 Baumsgaard 'triangle government' is an exception to this pattern; a shift to the right in the party composition of the cabinet is not associated with a shift to the right in cabinet policy (perhaps because of the need to win over the Radical Liberals). The reinstatement of an SD cabinet under Krag produces a leftward shift in 1971 and the taking office of the Venstre cabinet led by Hartling produces a shift to the right in 1973. The relatively right-wing policies of the SD governments led by Jorgensen are not explicable in these terms, however. Policy, as we argued above, was agreed between all the parliamentary parties and was orthodox and 'right-wing'.

These general patterns are summed up in Figures 6.1, 6.2 and 6.3, which shows the relationship between government policy and, in turn, the policy of the Social Democrats, the policy of the party controlling the median legislator and the mean policy of the government parties. It is the mean policy of the government parties that most closely tracks government policy outputs, though all indicators appear to track it quite closely. If an attempt is made, using regressions, to predict government policy from each of these three indicators, the results are not particularly impressive, being tabulated in Table 6.3. However, if the 'deviant' Jorgensen administrations are ex-

Table 6.3 Regressions of government policy (Y) on policy positions of Social Democrats (X_1), median legislators (X_2) and mean government member (X_3) all measures on the left–right dimension, Denmark, 1945–82

Predictor	a	$Y-a_1 + b_1x_1$ b	r^2
All cases			
SD policy	8.1	.64	.26
Median legislator	1.2	.39	.06
Mean government parties	0.7	.39	.28
Excluding Jorgensen cabinets			
SD Policy	+3.2	.51	.27
Median legislator	−1.8	.63	.18
Mean government parties	−3.6	.63	.76
Multiple regression, excluding Jorgensen		Beta	r^2=.80
SD Policy		.00	
Median Legislator		.31	
Mean government parties		.48	

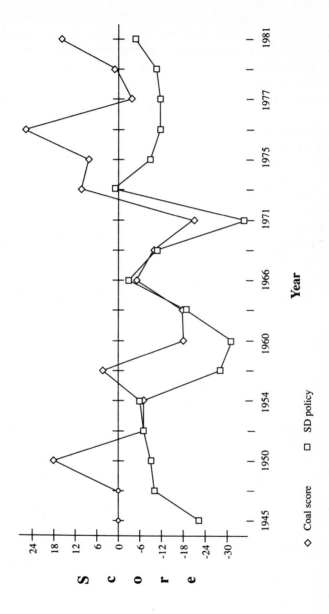

Figure 6.1 Relationship between Social Democratic and government policy on the left–right scale, Denmark, 1945–82

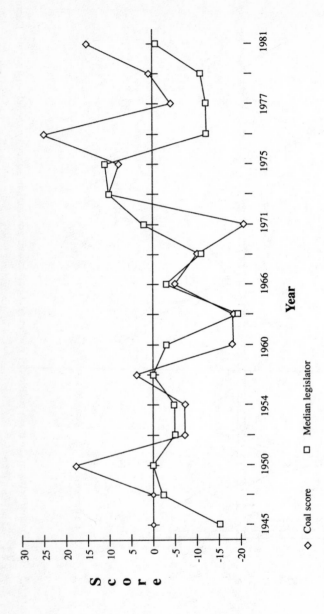

Figure 6.2 Relationship between the policy of the party with the median legislator and government policy on the left–right scale, Denmark, 1945–82

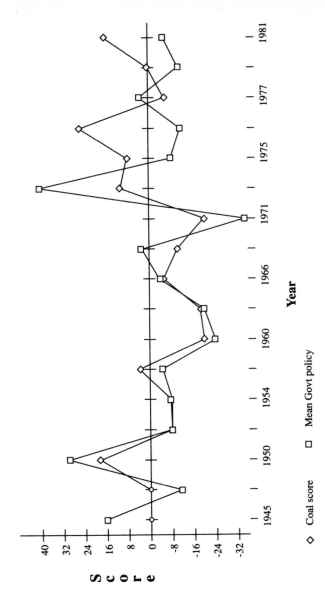

Figure 6.3   Relationship between the mean position of government parties and government policy on the left–right scale, Denmark, 1945–82

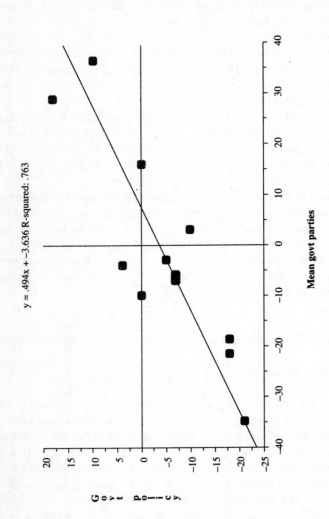

Figure 6.4 Regression of government policy on mean policy of government members, left–right scale, Denmark, 1945–82

y = 494x + -3.636 R-squared: .763

Mean govt parties

G
o
v
t

P
o
l
i
c
y

cluded, then the picture improves quite radically, with the mean policy of the government parties being a very good predictor of government policy. (A scatterplot of this regression is given in Figure 6.4). As the multiple regression reported in the final part of Table 6.3 shows, however, the policy constellation in the legislature as a whole (measured by the position of the party with the median legislator) appears to have an independent effect on government policy, over and above that produced by government member-ship. The multiple regression also shows that the impact of the SD on government policy outputs seems to be entirely a product of its generally central policy position.

The full set of distances between party and government policy is shown in Table 6.4. Clearly, the two large, 'centrist' parties, the Social Democrats and Radical Liberals (RV), get the best 'payoffs' from government in the sense that government policy is closest to their own party positions. The Radical Liberals, the more centrist, do a little better.

As might be expected from the previous analysis, however, government membership did have its own specific policy payoffs, as can be seen from Table 6.5, which contrasts the policy payoff going to particular parties when they were in government with that going to them when they were out. All parties did better when they were in government, and some did much better, reflecting the earlier result that government membership was quite strongly associated with coalition policy.

THE TWENTY-DIMENSIONAL ANALYSIS

Government formation

With the large and complex party system, the politics of coalition in Den-mark are difficult to analyse. Looking at the distance matrices as a whole we find confirmation of many of the points brought out in the one-dimensional analysis, though differences are also worthy of note. The Radical Liberals, for example, appear closer to the Agrarians and Conservatives in the multi-dimensional space then they were in the one-dimensional space, while the parties of the left also display more affinity for each other. The widening of party differences as the period progressed is well-reflected in the 20-dimensional distance matrices; differences over 100 (on a scale of 0 to 200) appear frequently in 1975, 1979 and 1981, but only rarely before this and never before 1953.

The clustering diagrams based on these distances provide us with some interesting insights into general patterns of coalition-formation in Denmark

Table 6.4 Distance between party and government policy on the left–right dimension, Denmark 1945–82

Year	Party											Prime minister
	DKP	SFP	VS	SD	RV	RF	VEN	KFP	FP	KrfP	CD	
1945	21			22	15	-6	-16	0				Kristensen
1947	10			10	2	-25	-3	-19				Hedtoft I
1950	44			27	18	8	-2	-20				Eriksen
1953:1	8			0	-2	-26	-12	-12				Hedtoft II
1953:2	27			6	5	-23	-14	-16				Hansen I
1957	45			32	4	-11	28	-34				Hansen II
1960	25	50		13	-6	-12	-40	-77				Kampman
1964	7	11		1	-5	-33	-24	-36				Krag II
1966	38	20		-2	10		-17	-40				Krag III
1968	40	21	34	1	2	-19	-18	-24				Baunsgaard
1971	10	7	-9	14	-23	-47	-28	-60		-42		Krag IV
1973	40	28	17	9	22	0	-27	-2	-2	-29	-63	Hartling
1975	38	30	24	17	-10	10	-3	0	-17	-17	-6	Jorgensen I
1977	48	53	47	37	37	18	5	3	17	-6	-4	Jorgensen II
	19	24	18	8	8	11	24	-26	-12	-35	-33	
1979	52	44	27	12	12	-17	-50	-35	-44	-31	-49	Jorgensen III
1981	52	52	40	20	16	7	-8	-36	-21	0	-27	Jorgensen IV
1982	60	60	48	28	22	15	0	28	13	8	19	Jorgensen V
	30.8	30.9	27.0	13.6	11.6	17.1	18.8	27.4	18.8	22.9	30.3	Mean absolute distance

Table 6.5 Distances between party policy and government policy on the left–right continuum, by membership and non-membership of the government, Denmark 1945–82

Party	DKP	SFP	VS	SD	RV	RF	VEN	KFP	FP	KrfP	CD
In government	n/a	n/a	n/a	13.2	4.0	11.0	17.4	22.0	n/a	n/a	n/a
Out of government	30.8	30.9	27.0	14.8	13.2	17.5	19.3	28.1	18.8	22.9	30.3

– notably, into the prevalence of Social Democratic minority governments. Because of the complexity of the case and the difficulty of making a clear analytic decision, we applied both hierarchical and non - hierarchical cluster algorithms simultaneously to the Danish case. In many cases, however, they lead to similar conclusions. According to either algorithm we can see the emergence of a tendency for 'rival' clusters of parties to form as mirror images of one another, with neither quite able to control a legislative majority. The pattern is most strikingly illustrated in 1977 but can be seen after nearly every election since 1957. There is a left wing cluster of parties centred on the SD, to which can be added the VS, DKP and SFP. The RV moves between this cluster and the other, which comprises the Venstre and KFP (typically very close to each other), to which are added RF, KrfP, FP and CD. If coalition formation proceeded solely in terms of policy based clustering, then the only winning coalitions possible would contain many parties, and sometimes be barely short of the grand coalition as a majority only emerges when the two rival blocs fuse. In this closely balanced set of contests between the two rival blocs, the SD is by far the largest party.

It would be very neat if power in Denmark ebbed and flowed with the policy position of the RV, as changes in its policy programme moved it from bloc to bloc, but this is not the case. The Venstre–KFP minority government in 1950, for example, occurred when the RV was closer to the SD, the two blocs were perfectly balanced with 71 seats each and the DKP closer to the SD than to the others. And the shift back to SD minority government in 1953 is associated with a move away from the SD by the RV. This movement continued through 1957, when the RV actually went into government with the SD and RF, a coalition that is not at all explained by the cluster diagrams. On the other hand, the coming together of the SD and RV for the 1960 Kampmann coalition predicted these. The SD's loss of power to the Baumsgaard coalition in 1968, is not associated with a shift away from the SD by the RV, though it is associated with electoral losses by both the SD and SFP. The complex bargaining situation that arose after the 1973 election presents a stiff challenge to any model. The clustering model, however, is unable to pick up any pattern that suggests that a single party Venstre government with far less than a majority would form. If anything the cluster of the parties on the left is 'tighter' than that on the right. Finally, the 'defection' of the Venstre from the right-wing bloc to go into government with the SD in 1978 is not picked up by the appropriate 20-dimensional distance matrix. (A glance at Table 6.2 will show that this defection is not picked up by the one dimensional analysis either.) The enduring cluster of KFP and Venstre seems as tight as ever at this stage.

Overall, therefore, the 20-dimensional analysis seems to be better at providing us with ideas about general patterns in, rather than the specific results of, coalition bargaining in Denmark. Applying the constraints in Table 6.1 is not much help, since the main effect is to eliminate parties like the Communist (DKP), Socialist People's Party (SFP), Left Socialists (VS) and Progress Party (FP) which are not central to the incipient coalitions in any case.

Distances between government and party policy

Representing party positions in twenty-dimensional as opposed to one-dimensional policy space does not add noticeably to our ability to explain the governments that form in Denmark. In the case of policy payoffs to parties, which we operationalise in terms of the distances between party policy positions and those of governments, the one-dimensional analysis gives very interesting results, showing not only that government members benefited in policy terms from their membership, but also that parties with a good strategic position in the legislature did so.

Table 6.6 reports corresponding results for the twenty-dimensional space. The pattern here is much less clear-cut. For example, if we rank-order parties in terms of their closeness to government policy position, we discover that government parties are closest to government policy only in eight out of seventeen cases. Even in these cases, some members of the government are less close than parties that are not members of the government.

Overall, the twenty-dimensional analysis, in contrast to the one-dimensional left–right one, suggests that government members do not gain particularly in policy terms relative to non-members. One possible interpretation is that Danish politics are best explained in terms of an underlying left–right confrontation reflected in the one-dimensional analysis rather than in a higher dimensional representation.

Table 6.6 Distances between party and government policy in 20-dimensional policy space Denmark, 1945–82

Year	Government	DKP	SFP	VS	SD	RV	RF	VEN	KFP	FP	KrfP	CD	Rank order
1945	Kristensen	59			80	69	64	*54*	54				1
1947	Hedtoft I	65			*32*	67	41	17	54				2
1950	Eriksen	59			43	30	40	*42*	*52*				2, 4
1953	Hedtoft II	75			*51*	44	46	32	56				4
1955	Hansen I	61			*43*	73	65	57	55				1
1957	Hansen II	76			*66*	*46*	*29*	37	53				1, 3, 5
1960	Kampman	–	73		*83*	*73*		105	106				1 =, 3
1964	Krag II	–	47		*39*	34		57	54				2
1966	Krag III	–	62		*48*	59		67	86				1
1968	Baunsgaard	–	64		31	*30*		*42*	*44*				1, 3, 4
1971	Krag IV	–	53		*77*	59		67	79				4
1973	Hartling	66	60		52	49	64	*60*	63	45	73	37	5
1975	Jorgensen I	77	78	72	*58*	31	63	69	56	81	98	59	3
1977	Jorgensen II	62	76	64	*59*	66	39	32	30	26	75	21	6
1978	Jorgensen III	57	65	75	*60*	67	44	*53*	45	49	86	64	4, 6
1979	Jorgensen IV	87	82	82	*38*	72	67	82	64	75	67	79	1
1981	Jorgensen V	70	84	61	*35*	47	38	59	88	67	72	70	1
1982	Schluter	77	79	72	58	48	67	*48*	*63*	56	*73*	*57*	1 =, 4, 5, 7

Note: Parties which form the government are italicised.
Governing party(ies) in terms of closeness to government policy (1 = closest)

THE DISAGGREGATED TWENTY-DIMENSIONAL ANALYSIS

Table 6.7 shows the position of the median legislator in the twenty dimensions taken separately. They show that the SD has potentially been a predominant party on only a few occasions and has not filled the role occupied, for example, by the Christian Democrats in Italy. The SD controlled the median legislator on nearly all dimensions for which there was an unambiguous median legislator after the 1960, 1964, 1966 and 1979 elections. In each case it was in government, and governed alone except for 1960, when it went into power with the RV, which controlled the median legislator on most of the other dimensions. This demonstrates the existence of a broad association between control of the median position and government participation.

The SD's fall from power in 1950 cannot be explained in these terms, but their substitution by the 'triangle' coalition in 1968 was associated with a dramatic turn-round in the number of policy dimensions on which the party controlled the median legislator. In 1968, the Venstre and the KFP between them controlled twice as many policy dimensions as the SD, and the analysis clearly predicts their move into government. The shift back to SD minority government in 1971 is not so easy to explain in these terms, neither is the single party Venstre government of 1973. But the Social Democrats were re-establishing their central role by 1975. The one lapse from this, where the Agrarian Liberals (Venstre) 'captured' a number of policy dimensions in 1977, was associated with the Social Democrats taking them into coalition in 1978–79. Again, the emergence of the 'Four-Leaf Clover' government in 1982 after a short Social Democratic interlude was foreshadowed by a revival of Agrarian (Venstre) and Conservative (KFP) control of several dimensions in 1981.

The role of the Conservatives is worth examining. It may be coincidence, but Conservative control of the median legislator on more than one dimension is associated with the emergence of a bourgeois government in three out of five cases (three out of four, if we discount the peculiar circumstances of 1973). The strategic position of the more extreme of the 'Right Centre' parties may indeed be a more useful indicator of how far power has passed to the bourgeois bloc than the position of the Agrarian Liberals (Venstre).

Overall, therefore, the disaggregated twenty-dimensional analysis, like the parallel one-dimensional one does give us useful insights into Danish government formation. Both are a little fuzzy, however, and it remains to be seen how far they help us to make a more exact analysis of the circumstances in which different types of government emerge.

Table 6.7 Party controlling median legislator on each of 20 policy dimensions, Denmark, 1945–82

Dimension	1945	1947	1950	1953:1	1953:2	1957	1960	1964	1966	1968	1971	1973	1975	1977	1979	1981
State intervention	VEN	SD	DKP	*	SD	VEN	RV	SD	SD	SD	SD	CD	SD	*	SD	SD
Quality of life	*	*	*	*	SD	*	RV	KFP	*	*	*	*	SD	*	SD	SD
Peace and co-operation	DKP	*	RV	SD	VEN	SD	SD	SD	SD	SD	*	FP	*	*	*	SD
Anti-establishment view	*	*	*	*	*	*	*	*	*	*	*	*	*	*	*	*
Capitalist Economics	KFP	SD	RV	VEN	RV	RV	SD	SD	RV	RV	RV	CD	RV	*	RV	Krfp
Social conservatism	SD	VEN	SD	RF	SD	VEN	SD	SD	*	*	VEN	*	FP	RV	SD	KFP
Productivity and Infrastructure	SD	SD	SD	RF	RV	*	SD	SD	SD	VEN	SD	*	VEN	VEN	SD	VEN
Military (positive)	KFP	*	SD	DKP	SD	VEN	SD	SD	*	KFP	*	*	*	SD	*	*
EEC (positive)	*	*	*	*	*	*	*	SD	SD	SD	*	FP	*	*	*	*
EEC (negative)	*	*	*	*	*	*	*	SD	SD	*	*	*	*	*	*	*
Freedom and human rights	SD	SD	SD	SD	SD	*	*	RV	SD	VEN	VEN	*	SD	*	KFP	KFP
Democracy	SD	RV	*	SD	*	*	SD	SD	SD	KFP	VEN	*	SD	*	KrfP	*
Decentralisation	*	*	*	*	*	*	*	SD	SD	*	SD	SD	*	*	*	*
Government efficiency	*	*	*	*	*	*	SD	*	SD	VEN	*	VEN	KFP	*	*	*
Social justice	RV	SD	KFP	VEN	SD	VEN	RV	SD	SD	KFP	RV	VEN	VEN	VEN	SD	RV
Social expansion	*	DKP	RV	RV	SD	*	RV	RV	RV	VEN	*	RV	FP	VS	SD	VEN
Education services +	*	*	*	*	SD	SD	SD	RV	SD	VEN	VEN	*	FP	VEN	SD	SFP

Table 6.7 (cont'd)

Dimension	Year															
	1945	1947	1950	1953:1	1953:2	1957	1960	1964	1966	1968	1971	1973	1975	1977	1979	1981
Labour Groups (+)	RV	*	RF	*	*	RV	SD	SFP	*	*	*	*	*	*	SD	*
Agriculture and farmers	*	RV	*	*	VEN	*	*	SD	*	KFP	*	*	*	*	*	SD
Minorities	*	RV	*	*	*	*	*	*	SD	*	KFP	*	*	*	*	*

No. of dimensions on which party controls median legislator:

	1945	1947	1950	1953:1	1953:2	1957	1960	1964	1966	1968	1971	1973	1975	1977	1979	1981
DKP	1	1	1	1	0	0	0	0	0	0	0	0	0	0	0	0
SFP	0	0	0	0	0	0	0	1	1	0	0	0	0	0	0	1
VS										4	2	1	4	1	8	4
SD	4	4	4	3	7	2	9	11	13	1	2	1	1	1	1	1
RV	2	3	2	1	2	2	3	3	0	0	0	0	0	0	0	0
RF	0	0	1	2	0	0	0	0	0	0	0	0	0	0	1	1
KrfP												1	2	3	0	2
VEN	1	1	0	2	2	4	0	0	1	4	5	1	1	0	1	2
KFP	2	0	1	0	1	0	1	1	0	4	1	0	3	0	0	0
FP												2	0	0	0	0
CD												2	0	0	0	0
No Party	10	11	11	11	8	12	13	4	6	7	10	13	9	14	9	9

CONCLUSIONS

We are now in a position to see how well the various policy-based models of government formation perform in the Danish case. In Table 6.8 we compare the performance of the four that have already been employed in the other Scandinavian countries. In light of the pervasive minority governments in Denmark, however, we add a variant to the Minimal Connected Winning formation, Theory D1. This relaxes the winning condition and predicts simply that coalitions will be connected on the left–right continuum. Superficially, in fact, this is the theory that performs best in the Danish case, covering 80 per cent of the governments that form. In fact, however, it is very much boosted by the single-party governments – which are connected only in a degenerate and trivial sense. If we look at real coalitions of two or more parties, we find they are connected in only three out of six occurrences. Minimal connected winning theory, performs absolutely disastrously in Denmark, as anticipated. Of the other theories tested, the two multi-dimensional Models – A and B – perform better than the uni-dimensional Model C. However, Model A – based on the idea that governments will be formed by one of the clusters identified by the average distance 'trees' shown in the Appendix to this chapter (Table D.4) – is also helped by the fact that single parties, trivially, form one of the modes of the tree. Thus their success rate, is 'artificially' boosted by the heavy predominance of single-party governments.

This is not a factor that affects either Model B or Model C critically. Both of these are based on the idea that the government will include the party that could form a policy-viable coalition in its own right, identified on the basis of either the proportion of all 20 policy dimensions on which it is pivotal (Model B) or on the basis of the standard left–right dimension (Model C). Model B predicts a higher number of the governments which actually form (60 per cent compared to 40 per cent) but C is more efficient since it includes fewer potential governments in its prediction set. It cannot be said, however, that the predictive efficiency of any model is very great – they range from 3 to 7 per cent. This is in spite of the fact that we have, in view of the constraints identified in Table 6.1, excluded from the prediction sets of all models any combination involving the 'ostracised parties': Communists (DKP), Left Socialists (VS), Socialist People's Party (SFP) and Progress Party (FP). With these included, the prediction sets would be much larger. Notwithstanding this, all models do better than random predictions. Given the large numbers of parties in Denmark, picking coalitions out of a hat would have a predictive accuracy of the order of one to three per cent.

Table 6.8 Success rates of policy-based coalition theories in Denmark 1945–82

Year	Number of Coalitions Arithmetically possible	Number of Coalitions Feasible under constraints	Theory A Predictions Set	Correct	Theory B Predictions Set	Correct	Theory C Predictions Set	Correct	Theory D1 Predictions Set	Correct	Theory D2 Predictions Set	Correct	Size*
1945	63	31	9	yes	15	no	5	no	2	no	15	yes	S
1947	63	31	9	yes	15	yes	5	no	2	no	15	yes	S
1950	63	31	9	no	15	no	5	no	2	no	15	yes	C
1953(1)	63	31	9	yes	15	yes	5	no	2	no	15	yes	S
1953(2)	63	31	9	yes	15	yes	5	no	2	yes	15	yes	S
1957	63	31	9	no	15	no	4	yes	2	no	15	yes	C
1960	31	15	7	yes	8	yes	4	yes	2	no	15	yes	C
1964	31	15	7	yes	8	yes	4	yes	2	no	8	yes	S
1966	31	15	7	yes	8	yes	4	yes	2	no	8	yes	S
1968	63	31	7	no	8	NA	4	no	2	no	8	no	C
1971	31	15	7	yes	8	no	7	no	2	no	8	yes	S
1973	1023	127	13	yes	42	NA	7	no	2	no	28	yes	S
1975	1023	63	12	yes	26	yes	6	no	2	no	28	yes	S
1977	2047	127	13	yes	42	no	7	yes	2	no	28	yes	S
1978	2047	127	13	no	42	yes	7	yes	2	no	28	yes	C
1979	1023	127	11	yes	42	yes	7	yes	2	no	28	yes	S
1981	511	63	12	yes	26	yes	6	no	2	no	21	yes	S
1982	511	63	12	no	26	no	6	no	2	no	21	no	C

* S = Single Party
  C = Coalition Parties

Table 6.8 (cont'd)

Predictive accuracy (No correct/No feasible cases)

| .72(13/18) | .60(10/16) | .40(7/18) | .06(1/18) | .80(14/18) |

Predictive efficiency (No correct/No predictions)

| .07(131/173) | .03(10/376) | .07(7/96) | .039(1/36) | .04(14/312) |

Notes: Constraints are that Communists, Socialist People's Party, Left Socialists and Progress Party are excluded from any potential government.

Theory A: will be at node on 20-dimensional cluster tree and policy viable on at least one dimension
Theory B: will include 20-dimensional predominant party
Theory C: will be policy viable based on one-dimensional clustering
Theory D1: will be minimal one-dimensional connected winning
Theory D2: will be one-dimensional connected

The overall success of the various policy-based models in predicting coalitions in Denmark is very limited. Much more clear cut is the relationship between party and government policy. Here we find clear confirmation that some governing parties do get payoffs, and above all that parties in a policy-dominant position get higher payoffs than others.

APPENDIX D

Table D.1   Seat distributions in the Danish legislature, 1945–84

Year	DKP	SFP	VS	SD	RV	RF	VEN	KFP	FP	KrfP	CD
1945	18			48	11	3	38	26			
1947	9			57	10	6	49	17			
1950	7			59	12	12	32	27			
1953:1	7			61	13	9	33	26			
1953:2	8			74	14	6	42	30			
1957	6			70	14	9	45	30			
1960	0	11		76	11	0	38	32			
1964	0	10		76	10	0	38	36			
1966	0	20		69	13	0	34	35			
1968	0	11	4	62	20	0	34	37			
1971	0	17	0	70	27	0	30	31		0	
1973	6	11	0	46	20	5	22	16	28	7	14
1975	7	9	4	53	13	0	42	10	24	9	14
1977	7	7	5	65	6	6	21	15	26	6	11
1979	0	11	6	68	10	5	22	22	20	5	6
1981	0	21	5	59	9	0	20	26	16	4	15
1984	0	21	5	56	10	0	22	42	6	5	8

Year	Total	Left Total	SD	Right Total	Government Composition
1945	149	18	48	78	V
1947	149	9	57	82	SD
1950	151	7	59	83	V-KFP
1953:1	151	7	61	81	SD
1953:2	179	8	74	92	SD
1957	179	6	70	98	SD-RV
1960	179	11	76	81	SD-RV
1964	179	10	76	84	SD
1966	179	20	69	82	SD
1968	179	15	62	91	RV-V
1971	179	17	70	88	SD

Year	Total	Left Total	SD	Right Total	
1973	179	17	46	112	VEN
1975	179	20	53	102	SD
1977	179	19	65	91	SD
IqYX	179	19	65	91	SD-VEN
1979	179	17	68	90	SD
1981	179	26	59	90	SD
1984	179	26	56	93	K, RV, CD, Krf

Table D.2   Danish governments, 1945–84

Government	Date government formed	Parties
Kristensen	8 November 1945	V
Hedtoft	31 November 1947	Soc
Eriksen	28 October 1950	V, K
Hedtoft II	1 October 1953	Soc
Hansen I	1 February 1955	Soc
Hansen II	27 May 1957	Soc, R, DR
Kampmann I	1 April 1960	Soc, R, DR
Kampmann II	18 November 1960	Soc, R
Krag I	3 September 1962	Soc, R
Krag II	24 September 1964	Soc
Krag III	September 1966	Soc, SF
Baunsgaard	2 February 1968	V, K, R
Krag IV	10 October 1971	Soc (SF)
Jorgensen I	7 October 1972	Soc (SF)
Hartling V	18 December 1973	V
Jorgensen II	13 January 1975	Soc
Jorgensen III	25 February 1977	Soc
Jorgensen IV	31 August 1978	Soc, V
Jorgensen V	26 October 1979	Soc
Jorgensen VI	30 January 1981	Soc
Schluter I	10 September 1982	K, R, CD, KrF

Key to Parties :

CD	Centre Democrats
DR	Danish Justice Party
K	Conservatives
KrF	Christian People's Party
R	Radical-Venstre (Liberals)
Soc	Social Democrats
SF	Socialist People's Party
V	Venstre (Agrarian Liberals)

Table D.3   Twenty-dimensional distances between Danish parties in election years 1945–75

1945

SD					
RV	43				
KFP	44	43			
VEN	56	57	38		
DKP	49	38	45	71	
RF	52	29	32	36	59
	SD	RV	KFP	VEN	DKP

1947

SD					
RV	43				
KFP	52	61			
VEN	25	50	45		
DKP	57	42	77	50	
RF	53	74	49	38	80
	SD	RV	KFP	VEN	DKP

1950

SD					
RV	41				
KFP	55	50			
VEN	45	46	32		
DKP	52	63	85	77	
RF	53	48	42	26	69
	SD	RV	KFP	VEN	DKP

1953

SD					
RV	60				
KFP	36	50			
VEN	40	56	10		
DKP	40	44	44	48	
RF	48	48	36	40	56
	SD	RV	KFP	VEN	DKP

1954

SD					
RV	55				
KFP	47	56			
VEN	48	57	39		
DKP	66	73	83	80	
RF	80	83	51	50	112
	SD	RV	KFP	VEN	DKP

1957

SD					
RV	96				
KFP	93	63			
VEN	81	69	24		
DKP	52	76	93	101	
RF	75	53	42	38	83
	SD	RV	KFP	VEN	DKP

1960

SD				
RV	68			
KFP	113	103		
VEN	92	68	59	
SFP	102	100	135	114
	SD	RV	KFP	VEN

1964

SD				
RV	41			
KFP	73	52		
VEN	52	39	53	
SFP	56	45	75	68
	SD	RV	KFP	VEN

1966

```
SD
RV  49
KFP 60  65
VEN 41  64  51
SFP 54  33  82  79
    SD  RV  KFP VEN
```

1968

```
SD
RV  37
KFP 51  44
VEN 37  44  32
SFP 30  47  71  57
VS  61  62  90  80  47
    SD  RV  KFP VEN SFP
```

1971

```
SD
RV  92
KFP 126 80
VEN 88  82  66
SFP 64  68  114 78
    SD  RV  KFP VEN
```

1973

```
SD
RV  49
KFP 61  74
VEN 80  75  55
DKP 64  59  91  86
RF  76  63  75  62  60
SFP 42  51  69  96  36  68
CD  61  46  72  67  63  61  65
KRF 95  88  92  103 115 89  97  70
FP  63  58  76  77  77  73  71  48  76
    SD  RV  KFP VEN DKP RF  SFP CD
```

KRP

1975

```
SD
RV  47
KFP 70  49
VEN 67  48  37
DKP 55  70  77  78
RF  55  40  61  58  58
SFP 52  73  64  71  41  49
CD  59  38  55  52  60  44  55
KRF 104 93  106 107 107 125 114 85
FP  56  65  76  81  27  61  40  53  100
    SD  RV  KFP VEN DKP RF  SFP CD  KRP
```

Figure D.1   Cluster diagrams of Danish coalition formation, 1945–82

1945

Average Linkage

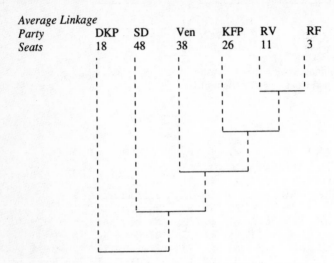

Party	DKP	SD	Ven	KFP	RV	RF
Seats	18	48	38	26	11	3

K-Means

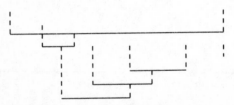

Winning MAP = Ven + KFP + RV + RF (Ave Linkage)
            = DKP + SD RV   (K-Means)
Actual Govt = Venstre (Kristensen)

1947

Average Linkage

Party	DKP	RV	SD	Ven	KFP	RF
Seats	9	10	57	49	17	6

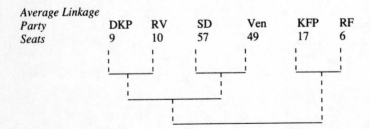

K-Means

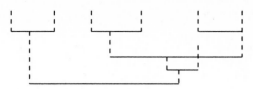

Winning MAP = SD + Venstre
Actual Govt = SD (Hedtoft I)

1950

Party	DKP	RV	SD	Ven	KFP	RF
Seats	7	12	59	32	27	12

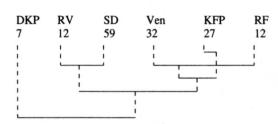

Winning MAP = RV + SD + Venstre + KFP + RF
Actual Govt = Venstre + KFP (Eriksen)

1953:1

Average Linkage

Party	DKP	RV	SD	Ven	KFP	RF
Seats	7	13	61	33	26	9

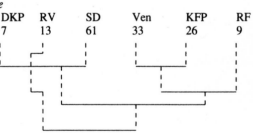

K-Means

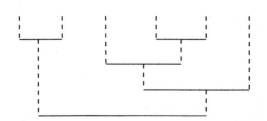

1953:2

Average Linkage

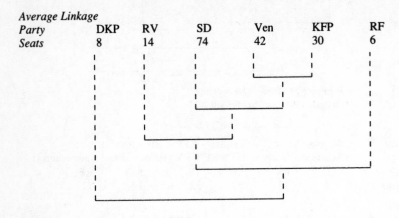

Party	DKP	RV	SD	Ven	KFP	RF
Seats	8	14	74	42	30	6

K-Means

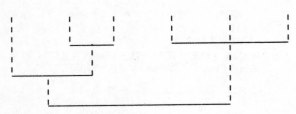

Winning MAP = SD + Venstre + KFP   (Average Linkage)
            = SD + RV DKP   (K-Means)
Actual Govt = SD (Hansen I)

1957

Average Linkage

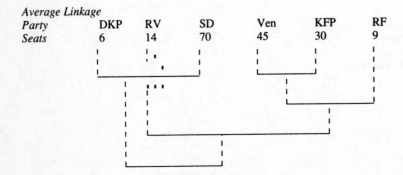

Party	DKP	RV	SD	Ven	KFP	RF
Seats	6	14	70	45	30	9

K-Means

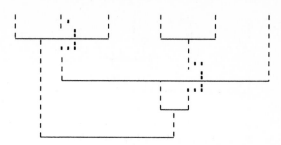

Winning MAP   = Venstre + KFP + RF + RV
Actual coalitions = SD + RF + RV (Hansen II and Kampmann I)

1960

K-Means

Party	SFD	SD	RV	Ven	KFP
Seats	11	76	11	38	32

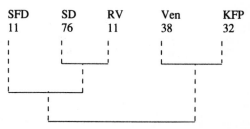

Winning MAP   = SD + RV + Venstre + KFP (Centroid)
            = SD + RV + SFP (Average and K-Means)
Actual Coalition = SD + RV Greenland Rep. (Kampmann II, Krag I)

1964

Centroid Linkage

Party	SFD	SD	RV	Ven	KFP
Seats	10	76	10	38	36

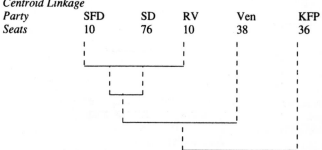

K-Means

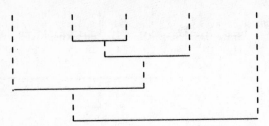

Winning MAP = SFP + SD + RV (Centroid)
                        SD + RV + Venstre (Average and K-Means)
Actual Govt   = SD (Krag II)

1971

Average Linkage

Party	SFP	SD	RV	Ven	KFP
Seats	17	70	27	30	31

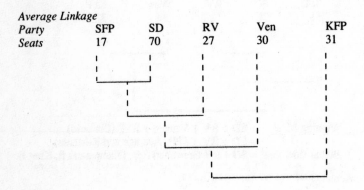

K-Means

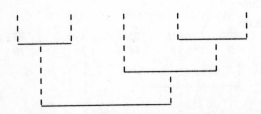

Winning MAP   = SFP + SD + RV (Average Linkage)
                            RV + Venstre + KFP (K-Means)
Actual Govt   = SD (Krag IV, Jorgensen I)
                            Venstre (Hartling I)

1973

Average Linkage

Party	SFP	DKP	SD	RV	CD	FP	RF	KFP	Ven	KRF
Seats	11	6	46	20	14	28	5	16	22	7

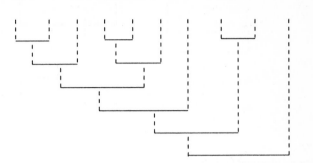

K-Means

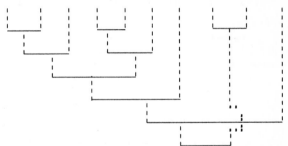

Winning MAP = SFP+DKP+SD+CD+RV (Centroid)
SFP+DKP+SD+CD+RV+FP (Average and K-Means)
Actual Govt = Venstre (Hartling II)

1975

Average Linkage

Party	SFP	VS	DKP	SD	RV	CD	FP	KFP	Ven	KRF
Seats	9	4	7	53	13	4	24	10	42	9

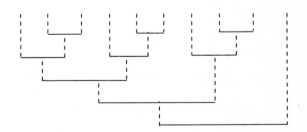

K-Means

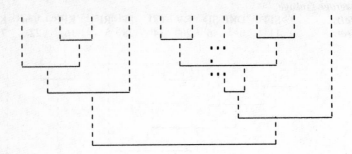

1977
Centroid, Average Linkage

Party	VS	SFP	DKP	SD	RV	CD	FP	RF	KFP	Ven	KRF
Seats	5	7	7	65	6	11	26	6	15	21	6

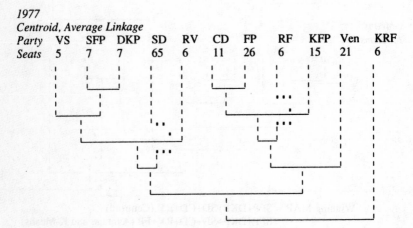

K-Means

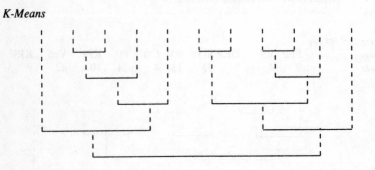

1979

Centroid, Average Linkage

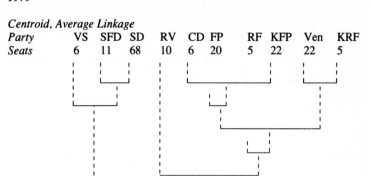

Party	VS	SFD	SD	RV	CD	FP	RF	KFP	Ven	KRF
Seats	6	11	68	10	6	20	5	22	22	5

K-Means

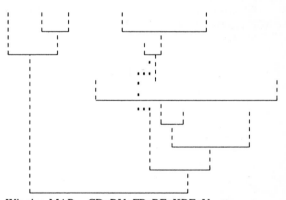

Winning MAP = CD+RV+FP+RF+KRF+Venstre
Actual Govt   = SD (Jorgensen IV)

1981

Average, Centroid Linkage

Party	SFP	VS	SD	RV	CD	FP	KFP	Ven	KRF
Seats	21	5	59	9	15	16	26	20	4

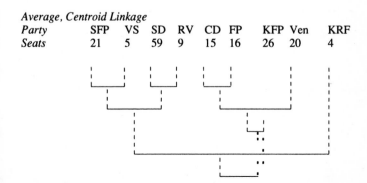

K-Means

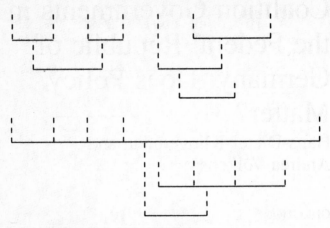

Winning MAP = SFP+VS+SD+RV
Actual Govt   = SD (Jorgensen V)

7 Coalition Governments in the Federal Republic of Germany: Does Policy Matter?

Hans-Dieter Klingemann and Andrea Volkens

INTRODUCTION

In West Germany majority coalitions are the characteristic mode of governing. The key role in those coalitions is played by the small Free Democratic Party (FDP). This has the crucial strategic role in deciding which of the two larger parties – the Social Democrats (SPD) or the Christian Democrats (CDU/CSU) will form the government.

In spite of a broad diversity over specific policy issues, the contemporary pattern of coalition politics follows the familiar left–right dimension. Most important in the context of the present volume, the structure of coalition governments has conformed remarkably well to a key prediction of coalition theory: the median legislator determines the composition of governments. Despite its smallness the FDP has been a permanent coalition actor because it occupies the position of a median legislator on the left–right dimension for most of the time.

PARTY SYSTEM DEVELOPMENTS AND COALITION GOVERNMENTS

Since the founding of the Federal Republic coalitions have been the usual form of government. Only once, in 1957, did a party – the Christian Democratic Party (CDU/CSU) – achieve an absolute majority of seats in the Bundestag, the most influential of the two parliamentary chambers of West Germany. The second major party, the Social Democratic Party (SPD), surpassed its competitor in 1972 but was second in all the other elections. The third important coalition actor, the Free Democratic Party (FDP), attained its best result in 1961 with 12.8 per cent of the valid votes cast and its low point with only 5.8 per cent in 1969. Compared to the Christian Democrats and the Social Democrats the Liberals (FDP) are clearly a much smaller party. Table E.1 and E.2, in the chapter appendix, show the results of West German federal elections based on the total population entitled to vote and the distribution of seats in the Bundestag from 1949 to 1987.

Three stages of party system development can be distinguished according to the number of parties represented in parliament. First, there was a phase of concentration during which the number of parties declined from ten in 1949 to three in 1961; second, the period of a stable three party system from 1961 to 1982, with the CDU/CSU, the SPD and the FDP; and third, a new differentiation of the party system with four parties after the Green party entered parliament in 1982.

These stages of party system development shaped the composition of coalition governments. During the first phase, a classic multi-party situation, coalition governments were composed of the CDU/CSU as the major party and several smaller centre-right parties. This phase was dominated by Adenauer, the first chancellor of the FRG. Adenauer followed the successful strategy of enlarging coalitions beyond what was needed for a legislative majority, thereby absorbing most of the smaller parties both at the elite and the voter levels. During this period coalition changes were due to quarrels between party wings within the minor coalition partners which resulted in the parties breaking up into fractions. The so called 'minister-wings' either joined the CDU or created a new party. These parties faded into oblivion very quickly due to the 5 per cent hurdle for entering parliament.

The only small party which survived this strategy of absorbing smaller coalition partners was the Free Democratic Party. During the period of the stable three party system from 1961 to 1983 the FDP gained the position of a pivotal party, making and breaking governments. The Green Party has only recently become an acceptable coalition partner for the SPD at the Laender level, but up to now the two parties have never gained a majority of seats at federal level.

Majority government is the rule in Germany. It is almost enforced by institutional rules (see below for details). Public opinion also favours coalitions with clear absolute majorities. Minority governments occurred three times as interim bargaining situations during coalition crisis but were never meant to last. Table E.3 identifies 23 governments in West Germany for the period between 1949 and 1990.

Coalitions have been quite stable in Germany. Out of the 23 different governments 11 were formed after elections, and the three minority cabinets do not qualify as 'real' governments in the German case. Apart from slight variations in coalition partners during the concentration phase of the party system, only two major changes in coalition partners occurred during legislative periods: in 1966, when the Grand Coalition was established, and in 1982, when the FDP changed its coalition partner from the SPD to the CDU/CSU. Because of the decisive position of the German chancellor, the two changes in chancellorship without changes of coalition parties (1963: Adenauer – Erhard; 1974: Brandt – Schmidt) may also be viewed as having a crucial impact on coalition policy.

Since 1961 the typical government has been a coalition composed of either the CDU/CSU or the SPD as the major coalition partner with the FDP. Only once, in 1966, was a Grand Coalition established when no agreement could be reached between the CDU/CSU and the FDP on how to cover the budgetary deficit. This was the first time the SPD participated in a coalition government at federal level. After an election in 1969, the SPD and the FDP agreed to form a Social–Liberal coalition. Similar coalitions at the state level as well as the election of Gustav Heinemann to the federal presidency by an alliance of the SPD and the FDP, signalled a changing coalition pattern. The Social–Liberal alliance lasted 13 years. Schmidt, successor to the first post-war SPD chancellor Brandt, was dismissed by a constructive vote of no-confidence. Helmut Kohl, party chairman of the Christian Democrats, formed a new coalition with the support of the FDP, which went on to win the subsequent elections of 1983 and 1987.

Thus the characteristic of German coalitions is that the smallest party has the most strategic role in deciding which of the two larger parties will form the government.

HISTORICAL ROOTS

The crucial importance of the FDP is due to its central position between the CDU/CSU to its right and the SPD to its left, when placed along an overall left–right dimension. This constellation of the three dominant players in German governmental politics had already emerged before the founding of the Federal Republic in 1949. Dimensions of policy consent and dissent were particularly evident in the operation of two planning bodies established in 1947 and 1948, the Economic Council and the Parliamentary Council. In these institutional settings one can discern the harbingers of coalition behaviour that would later become the norm.

Each of these bodies was initially composed of roughly 50–65 members appointed by the Land parliaments. The mandate of the Economic Council was to formulate policies for economic and infrastructural organisation. The Parliamentary Council was instigated by the Allies in the wake of the Berlin Blockade as a recognition of, first, the need for permanent institutions of governance and, second, the clear impossibility of co-operating with the Soviets and including the Eastern Zone. It was within these two bodies that the issues shaping future coalitions clearly emerged.

Within the Economic Council German politicians accommodated partisan orientations toward general economic policy. They arrayed rather clearly along what would eventually be the general left–right dimension, opposing a more market oriented to a more centrally planned economy. Here, the more bourgeois groups – most particularly the CDU/CSU and the FDP – carried the day. This alliance clearly presaged the coalition most common in the Federal Republic.

The Parliamentary council saw the genesis of the second most common coalition arrangement, including the FDP, again, but this time in co-operation with the Social Democrats. The central task of the Parliamentary Council was to write a constitution. Two sets of issues tended to divide the participants: first, the relative degree of permanence the document would have produced, and second, the relative distribution of authority between the projected central government and the constituent Laender. Since reunification was likely to work to the advantage of the SPD, it resisted all efforts to treat the document as anything other than tentative or provisional. While accepting its provisionality, the CDU and other centre-right groupings saw the task as building a structure which could serve as a model for a reunited Germany.

The second dominant conflict among the partisan groups was the form and structure of federalism, ranging from the Bavarian Party's advocacy (with French encouragement) of a rather loose confederation, through the CDU (and American-supported) push for a more clearly federal structure, to the SPD's advocacy of a strong central government and only semi-autonomous Laender (a stance supported by the British Labour Party). Closely associated with the institutional frame of central/Laender responsibilities was the question of fiscal power, and in particular which governmental level would have the primary taxing and spending authority. Again, the SPD and the FDP, favouring a more centralized structure, found themselves in alliance.

Nonetheless, there was much inter-party compromise (excluding the Communists) in the working of the Parliamentary Council, which was important for the legitimacy of the Basic Law, the 'Grundgesetz', which still serves as the West German constitution.

STRUCTURAL INFLUENCES AND CONSTRAINTS

The historical experiences of the Weimar Republic with unstable governments in a polarized and fragmented party system led to the adoption of the three central features of the Basic Law which impact on governments: first, the 5 per cent hurdle; second, the two-thirds majority requirement for constitutional amendments; and third, the unusually strong position of the German chancellor.

The West German election law operates on the principle of proportional representation which tends to give rise to a multi-party system. This was prevented, however, by the introduction of a five-per cent hurdle to avoid the recurrence of the Weimar situation. The five-per cent criterion was applied at the Laender level in the 1949 election, and in this form favoured regionally strong, small parties (BP,WAV,DP,SSW,DZ). This provision was changed with the election law of July 1953. It was now applied at the federal level and eliminated many of the smaller parties mentioned above. It can be regarded as an important institutional condition of the concentration of the party system which, over time, minimised the coalition possibilities.

The two-thirds requirement for constitutional amendments led Adenauer to form the oversized coalition of 1953 to anticipate the disputed rearmament legislation. The necessity of constitutional amendments was also an argument for the formation of the Grand Coalition which actually passed twelve such amendments – more than any other German government.

German chancellors have a strong political position. This has led many observers to describe the German political system as a 'chancellor democracy' (Kanzlerdemokratie). The Chancellor decides on the number of ministries, appoints all cabinet members, who become directly responsible to him and, by the constitution, sets the 'national policy guide-lines' (Richtlinienkompetenz). Moreover, the chancellor can only be dismissed if another chancellor is presented by a new parliamentary majority (vote of no-confidence). On the other hand, the chancellor lacks the power to dissolve parliament – a major weapon when it comes to disciplining his own coalition.

These institutional provisions serve the following functions:

- restricting coalition choices by eliminating small parties,
- requiring governments to have a majority of seats,
- stabilizing coalition governments by increasing the likelihood that the coalition will continue for the whole legislative period.

Electoral pacts can be considered the most important constraint on coalition formation in the German context. In eight out of eleven elections the parties announced beforehand which coalitions they would form after the election. This strategy of pre-election coalition pacts finds a basis in the West German electoral system '. . . [which] with its provision both for a constituency candidate, and for a party list – allows a coalition government to appeal explicitly for endorsement as a coalition' (Bogdanor, 1986). Formal coalition theories which exclude this consideration ignore the realities of West German coalition politics.

The negative versions of the coalition pact are (a) the self-imposed refusal to enter a coalition and (b) the refusal of a party to consider another party as its coalition partner. The former was the case with the Bavarian Party (BP) and the Economic Reconstruction League (WAV) in 1949 as well as with the FDP in 1957. The veto operated in 1949 when all parties refused the Communists as a potential ally and the CSU rejected the SPD. Similarly, in 1953 the CDU/CSU also announced that it would not ally with the SPD.

Table 7.1 summarises the institutional constraints and other restrictions on the choice of coalition partners.

PATTERNS OF COALITION BARGAINING

Before turning to the quantitative analyses of policy based coalition formation we want briefly to describe the changing patterns of coalition bar-

Table 7.1   Constraints and influences on coalition bargaining in Federal Germany 1949–87

	Period	Effects
1. Pre-election pacts commit FDP and partner to form coalition together	1953–87	Composition of coalition predetermined by election results
2. Refusal to go into coalition with specific other parties	1949–60	Reduced range of coalition possibilities
3. Communists banned	1952–87	Little practical effect
4. Electoral threshold eliminates small parties	1953–87	Typically restricts choices to three main parties, with FDP at median position
5. Constructive vote of no confidence	1949–87	Renders incumbent government more stable.
6. Chancellor lacks power of dissolution of Bundestag	1949–87	Makes it more probable coalition will continue for life of legislature.

gaining. There is no institutional regulation of the bargaining process nor of the way its results are registered. Thus, some coalition agreements are summarised in separate documents (Kaolitionsvertraege), others found expression in the government declaration (Regierungserklaerung) and still others were merely sealed by a handshake. Some have been kept secret, others have been published. Empirically, we find a wide variation in these respects.

The major players are and have always been the respective party leaders and the top party politicians. And each coalition negotiation has to answer at least these two questions: (1) What are the major policy goals and how should they be reached ("Sachverhandlungen")? and (2) How should the ministries be divided between the coalition parties and which politicians are acceptable for cabinet and other top level positions in the government ('Personalverhandlungen')? These questions have always been tackled in that order: that is, policies first and political personnel second.

In the early period Adenauer settled these questions mainly by himself. However, what we can observe over time is a growing differentiation and bureaucratisation of the negotiation process. More politicians and more staff are incorporated in decision making. Committees and sub-committees debate the diverse policy questions in great detail.

It is difficult to decide whether office-seeking or policy-pursuit is the more important consideration which tips the scale in bargaining. The negotiations do not take place in the public domain. And the account given by the politicians themselves, in autobiographies and other statements, is more often than not contradictory. The media have to cope with the same lack of information although they may have a broader range of informants. They tend to report the potentially most divisive issues, issues that generate the greatest difficulties for the final agreement. From a systematic survey of press reports about coalition bargaining we observe that conflict over issues is rated as more important than conflict over the distribution of portfolios. The only time when the latter was controversial was in the 1950, where the general structure of the federal government was still to be created.

Coalition termination also indicates the importance of policy-seeking in Germany: not a single coalition has broken down because of disagreement over the distribution of ministries. Coalition crises have always been provoked by policy quarrels. Obviously it was easier to create new ministries or cabinet rank positions to satisfy demands than to compromise over the important issues which were on the agenda of national politics. Thus, the evidence we have from these albeit fragmentary accounts is that policy-seeking is at least as important as office-seeking when it comes to explaining coalition behaviour in Germany.

DOCUMENTS CODED

The convention in the Federal Republic is for the Chancellor to make a formal declaration of policy (Grosse Regierungserklarung) at the beginning of each clearly demarcated new (coalition) government. The qualification is important, as some governments which emerge as separate by our definition were not clearly demarcated and constitute only minor changes. Most of these occurred in the 1950s and the early 1960s when the same Chancellor had to cope with coalition partners who were in the process of splitting up (Adenauer 2b, 2d, 3b). In other cases the governments were brief and transitional (Adenauer 2c, Erhard 2b, Schmidt 3b). New governments have been formed and declarations made after each of the eleven federal elections. Four major changes occurred during the legislature (Erhard 1, Kiesinger 1, Schmidt 1, Kohl 1) which were also accompanied by government declarations. Thus, our analysis will rest on all 15 formal government declarations made in the period between 1949 and 1987. Sometimes, the parties in the coalition have made formal coalition agreements (Koalitionsvertrag). However, not all coalition governments have done that. It is therefore, better to operate on the basis of the Chancellor's presentation which is always made for a clearly constituted and permanent government.

As far as party programmes are concerned we have included all 13 political parties which entered the Bundestag in the eleven elections held since 1949. Thus, we can compare the policy positions between parties for these eleven electoral situations.

Formally there is another party represented in Bonn: the Christian Democratic Party (CSU), sister party of the CDU in Bavaria where the CDU leaves it a free field. More right-wing than the CDU, this party has been dominated by the figure and aspirations of Franz-Josef Strauss, joint Chancellor candidate with the CDU in 1980. Most of the time the two parties also presented joint election programmes. For purposes of analysis we can regard the CSU as basically a faction within the CDU.

Comparisons between election programmes and government declarations pose no problems for the governments formed after each election. In those cases, however, where governments have been formed during the period of the legislature we systematically compare the government declaration with the party programmes for the preceding election.

Government declarations and party programmes have been coded into the same categories which applied throughout our analysis, though the unit of analysis is slightly different, being based on 'problems' rather than (quasi) sentences. The differences are not great however, and do not preclude systematic comparisons with the other countries in this book.

Dimensions of party competition

Previous factor analysis of election programmes produced dimensions which related to pertinent problems of any political system, namely the organisation of the polity, the organisation of society, the organisation of the economy and the general issue of preservation and survival. A left–right pattern emerged particularly with respect to the economic domain.

The standard left–right scale which is used for the analyses presented in this book also clarifies the political situation for Germany. The scores for both parties and governments on this one dimension are reported in Table 7.2 and Figure 7.1.

Table 7.2 and Figure 7.1 show that party positions on the common left–right dimension are very much what might have been expected, with the SPD on the left, the CDU on the right and the FDP generally in between. It adds to the credibility of the scale that the FDP was located to the right of the CDU in 1949 and 1953, given the relatively high influence of the North Rhine-Westphalia-based social wing of the CDU (Sozialausschusse) and the economic conservatism of the FDP. In 1957, the CDU shows a drastic shift to the right. This shift expresses Adenauer's firm stand on the issue of defence as well as a more conservative view of economic and social problems. The formation of the Grand Coalition is nicely anticipated by a move of the Social Democrats to the right and the Christian Democrats to the left. The move to the right by the Social Democrats also reflects the new principles as formulated in their 1959 Bad Godesberg basic programme. From 1965 to 1969 all three parties drift to the left, the Free Democrats in particular. The move to a Social–Liberal coalition government becomes clearly visible. While the SPD's position remained relatively stable from 1969 both the Christian Democrats and the Free Democrats started moving to the right. In 1987, five years after the formation of the Christian–Liberal coalition government in 1982, the two parties occupied almost the same position on the left–right dimension.

The left–right positions of many of the small parties in 1949, 1953 and 1957 are difficult to interpret. Some of them were mainly concerned with issues of federalism and regional autonomy (Deutsche Zentrumspartei, Baeyernpartei, Suedschleswigscher Waehlerverband, Deutsche Partei) or the specific interest of the refugees (Bund der Heimatvertriebenen und Entrechteten). Two of the smaller right-wing parties appear more leftist than expected (Deutsche Rechtspartei, Wirtschaftliche Aufbauvereinigung). Closer inspection reveals that this is mainly due to massive social-service demands made on behalf of their specific clientele. On the other side of the scale we should have expected the Communists to be further to the left. This

Table 7.2 Party and coalition policy in the Federal German Republic on the common left–right dimension, 1949–87

Election year					Party scores								Coalition/ policy score	
	KPD	GRNS	SPD	FDP	CDU	DP	BHE	DZ	WAV	DRP	BP	SSW		
1949	-24		-25	2	-15*	*14*		-17	-29	5	19	32	Adenauer 1	-7
1953			-36	-3	-12*	*-26*	-20	-23					Adenauer 2	-3
1957			-29	1	29*	*-23*							Adenauer 3	5
1961			-13	-4*	5								Adenauer 4	4
			-13	-4*	5								Erhard 1	12
1965			- 8	4	-5*								Erhard 2	13
			- 8	4	-5*								Kiesinger	9
1969			-21	-16*	-8								Brandt 1	-8
1972			-17	-5*	-1								Brandt 2	-12
			-17	-5*	-1								Schmidt 1	-1
1976			-23	-11*	5								Schmidt 2	-7
1980			-27	-8*	14	*17*							Schmidt 3	1
			-27	-8*	14								Kohl 1	15
1983			-40	-18	-5*								Kohl 2	9
1987		-33	-24	2	2*								Kohl 3	1

Notes: Government parties italicised.
*Party with control of the median legislator.

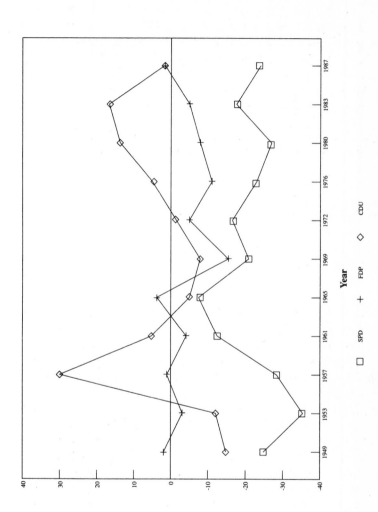

Figure 7.1 Left–right positions in the Federal German Republic, 1949–87

can be explained mainly by their frequent mentioning of 'freedom' which, however, in their understanding was framed as 'freedom from the Western allies' and the freedom to join the GDR. By 1961 none of these smaller parties survived, West Germany entered its phase of a stable three party system. This phase came to an end when, in 1983, the Greens entered the federal parliament. As Table 7.2 shows, the Green party takes up a position to the left of the SPD.

The changes in the three major parties' positions on the left–right dimension are highly comparable with changes in their coalition preferences. The Free Democrats in particular seem to signal to the electorate which coalition they are likely to enter. All of these movements are in accord with conventional accounts of the development of the German party system over the post-war period, and we therefore feel confident in applying the standard left–right dimension in the German case.

ONE-DIMENSIONAL ANALYSES OF GERMAN COALITION BARGAINING

Government formation

The membership of government coalitions and the party controlling the median legislator are also given in Table 7.2. The results are quite striking. The party controlling the median legislator is invariably in government. As can be seen from Table 7.2, the party with the median legislator is usually the FDP, especially in the period after 1969 – a finding that not only confirms but explains why the FDP has been such a permanent feature of governmental politics in West Germany.

Considering only the two party governments that formed after the German party system had reached substantially its present shape, in 1961, Table 7.2 shows that governments nearly always comprised the parties that were closest together on the left–right scale. The FDP was exactly half way between the other two in 1961. In 1965, the two closest parties were the CDU and SPD, which was in fact the coalition that eventually prevailed. In 1969, the two closest were SPD and FDP, which formed the government. In 1972, however, the left–right positions of the parties indicate a FDP–CDU coalition which did not in fact form. In 1976, the continuation of Schmidt's SPD–FDP coalition is accurately predicted, as it its continuation again in 1980. However, the FDP had moved to a position almost half way between the two larger parties in 1980, presaging the change in alignment that did indeed occur before the next election in 1983. In 1983 and 1987, the FDP and CDU were the two closest parties and did indeed form the government.

All in all, therefore, the one-dimensional analysis paints a very clear picture of government formation in the Federal Republic. The median party is nearly always in government, and the government usually comprises the two parties closest to each other on the left–right dimension. The pattern is summarised in Table 7.3, which shows mean party and government policy positions during the four basic 'eras' of government formation in West Germany. During the first era, that of CDU dominated coalitions, mostly including the FDP, the FDP and CDU are very close together and the SPD is well away from them on the left. During the era of the Grand Coalition between the CDU and SPD, the two parties are very close together, and the FDP has a distinct position. During the era of SPD–FDP coalitions, the two government parties are the closest pair, both appearing on the left of the scale. And the second era of CDU–FDP coalition also has the two government parties as the closest pair, the result of a rightwards move by the FDP. The one dimensional analysis thus very neatly captures the periodisation of coalition formation in West Germany.

Policy payoffs on the left–right dimension

The policy position of each West German government is also given in Table 7.2, and summarised in Table 7.3. They show that government policy followed the policy of government members quite closely. In particular, as the SPD stayed out of office during the 1980s, government policy moved

Table 7.3 One-dimensional coalition bargaining in the Federal Republic by 'Coalition era'

	Government Declaration	CDU	FDP	SPD
Left–right position	2.4	2.1	–3.7	–20.3
in periods				
CDU 1	4.8	0.0	–0.7	–20.7
GC	9.0	–5.1	3.7	– 8.2
SPD	–5.4	8.4	–9.0	–21.4
CDU 2	8.3	11.9	–3.4	–22.7

steadily rightwards, leaving the SPD increasingly isolated. Table 7.3 quantifies this, and shows that the only period that does not fit in with this analysis is that of the Grand Coalitions. The two periods of CDU dominated coalitions produce government policies that are relatively on the right. The period of SPD dominated coalitions produces policies that are relatively on the left. But the era of Grand Coalition produces the most right wing policies of all, which is difficult to explain in terms of the theories.

Table 7.4 operationalises the policy payoffs going to each party in terms of the distance between party and government policy (the smaller the distance, the greater the payoff). From this we can see that the CDU and FDP have consistently done better than the SPD as a result of the coalition game in West Germany. Whether in or out of office, there tends to be a larger distance between SPD and government policy than there is for the other parties. Getting into office does make some difference for the SPD, however – it seems to do less badly. The other two parties do quite well all the time in policy terms, so getting into government makes little difference to them.

MULTI-DIMENSIONAL ANALYSIS OF COALITION BARGAINING IN WEST GERMANY

Government formation

Only 16 of the 20 policy coding categories were populated in the German case. Table E.4 in the Appendix to this chapter shows both the city block distances between parties and the results of the standard average linkage hierarchical cluster analysis based upon these.

The cluster figures show that the multi-dimensional analysis consistently fails to predict the coalition which actually formed in Germany. Often, this is because the two closest parties are in fact the CDU and SPD. A Grand Coalition of these two big parties is predicted in 1949, 1961, 1965, 1969, 1972 and 1987. Only once, in the 1965–69 inter-election period, did this coalition form. Accurate predictions were made in 1953, 1957 (trivially, since the CDU had a majority, though the DP was correctly identified as the most likely CDU partner in the event of a surplus majority coalition) and 1980. All in all the cluster predictions using the multi-dimensional policy space are markedly less successful than those based on the standard left–right continuum. Policy does seem to be important in coalition formation in West Germany, but policy defined in terms of the major left–right dimen-

Table 7.4 Distances between party and coalition policy in the Federal German Republic on the common left–right dimension, 1949–87

Government No.	Election Year	KPD	GRN	SPD	FDP	CDU	DP	BHE	DZ	WAV	DRP	BP	SSW
							Party Score						
1	1949	−17		−18	9	−8	21		−10	−22	12	26	39
2	1953			−39	−6	−15	−29	−23	−26				
3	1957			−34	−4	24	−28						
4	1961			−17	−8	1							
5				−25	−16	−7							
6	1965			−21	−9	−18							
7				−17	−5	−14							
8	1969			−13	−8	0							
9	1972			−5	7	11							
10				−16	−4	0							
11	1976			−16	−4	12							
12	1980			−28	−9	13							
13				−42	−23	−1							
14	1983		−49	−27	−14	8							
15	1987		−34	−25	1	1							

Table 7.4 (cont'd)

Government No.	Election Year	Party Score												
		KPD	GRN	SPD	FDP	CDU	DP	BHE	DZ	WAV	DRP	BP	SSW
Absolute mean distance				23	9	9							
Means when in office				16	9	10							
out of office				28	5	7							
Means when median party				19	10	13							
not median party				24	6	9							
Means when in coalition with: CDU					11								
SPD					6								

sion of party competition, not the broader policy provisions in the party manifesto as a whole.

Multi-dimensional policy payoffs

Policy payoffs in the multi-dimensional space, once more operationalised as the distance between party and coalition policy, are given in Table 7.5.

On aggregate, the CDU does rather better than the other parties, and the FDP rather worse. While the FDP appears to get a higher payoff when in office than when out, the CDU seems to do better when out of office. Once more, the multi-dimensional analysis is less easy to interpret than the one-dimensional analysis, given the FDP's central position in so many post-war German governments. The low multi-dimensional policy payoffs to the FDP, taken together with the fact that it often appeared as the most remote party in the distance matrices, suggests that the content analyses were systematically coding aspects of party policy on which the FDP differed from the other parties, and from the governments which eventually formed, but which had no real bearing on party competition.

DISAGGREGATED MULTI-DIMENSIONAL ANALYSIS

Instead of dealing with aggregate policy distances in the multi-dimensional policy space, Table 7.6 looks at the parties controlling the median legislator on each dimension taken one at a time. Obviously, with a majority of seats the CDU dominates all dimensions in 1953 and 1957. Other than this, however, three is no obviously predominant party in West Germany. The CDU generally controls the median legislator on more dimensions than any other party, though the SPD's emergence into a dominant position in 1969 is shown quite clearly. After 1969, however, each of the three parties controls more comparable numbers. The FDP reached its maximum in 1965 and 1980. In each case the party changed coalitions shortly afterwards.

Table 7.6 also shows that particular parties tend to control particular policy dimensions throughout the study period. The most dramatic example of this is the 'social welfare' dimension, controlled on all but one occasion by the CDU. The CDU has also dominated policy dimensions dealing with freedom and human rights, economic infrastructure, education, social justice and social services. No other party has as consistent a record at dominating particular dimensions, though the SPD does best on the quality of life, the social conservatism and the various foreign policy dimensions.

Table 7.5 Distances between party and coalition policy in the Federal German Republic, on 16 dimensions, 1949–87

Election Year	KPD	GRN	SPD	FDP	CDU	Party score DP	BHE	DZ	DRP	WAV	BP	SSW
1949	64		55	38	60	61		73	68	51	66	85
1953			48	55	43	72	90	62				
1957			78	75	76	70						
1961			54	57	48							
1963			42	59	57							
1965			46	53	50							
1966			71	65	47							
1969			46	57	38							
1972			43	84	32							
1974			60	84	33							
1976			53	43	34							
1980			35	45	47							
1982			56	59	36							
1983		81	37	47	33							
1987		57	51	60	46							

Table 7.5 (cont'd)

Election Year	KPD	GRN	SPD	FDP	Party score CDU	DP	BHE	DZ	DRP	WAV	BP	SSW
Absolute mean distance			52	59	46							
Means when												
in office			51	57	50							
out of office			52	70	37							
Means when												
median party*			51	53	45							
not median party			52	62	48							
Means when in coalition with												
SPD				63								
CDU				53								

* Median Party = party with median legislator in most dimensions.
1976: FDP and CDU

An analysis not reported here shows that these policy dimensions are also ones where relevant ministries go disproportionately to parties dominant on them.

CONCLUSIONS: THE ROLE OF POLICY IN WEST GERMAN COALITION FORMATION

Table 7.7 provides a synopsis of the success rates of various policy-based hypotheses about coalition formation in West Germany. The success of each theory is recorded for each post-war government and aggregate success rates over all of them. Since some hypotheses make more predictions than others, we have also included figures for the 'predictive efficiency' of each hypothesis. This is the number of successfully predicted coalitions as a proportion of *all* the coalitions predicted to form by the theory in each situation. The predictive efficiency shows how much of the success of a theory is due to a blunderbuss approach in which practically all possible coalitions are postdicted. In this case theories which make unique predictions are favoured and score highest.

As might have been expected from our discussion of the cluster models, these did very badly overall, actually performing worse in the West German case than picking coalitions out of a hat. One possible source of systematic misprediction, as we suggested above, is that the FDP has consistently emphasised policy categories in its manifestos that are captured by our coding but which for some reason are not salient in coalition formation. This would explain why the one-dimensional analysis, which puts the FDP at the centre of things, does better than the multi-dimensional analysis, which tends, less plausibly, to put the FDP on the fringe.

All the other policy-based hypotheses did substantially better than chance. Predictions that the coalition would contain a predominant or median party performed very well, though it should be noted that about one half of all possible coalitions were in their prediction sets. The same is true for Axelrod's connectedness hypotheses (Theory F). Overall, the one-dimensional 'proximity' hypotheses (A and E) performed best, especially as they generated unique predictions which improved their efficiency rate.

The figures in Table 7.7 strongly support the idea that policy competition between the West German parties is organised along a single left–right dimension. All of the hypotheses that do well are defined in terms of a single dimension of ideology. The hypothesis that does by far the worst is defined in terms of a multi-dimensional policy space. The unidimensional

Table 7.6 Party controlling median legislator on 16 dimensions Federal Republic of Germany, 1949–87

Year	49	53	57	61	65	69	72	76	80	83	87	SPD	FDP	CDU
Government	KPD	CDU	CDU	FDP	SPD	*	CDU	CDU	FDP	GRU	CDU	1	2	5
Freedom	SPD	CDU	CDU	CDU	SPD	SPD	CDU	CDU	CDU	CDU	SPD	4	—	7
Democracy	*	CDU	CDU	FDP	FPD	CDU	*	FDP	SPD	SPD	FDP	2	4	3
Economic Infrastructure	WAV	CDU	CDU	CDU	FDP	SPD	SPD	CDU	FDP	CDU	CDU	2	2	6
Capitalist Economics	DP	CDU	CDU	SPD	FDP	SPD	CDU	FDP	FDP	FDP	CDU	2	4	4
State Intervention	*	CDU	CDU	CDU	SDP	SPD	CDU	CDU	SPD	GRU	CDU	3	—	6
Agriculture	SPD	*	CDU	CDU	FDP	SPD	CDU	CDU	FDP	CDU	*	2	2	5
Education	*	CDU	CDU	CDU	CDU	SPD	CDU	FDP	CDU	CDU	CDU	1	1	8
Quality of Life	*	CDU	CDU	FDP	*	SPD	SPD	SPD	SPD	SPD	*	5	1	2
Social Conservatism	FDP	CDU	CDU	SPD	*	FDP	CDU	FDP	SPD	SPD	SPD	4	3	3
(Welfare State†)	CDU	CDU	CDU	CDU	SPD	CDU	CDU	CDU	CDU	CDU	CDU	1	—	10
a. Social Justice	CDU	CDU	CDU	CDU	FDP	CDU	SPD	*	CDU	CDU	CDU	1	1	8
b. Social Services	CDU	CDU	CDU	CDU	SPD	CDU	CDU	CDU	CDU	SPD	CDU	2	—	9
c. Labour	SPD	CDU	CDU	FDP	SPD	CDU	*	FDP	FDP	FDP	CDU	1	5	4

Table 7.6 (cont'd)

Year	49	53	57	61	65	69	72	76	80	83	87	SPD	FDP	CDU
European Co-operation	*	CDU	CDU	SPD	SDP	SPD	SPD	FDP	FDP	CDU	SPD	4	3	3
Military Strength	*	CDU	CDU	SPD	FDP	SPD	SPD	SPD	FDP	FDP	SPD	5	3	2
Peace and Detente	*	CDU	CDU	CDU	FPD	SPD	SPD	SPD	FDP	SPD	FDP	4	3	3
No:														
SPD	3	—	—	4	6	10	6	3	4	5	4	45		
FDP	1			4	7	1	—	6	8	3	2		32	
CDU	2	15	16	8	1	4	8	6	4	6	8			78

Note: * means unpopulated for that year
† Aggregated over three succeeding dimensions.

Table 7.7 Success rates of policy-based coalition theories in the Federal German Republic, 1961–87

Govt No.	1	2	3	4	5	6	7	8	9	10	11	12	13	14	15	Predictive success	efficiency
Election Year	1949	1953	1957	1961		1965		1969	1972		1976	1980		1983	1987		
No. of Parties	10	6	4	3	3	3	3	3	3	3	3	3	3	4	4		
No. of Possible Governments	1023	63	15	7	7	7	7	7	7	7	7	7	7	15	15		
Prediction:																	
Theory A	No	No	No	Yes	Yes	No	Yes	Yes	No	No	Yes	Yes	No	No	Yes	.47 (7/15)	.47 (7/15)
Theory B	Yes	Yes	Yes	Yes	Yes	No	Yes	Yes	Yes	Yes	Yes	Yes	Yes	Yes	Yes	.93 (14/15)	.08 (14/162)
Theory C	No	Yes	Yes	Yes	Yes	Yes	No	Yes	No	No	(No)	Yes	No	Yes	Yes	.67 (10/15)	.06 (10/162)
Theory D	No	No	Yes	Yes	No	Yes	No	No	No	No	No	Yes	No	No	No	.20 (3/15)	.20 (3/15)
Theory E	No	Yes	No	Yes	Yes	Yes	No	Yes	No	No	Yes	Yes	No	No	Yes	.53 (8/15)	.53 (8/15)
Theory F	No	No	No	Yes	Yes	No	Yes	Yes	Yes	Yes	Yes	Yes	Yes	Yes	Yes	.73 (11/15)	.07 (11/173)

Theory A: Coalition will be the closest parties which form a majority on the left–right dimension
Theory B: Coalition will contain the party with the median legislator on left–right dimension
Theory C: Coalition will contain the party with the median legislator on most of the disaggregated 16 dimensions
Theory D: Coalition will be at the first majority node on cluster tree of 16 dimensions and policy viable on at least one dimension
Theory E: Coalition will contain the FDP and its closest neighbour on left–right dimension
Theory F: Coalition will be connected majority on left–right dimension

Note : No constraints included as they would in most cases eliminate any purely policy-based choice.

hypotheses, moreover, do particularly well in the West German context, compared with other countries, a product largely of the responsiveness of the coalition system to the role of the party controlling the median legislator.

APPENDIX E

Table E.1 Results of West German Federal elections: second votes as a proportion of the electorate

	1949	1953	1957	1961	1965	1969	1972	1976	1980	1983	1987
KPD	4.4	1.8	—	—	—	—	—	—	—	—	—
SPD	22.2	23.9	26.9	30.5	33.3	36.4	41.4	38.3	37.6	33.7	31.0
FDP	9.1	7.9	6.5	10.8	8.0	4.9	7.6	7.1	9.3	6.1	7.6
CDU/SDU	23.6	37.5	42.4	38.2	40.3	39.3	40.5	43.8	39.0	43.1	37.0
CDU	19.2	30.2	33.5	30.1	32.2	31.2	31.8	34.2	30.0	33.7	28.8
CSU	4.4	7.3	8.9	8.1	8.1	8.1	8.7	9.6	9.0	9.4	8.2
DZ	2.3	0.7	—	—							
DP	3.0	2.7	2.8	—							
WAV	2.2	—	—	—							
DKP/DRP	1.4										
GB/BHE	—	4.9	3.9								
BP	3.2	1.4									
SSW	0.2	0.1	0.1	0.1	—	—	—	—	—	—	—
Die Gruenen	—	—	—						1.3	4.9	6.9
Others	4.5	2.1	2.0	4.6	3.1	4.7	0.9	0.7	0.6	0.5	0.3
Invalid votes	2.4	2.8	3.3	3.5	2.1	1.4	0.7	0.8	0.8	0.8	0.8
Non-voters	21.5	14.2	12.2	12.3	13.2	13.3	8.9	9.3	11.4	10.9	16.4
Electorate	31208	33202	35401	37441	38510	38677	41446	42058	43232	44089	45291

Table E.1 (cont'd)

Key to Parties :

KDP	Kommunistische Partei Deutschlands (Communist Party)
SPD	Sozialdemokratische Partei Deutschlands (Social Democrats)
FDP	Freie Demokratische Partei Deutschlands (Free Democratic Party)
DA/FVP	Demokratische Aktion/Freiheitliche Volkspartei (Democratic Action/Free Peoples' Party)
CDU/CSU	Christliche Demokratische Union/Christlich Soziale Union (Christian Democratic Union/Christian Social Union)
CDU	Christliche Demokratische Union (Christian Democratic Union)
CSU	Christlich Soziale Union (Christian Social Union)
DZ	Deutsche Zentrumspartei (Centre Party)
DP	Deutsche Partei (German Party)
WAV	Wirtschaftliche Aufbauvereinigung (Economic Reconstruction League)
DKP/DRP	Deutsche Konservative Partie/Deutsche Reichspartei (German Reich Party)
GB/BHE	Gesamtdeutscher Block/Block der Heimatvertriebenen und Entrechteten (Refugee Party)
BP	Bayern Party (Bavarian Party)
SSW	Suedschleswigscher Waehlerverband (South Schleswig Voters League)
Die Gruenen	The Greens

Table E.2 The German parties' power in parliament: distribution of seats in the Bundestag

	1949		1953		1957		1961		1965		1969		1972		1976		1980		1983		1987	
	N	%	N	%	N	%	N	%	N	%	N	%	N	%	N	%	N	%	N	%	N	%
KPD	15	3.7	—		—		—		—		—		—		—		—		—		—	
SPD	131	32.6	151	31.0	169	34.0	190	38.1	202	40.7	224	45.2	230	46.4	214	43.1	218	43.9	193	38.8	186	37.4
FDP	52	12.9	48	9.9	41	8.2	67	13.4	49	9.9	30	6.0	41	8.3	39	7.9	53	10.6	34	6.8	46	9.3
CDU/CSU	139	34.6	243	49.9	270	54.4	242	48.5	245	49.4	242	48.8	225	45.4	243	49.0	226	45.5	244	49.0	223	44.9
/CDU	115	28.6	191	39.2	217	43.7	192	38.5	196	39.5	193	38.9	177	35.7	190	38.3	174	35.0	191	38.4	174	35.0
/CSU	24	6.0	52	10.7	53	10.7	50	10.0	49	9.9	49	9.9	48	9.7	53	10.7	52	10.5	53	10.6	49	9.9
DZ	10	2.5	3	0.6	—		—		—		—		—		—		—		—		—	
DP	17	4.2	15	3.1	17	3.4	—		—		—		—		—		—		—		—	
WAV	12	3.0	—		—		—		—		—		—		—		—		—		—	
DKP/DRP	5	1.2	—		—		—		—		—		—		—		—		—		—	
GB/BHE	—		27	5.5	—		—		—		—		—		—		—		—		—	
BP	17	4.2	—		—		—		—		—		—		—		—		—		—	
SSW	1	0.3	—		—		—		—		—		—		—		—		—		—	
Die Gruenen	—		—		—		—		—		—		—		—		—		27	5.4	42	8.4
Others	3	0.8	—		—		—		—		—		—		—		—		—		—	
Total	402	100	487	100	497	100	494	100	496	100	496	100	496	100	496	100	497	100	498	100	497	100

Table E.3 Coalition Governments in the Federal Republic of Germany

Election Date	Time Period	Coalition	Chancellor
14 August 1949	20.09.49-19.10.53	CDU/CSU FDP DP	Adenauer 1*
06 September 1953	20.10.53-23.07.55	CDU/CSU FDP DP GB/BHE	Adenauer 2a*
	24.07.55-25.02.56	CDU/CSU FDP DP	Adenauer 2b
	26.02.56-20.03.56	CDU/CSU DP	Adenauer 2c
	21.03.56-28.10.57	CDU/CSU DP DA/FVP	Adenauer 2d
15 September 1957	29.10.57-01.07.60	CDU/CSU DP	Adenauer 3a*
	02.07.60-13.11.61	CDU/CSU	Adenauer 3b
17 September 1961	14.11.61-19.11.62	CDU/CSU FDP	Adenauer 4a*
	20.11.62-10.12.62	CDU/CSU	Adenauer 4b
	11.12.62-15.10.63	CDU/CSU FDP	Adenauer 4c
	16.10.63-19.10.65	CDU/CSU FDP	Erhard 1*
19 September 1965	20.10.65-28.10.66	CDU/CSU FDP	Erhard 2a*
	29.10.66-30.11.66	CDU/CSU	Erhard 2b
	01.12.66-20.10.69	CDU/CSU SPD	Kiesinger*
28 September 1969	21.10.69-13.12.72	SPD FDP	Brandt 1*

Table E.3 (cont'd)

Election Date	Time Period	Coalition	Chancellor
19 November 1972	14.12.72-15.05.74 16.05.74-14.12.76	SPD FDP SPD FDP	Brandt 2* Schmidt 1*
03 October 1976	15.12.76-04.11.80	SPD FDP	Schmidt 2*
05 November 1980	05.11.80-17.09.82 18.09.82-30.09.82 01.10.82-28.03.83	SPD FDP SPD CDU/CSU FDP	Schmidt 3a* Schmidt 3b Kohl 1*
06 March 1983	29.03.83-10.03.87	CDU/CSU FDP	Kohl 2*
25 January 1987	11.03.87-	CDU.CSU FDP	Kohl 3*

* Government declarations coded.

Table E.4   Matrices for West German parties on 16 dimensions, 1949–87 (city block metric)

1949

SPD	59								
FDP	96	78							
CDU	107	58	66						
DZ	80	64	79	93					
DP	57	71	80	81	65				
WAV	87	53	68	54	75	87			
DRP	57	60	95	107	74	61	95		
BP	88	81	84	108	77	77	93	49	
SSW	70	91	93	127·	86	79	110	66	65
	KPD	SPD	FDP	CDU	DZ	DP	WAV	DRP	BP

1953

FDP	65				
CDU	40	39			
DZ	65	88	74		
DP	61	62	51	63	
BHE	84	67	77	90	80
	SPD	FDP	CDU	DZ	DP

1957

FDP	75		
CDU	94	77	
DP	93	85	77
	SPD	FDP	CDU

1961

FDP	47	
CDU	46	47
	SPD	FDP

1965

FDP	53	
CDU	52	45
	SPD	FDP

1969

FDP	60	
CDU	32	71
	SPD	FDP

1972

FDP	96	
CDU	45	84
	SPD	FDP

1976

FDP	50	
CDU	61	44
	SPD	FDP

1980

FDP	42	
CDU	54	50
	SPD	FDP

1983

SPD	67		
FDP	57	47	
CDU	94	58	67
	GRU	SPD	FDP

1987

SPD	51		
FDP	65	56	
CDU	71	44	67
	GRU	SPD	FDP

Figure E.1   Cluster diagrams for West German parties on 16 dimensions, 1949–87
(City-block metric)

1949

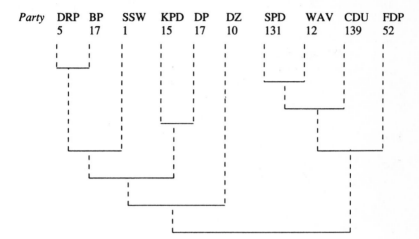

Party	DRP	BP	SSW	KPD	DP	DZ	SPD	WAV	CDU	FDP
	5	17	1	15	17	10	131	12	139	52

Winning MAP   = PD + WAV + CDU
Actual coalition = Adenauer 1: CDU + FDP + DP

1953

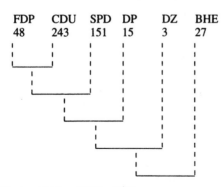

Party	FDP	CDU	SPD	DP	DZ	BHE
Seats	48	243	151	15	3	27

Winning MAP + CDU + FDP
Actual coalition = Adenauer 2a: CDU + FDP + DP + BHE
　　　　　　　　　　Adenauer 2b: CDU + FDP + DP
　　　　　　　　　　Adenauer 2c: CDU + DP
　　　　　　　　　　Adenauer 2d: CDU + DP + DA/FVP

1957

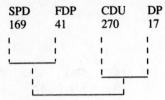

Winning MAP   = CDU
Actual coalition = Adenauer 3a: CDU + DP
                   Adenauer 3b: CDU

1961

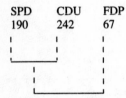

Winning MAP   = CDU + SPD
Actual coalition = Adenauer 4a: CDU + FDP
                   Adenauer 4b: CDU
                   Adenauer 4b: CDU + FDP
                   Erhard I: CDU + FDP

1965

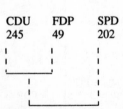

Winning MAP   = CDU + FDP
Actual coalition = Erhard 2a: CDU + FDP
                   Erhard 2b: CDU
                   Kiesinger: CDU + SPD

1969

Party
Seats

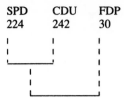

Winning MAP   = SPD + CDU
Actual coalition = Brandt 1: SPD + FDP

1972

Party
Seats

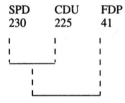

Winning MAP   = SPD + CDU
Actual coalition = Brandt 2: SPD + FDP
                   Schmidt 1: SPD + FDP

1976

Party
Seats

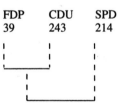

Winning MAP   = CDU + FDP
Actual coalition = Schmidt 2: SPD + FDP

1980

Party   SPD   FDP   CDU
Seats   218   53   226

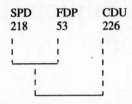

Winning Map   = SPD + FDP
Actual coalition = Schmidt 3a: SPD + FDP
                     Schmidt 3b: SPD
                     Kohl 1: CDU + FDP

1983

Party   SPD   FDP   GRU   CDU
Seats   193   34   27   244

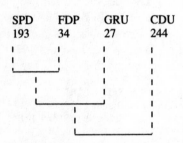

Winning MAP   = SPD + FDP + Greens
Actual Coalition = Kohl 2: CDU + FDP

1987

Party   SPD   CDU   GRU   FDP
Seats   186   223   42   46

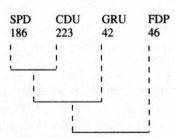

Winning MAP   = CDU + SPD
Actual coalition = Kohl 3: CDU + FDP

8 Party and Coalition in Luxembourg
Derek John Hearl

Luxembourg has, for many years, had a very stable pattern of coalition government dominated by coalitions between the Chrestlech–Sozial Vollekspartei (CSV) and either the Letzeburger Sozialistech Arbechter Partei (LSAP) or the (Liberal) Demokratesch Partei (DP). Indeed, the CSV has led almost every cabinet since the Second World War, alternation being confined to its more or less regular switching between the LSAP and the DP. The two exceptions to this rule of CSV-led two-party governments were the Dupong Government of National Union in which all three traditional parties together with the Communists took part during the immediate post-war year, and Gaston Thorn's Government of 1974–79, the only one since the First World War to have excluded the CSV. In this respect, the CSV must clearly qualify as the predominant party in the system.

Procedures for government formation in Luxembourg are similar both in theory and in practice to those in Belgium although there are a number of minor differences. The two most important are, firstly, that the institution of *informateur* arrived rather late in the Grand duchy, being first employed at the time of the formation of the Thorn Government in 1974. This is a consequence of the rise of the DP to major party status and the associated increase in coalition possibilities following each election. In this changed situation the appointment of a *formateur* at the beginning of the government formation process, as was the previous practice, might well give the party concerned a marked advantage in the subsequent inter-party bargaining, bringing the Grand Duke into direct political controversy. The appointment of an *informateur* is designed to obviate this danger.

A second important difference between practice in Luxembourg and Belgium concerns the requirement that any inter-party agreement be ratified by the appropriate party organs. This was dramatically illustrated in 1969 for example, when a specially convened LSAP party congress refused to ratify the coalition deal its own leaders had drawn up with the CSV. The CSV then turned to the DP and the Werner-Schaus II Government was formed as a result.

THE ROLE OF POLICY IN COALITION BARGAINING

As our previous analysis (Hearl, 1987) showed, party policy as expressed in election programmes, plays a central part in Luxembourg politics. Parties take their electoral promises very seriously and these are widely disseminated to the public at election time. Luxembourg has no tradition of pre-electoral pacts or agreements, and even outgoing government parties seek to emphasise their own record and that of their ministers rather than that of the government as a whole. Each party fights each election entirely independently, promising to get as much of its programme as possible implemented by any government in which it might subsequently hold office.

In a country as small as Luxembourg, where virtually every member of the political elite knows every other member personally, individuals and inter-personal relationships probably count for more than might be the case in larger, more anonymous systems. This might on the face of it appear to undermine the role of programmatic differences between parties during coalition bargaining. Nevertheless, policy differences do remain important, as do what we have termed 'instrumental' office-seeking, whereby particular parties value particular ministries which control policy areas of importance to them. There is a wealth of evidence for this latter point. The CSV has virtually monopolised portfolios having responsibility for agriculture, economics, family affairs and church–state relations; the Socialist LSAP, when in government, has almost always held the social services and labour relations portfolios; the DP has usually successfully bid for the education, middle classes and interior portfolios. On the other hand, the foreign affairs portfolio, presumably because it is seen as number two in the cabinet pecking order, seems in recent years to have become the prerogative of the junior partner in government, whichever party that might happen to be.

Very little has been written about the actual coalition negotiation process in Luxembourg. This seems to involve four basic stages. First, following the declaration of the results of the general election, the parties which are to negotiate with one another must be identified. Formally, this is the task of the Grand Duke himself although in practice he acts through an *informateur* and/or *formateur*. The actual choice of negotiating partners is heavily influenced by the election result, a point to which we return later.

Second, formal negotiations take place. These are generally completed very quickly, often in less than a week, and seem on the face of it to deal first with policy and then only secondly with the distribution of portfolios. However, in view of the fact that negotiating teams are rather small, perhaps less than a dozen participants altogether, it is almost inconceivable that there is not at least a measure of informal blurring of this distinction, leading to direct trade-offs between the 'payoffs' of portfolios and policy. It is very rare for formal negotiations to break down. Even when coalition formation was derailed in 1969, a deal between the leadership of both the CSV and LSAP had been successfully struck, prior to its repudiation by the LSAP congress.

Third, following a successful outcome to negotiations and the *formateur*'s formal report on these to the Grand Duke, the outcome (in the form of a policy statement and list of proposed ministerial posts) is presented for ratification to the constitutional organs of the parties involved. In the case of the CSV and LSAP this is a special meeting of the full Party Congress, but the DP has sometimes used its National Council instead. Although outright rejection of a package is rare, the rejection of a fully agreed coalition deal at the LSAP's 1969 Special Congress underlines that the procedure is by no means a formality for any party. (As we have seen, a quite different coalition formed as a result of this procedure.) Clearly, this provision is of considerable importance during the coalition negotiations, since party negotiators must always anticipate the likely reactions of their rank-and-file members and activists.

Finally comes the investiture stage. The new Ministers receive their formal appointment from the Grand Duke and then to seek the approval of the Chamber vun Deputeirten on the basis of a Government Declaration.

STRUCTURAL INFLUENCES AND CONSTRAINTS ON COALITION BARGAINING

Exogenous constraints

Generally speaking, Luxembourg is not a country in which there are external constraints on the party composition of governments. The only potential exception is purely speculative; it relates to the possibility that, during the cold war period, the country might have been effectively prevented by its NATO allies from having Communist ministers in the government. Certainly, the Kommunistesch Partei vu Letzeburg (KPL) was for a long time Western Europe's most pro-Soviet Communist Party and its participation in the government of a NATO Member State would certainly have met with considerable external opposition from the rest of the Western Bloc. However, since election results in Luxembourg left the KPL peripheral to government formation, the question is academic.

Endogenous constraints

Not only was the KPL the most pro-Soviet Communist party in Western Europe, but it remained overtly Stalinist well into the 1970s. As an explicitly 'anti-system' party, there is little possibility that any of the three other main parties in Luxembourg would have seriously considered going into coalition with the KPL at any time after the immediate post-war period.

Structural influences

The relatively recent procedural innovation of *informateur* lessens the Grand Duke's role in specifying the party leader who is to spearhead the coalition formation process. This provides an incentive for informal bargaining between the various parties before to the actual appointment of a *formateur*.

The necessity for any coalition agreement to receive formal approval from each party's formal decision making structure is a very good example of an endogenously imposed structural feature. Given the general pattern for the rank-and-file members of political parties to be more concerned with policy than with office benefits (they are not, after all, the ones who get into office) this feature ought to have the effect of making Luxembourg a more policy-oriented system.

The influences and constraints mentioned above are listed in Table 8.1.

DIMENSIONS OF PARTY COMPETITION

As has already been pointed out, the received wisdom about Luxembourg politics is that, with the exception of the Communists, political parties are not very far apart ideologically. This impression was confirmed by our

Table 8.1   Constraints and influences on coalition bargaining in Luxembourg

1. Refusal of three principal parties to consider coalitions with Communists or other minor parties.
2. Expectation that electoral gains and losses for parties in outgoing government will be reflected in government formation process.
3. Introduction of *informateur* has lessened Grand Duke's role in specifying the nucleus of the coalition formation process. This has led to more 'free-style' bargaining.
4. Necessity for coalition agreement to receive approval of representative party bodies.

earlier manifesto analyses, in which the Grand Duchy was one of the few developed countries which did not exhibit a classic left–right socio-economic dimension (Hearl, 1987). Rather, a two-dimensional picture emerged. The first dimension contrasted the isolationism typical of the Luxembourg Communist party with a concern for 'new' issues such as technology, the environment, culture and decentralisation. The second dimension was concerned with the valence issues of social justice, freedom and democracy.

Table 8.2 shows the positions of the main parties in Luxembourg after each election during the study period on the common left–right dimension used throughout this book. They also show the scores of each of the governments formed. Unfortunately, no Communist manifesto be traced for 1945 or for the Demokratesch Partei's predecessor the Groupement Democratique for either 1945 or 1948. This means that the analysis has really to be confined to the period from 1951 onwards.

The rankings of the parties generated by the common left–right scale do not always conform to the received wisdom about Luxembourg, at least as far as this is captured by previous studies based on expert judgements. Both Dodd (1976) and Morgan (1976) place the DP to the right of the CSV in their tests of coalition theories. However, Inglehart and Klingemann (1976),

Table 8.2 Party and government scores on standard left–right dimension, Luxembourg

Year	Left–Right Score				
	KPL	LSAP	CSV	DP	Government
1945	n/a	*–44*	27	n/a	14
1945	n/a	–44	27	*n/a*	48
1948	–38	–24	*–17*	*n/a*	–16
1951	–38	– 4	– 1	– 3*	–28
1954	–44	*–47*	11	–13*	– 2
1959	–35	–41	9	– 8*	– 5
1964	–13	–40	–22*	– 9	–23
1964	–13	–40	–22*	– 9	4
1968	–40	–31	–20	– 7*	–21
1974	–46	*–45*	–20	–24*	–14
1979	–74	–28	–10	–16*	2
1984					–14

Government parties italicised.
* Median party.

analysing the ideological self-placement of party voters, place the CSV to the right of the DP, the ranking typically generated by our manifesto analyses. Laver and Hunt (1991), in a comparative analysis using a large number of expert judgements, provide data which suggests the source of this ambiguity. On general economic strategy (dealing with policies on matters such as public spending, taxation and public ownership) the CSV is placed to the left of the DP. On social affairs (dealing with policies on church–state relations, divorce and homosexuality), the CSV is placed markedly to the right of the DP. The standard left–right scale, which combines both aspects of policy, may thus be muddying the water on these matters.

Further evidence that our left–right scale does not apply to the Luxembourg case as well as to some others follow from the fact that party positions on this scale are rather more unstable than those generated in earlier, country-specific factor analyses (Hearl 1987). Notwithstanding these potential problems, our standard scale does go quite a long way towards helping us to interpret government formation in Luxembourg, while its face validity finds some support in other empirical work.

THE DOCUMENTS CODED

As has already been pointed out, Luxembourg Prime Ministers go before the Chamber vun Deputeirten as soon as possible following their appointment to make a *declaration gouvernementale* setting out the new Government's policy. This Declaration is always read out by the Prime Minister in the form of a speech and, as such, is recorded in the *compte rendu* (that is, the Chamber's verbatim record). The text is also always separately printed and circulated to Deputies, before it is debated. Following this debate, the Declaration is voted on (and invariably approved) as a result of which the new Government is considered as having received the Chamber's confidence and henceforth as legitimately able to govern.

Coding was straightforward. As in the Belgian case, Prime Minister – particularly in recent years – sometimes devoted two or three paragraphs to the history of the government formation itself and these sentences have generally been treated as uncoded. Mostly, however, the various manifesto coding conventions could be applied with no more difficulty than they had been to the election programmes themselves. (Incidentally, unlike the manifestos which were almost all in German, the government declarations are exclusively in French with the exception of the one made by Jacques Santer in 1984, in which the final six paragraphs are in Luxembourgish.)

The documents, although short compared to the manifestos, are rather longer on average than their Belgian counterparts. In common with the manifestos, they have been getting steadily longer over time. The shortest is that of the Dupong I Government in 1947; the longest that of the Santer-Poos Government in July 1984.

ONE DIMENSIONAL ANALYSIS OF COALITION FORMATION AND PAYOFFS

Government formation

Table 8.2 indicated the party controlling the median legislator on the left–right dimension after each election in the study period. This was rarely the CSV, contrary to the received wisdom. In fact it was the CSV only in 1964 and 1967, and the DP in all other cases after 1948, barring one occasion, 1954, when technically both parties contained a median legislator since the CSV held exactly half the seats. In this case, given the CSV's position, we have designated this as the party with the median legislator.

It will be seen from Table 8.2 that the party with the median legislator was a member of the government in seven of the eight applicable cases. The success of the 'median legislator' hypothesis is secured because the DP gets into office whenever it controls the median (except in 1951). When the DP does not control the median, then it does not get into office, and a centre left coalition forms instead. We can also see from Table 8.2 that, on the only occasion when the CSV was forced from office, it was not the median party. In other words, Table 8.2 paints a picture of a numerically predominant party, the CSV, being a more or less permanent fixture in government, though needing a coalition partner because it does not control the median legislator. When the DP is at the median, the CSV must take it into coalition. When the DP is not at the median, the CSV takes the chance to alternate partners and brings in the LSAP. Note that the predominant status of the CSV is not explained by Table 8.2, and must be taken as exogenous. Given this, Table 8.2 provides some intriguing insights into its choice of partners.

Policy payoffs and government policy

Table 8.2 gives the policy positions of each government on the left–right dimension, and Table 8.3 gives the 'policy payoff' to each party, operationalised as the distance between party and government policy. These show that government policy in Luxembourg follows quite closely the policies of the two parties which between them always control the median legislator and that government policy tracks CSV policy particularly closely, and does so even on the single occasion when the CSV was out of office. As Table 8.3 shows, when it was forced out of office in 1974, the CSV did better, in policy terms, than either of the government parties.

This relationship is summarised in Figure 8.1, which plots CSV policy against government policy and fits a regression line. It seems to be reasonably easy to predict government policy from CSV policy, though it would be dangerous to concluded from this that the CSV always calls the shots in Luxembourg. This is because both the CSV and the DP did much better than the other main parties over the post-war period taken as a whole, while their policies tracked one another reasonably closely also. There are insufficient observations to allow us to disentangle the interdependent policy effects of these two parties. The broad pattern, however, is quite clear. Note that the LSAP never controlled the median legislator, and that it did far less well in terms of government policies on the left–right dimension than parties that did control the median legislator. Thus policy payoffs on the left–right dimension are clearly related to the relative policy positions of the various parties.

Table 8.3   One-dimensional distances between party and government, Luxembourg

Year	Left–right score			
	KPL	LSAP	CSV	DP
1945	n/a	*58*	*14*	n/a
1945	n/a	92	*21*	*n/a*
1948	16	8	*1*	*n/a*
1951	28	24	27	26
1954	36	*45*	13	11
1959	33	36	13	*3*
1964	21	*17*	*1*	14
1964	39	*44*	26	13
1968	8	10	*1*	*13*
1974	1	*31*	6	*10*
1979	41	30	*12*	*18*
Mean all cases	25	36	12	13
Mean in government		36	13	11
Mean out of government	25	35	6	16

Parties in government italicised.

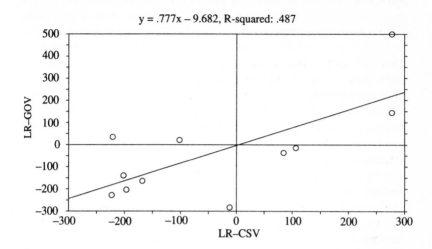

Figure 8.1   Government and CSV policy, Luxembourg, 1945–80

Table 8.3 also compares the policy payoff to each party when it is in government with policy payoffs when it is out of office and the patterns here are far less clear-cut. Government membership in itself makes little difference to policy payoffs in Luxembourg. We have already seen that the CSV did very well even when out of office. This pattern extends to the other parties. The LSAP does equally badly when in government as when out, reflecting the fact that coalitions that include the LSAP, the main socialist party, simply do not adopt more left wing policy positions than coalitions that exclude it. At the other end of the scale, there is very little difference between coalitions that include the DP and coalitions that exclude it.

Overall, then, we can conclude that control of the median legislator appears to be a major factor in getting into office in the first place – almost never are parties that control the median legislator excluded from government in Luxembourg – but that this power does not translate into an ability to shift the direction of government policy. If anything to do with party policy affects government policy in Luxembourg, it seems to be a general shift in the policy constellation of the party system taken as a whole, rather than a change in the party composition of the government.

TWENTY-DIMENSIONAL ANALYSIS

Government formation

Figure F.1 in the appendix to this chapter shows both the inter-party city-block policy distances and the results of the standard cluster analysis based upon these distances. As the figure shows, the choice of clustering algorithm makes very little difference to the results, though we feel that non-hierarchical models are more appropriate on *a priori* theoretical grounds in a small party system in which governments tend to comprise two out of three main parties.

Five of the eight coalition governments that were formed between 1951 and 1979 are correctly predicted by the analysis, leaving three (1953, 1974 and 1979) that were not. The cluster models predict a continuation of the outgoing CSV–DP coalition in 1974 but it was in that year that the CSV was ousted from office by the Thorn Government formed by the DP and the LSAP. Nothing in the policies of the parties indicated this change. While the CSV suffered disastrous electoral losses, it could in theory have continued with the incumbent government. In 1979, in contrast, the 20-dimensional policy analysis suggests a continuation of the outgoing Thorn Government. Formally, this government had lost its majority but, given the very distant location of the KPL, the LSAP–DP coalition appears to remain policy viable. Nonetheless, it fell, and was replaced with a CSV–DP coalition.

Policy payoffs

Table 8.4 shows the 20-dimensional city-block distances between each party's manifesto position and that of each government policy statement, listed in ascending order, so that those whose payoffs are greater appear first. Again, since early Communist and DP Manifestos are missing, the evaluation begins in 1951.

The results closely parallel the one-dimensional analysis in that government membership seems to have little effect on policy payoffs. Typically, the CSV does best, even on the one occasion when it was out of office. When it does not, then the DP tends to do best, even when it is out of office, and both of these parties do significantly better than the LSAP. Even when the LSAP is in office, it does not do any better than when it is out. All in all, government membership in Luxembourg has little impact on policy payoffs, which seem to be more related to the overall policy constellation of the system.

Table 8.4 Twenty-dimensional city-block policy distances between party manifestos and government statements in Luxembourg

Government	Composition		20-dimensional city-block	Rank order of government parties in terms of distance to government position (1 = closest)
1	All Party	*CSV*	54.60	Not relevant
		LSAP	84.66	
2	CSV + DP	*CSV*	74.53	1
		LSAP	92.24	
3	CSV + DP	*CSV*	63.51	1
		KPL	105.73	
		LSAP	133.99	
4	CSV + LSAP	DP	55.74	3, 4
		KPL	63.51	
		CSV	71.53	
		LSAP	79.84	
5	CSV + LSAP	*CSV*	78.34	1, 2
		LSAP	83.97	
		DP	85.26	
		KP	11.10	
6	CSV + DP	*CSV*	42.91	1, 2
		DP	66.01	
		LSAP	92.38	
		KPL	111.02	
7	CSV + LSAP	DP	31.89	2, 3
		LSAP	36.53	
		CSV	40.86	
		KPL	37.57	
8	CSV + LSAP	DP	44.42	2, 3
		CSV	69.27	
		LSAP	69.54	
		KPL	87.90	
9	CSV + DP	LSAP	58.52	3, 4
		KPL	65.11	
		CSV	69.97	
		DP	76.19	
10	DP + LSAP	CSV	59.79	2, 3
		DP	66.28	
		LSAP	85.75	
		KPL	116.88	
11	CSV + DP	*CSV*	43.09	1, 2
		DP	44.22	
		LSAP	61.64	
		KPL	164.41	
12	CSV + LSAP	*CSV*	NA	NA
		LSAP	NA	
		DP	NA	
		KPL	NA	

Note: Government parties are italicised.

DISAGGREGATED 20-DIMENSIONAL ANALYSIS

Table 8.5 identifies the party with the median legislator on each of the twenty main policy dimensions taken one at a time. If we define as 'predominant' whichever party has the median legislator on most dimensions following each election, we find that the predominant party is a member of every post-war government.

The predominant party in these terms is nearly always the CSV, a position in which it was especially secure in 1951, 1959, and 1967. The DP had a much stronger position in 1968 and 1974. In 1974, both DP and LSAP controlled more policy dimensions than the CSV, and did succeed in keeping it out of office. In the later part of the period, furthermore, Table 8.6 does help us to identify the CSV's coalition partners. In the years when the DP controlled the median legislator on more policy dimensions than the LSAP – in 1959, 1968 and 1979, for example – the DP went into government. When the LSAP controlled more dimensions – in 1964, for example – then the LSAP went into government. Note that this multi-dimensional analysis provides a rationale for CSV–LSAP coalitions, since the LSAP does often occupy a key position on particular policy dimensions that might be important in coalition bargaining. (In contrast, the one-dimensional analysis makes it much harder to explain the role of the LSAP, since it is never pivotal on the main left–right dimension.)

Overall, the disaggregated twenty-dimensional analysis clearly adds something to our understanding of the politics of coalition in Luxembourg. As well as providing an interpretation of the role of the LSAP, the manifesto positions of the various parties highlight the central role of the CSV. The role of the CSV certainly appears to be important in practice, given the more or less permanent position of the party in government. It will be remembered that, in the one-dimensional analysis, this central role had to be assumed, but could not be inferred from the policy data. The twenty-dimensional analysis shows that the CSV was pivotal on a wide range of policy dimensions throughout the period, and thereby explains its predominant position. All of this is further evidence in favour of the argument that a single left-right dimension does not capture the full richness of policy bargaining in Luxembourg.

CONCLUSIONS

Table 8.6 summarises the results of the policy-based analyses of coalition bargaining in Luxembourg, indicating how each of four particular theories performs in each of the eight government formation situations in which it is

Table 8.5 Parties with the median legislator over 20 dimensions, Luxembourg

	1951	1954	1959	1964	1968	1974	1979
1. State intervention	CSV	—	CSV	LSAP	LSAP	CSV	DP
2. Quality of life	DP	—	CSV	LSAP	DP	CSV	CSV
3. Peace and co-operation	DP	CSV	CSV	CSV	DP	LSAP	DP
4. Anti-establishment	—	—	CSV/LSAP	—	—	LSAP	CSV
5. Capitalist economics	CSV	LSAP	DP	CSV	DP	DP	DP
6. Social conservatism	CSV	KPL	DP	KPL	DP	LSAP	DP
7. Productivity	DP	—	DP	CSV	DP	LSAP	LSAP
8. Military: positive	—	—	LSAP	CSV	—	—	—
9. EEC: positive	—	—	CSV	LSAP	DP	DP	CSV
10. Internationalism: negative	—	—	—	—	—	DP	—
11. Freedom and human rights	CSV	CSV	DP	LSAP	CSV	DP	CSV
12. Democracy	CSV	DP	LSAP	CSV	DP	DP	CSV
13. Decentralisation: positive	—	—	LSAP	CSV	DP	DP	DP
14. Government efficiency	—	—	CSV	LSAP	—	LSAP	DP
15. Social justice	CSV	DP	DP	CSV	LSAP	DP	CSV
16. Social services: positive	LSAP	CSV	CSV	CSV	DP	CSV	DP
17. Education: positive	—	—	CSV	CSV	LSAP	LSAP	CSV
18. Labour: positive	LSAP	DP	CSV	DP	DP	DP	LSAP
19. Agriculture and farmers	CSV	CSV	DP	DP	LSAP	CSV	CSV
20. Underprivileged minorities	LSAP	—	CSV	CSV	CSV	DP	LSAP
CSV	7	4	10	10	2	4	8
LSAP	3	1	4	5	4	6	3
DP	3	3	6	2	10	8	7
KPL	—	1	—	1	—	—	—

Table 8.6 Success rates of policy-based coalition theories in Luxembourg

	1951	1954	1959	1964	1967	1969	1974	1979	Predictive success	efficiency
No. of Parties	4	4	4	4	4	4	5	6		
No. of possible coalitions	15	15	15	15	15	15	15	15		
No. of feasible coalitions (given constraints)	4	3	4	3	3	4	4	4		
Accuracy of Prediction										
Theory A	Yes	No	Yes	Yes	Yes	Yes	No	No	.62 (5/8)	.62 (5/8)
Theory B	Yes	Yes	Yes	Yes	Yes	Yes	Yes	Yes	1.00 (8/8)	.33 (8/24)
Theory C	Yes	No	Yes	No	No	No	No	No	.25 (2/8)	.25 (2/8)
Theory D	No	No	Yes	Yes	Yes	Yes	Yes	Yes	.75 (6/8)	.50 (6/12)

Theory A: Coalition will be at first majority node on cluster tree and policy-viable on at least one dimension.
Theory B: Coalition will contain predominant party over disaggregated 20 dimensions.
Theory C: Coalition will consist of predominant party plus next closest party (City Block).
Theory D: Coalition will consist of adjacent parties on single dimension.

possible to make an assessment. Insofar as the twenty-dimensional analyses are concerned, the cluster analysis (Theory A) as we have seen earlier, certainly does have considerable success as does the one-dimensional Theory D (that governments will consist of parties that are, in policy terms, adjacent on the dimension). Theory C, (that the coalition will consist of the predominant party plus the one with the closest city block distance from it) is least successful; and Theory B (that the coalition will include the predominant party) most successful with all its characterisations correct. Models A and C generate unique predictions so their predictive efficiency is also high. The two most successful models form the point of view of postdiction (B and D) on the other hand generate wider and looser expectations about possible governments, so their efficiency is lower.

Overall, the policy based analyses do better in Luxembourg that might be expected from the apparent inapplicability of the common left–right scale. Even the one dimensional analysis, however, does add quite a bit to our ability to interpret the politics of coalition in Luxembourg. Coalitions almost invariably include the party controlling the median legislator. While the pivotal position of the CSV must be assumed, the one-dimensional analysis does offer an explanation of the CSV's choice of coalition partner. The disaggregated twenty-dimensional analysis goes beyond this, however, to provide an empirical interpretation of the key role of the CSV, as well as its choice of partners. Combining this with the fact that all three pairings of the three main parties have gone into government, we have clear evidence that it takes at least two dimensions to capture the salient features of coalition bargaining in Luxembourg.

APPENDIX F

Table F.1　Results of Luxembourg legislative elections, 1945–84

Date of Election	Seats won (and estimated percentage vote)[1]					
	CSV	LSAP	DP[2]	KPL	SDP	OTHERS
21 October 1945	25 (44.7)	11 (23.3)	9[2] (18.0)	5 (11.0)	—	1[3] (2.9)
(South and East) 6 June 1948 (centre and North)	9	10	3[2]	4		
3 June 1954	12 (39.4)	9 (35.7)	5[2] (16.4)	— (8.5)		
20 May 1954	26 (47.9)	17 (30.3)	6[2] (13.0)	3 (7.7)		
1 February 1959	21 (38.9)	17 (33.1)	11 (20.3)	3 (7.2)		
7 June 1964	23 (35.7)	21 (35.9)	6 (12.2)	5 (10.4)		
15 December 1968	21 (37.5)	18 (31.0)	11 (18.0)	6 (13.1)		
26 May 1974	18 (29.9)	17 (27.0)	14 (23.3)	5 (8.8)	5 (10.0)	
10 June 1979	24 (37.4)	14 (20.4)	15 (22.5)	2 (5.0)	2 (6.6)	2[4] (8.2)
17 June 1984	25 (36.6)	21 (31.8)	14 (20.4)	—	—	2[5] (4.2)

[1] Percentages are of 'adjusted national vote' which is calculated by dividing total vote for the candidates of each party in each constituency by the mean number of votes cast by each elector in that constituency; the resulting quotients are then summed nationally.

[2] 1945, 1948 and 1951: Groupement Patriotique et democratique; 1954: Groupement democratique; thereafter Demokratesch Partei.

[3] Parti des Independants de l'Est.

[4] 1979: One seat won by 'Enroles de force' and one by Independent Socialist.

[5] 1984: Two seats won by 'Di Greng Alternativ'.

Table F.2   List of Luxembourg governments, 1945–81

Government and Date of Declaration			Composition
1	Dupong (National Union)	20 November 1945	C S L K
2	Dupong I	5 March 1947	C L
3	Dupong II	21 July 1948	C L
4	Dupong III	11 July 1951	C S
5	Bech/Frieden	7 July 1954	C S
6	Werner–Schaus I	10 March 1959	C L
7	Werner–Cravatte I	22 July 1964	C S
8	Werner–Cravatte II	22 July 1967	C S
9	Werner–Schaus II	11 February 1969	C L
10	Thorn	4 July 1974	S L
11	Werner–Flesch	24 July 1979	C L
12	Santer–Poos	23 July 1984	C S

Key:

C = CSV; S = LSAP; L = DP; K = KPL

Notes:
Frieden replaced Bech as Prime Minister on 29 March 1959, when the LSAP refused to allow the latter to restructure the Government. Frieden made a speech about this to the Chamber but did not make a new Declaration.

Werner–Cravatte II was the outcome of a renegotiation between the two parties comprising the Government which then made a new declaration.

Table F.3   Matrices for cluster diagrams for Luxembourg parties in 20 dimensions, 1951–79 (city-block Metric)

1951				1953			
LSAP	46			LSAP	106		
DP	64	64		DP	83	73	
KPL	83	93	81	KPL	98	72	129
	CSV	LSAP	DP		CSV	LSAP	DP

1959				1964			
LSAP	89			LSAP	44		
DP	57	70		DP	39	43	
KPL	108	119	81	KPL	90	88	77
	CSV	LSAP	DP		CSV	LSAP	DP

1968				1974			
LSAP	76			LSAP	49		
DP	62	60		DP	36	43	
KPL	70	36	70	KPL	90	81	98
	CSV	LSAP	DP		CSV	LSAP	DP

1979			
LSAP	55		
DP	38	33	
KPL	155	158	149
	CSV	LSAP	DP

Figure F.1   Cluster diagrams for Luxembourg, 1951–79

1951

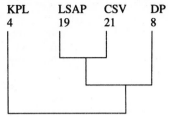

Party   KPL   LSAP   CSV   DP
Seats   4   19   21   8

Winning MAP   = LSAP + CSV
Actual Government = LSAP + CSV (Dupong)

1953

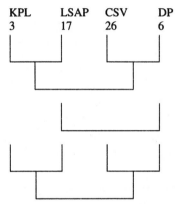

Party   KPL   LSAP   CSV   DP
Seats   3   17   26   6

Winning MAP   = CSV + DP
Actual Coalition = LSAP + CSV (Bech/Frieden)

1959

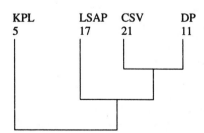

Party   KPL   LSAP   CSV   DP
Seats   5   17   21   11

Winning MAP   = CSV + DP
Actual coalition = CSV + DP (Werner I)

1964

Centroid, Average Linkage

Party	KPL	LSAP	CSV	DP
Seats	5	21	22	6

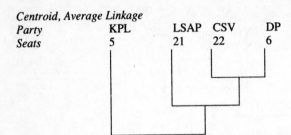

K-Means

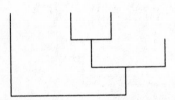

Winning MAP   = LSAP + DP (Centroid, average linkage)
                         LSAP + CSV (K-Means)
Actual coalitions = LSAP + CSV (Werner II)
Actual coalitions = LSAP + CSV (Werner III)

1968

Party	KPL	LSAP	CSV	DP
Seats	6	18	21	11

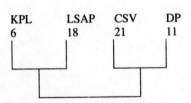

Winning MAP   = CSV + DP
Actual coalition = CSV + DP (Werner IV)

1974

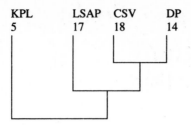

Winning MAP   = CSV + DP
Actual coalition = LSAP + DP (Thorn)

1979

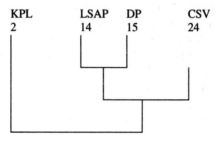

Winning MAP   = LSAP + CSV + DP
Actual coalition = CSV + DP (Werner V)

9 Policy and Coalition in Belgium

Derek John Hearl

Governments in Belgium tend to be short-lived, though government stability has risen significantly since the 1970s. As a consequence, there have been 35 cabinets during the study period, 1945–87 (see Table G.2). All but five of these have been coalitions; twenty–five of them have been formed by various combinations of the 'traditional' Catholic, Socialist and Liberal Parties without the participation of any other party. The most typical combination, accounting for sixteen out of the thirty-five governments, has been a two-party coalition comprising the Catholics (PSC/CVP) and either the Liberal PRL/PVV or the Socialist PS/SP. Government stability was relatively low during the immediate post-war period but rose steadily during the 1950s and 1960s, fell dramatically during the 1970s and is now rising once more. Broadly speaking then, periods of government stability have tended to coincide with periods of coalition between the PSC/CVP and one other traditional party; periods of low stability have coincided with other combinations.

Dramatic changes have taken place in Belgian politics during the post-war period. The most striking of these was the splitting of the three main parties along linguistic lines, coupled with the rise of explicit language parties during the 1960s. This led to an 'explosion' in the party system; in 1946 only four parties were represented in Parliament, by 1978 there were 13. However, the effect of this multiplication of parties on government formation has been limited, for two main reasons. First, the various linguistic 'wings' of the three traditional political 'families' (with one very minor exception in 1974) have always negotiated as undivided units, just as they did prior to their splitting. Second, apart from the immediate post-war years when the Communists were admitted to government and between 1974 and 1980 when the federalist parties sometimes were, there has been a firm consensus among these same three party families that they and only they had a legitimate right to govern. Indeed, some observers subscribe to the view that the traditional party elites never did accept the federalists as legitimate, admitting them to government only to undermine them.

Either way, both coalition bargaining and government participation in Belgium have generally been confined to the three traditional parties and their present-day successors. Consequently, since the same party families have very nearly monopolised Parliament over most of the same period, the single most common pattern has been a coalition of the two parties or families. Twelve post-war governments have been formed (or dominated) by the Catholic and Socialist Parties; nine by Catholics and Liberals and four by the Socialists and Liberals. This pattern, in which any pair of the three parties is a feasible option, may well be declining. It was made possible in the first place by the two-dimensional structure of Belgian politics, dating from the 1920s. Both a left–right and a clerical–anticlerical cleavage were more or less equally salient, giving the two anticlerical parties enough in common with each other to permit them to coalesce against the Catholics. The virtual disappearance of the clerical dimension after 1960 effectively removed this avenue of co-operation; a new policy dimension became salient. The two tripartite governments that included all of the traditional parties were made necessary by the rise of the unitarist–federalist dimension during the 1970s, a rise which threatened all the traditional parties.

PROCEDURES FOR GOVERNMENT FORMATION

In Belgium, procedures for cabinet formation are almost wholly a matter of convention. Nowhere are they laid down in the Constitution which merely states the strictly formal position that 'The King appoints and dismisses his Ministers'. Nevertheless, the conventions are very strong and are always rigidly adhered to. Owing to the increasing complexity of the political situation in recent years, the institution of *informateur* has been borrowed from the Netherlands. Otherwise, procedures have been virtually unchanged since the *de facto* emergence of the office of Prime Minister around the turn of the century.

Following his acceptance of a government's resignation, the King first appoints an *informateur* whose function is merely to hold discussions with all relevant political actors and to report back. Unlike the Dutch case, however, where the informateur is usually a rather independent figure, in Belgium he is invariably a senior politician, albeit one who is unlikely to head the new government. (However, following the 1983 election the Prime Minister in office, Wilfried Martens, was not only appointed a informateur but actually went on to head the subsequent government).

Occasionally, when the political situation following an election is particularly difficult, the King may first appoint a 'negotiator' (*mediateur/underhandelaar*) instead. This was the case, for example, following the

1979 and 1987 elections. Clearly a negotiator has the rather different and more politically sensitive task of actually trying to bring about a measure of inter-party agreement rather than simply reporting on the potential for this. (See De Meyer in Bogdanor, 1986, p.192).

Usually, in the light of the reports of the *informateur* or negotiator the King appoints a *formateur* who is actually charged with the task of forming a government. Technically, there is nothing to prevent a *formateur* from forming a government under someone other than himself but that is very rare. In effect, a Belgian *formateur* is Prime Minister designate and most often forms a government under his own leadership. If he should fall, the King appoints a new *formateur* who tries again. Although this process has taken longer in recent years, Belgian governments are formed in days rather than weeks.

Of course, the formal processes of consultation between the *informateur, formateur* and the various party leaders are only part of the story. Extensive informal negotiations obviously take place between and within parties. Activist influence has become much more important in recent years, a phenomenon which partly explains the difficulty of putting governments together in the first place and of maintaining them in office thereafter. Nowadays, all parties require that any coalition deal be ratified by the party's internal decision making bodies and, although this is largely a rubber-stamping process, it does present a new obstacle for negotiators to surmount. Since party activists tend to be more interested in policy concessions than in the perks of ministerial office, increasingly in recent years leaders have had to take these feelings into account. Whatever leader's personal desire for office, there is no doubt that policy considerations take precedence in providing a basis for coalition formation.

THE DIMENSIONS OF PARTY COMPETITION IN BELGIUM

Of all the countries in this study, we might expect the 'common' left–right dimension to capture rather less of what is going on in Belgium although it is clearly relevant to the class division which forms one basis of coalition politics there. Two other policy dimensions have also clearly been highly salient during the post-war period. The first is a classic 'clerical–anticlerical' dimension which has been long-standing but is now declining. The second, and most striking dimension, is the 'unitarist–federalist' division which came to prominence during the 1960s and 1970s as a preliminary to the standard analysis reported below. Belgian party and government positions on these dimensions were estimated from the programme material in a manner analogous to that used to estimate positions on the common left–right dimension used elsewhere in this volume. In addition, left–right scale positions were re-estimated on a slightly different basis, taking account of the variables used in the specific Belgian dimensions.

What the analysis showed was that relevant two-dimensional representations of Belgian politics changed from one incorporating class and religious dimensions up to and including 1958, to one incorporating class and regional dimensions after that time. Class divisions have thus been a constant of Belgian politics over the whole post-war period, while changes in the second dimension have produced confusion and realignments, particularly in the 1960s and 1970s. For a full representation of Belgian politics clearly two dimensions are preferable, but these results also indicate that our one-dimensional left–right summary may not distort the picture too much and many indeed capture quite accurately some longer-term trends.

Besides the one-dimensional representation we also conducted an analysis of the politics of coalition on the basis of the twenty-dimensional policy spaces used throughout the rest of this book, which mirror some of the regional and religious divisions as well as class ones. This is presented below.

The positions of the Belgian parties on the common left–right dimension are given in Table 9.1 The positions of the 'big three' party families on this dimension are highly interpretable, with the Liberals firmly on the right, the Socialists on the left and the Christian Democrats in the centre. Table 9.1 shows that the two Francophone parties took up stable positions on centre-left after they entered the scene. The Volksunie, in contrast, veered to the left and then to the right, according to our analysis of its manifestos. All in all, therefore, the standard left–right dimension provides an eminently interpretable one-dimensional view of Belgian politics during the study period.

GOVERNMENT POLICY STATEMENTS

Immediately following his formal appointment as the head of an incoming government, the new Prime Minister goes before the two Houses of Parliament in turn to present what has become known as the 'Government Declaration' (Declaration du Gouvernement or Regeringsverklaring). In earlier years this was a fairly general and rather wide-ranging speech setting out the new Government's general policy orientation; nowadays it tends to be longer and more detailed–sometimes, as in 1974, even accompanied by a number of annexes.

Table 9.1 Party and government positions on common left–right dimension, Belgium

Year	Party						
	BSP	PSC	Lib	VoLKS	RW	FDF	Govt
1946	*–13*	30	*15**				4
1946	*–13*	30	*15**				11
1946	*–13*	30	*15**				–15
1946	*–13*	*30*	15*				0
1949	–50	2*	*32*				6
1950	–14	2*	22				3
1950	–14	2*	22				38
1950	–14	2*	22				12
1954	*–31*	4*	*39*				22
1958	–20	*–4**	5				5
1958	–20	*–4**	5				7
1961	*–20*	*–10**	18	1			6
1965	–31	*–4**	8	–2			19
1965	–31	*–4**	*8*	–2			34
1968	*1*	*–13**	28	–25			–26
1971	–22	*–17**	*–3*	–24	–17	3	–17
1971	–22	*–17**	*–3*	–24	–17	*3*	6
1974	–39	*–15**	*14*	–19	*–9*	–12	5
1974	–39	*–15**	*14*	–19	*–9*	–12	6
1974	–39	*–15**	*14*	–19	*–9*	–12	0
1977	–13	*–14**	9	–6	–10	*–1*	0
1977	*–13**	*–14*	9	–6	–10	*–1*	46
1978	*–18**	2	18	*15*	–14	*–1*	56
1979	*–18*	2*	18	15	–14	*–1*	18
1980	*–18*	2*	*18*	15	–14	–1	0
1981	*–18*	2*	*18*	15	–14	–1	5
1981	*–18*	2*	18	15	–14	–1	1
1981	–22	5*	*28*	3	–12	–11	22
1981	–22	5*	*28*	3	–12	–11	12

Median party marked with an asterisk
Parties in government italicised

The full text of each government declaration is reproduced verbatim in the *Annales Parlementaires* or *Parlementaire Handelingen*, which is easily accessible. Thus it is the formal Government Declarations that have been coded as the most authorative statement of government policy. The list of those which have been obtained and coded for Belgium can be found in Table G.2.

While no more difficult than the coding of election programmes, the coding of government declarations did highlight one or two peculiarities which stem from the different nature of the two types of document. First, government declarations often contain some mention of the history of the Government's formation, the election result, the appointment of *informateur* and *formateur*, details of the various inter-party discussions that were held (sometimes including the abortive ones) and so on. Such statements have not been coded although they sometimes constitute a large proportion of the whole document. Second, a Prime Minister often devotes a lot of space to technically complicated proposals, such as tax reforms, which may not be very politically salient or controversial. The reverse effect can also be noticed on occasion. A statement such as 'the Government will fulfil its obligations under the NATO Treaty' (which, translated, means 'will accept Cruise Missiles') is not only more obscure than the equivalent manifesto commitment would have been, but also takes up a much smaller percentage of the total declaration than one might expect such a controversial policy proposal to occupy in an election programme, where it would have to be argued at some length. Thus one explanation for differences between election manifestos and government declarations is thus that, because of the latter's formal and official status, every single statement, however short, constitutes a solid and bankable commitment on behalf of the entire government. Major policy initiatives can sometimes be announced in a single sentence.

STRUCTURAL INFLUENCES AND CONSTRAINTS ON COALITION BARGAINING

Structural influences and constraints on coalition-making in Belgium are best considered in two distinct periods. Table 9.2 is thus divided into two parts; the first from 1946 to 1960, and the second from 1960 to 1980.

During the 1946–60 period we identify one full scale 'constraint', on the range of coalitions that can form, together with two important structural 'influences'. The first constraint has to do with the exclusion of particular parties. The exclusion of the Communist Party as a coalition partner needs some qualification since, like many of its sister parties in newly-liberated Europe, it was a member of the first three post-liberation governments. Following the 1946 election, however, at the start of the Cold War period, the party went into a political exile from which it was never to re-emerge. Indeed, its long period of electoral decline which began in 1946 culminated in 1985 when it lost its remaining seats in Parliament. Much less equivocal

Table 9.2   Constraints and influences on coalition bargaining in Belgium

---

First period (1946–60)

1.   Refusal of three traditional parties to consider coalitions with Federalist or Communist parties.
2.   Two-thirds majority needed for Constitutional Amendment.
3.   Doctrine of collective cabinet responsibility forces coalition partners defeated in cabinet decisions to defend coalition policy or leave government.

Second Period (1960–88)

1.   Constitutional requirement for linguistic parity among Ministers means that parties from both Communities must be included in all governments.
2.   Two-thirds majority needed for Constitutional Amendent.
3.   Since 1980, perceived need for Regional/Community Councils to have same political majority as national government.
4.   Necessity for coalition agreement to receive approval of representative party bodies.
5.   Doctrine of collective cabinet responsibility forces coalition partners defeated in cabinet decisions to defend coalition policy or leave government.

---

is the classification of the various federalist parties as having 'pariah' status. Indeed, until the advent of the first Tindemans Government in 1974, none of these parties was considered by any of its traditional rivals as being in any way fit to govern. The federalists were widely seen by the political establishment of the day not only as being anti-system but, in some quarters at least, as being downright anti-patriotic as well.

Among structural influences on coalition formation during this period is the doctrine of collective cabinet responsibility, as important in Belgium as it is in almost all other West European parliamentary systems. Parties defeated in cabinet must nonetheless defend policy decisions in public. This should encourage coalitions between parties that are closer together on policy.

Another major structural influence concerns the procedure for amending the Belgian constitution. Amendments require the assent of two-thirds of the members of both Houses of Parliament. The fact that so much of the country's politics has been dominated by constitutional issues has ensured that parties and governments have frequently pledged constitutional reform of various kinds. Consequently, they have from time to time effectively needed a two-thirds majority in parliament when forming coalitions. Even when government parties have not sought to control a two-thirds majority themselves, the need for government policy to be acceptable to parties outside the government has sometimes been very evident.

The lower half of Table 9.2 relates to the second post-war period after 1960. The list of influences and constraints differs from that in the first period. Perhaps the most important difference is that the constraint preventing the admission of the federalist parties to government disappeared during the second period. It is difficult to know precisely when the various traditional parties began to drop their opposition to the federalists but this must clearly have been before 1974, the first year in which any was admitted to a Belgian Cabinet.

Second, we note the emergence of a more rigid requirement that coalition negotiators seek the approval of their own party organisation before any deal can take effect. This became much less of the formality it had been in the previous period–particularly (but not only) among the traditional parties. It remains true that no party has yet repudiated a coalition agreement struck by its leaders, but there have been one or two close votes in party congresses in recent years. There can be little doubt that the need to keep an eye on party supporters and activists is nowadays of considerable significance and that the details of some coalition negotiations have been materially affected.

Conditions governing coalition making have also been influenced by constitutional changes. The first of these was the formal insertion into the constitution of the already well-established convention that governments must contain equal numbers of French and Flemish-speaking ministers. This is one of the clearest examples in Western Europe, of a rigid and explicit side constraint on possible conditions. It means, of course, that the inclusion of one of the language parties in a coalition must be balanced by appropriate ministerial appointments among the others. This, presumably, makes the inclusion of single language parties more disruptive. Now that the various parties have divided along language lines, however, it is probably this provision as much as any other factor which accounts for the continued strength of 'family' ties between parties across the linguistic divide. If parties must give an equal number of cabinet posts to others from across the language frontier, they will presumably prefer to cede these to their natural allies.

The long-term significance of one other recent constitutional change is more difficult to assess, precisely because it is so recent. It has certainly been important in the short-term, however. Following the start of the definitive phase of the Constitutional Revision of August 1980, Belgium has a system of devolved government in which Flemish, Francophone and Walloon Councils have their own 'Executives' responsible to the local political majorities on these Councils. So far, Belgian parties have refused to allow coalition building at community and regional levels to take place independently of coalition building at national level; this ensures that the same coalitions are formed at all levels. It follows from this that certain combinations which might be viable at one level are precluded because they are not viable at another.

COALITION BARGAINING ON THE COMMON LEFT–RIGHT DIMENSION

Government formation

As well as showing the positions of the parties, Table 9.1 also shows the position of each post-war government declaration on the common left–dimension, and identifies government members and the party controlling the median legislator. The party controlling the median legislator was in virtually every post-war Belgian government. This party was usually the PSC–CVP. Even when the PSC–CVP was not the median party, however, the party that did control the median legislator was nearly always in government. However, Table 9.1 does not help us to identify the other partners in the coalition. It is by no means inevitable that coalitions consist of the pivotal (median) party and its closest ideological neighbour (See Table 9.7 below).

Once the federalist parties had established themselves, we see that coalitions did not tend to be connected on the left–right dimension. Often, one of the main parties was left out in favour of a federalist party that was further away on the left–right scale. Obviously, the inclusion of such parties in government had little to do with their positions on the left–right dimension.

Overall, the dominance of the PSC–CVP–nearly always in control of the median legislator and nearly always in government is the most striking feature of the standard one-dimensional analysis.

Government policy

We now turn to the relationship between government and party policy. Table 9.1 also shows the positions of Belgian governments on the left–right scale. It can easily be seen that these positions veer around quite wildly, with little apparent logic. Even when two governments form one after the other with the same members, government policy is liable to change quite sharply. Changes in coalition members, furthermore, can be 'perverse' in the sense of moving away from rather than towards the policies of parties joining the coalition. This means that policy payoffs, operationalised as the distance between coalition and party policy and reported in Table 9.3, do not respond in any systematic manner to government membership. All in all, Tables 9.1 and 9.3 suggest strongly that factors other than party policy on the left–right dimension determine the content of Belgian government policy declarations.

Table 9.3　One-dimensional differences between party and government policy, Belgium

Year	Party					
	BSP	PSC	Lib	VoLKS	RW	FDF
1946	*17*	26	11			
1946	*24*	19	*4*			
1946	*2*	45	*30*			
1946	*13*	30	15			
1949	56	*4*	26			
1950	17	*1*	19			
1950	52	*36*	16			
1950	26	*10*	10			
1954	*53*	17	*17*			
1958	25	9	0			
1958	27	*11*	2			
1961	26	*16*	12	5		
1965	*50*	23	10	20		
1965	65	*38*	26	36		
1968	26	*13*	53	0		
1971	*5*	*0*	14	7	0	20
1971	*28*	*23*	9	30	23	*3*
1974	44	*20*	8	24	14	17
1974	45	*20*	8	24	*15*	17
1974	39	*15*	14	19	*9*	12
1977	13	*14*	9	*6*	10	1
1977	59	*60*	37	*52*	55	47
1978	73	*54*	38	*41*	70	*57*
1979	*36*	*17*	1	3	33	20
1980	*18*	*2*	18	15	14	1
1981	22	*3*	*13*	11	19	6
1981	*19*	*1*	17	14	15	2
1981	44	*17*	7	19	34	32
1981	34	7	*17*	9	24	22
Mean	33	19	16	19	24	18

Parties in Government are italicised.

TWENTY DIMENSIONAL ANALYSIS OF COALITIONS IN BELGIUM

Government formation

Figure G.1, in the Appendix to this chapter, shows inter-party city-block distances calculated over the twenty standard dimensions used throughout this volume, as well as the cluster models based upon those distances. Given the very fluid Belgian party system and the various earthquakes through which it has passed, we feel that a non-hierarchical clustering model is more suitable. There have been a sufficient number of radical realignments for us to suppose that the Belgian parties are likely to optimise in their coalition building, rather than to proceed incrementally.

The full results of the 20-dimensional cluster analyses are summarised in Table 9.4 which shows predictions for each post-war Belgian Parliament between 1949 and 1981. The PCB–KPB manifesto data is lacking for the 1946–49 legislature, but since we assume it is excluded as a pariah in any case, we make characterisations on the basis of the positions of the three main parties in this period. Of the thirteen programmatic characterisations of likely governments, nine were to come wholly or substantially true at some point during the lifetime of the legislature concerned. The ones that did not are those for 1954, 1958, 1968 and 1974, all years in which special circumstances can be said to have intervened.

It is noteworthy that all four occurred when the normally dominant left–right dimension was temporarily eclipsed by another. In 1954 and again in 1958, for example, the other dimension was the clerical-anticlerical divide, which set the Socialist and Liberal parties on the one hand against the Social-Christians on the other over the question of the level of public support to be given to religious education. Similarly, the elections of 1968 and 1974, represent the years when the intensity of the federalist-unitarist dimension was at its height. Even allowing or the fact that these other dimensions do find some measure of expression in the twenty-dimensional space upon which this analysis is based, the fact remains that left–right issues continue to predominate. We should not be surprised, when the normal dimensional structure should sometimes fail to predict actual outcomes.

Even without making allowances for such special circumstances, however, the prediction rate of the multi-dimensional cluster models is quite high. Insisting on a governmental majority, about half of the governments that form are identified by a model making a unique prediction out of a wide

Table 9.4   Summary of results of 20-dimensional analyses, Belgium, 1946–81

Election year	Cluster prediction**	Actual government(s)		Total government seats	correct prediction
1946	C+S	4	S, L, K	109	No
		5	S, L, K	109	No
		6	C, S	161*	Yes
		7	C, S	161*	Yes
1949	C, L	8	C, S	134	Yes
1950	C (Majority)	9	C	108	Yes
		10	C	108	Yes
		11	C	108	Yes
1954*	C, S	12	S, L	111	No
1958**	C, S	13	C (Minority)	(104)	—
		14	C, L	125	No
1961	C, S	15	C, S	180	Yes
1965*	C, L	16	C, S	141	No
		17	C, L	125	Yes
1968*	S, L	18	C, S	128	No
1971*	C,S,L,V	19	C, S	128	(Yes)
		20	C, S, L	159*	(Yes)
1974	C,V,R	21	C, L (Minority)	(102)	—
		22	C, L, R	116	No
		23	C, L, R	115	No
		24	C, L (Minority)	(102)	—
1977*	C, S	25	C, S, V, F	172*	(Yes)
		26	C, S, V, F	172*	(Yes)
1978*	C, L	27	C, S, F	151*	No
		28	C, S	140	No
		29	C, S, L	176*	(Yes)
		30	C, S	140	No
		31	C, S	140	No
1981	C, L	32	C, L	113	Yes

Minority governments are in parentheses.
*   = Two-thirds Majority
** First cluster with majority status and policy viable on at least one dimension.

range of alternatives. Relaxing the formation requirement to cover viability rather than majority status, several other governments are accurately forecast. This record is very much better than could be expected by chance and shows that the multi-dimensional cluster models add considerably to the interpretation of government formation in Belgium.

Government policy

We now turn our attention to government policy, as defined in the full 20-dimensional policy space. Table 9.5 shows the results of an analysis of the 20-dimensional city-block distances between each party's position at each election and that of each government's policy declaration. The second column of Table 9.5 shows the parties which formed each govern-

Table 9.5   Summary of policy payoffs in 20-dimensional space, Belgium, 1945–81

Government No.	Parties comprising government	Parties closest to government policy position
3	S	S
4	S, L, K	–
5	S, L, K	–
6	C, S	–
7	C, S	–
8	C, S	L, C
9	C	C
10	C	L
11	C	C
12	S, L	C, L
13	C (Minority)	S
14	C. L	L, C
15	C, S	C, L
16	C, S	C, (V), S
17	C, L	L, C
18	C, S	L, (V), S
19	C, S	L, (V), C
20	C, S, L	(V), (F), S,(R), L, C
21	C, L (Minority)	L, (F), (V), (R)C
22	C, L, R	F, L, V
23	C, L, R	–
24	C, L (Minority)	–
25	C, S, V, F	F, S, V, C
26	C, S, V, F	L, F, C.S
27	C, S, F	C, R, F
28	C, S	–
29	C, S, L	C, S, R
30	C, S	C, S
31	C, S	C, L
32	C, L	C, L

Note: Parties in parentheses excluded from coalition formation before 1974.

ment while the third column rank-orders the parties according to their 20-dimensional city-block policy distance from the government. The first party in the third column is the one closest to government policy, the second party is the second closest, and so on.

The results are quite impressive. Eleven of the twenty-three governments for which the calculation is possible consist of precisely those parties which obtain the highest payoffs while in a further ten cases at least one of the coalition partners does so. This leaves only two governments, both single party PSC–CVP governments as it happens, where the government party did not itself obtain the greatest policy payoff. This evidence supports the notion that government participation is important to Belgian parties in policy terms.

DISAGGREGATED TWENTY-DIMENSIONAL ANALYSIS

Table 9.6 identifies the party with the median legislator after each election on each of the twenty policy dimensions viewed separately. While the PSC–CVP is well-positioned the 20-dimensional analysis does not suggest a position of overwhelming dominance, although the party typically controlled the median legislator on more policy dimensions than any other. Its position was, however, much weaker in 1946, 1958 and 1971.

As we know, the CVP–PSC has been in most post-war Belgian coalitions, so its predominance has certainly been reflected in government formation. The fact that the party is not totally dominant, however, is better reflected in the 20-dimensional than the one-dimensional analysis, and corresponds with the formation of occasional governments that have excluded the PSC–CVP altogether.

CONCLUSIONS

Belgium must be the most clear-cut example in Western Europe of a multi-dimensional party system. Nonetheless, the standard one dimension analysis performed on the other party systems in this book also threw up some interesting insights in the Belgian case. In particular, the one-dimensional analysis documents quite unequivocally the dominant position of the CVP–PSC throughout the post-war period, as well as highlighting those times when this hegemony was most under threat. The party typically controlled the median legislator, and was more or less continuously in government as a result.

Table 9.6 Parties with median legislator over 20-dimensions, Belgium, 1946–81

	1946	1949	1950*	1954	1958	1961	1965	1968	1971	1974	1977	1978	1981
1 State intervention	S	S	C	C	L		L	C	L	R	C	C	C
2 Quality of life	S	S	C	C	L	C/L	L	C	L	F	L	S	C
3 Peace & co-operation	S	L	C	C	L	L	C	S	L	C	C	C	C
4 Anti-establishment	C/L	C/L	C	C/S	S/L	C/S/L	C	C/S/L	R	C/S	S	C	S
5 Capitalist	C	C	C	C	C	C	C	S	C	C	C	C	C
6 Social conservatism	L	L	C	L	C	C	L	L	C	S	C	L	C
7 Productivity	S	L	C	L	C	S	S	C	S	S	L	S	C
8 Military: positive	C/L	S	C	C	C	C/L/V	S	C	S	C	C	C	C
9 EEC: positive	—	C/L	C	C	C	L	L	C	V	S	C	C	C
10 Internationalism (+)			C	C/S	—	C/S/L		C/L				C/L/V	C/L/V/F
11 Freedom/human Rights	S	C	C	C/L	S	S	C	C	C	C	S	L	L
12 Democracy	C	S	C	C	C/S	S	S	C	C	C	C	C	C
13 Decentralisation: (+)	L	S	C	C	L	C	L	C	V	V	S	L	L
14 Government efficiency	C/L	C	C	C	S/L	C	C	C	C/S	V	C	C	C
15 Social justice	L	C	C	C	S	C	S	S	S	C	C	C	C
16 Social services: (+)	S	C	C	S	C	C	C	S	S	S	S	S	C
17 Education: (+ve)	L	C	C	C	L	C	C	C	C	C	L	C	C
18 Labour: (+ve)	L	C	C	L	S	C	C	C	S	C	L	C	C
19 Agriculture	C	L	C	C	L	C	S	C	S	V	L	C	S
20 Underpriviledged minorities	S	C	C	C	L	S	L	S	C	L	S	F	S
C (PSC–CVP)	7	10	20	15	6	14	9	13	6	9	9	14	15
S (PSB–BSP)	7	5		3	8	6	5	6	8	6	6	2	3
L (PLP–PVV)	7	6		4	8	6	5	3	2	1	4	4	3
V (Volksunie)						1			2	2		1	1
R (RW)									1	1			
F (FDF)												1	1

* Social Christian majority.

However, the one-dimensional analysis was of limited use in predicting either the party composition of the government or the locus of government policy, as Tables 9.7 and 9.8 indicate. In contrast, the 20-dimensional analyses were rather successful in making sense of the policy 'payoffs' going to the various parties. The policy positions of governments can be

Table 9.7 Results of testing hypotheses derived from unidimensional analysis, Belgium

Hypothesis 1: Coalition will contain party with median legislator.
Hypothesis 2: Coalition will consist of party with median legislator plus next closest party.
Hypothesis 3: Coalition will consist of PSC/CVP plus next closest party.
Hypothesis 4: Coalition will consist of adjacent parties on dimension.
Hypothesis 5: Government policy will lie between those of coalition partners.
Hypothesis 6: Government policy will be closest to that of party with median legislator.
Hypothesis 7: Government policy will be closest to that of PSC/CVP.
Hypothesis 8: Government policy will lie in expected direction.
Hypothesis 9: Government policy will move in same direction as PSC/CVP.

Election Year:	1946					1949	1950			1954
Government number	3	4	5	6	7	8	9	10	11	12
Coalition	S	SLK	SLK	CS	CS	CL	C	C	C	SL
Hypothesis 1:	F	T	T	F	F	T	T	T	T	F
Hypothesis 2:	F	F	F	F	F	T	F	F	F	F
Hypothesis 3:	F	F	F	F	F	T	F	F	F	F
Hypothesis 4:	NA	T	T	F	F	T	NA	NA	NA	F
Hypothesis 5:	NA	T	F	NA	NA	T	NA	NA	NA	T
Hypothesis 6:	T	T	F	NA	NA	T	NA	NA	NA	F
Hypothesis 7:	F	F	F	NA	NA	T	T	F	F	F
Hypothesis 8:	T	T	T	NA	NA	F	NA	NA	NA	F
Hypothesis 9:	NA	NA	NA	NA	NA	NA	T	NA	NA	T

Election Year:	1955		1961	1965		1968	1971		1974	
Government number	13	14	15	16	17	18	19	20	21	22
Coalition	C	CL	CS	CS	CL	CS	CS	CSL	CL	CLR
Hypothesis 1:	T	T	T	T	T	T	T	T	T	T
Hypothesis 2:	F	T	T	F	T	T	T	T	F	F
Hypothesis 3:	F	T	T	F	T	T	T	T	F	F
Hypothesis 4:	NA	T	T	T	F	F	T	F	F	F
Hypothesis 5:	NA	F	F	F	F	F	F	T	T	T
Hypothesis 6:	NA	F	F	F	F	T	T	F	F	F
Hypothesis 7:	F	F	F	F	F	F	T	F	F	F

Hypothesis 8:	NA	F	T	F	T	T	T	T	F	F
Hypothesis 9:	T	NA	T	T	NA	T	F	NA	F	NA

Election Year:				1977		1978				1981
Government number	23	24	25	26	27	28	29	30	31	32
Coalition	CLR	CL	CSVF	CSVF	CSF	CS	CSL	CS	CS	CL
Hypothesis 1:	T	T	T	T	T	T	T	T	T	T
Hypothesis 2:	F	F	T	T	F	F	F	F	F	T
Hypothesis 3:	F	F	T	T	F	F	F	F	F	T
Hypothesis 4:	F	F	F	F	F	F	F	F	F	F
Hypothesis 5:	NA	NA	F	F	F	NA	T	F	F	T
Hypothesis 6:	NA	NA	F	F	F	NA	T	T	F	T
Hypothesis 7:	NA	NA	F	F	F	NA	T	T	F	T
Hypothesis 8:	NA	NA	F	F	F	NA	F	T	F	T
Hypothesis 9:	NA	NA	T		NA	F	NA	NA	NA	NA	NA

Summary of *hypothesis testing*

	True	False
Hypothesis 1:	26	4
Hypothesis 2:	10	20
Hypothesis 3:	10	20
Hypothesis 4:	7	18
Hypothesis 5:	8	12
Hypothesis 6:	7	14
Hypothesis 7:	6	19
Hypothesis 8:	10	11
Hypothesis 9:	7	4

Table 9.8   Summary of results of test of one-dimensional hypotheses (from Table 9.7)

	Overall result		1946–58		1961–81		'First' governments after election	
	True	False	True	False	True	False	True	False
Hypothesis 1:	26	4	8	4	18	0	11	2
Hypothesis 2:	10	20	2	10	8	10	6	7
Hypothesis 3:	10	20	2	10	8	10	6	7
Hypothesis 4:	7	18	4	3	3	15	4	5
Hypothesis 5:	8	12	3	2	5	10	4	6
Hypothesis 6:	7	14	3	1	4	13	5	6
Hypothesis 7:	6	19	2	8	4	11	4	8
Hypothesis 8:	10	11	3	3	7	8	5	6
Hypothesis 9:	7	4	3	0	4	4	7	4

Hypothesis 1: Coalition will contain party with median legislator.
Hypothesis 2: Coalition will consist of party with median legislator plus next closest party.
Hypothesis 3: Coalition will consist of PSC/CVP plus next closest party.
Hypothesis 4: Coalition will consist of adjacent parties on dimension.
Hypothesis 5: Government policy will lie between those of coalition partners.

Hypothesis 6: Government policy will be closest to that of party with median legislator.
Hypothesis 7: Government policy will be closest to that of PSC/CVP.
Hypothesis 8: Government policy will lie in expected direction.
Hypothesis 9: Government policy will move in same direction as PSC/CVP.

reasonably well predicted from the policy positions of their members: together with the unique predictions that can be generated by using the majority criterion, which is realistic for Belgium, this produces quite high success and efficiency rates for the multi-dimensional models as the summary Table 9.9 illustrates.

All in all, these results demonstrate that Belgian coalitions seem to give high priority to policy considerations, but these are best represented multi-dimensionally rather than on the unidimensional left–right continuum which seems to fit most other European countries.

Table 9.9 Success of policy-based hypotheses on government formation in Belgium

Government	Number of possible coalitions	Number of feasible coalitions given constraints	Does Theory A predict correctly?	Does Theory B predict correctly?	Does Theory C predict correctly?
3	15	7	n/a	NA	NA
4	15	7	No	Yes	No
5	15	7	No	Yes	No
6	15	7	Yes	Yes	Yes
7	15	7	Yes	Yes	Yes
8	15	7	Yes	Yes	Yes
9	15	7	Yes	Yes	*
10	15	7	Yes	Yes	*
11	15	7	Yes	No	*
12	15	7	No	No	No
13	15	7	No		*
14	15	7	No	Yes	No
15	15	7	Yes	Yes	Yes
16	127	7	No	Yes	No
17	127	7	Yes	Yes	Yes
18	127	7	No	Yes	Yes
19	127	7	Yes	Yes	Yes
20	127	7	Yes	Yes	No
21	127	63	No	Yes	No
22	127	63	No	Yes	No
23	127	63	No	Yes	No
24	127	63	No	Yes	No

Table 9.9 (cont'd)

Government	Number of possible coalitions	Number of feasible coalitions given constraints	Does Theory A predict correctly?	Does Theory B predict correctly?	Does Theory C predict correctly?
25	127	63	Yes	Yes	No
26	127	63	Yes	Yes	No
27	127	63	No	Yes	No
28	127	63	No	Yes	No
29	127	63	Yes	Yes	Yes
30	127	63	No	Yes	Yes
31	127	63	No	Yes	Yes
32	127	63	Yes	Yes	No
Predictive success			.49 (14/29)	.93 (27/30)	.41 (10/25)
Predictive efficiency			.49 (14/29)	.15 (27/192)	.41 (10/25)

*Single party majority

Hypothesis A: Coalition will be at first majority node on cluster tree and policy-viable on at least one dimension.

Hypothesis B: Coalition will contain predominant party over disaggregated 20 dimensions.

Hypothesis C: Coalition will consist of predominant party plus next closest party (city block).

APPENDIX G

Table G.1   Results of post-war legislative elections in Belgium (Chambre des Represenants/Kamer van Volksvertegenwoodigers)

Election year	PSC–CVP	PSB BSP	PLP PVV	PCB KPB	VoLKS	RW	FDF	*Others*
1946	92	69	17	23				1
1949	105	66	29	12				
1950	108	77	20	7				
1954	95	86	25	4	1			
1958	104	84	21	2	1			
1961	96	84	20	5	5			2
1965	77	64	48	6	12	3	2	
1968	69	59	47	5	20	7	5	
1971	67	61	34	5	21	14	10	
1974	72	59	33	4	22	13	9	
1977	80	61	33	2	20	5	10	
1978	82	58	37	4	14	4	11	2
1981	61	61	52	2	20	6	2	8
1985	69	67	46	0	16		3	11
1987	62	72	48	0	16		3	11

Seats gains and losses								
1949	13	–3	12	–11				–1
1950	3	11	–9	–5				
1954	–13	9	5	–3	1			1
1958	9	–2	–4	–2	0			–1
1961	–8	0	–1	3	4			2
1965	–19	–20	28	1	7	3	2	–2
1968	–8	–5	–1	–1	8	4	3	
1971	–2	2	–13	0	1	7	5	
1974	5	–2	–1	–1	1	–1	–1	
1977	8	2	0	–2	–2	–8	1	
1978	2	–3	4	2	–6	–1	1	2
1981	–21	3	15	–2	6	2	–9	6
1985	8	6	–6	–2	–4	–6	1	3
1987	–7	5	2	0	0		0	0

Table G.2   List of Belgian governments

		Date of formation	Parties in government	Coded
00	Frielen (London)	1940		
01	Van Acker I	February 1945	C, S, L, K	Yes
02	Van Acker II	August 1945	S, L, K	No
General election: February 1946				
03	Spaak I	March 1946	S	Yes
04	Van Acker III	April 1946	S, L, K	Yes
05	Huysmans	August 1946	S, L, K	Yes
06	Spaak II	March 1947	C, S	No
07	Spaak III	November 1948	C, S	No
General election: June 1949				
08	Eyskens I	August 1949	C, L	Yes
General election: June 1950				
09	Duviesart	June 1950	C	Yes
10	Frolien	August 1950	C	Yes
11	Van Houtte	January 1952	C	Yes
General election: April 1954				
12	Van Acker IV	April 1954	S, L	Yes
General election: June 1958				
13	Eyskens II	June 1958	C	Yes
14	Eyskens III	November 1958	C, L	Yes
General election: March 1961				
15	Lefevre	April 1961	C, S	Yes
General election: May 1965				
16	Harmel	July 1965	C, S	Yes
17	Van den Boeynants I	March 1966	C, L	Yes
General election: March 1968				
18	Eyskens IV	June 1968	C, S	Yes
General election: November 1971				
19	Eyskens V	January 1972	C, S	Yes
20	Leburton	January 1973	C, S, L	Yes
General election: March 1974				
21	Tindemans I	April 1974	C, L	Yes
22	Tindemans II	June 1974	C, L, R	Yes
23	Tindemans III	December 1976	C, L, R	No
24	Tindemans IV	March 1977	C, L	No

General election: April 1977

25	Tindemans V	June 1977	C, S, V, F	Yes
26	Van den Boevnants II	April 1978	C, S, V, F	Yes

General election: April 1978

27	Martens I	April 1979	C, S, F	Yes
28	Martens II	January 1980	C, S	No
29	Martens III	May 1980	C, S, L	Yes
30	Martens IV	October 1980	C, S	Yes
31	Mark Eyskens	April 1981	C, S	Yes

General election: November 1981

32	Martens V	December 1981	C, L	Yes

General election: October 1985

33	Martens VI	November 1985	C, L	No
34	Martens VII	October 1986		No

General election: December 1987

35	Martens VIII	May 1988	C, S, V	No

Key to Coalition Parties:	Uncoded Documents:	
C = PSC/CVF	02	Document not yet obtained
S = PS(B)/(B)SF	06	Document not yet obtained
L = Liberals	07	Document not yet obtained
K = FCB/KPB	23	No document found
R = Rass. Wallon	24	No document found
V = Volsunie	28	Obtained but not coded (Note)
F = FDF	33	Document not yet obtained
	34	Document not yet obtained
	35	Document not yet obtained

Note:

Not only is Document No. 29 entitled Communication du Gouvernment/Mededline van de Regerina (instead of the usual Declaration gouvernementale/ Regeringsverklaring, but it contains the following statement: 'Un nouvel accord du gouvernement n'a pas ete negocie a cette occasion. Le gouvernement reste fidele a sa declaration gouvernementale . . .' In addition, although the 'Communication' is of considerable constitutional interest and importance, very little if any of it can be coded in terms of the coding frame. Consequently, it should not be treated as a 'Declaration' for the purpose of the current analysis.

Table G.3   Twenty-dimensional city-block policy distances between party manifestos and government declarations

Government	Composition	20-dimensional city-block distances	
3	S	S	48.77
		C	72.27
		L	86.43
4	S,L, K	S	62.75
		C	63.57
		L	66.41
5	S, L, K	S	59.32
		C	73.00
		L	79.48
6	C, S		
7	C, L		
8	C, L		
9	C	C	50.02
		L	59.04
		S	93.40
10	C	L	63.30
		C	78.62
		S	98.00
11	C	C	41.69
		L	42.61
		S	77.27
12	S, L	C	47.99
		L	69.82
		S	99.50
13	C	S	52.43
		C	54.66
		L	54.71
14	C, L	L	67.11
		C	76.00
		S	80.25
15	C, S	C	55.08
		L	61.31
		S	67.55
		V	94.37
16	C, S	C	57.41
		V	68.93
		L	83.36
		S	98.02
17	C, L	L	63.12
		C	75.83
		S	104.24
		V	117.67

18	C, S	L	69.91
		V	70.03
		S	76.70
		C	76.84
		F	89.77
19	C, S	L	47.50
		V	49.86
		C	54.24
		S	55.00
		F	66.28
		R	87.27
20	C, S, L	V	61.62
		F	64.98
		S	69.02
		R	71.81
		L	73.90
		C	83.84
21	C, L	L	55.98
		F	60.66
		V	60.72
		R	64.04
		C	69.73
		S	71.44
22	C, L, R	F	58.25
		L	68.67
		V	74.73
		R	76.91
		C	83.60
		S	91.87
23	C, L, R		
24	C, L		
25	C, S, V, F	F	108.66
		S	111.18
		V	111.40
		C	112.00
		L	114.02
		R	130.24
26	C, S, V, F	L	97.30
		F	115.08
		C	118.30
		S	118.34
		V	118.54
		R	140.66
27	C, S, F	C	63.25
		R	70.22
		F	74.44
		S	74.83
		L	80.30
		V	87.57

28	C, S		
29	C, S, L	C	48.08
		S	60.94
		R	64.11
		L	64.29
		F	72.91
		V	73.22
30	C, S	C	51.97
		S	61.41
		R	65.88
		F	71.24
		L	76.44
		V	88.35
31	C, S	C	79.45
		L	90.62
		F	90.64
		V	90.75
		R	98.26
		S	100.17
32	C, L	C	40.92
		L	54.49
		V	61.98
		S	71.09
		F	78.35
		R	83.16

Table G.4   City-block matrices for Belgium, 1946–81

1946

PSB	66	
Lib	82	74
	PSC	PSB

1949

PSB	106	
Lib	69	133
	PSC	PSB

1950

PSB	64	
Lib	47	65
	PSC	PSB

1954

PSB	64	
Lib	82	108
	PSC	PSB

1958

PSB	62	
Lib	63	69
	PSC	PSB

1961

PSB	38		
Lib	78	86	
Volks	74	90	114
	PSC	PSB	Lib

1965

PSB	59		
Lib	49	78	
Volks	81	94	98
	PSC	PSB	Lib

1968

PSB	69			
Lib	71	64		
Volks	68	79	79	
FDF	76	103	93	80
	PSC	PSB	Lib	Volks

1971

PSB	45				
Lib	49	50			
Volks	58	41	57		
RW	85	68	86	57	
FDF	86	61	81	70	75
	PSC	PSB	Lib	Volks	RW

1974

PSB	63				
Lib	64	69			
Volks	43	52	53		
RW	67	72	65	54	
FDF	60	75	72	47	65
	PSC	PSB	Lib	Volks	RW

1977

PSB	20				
Lib	43	47			
Volks	63	57	54		
RW	113	107	102	72	
FDF	58	66	47	47	79
	PSC	PSB	Lib	Volks	RW

1978

PSB	49				
Lib	47	64			
Volks	68	75	57		
RW	57	40	66	73	
FDF	62	73	81	54	55
	PSC	PSB	Lib	Volks	RW

1981

PSB	48				
Lib	49	87			
Volks	52	64	59		
RW	56	36	91	50	
FDF	60	48	93	56	34
	PSC	PSB	Lib	Volks	RW

Figure G.1 Coalition cluster diagrams for Belgium, 1946-81

1946

Average Linkage

K-Means

(Missing crucial Communist programme)
Actual coalition = PSB+Lib+Comm (Van Acker 3, Huysmans) (4,5).
PSC+PSB (Spaak 2,3) (6,7)

1949

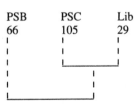

Winning Map   = PSC+Lib
Actual Coalition = PSC+Lib (Eyskens 1) (8)

1950

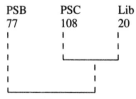

Smallest MAP   = PSC
Actual Governments = PSC (Duviesart) (9)
                   = PSC (Pholien) (10)
                   = PSC (van Houtte) (11)

1954

Party	PSB	PSC	Lib
Seats	86	95	25

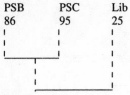

Winning MAP   = PSB + PSC
Actual coalition = PSB + Lib (Van Acker 4) (12)

1958

Party	PSB	PSC	Lib
Seats	84	104	21

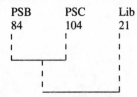

Winning MAP   = PSB + PSC
Actual coalition = PSC (Eyskens 2) (13)
                 PSC + Lib (Eyskens 3) (14)

1961

Party	PSB	PSC	Lib	Volks
Seats	84	96	20	5

Centroid Linkage

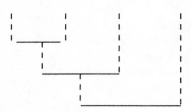

K-Means; Average Linkage

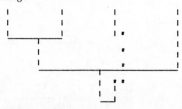

Winning MAP   = PSB + PSC
Actual coalitions = PSB + PSC (Lefevre) (15)

1965

Party	PSB	PSC	Lib	Volks
Seats	64	77	48	12

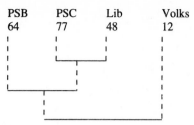

Winning MAP   = PSC + Lib
Actual coalitions = PSC + PSB (Harmel) (16)
                          PSC + Lib (Vanden Boeynants 1) (17)

1968

Average, K-means and centroid linkage

Party	PSB	Volks	PSC	Lib	FDF
Seats	59	20	69	47	7

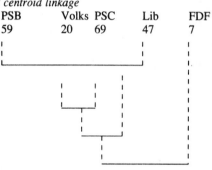

Winning MAP   = PSB + Lib
Actual coalitions = PSB + PSC (Eyskens 4) (18)

1971

Average linkage

Party	PSB	Volks	PSC	Lib	RW	FDF
Seats	61	21	67	31	14	10

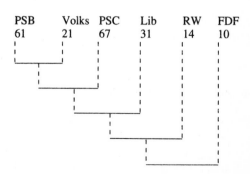

K-Means

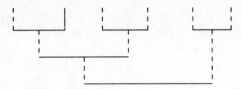

Winning MAP   = PSB + Volks + PSC + Lib
Actual coalitions = PSB + PSC (Eyskens 5) (19)
                          PSB + PSC + lib (Leburton) (20)

1974

Party	PSB	Volks	PSC	Lib	RW	FDF
Seats	59	22	72	30	13	9

Average Linkage

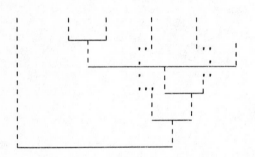

K-Means

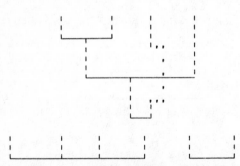

Winning MAP   = PSC + Volks + RW + FDF (Average Linkage)
                          PSC + Volks + RW (K-Means)
Actual coalitions = PSC+ Lib   (Tindemans 1) (21)
                          PSC + Lib + RW   (Tindemans 2) (22)
                          PSC + Lib + RW   (Tindemans 3) (23)
                          PSC + Lib   (Tindemans 4) (24)

1977

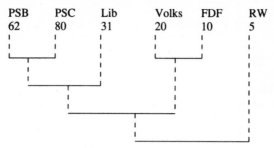

Parties	PSB	PSC	Lib	Volks	FDF	RW
Seats	62	80	31	20	10	5

Winning MAP   = PSB + PSC
Actual coalition = PSC + PSB + VU + FDF (Tindemans 5) (25)
                   PSC + PSC + VU + FDF (Vanden Boeynants) (26)

1978

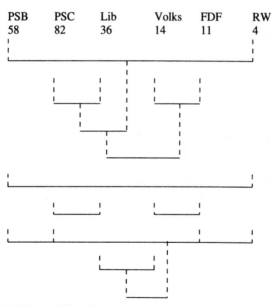

Parties	PSB	PSC	Lib	Volks	FDF	RW
Seats	58	82	36	14	11	4

Winning MAP   = PSC + Lib
Actual coalition = PSC + PSB + FDF (Martens 1) (27)
                   PSC + PSB   (Martens 2) (28)
                   PSC + PSB + Lib (Martens 3) (29)
                   PSC + PSB   (Martens 4) (30)
                   PSC + PSB   (Mark Eyskens) (31)

1981

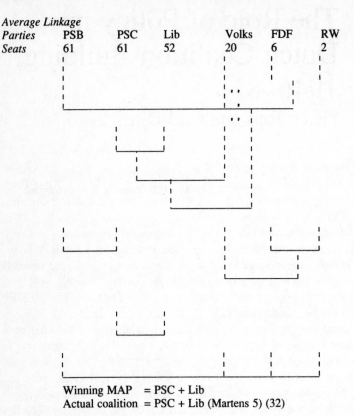

Average Linkage *Parties*	PSB	PSC	Lib	Volks	FDF	RW
Seats	61	61	52	20	6	2

Winning MAP   = PSC + Lib
Actual coalition = PSC + Lib (Martens 5) (32)

10 The Role of Policy in Dutch Coalition Building, 1946–81
Pieter Tops and Karl Dittrich

By far the most striking feature of the politics of coalition in the Netherlands is the permanent presence of one party in government. After 1945, not a single government has been formed without the Catholic People's party (KVP) or its successor, the Christian Democratic Appeal (CDA). The confessional parties have provided an element of continuity in Dutch politics. However, they have, after 1945, never opted for a cabinet consisting solely of confessional ministers. They have formed coalition cabinets with either the Social Democratic Party (PvdA) or the Conservative-Liberals (VVD). Only once, in 1948, was there a cabinet consisting of the KVP and both the PvdA and the VVD.

A second striking feature of Dutch cabinet-building after 1945 has been the greater success of the Liberals compared to the Social Democrats in forming a coalition with the religious parties. The PvdA has been in government for about 19 years, the VVD for nearly 24 years over the post-war period. Moreover, the Social Democrats spent most of their time in government during the 1940s and 1950s. After 1958 the confessional parties preferred co-operation with the VVD.

In this chapter we will look at the question of whether party policies can be used to explain the composition of Dutch cabinets. Does party policy account, for example, for the permanent presence of the KVP and CDA in Dutch cabinets? Is it possible to use policy distances to explain the relative absence from coalitions of the Social Democrats and the greater participation in coalitions of the Liberals?

We will also investigate the way in which policy payoffs are distributed among parties. Do coalition programmes constitute a 'fair' deal between the coalition partners, or do they favour some parties more than others? Does it really matter, as far as policy payoffs are concerned, whether a party is in or out of government? Before we can do anything else, however, we must begin with a brief description of the main features of the Dutch party system.

THE DUTCH PARTY SYSTEM

The total number of parties in the Dutch parliament has varied since 1945 between seven and fourteen. There has never been a party with a majority of the seats in the Tweede Kamer (Second Chamber), nor has there been a party that had a realistic hope of reaching a majority on its own. Thus, in order to form a government, Dutch parties have always needed to form coalitions.

After 1945, the Dutch party system passed effectively through three phases. The first, which lasted from 1946 until 1963, saw the well-known politics of accommodation (Lijphart, 1968). The Netherlands was a strongly segmented society, divided into four subcultures – Protestant, Catholic, Socialist and Liberal – each of which was rather hostile towards, and isolated from, the others. Each had its own organisational infrastructure, with the main parties acting as the political branches of these organisational 'pillars' – (zuilen): the KVP for the Catholics, the ARP and CHU for the Protestants, the PvdA for the socialists and the VVD for the Liberals. The degree of 'pillarisation' (verzuiling) was however not similar in all the subcultures: it was very developed with the Catholic and Protestant subcultures, quite developed among the Socialist minority but less so among the liberal groups. Pillarisation did not destablise Dutch politics and society, because there was a high degree of co-operation and 'accommodation' between the leaders of the pillars.

In this period the political climate was very stable. The five main parties did not win or lose many votes and after each election they got about 90 per cent of the seats between them. The three religious parties in particular were very stable; their seats in the Tweede Kamer varied between 50 per cent and 54 per cent of the total. They never used this narrow majority to form a government on their own and, although they had a lot of things in common, it would be wrong to see them as a monolithic political bloc.

The first regular post-war coalition (Beel, 1946–48), consisting of PvdA and KVP, had to resign early on the question of withdrawal from Indonesia. For a long period after this (1948–59) oversized 'broad-based' coalitions were formed (for example, Drees I–IV). The heart of these coalitions consisted of the KVP and the PvdA; they were supplemented by the CHU, the ARP (after 1952) and the VVD (Between 1948 and 1952). Even a grand coalition between the five major parties was a real possibility during this period. In 1959, however, the broad based coalitions came to an end; the KVP and other confessional parties exchanged the PvdA for the VVD as a coalition partner (starting with the De Quay cabinet, 1959–63).

The end of this first phase in Dutch post-war politics is marked by some very turbulent coalition developments. The KVP–ARP–CHU–VVD coalition originally formed after the elections of 1963 broke down after nearly two years. Without new elections, a completely new coalition emerged, consisting of the KVP, PvdA and ARP, but this collapsed after a short time. It was brought down by the KVP in the so-called 'Night of Schmelzer', named after the parliamentary chairman of the KVP. This event had a tremendous impact on Dutch politics. The Socialists accused the KVP of 'unreliability' and it was one of the main reasons they started a 'polarisation strategy' against the Catholic party. This polarisation was a main feature in the second phase of post-war Dutch politics.

The second phase of post-war political history in the Netherlands was a short but exciting period that takes in the elections of 1967, 1971 and 1972. As in the rest of the Western world ideological, sociological and moral changes had a huge impact. As a consequence the pillars began to crumble. Secularisation and the rapidly declining loyalty of religious voters to their respective parties ate away the strength of the KVP and, to a lesser extent, of the CHU and the ARP. In three elections the KVP saw about half of its voters shift to non-voting or to other parties. As a consequence, the three confessional parties were pushed towards each other. They strengthened their ties, co-operated more often than they did before and finally started a process of merger (De Jong and Pijnenburg, 1988).

The other two traditional parties, the PvdA and the VVD, tried to profit from the electoral decline of the confessional parties, adopting a 'polarisation strategy' in an attempt to force the confessional parties into 'political clarity' (in other words, to declare a preference for co-operation with one of the other two parties). The polarisation strategy combined with an internal process or radicalisation in the PvdA (Van den Berg, 1986). The 'new left' took control of the party and adopted a very firm stand towards the confessional parties. In 1971 and 1972 the PvdA entered into a pre-electoral alliance with D'66 and PPR, aiming at a majority in the elections. Electoral volatility also provided leeway for new political parties. In 1971 and 1972 as many as 14 parties won seats in the Tweede Kamer. The most important new parties were D'66, a radical democratic party with the explicit goal of 'exploding' the existing party system; the PPR, a leftist party founded by ex-members of KVP and ARP; and DS'70, a party of rather conservative social democrats who left the PvdA out of dissatisfaction with its radicalisation.

The first coalition of this phase was the KVP–ARP–CHU–VVD cabinet headed by De Jong. This was the first post-war cabinet to complete the full four-yearly parliamentary period without formal interruption. In the elections of 1971 these four parties lost their majority and could continue in government only with the help of one of the new parties (DS'70). The consequent Biesheuvel cabinet broke down after a year. New elections were held, and after a very turbulent process of coalition formation, the cabinet of Den Uyl came into existence. This was the first cabinet in Dutch history in which the left had a majority of the ministers.

The Den Uyl cabinet was followed by a great election victory for the socialists in 1977. They gained ten extra seats, which was unprecedented in Dutch political history. At the same time, however, the new interconfessional party, the CDA, stemmed the heavy losses of the former confessional parties. It won one seat more than the KVP, ARP and CHU jointly in 1972.

After these elections attempts were made, over a very long negotiating period, to form a new government of the PvdA, CDA and D'66. However, after more than five months, the attempt had to be given up. The differences in political style and in policy preferences between the PvdA and the CDA as well as the antagonisms between their leaders, Den Uyl (PvdA) and Van Agt (CDA), could not be bridged. The negotiations finally broke down on differences about the personal composition of the new cabinet. Subsequently, the CDA formed a new cabinet with the VVD (Van Agt I, 1977–81) after a relatively short period of negotiation. The formation of this cabinet marks the turning point between the second and third phases of Dutch post-war politics.

The most important feature of the third phase in Dutch post-war politics is the success of the new interconfessional party, the CDA. Although it suffered from many growing pains, the CDA gave stability to the confessional bloc and therefore to the centre of the Dutch political system. The CDA stopped the heavy electoral losses of the former confessional parties and, after a small decline in 1982, made major gains in the elections of 1986. In 1981 and 1986 the CDA became the largest party in the Dutch parliament.

For ten of the eleven years between 1977 and 1988 the CDA has governed with the VVD. The CDA–VVD regnum was only interrrupted after the elections of 1981, when the two parties lost their majority in parliament. Subsequently, a coalition was formed with CDA, PvdA and D'66 (Van Agt II, 1981–82), which had already broken down by the time it presented itself to parliament. The coalition was repaired but it crumbled once more after another six months, finally coming to an end in April 1982. Since then, the Netherlands has been governed by a CDA–VVD coalition (Lubbers I and II, 1982–90).

THE ROLE OF POLICY IN COALITION BARGAINING

Put very crudely, the Netherlands can probably be characterised as a policy-seeking rather than as an office-seeking system. There exists a rather strong left–right dimension (see below) and parties invest a lot of time in developing a clear and consistent policy profile on this dimension. Ideological competition between the parties has intensified since the mid-1960s, but even in the phase of the politics of accommodation, when traditional loyalties strongly determined the patterns of party support, political parties maintained characteristic policy profiles. Conversely, the absence of clientelistic practices in Dutch politics renders pure office-seeking strategies less rewarding. Policy, therefore, is more than just one of the matters that a Dutch politician must deal with; it is at the heart of Dutch politics.

Parties in the Netherlands pay a lot of attention to the drafting of manifestos (Dittrich, 1987). All the main party organs are involved and there are elaborate procedures, in which the role of each party organ is clearly described. An initial draft programme is drawn up by the party councils, after which local and regional branches and interest groups may propose as many amendments as they wish. Final decisions are taken by the party congresses, usually after extensive discussions.

A very important function of manifestos is to form a basis for (often detailed) negotiations with other parties on government policy. Partly because of the extensiveness of the party platforms, government programmes have become more comprehensive and elaborate and their impact on Dutch politics has become rather sweeping. They have become more than just agreements at the start of the coalition that express a willingness to co-operate, as was perhaps the case at the beginning of the post-war period. Instead, they now have a fundamental influence on nearly all important decisions that a government must take. Government proposals are usually evaluated in terms of the relevant agreements in the government programme. Deflections from the programme are usually taken very seriously by the coalition partners.

Generally, coalition building processes in the Netherlands can be divided into three phases. In the first phase, a provisional decision is taken on the composition of the coalition. In the second phase, negotiations on the government programme are conducted between the proposed coalition partners. In the third and last phase decisions are taken on the portfolio distribution and on the personal composition of the cabinet. Of course this is a simplification; in reality there is always some overlap between the phases, but in general it is an acceptable characterisation of Dutch coalition building.

Programme negotiations are therefore not as a rule decisive for the composition of the cabinet. In this way politicians avoid having to conduct negotiations on composition and programme at the same time. Only after the elections in 1956 and 1972 did the two phases intermingle. In 1951, when the Drees I cabinet was reconstructed after a severe conflict between one of the ministers and his own party, agreement on the government programme preceded agreement on the composition of the cabinet. In most cases the coalition originally contemplated became the ultimate government that formed. The only exception to this occurred in 1977. In that year, as we have mentioned, very laborious negotiations between CDA, PvdA and D'66 broke down after more than five months, as a result of conflict about the personal composition of the cabinet. Subsequently, a coalition between CDA and VVD was formed.

In the second phase coalition building starts: here, the programme negotiations are central. The composition of the cabinet has already been more or less decided but this phase is very important for the distribution of policy payoffs.

Until the formation of the Biesheuvel cabinet in 1971, negotiations over the programme were the least time-consuming phase of Dutch coalition building, in spite of the important role of policy. From then on, however, it has taken relatively more time to come to a policy agreement. In 1971 and 1977 it was the most time-consuming phase. Of course the increase in the length of government programme is closely connected with this development.

In the third phase of coalition building, agreements are worked out on the portfolio distribution and the personal composition of the cabinet. In general this is the most time-consuming phase of coalition building, despite the fact that the well-known proportionality rule is also valid for the distribution of cabinet portfolios in the Netherlands. Usually portfolios – cabinet ministers as well as state secretaries – are roughly distributed among the coalition members in accordance with their relative numerical size (measured by legislative seats). Of course, there is disagreement sometimes about the actual application of the proportionality rule. But, in general, considerable time is needed to come to an agreement on the portfolio distribution even after the exact number of ministers and portfolios has been agreed upon. The wish of parties to be represented in relevant policy areas together with the availability of capable candidates, and the personal preferences of the candidates usually make for an intricate and time-consuming process.

The total length of the formation process varies from cabinet to cabinet, but is generally long when compared with countries that have a similar political system. The formation processes in 1956, 1972, 1977 and 1981 were of exceptional length, even by Dutch standards.

CONSTRAINTS ON BARGAINING

Before we can take account of the policy distances between parties, we first have to define the range of potential coalitions for which those policy distances are relevant. Not all possible coalitions are viable in the Netherlands. Some coalitions are impossible because of general or party-specific constraints on bargaining.

General constraints

There are no formal exogenous constraints on coalition bargaining in the Netherlands. We should, however, reckon with three informal 'rules of the game' that act as general endogenous constraints on the coalitions which can form and are agreed by each of the major players in the coalition formation game.

To begin with, there are no regular minority coalitions in the Netherlands. Each of the three minority cabinets after 1945 (Zijlstra, Biesheuvel II and Van Agt III) was a short-lived interim or caretaker cabinet, formed to bridge the period between the breakdown of one government and the installation of another. A second informal rule of the game is constituted by the reluctance of the religious parties to govern alone (with the exception of two caretaker cabinets). In spite of their numerical parliamentary majority in the period between 1946 and 1963 (see Table H.1 in the appendix to this chapter) they have never opted for a cabinet composed of religious parties only. A reason for this may be found in the extraordinary politico-economic situation after the end of the Second World War. There was a general feeling that the post-war reconstruction of the Netherlands needed broadly-based political support, including at least the most important religious and non-religious parties. A more important reason however, has its origins in the history of Dutch politics. The Dutch political system – and society – was at the end of nineteenth and the beginning of the twentieth century deeply divided between religious and non-religious political groups. During the Pacificatie of 1918 the most important issues were resolved, in the sense that the equal position of each religious group was legalised. Since then no government has formed on the basis of religion alone: secular parties have always been represented in government. A last reason has to do with the fact that the three religious parties were not a monolithic political bloc. Although they had a lot of things in common, the political and cultural differences between the KVP and the ARP especially would have rendered a confessional majority-government difficult.

A third informal rule of the game is the strong tradition against admitting to the coalition small parties (parties with less than three or so seats) or extreme parties. To this rule there is only one exception. In 1971 the PPR formed a pre-electoral pact with PvdA and D'66. Although the PPR got only two seats in parliament, the other parties stuck to the previous agreements by doing so, they gave the PPR coalition-potential in this instance. On all other occasions the small parties have not played an important role, no matter how crucial their seats might have been for one or the other coalition (and they were indeed crucial in 1972 and 1981). Extreme parties, such as the Communist Party (CPN) or the farmer's party (BP), will not be admitted to a coalition.

Party-specific constraints

These three general endogenous constraints on bargaining agreed by the three main parties, which between them control government formation, allow us to select a much smaller subset out of the thousands of arithmetically possible coalitions that would have formed in the Netherlands after each election since 1945. A further reduction in the range of possible coalitions, however, is produced once we consider a number of party-specific endogenous constraints on bargaining. Typically, these are formal public commitments by particular parties about which partners are, and are not, acceptable. Obviously, these commitments are not 'given' but arise as a result of party competition. Once made, however, such commitments do act as constraints on bargaining. These have been both prescriptive – on the basis of pre-electoral alliances such as that between PvdA, PPR and D'66 in 1971 and 1972, and proscriptive – as specific parties have excluded co-operation with specific opponents. Table 10.1 lists these constraints in Dutch politics after 1945.

The most striking aspect of the bottom part of Table 10.1 is the protracted mutual exclusion of the PvdA and the VVD. The VVD started this polarisation in 1959 and ended it formally on the eve of the election of 1977. The Socialists adopted the polarisation strategy in 1967 and ended it in 1982. Many students of Dutch politics have pointed out that this polarisation between PvdA and VVD, although intended to hit the confessional parties, in fact strengthened them, since they were always needed for any legislative majority (Van den Berg, 1986).

Table 10.1   Structural influences and constraints on Dutch coalition formation

A: General constraints (informal rules of the game)

 1. No minority cabinets
 2. No exclusive religious cabinet
 3. No small or extreme parties in cabinet

B. Party-specific constraints

 1. PvdA, D'66, PR (also known as progressive three) formed pre-electoral alliance in 1971, 1972
 2. VVD excluded co-operation with PvdA in 1959, 1963, 1967, 1971, 1972
 3. PvdA excluded co-operation with VVD in 1967, 1971, 1972, 1977, 1981
 4. Progressive three excluded co-operation with all other parties in 1971, 1972
 5. D'66 excluded co-operation with CDA and VVD, but not with CDA or VVD in 1977, 1981.

The situation was further polarised by the PvdA in 1971 and 1972 when they entered a pre-electoral alliance with D'66 and PPR and declared they would not be prepared to form a coalition with any other parties after the elections. This attempt to give 'clarity' to the voters caused the socialist party a lot of embarrassment, especially in 1972 when the so-called 'progressive three' again fell far short of a majority (Daalder, 1986).

Finally, in 1977 and 1981 D'66 excluded co-operation with both the CDA and VVD, but not with either one on its own. In practice, this meant that they would not participate in a government without the PvdA; because of the exclusion of the VVD by the PvdA it meant that D'66 tied itself to a coalition of PvdA, CDA and D'66.

Table 10.2 shows the impact of general and specific bargaining constraints on the total number of possible coalitions in Dutch politics. The figures speak largely for themselves, although we should note the dramatic reduction in the range of possible coalitions that is produced by the constraints. This reduction is at its most spectacular in 1971 and 1972 when several thousand arithmetically possible coalitions are reduced to one, once bargaining constraints are considered. This peculiar situation was caused by the uncompromising position of the progressive three, discussed above.

In 1971 and in 1972 the only possible coalition consisted of KVP, ARP, CHU, VVD and DS'70. In 1971 this coalition actually came into being, but it collapsed after a year, in a crisis provoked by DS'70. Due to this exercise, the other parties in 1972 refused to join a coalition with DS'70 again. There was thus an unprecedented stalemate in the cabinet formation process since

Table 10.2   Total number of conceivable and feasible coalitions after each election, Netherlands, 1946–81

Year	Number of arithmetically possible coalitions	Number of possible winning coalitions	Number of possible coalitions according to general constraints	Number of possible coalitions eliminated by party-specific constraints	Remaining possible coalitions
1946	127	64	10	—	10
1948	255	128	10	—	10
1952	255	128	10	—	10
1956	127	64	13	—	13
1959	255	128	12	6	6
1963	1023	512	11	4	7
1967	2047	1024	23	12	11
1971*	4095	2048	23	22	1
1972*†	4095	2048	14	13	1
1977	2047	1024	7	4	3
1981	1023	512	5	3	2

* Progressive three counted as one party.

† Progressive three counted as one party, confessional three counted as three parties.

all arithmetically possible coalitions were excluded by existing constraints. This could only be solved after the progressive three moderated their position on non-participation in a 'post-electoral' coalition. After a very turbulent formation-process a new government came into being, that consisted of members of the progressive three and KVP and ARP. This cabinet was supported by the parliamentary parties of PvdA, PPR and D'66 and tolerated by KVP and ARP.

Having limited the range of arithmetically possible coalitions by applying the bargaining constraints listed, we now explore the extent to which the policy positions of the parties can be used to account for the coalitions which actually formed.

DOCUMENTS CODED

In order to establish these policy positions of coalition governments, we coded the formal government policy statement rather than the government programme agreed between the parties in the period of cabinet formation. This policy statement is made before parliament by the prime-minister in the so-called installation debate. It is a verbal reproduction of the formal government programme written into the official record of parliament. Only one cabinet (Drees III in 1952) did not make an autonomous policy statement. The announcement of its policy intentions was made in conjunction with the general discussions on the budget for 1953. We therefore had to exclude it from our analysis. Because of the very minor importance of the four caretaker cabinets, we have also excluded these from further discussions. Furthermore, we left out the Drees II government of 1950. This was a reconstruction of the Drees I government, which had collapsed after an internal conflict between the VVD minister of Foreign Affairs and his own party in the Tweede Kamer. No new elections were held, no changes occurred in the political composition and only minor changes took place in the personal composition of the cabinet. Moreover, the policy statement of the new government had a very peculiar character (Visser, 1986). It emphasised only three policy issues (enlarging defence expenditures, balancing the budget, stabilizing the balance of payments) and did not mention other plans. The party manifestos that we used for our analysis are described in Dittrich (1987).

DIMENSIONS OF POLICY-COMPETITION

While it is certainly quite common to describe the Dutch party system in terms of a single ideological dimension (see, e.g. de Swaan 1973), some evidence exists that it was for a certain period of time a 'one-and-a-half' dimension system, involving a (strong) socio-economic dimension and a (rather weak) religious dimension. This last dimension relates solely to the manifestos of the confessional parties and was not relevant for the other parties. By the beginning of the 1960s, the religious dimension had almost faded away (Dittrich, 1987). The policy coding categories used by Dittrich as indicators for the religious dimension in his original analysis of Dutch party manifestos, are incorporated in the standard left–right dimension used in this study. The weakness of the religious dimension is illustrated by the fact that this seems to influence the relative positions of the respective parties only in a very limited way (only ARP and CHU have a slightly different position). Most probably, the religious 'half-dimension' was not a very important determinant of coalition behaviour.

Table 10.3 shows the policy positions of those parties with coalition potential under our constraints on the standard left–right dimension used

Table 10.3 Policy positions of Dutch parties and governments in one-dimensional space, 1946–81

Party	1946	1948	1952	1956	1959	1963	1967	1971	1972	1977	1981
KVP	4	7	20	9	-9	-13	7	-26			
ARP	21	18	16	9	17	2	-5	-18			
CHU	22	21	21*	27	14	-2	10	-22			
'CDA'†									-14		
CDA										-12	-19
PvdA	-20	-15	-23	-21	-28	-31	-25	-40		-45	-29
D'66							-18	-21	-13	-27	-22
PPR								-36			
Progressive three									-44		
VVD	19	20	33	10	17	10	10	-2	21	14	8
DS'70								-13	-13		
Government	10	0	3	-3	7	-10	11	1	-18	-1	1

* No data for CHU; policy position assumed unchanged since 1948
† In 1972, KVP, ARP and CHU only had a common programme

with other countries in this book. During the whole period after the Second World War the PvdA occupied a rather isolated position on the left wing of the Dutch party system. Only in 1971 and 1972, and perhaps in 1981, did the socialists find a party neighbour, in the shape of D'66 or the PPR, within a relatively short ideological distance. Table 10.3 clearly documents, moreover, the rapid radicalisation of the PvdA in the period between 1967 and 1972.

The right-wing position on the scale was for most of the time occupied by the VVD, the liberal-conservative party. Only 1956 seems to be a real exception, with the CHU clearly occupying the right wing position. In contrast, to the PvdA, the position of the VVD initially was not an isolated one. In most of the elections the VVD was close to CHU and ARP (in 1946, 1948, 1959 and 1963) or KVP and CHU (1967). Beginning in 1971, however, the VVD lost its close ideological neighbours. Especially after the start of Christian-Democratic co-operation, the VVD became the sole occupier of the right-wing position in the Dutch party system.

The position of the KVP, the catholic party and, after 1972, the CDA, the Christian Democratic Party, was always between the positions of the PvdA and VVD. In most elections the KVP is the most left-oriented confessional party (1946, 1948, 1959, 1963 and 1971); in 1956 it had to share this position with the ARP, while the ARP was the most left-oriented confessional party in 1952 and 1967. Moreover, it is interesting to note that the KVP took its most right-wing positions in 1946, 1948, 1952, 1956 and 1967; in each of those years the KVP had just been involved in a coalition with the PvdA. In 1959, 1963 and 1971 the KVP took its most left-wing position; in 1963 and 1971 the KVP had just been in coalition with the VVD. This suggests that the KVP may have used its manifestos as a counterbalance to the position of the outgoing government.

A party can 'control' a particular policy dimension if it controls the median legislator on that dimension. In a one-dimensional policy space control of the median legislator, as we saw in Chapter 1, places it in the core position. If, over a period of time, the same party occupies this position, we might think of it as a 'predominant' party in the system as a whole. In Dutch terms we can think of the predominant party as one that tends to control the median legislator among those parties with coalition potential. The core position in the Dutch party system always was occupied by the catholic party (KVP) and its successor, the CDA. These parties therefore can be considered as the predominant parties in the Netherlands.

ONE-DIMENSIONAL ANALYSIS

Government formation

The first and most obvious conclusion from this analysis has already been alluded to – the party with the median legislator on the left–right scale, the KVP or CDA, was never out of government in the post-war era. The evidence in this is quite unequivocal. Given this, the next matter to settle is whether the KVP/CDA core parties select coalition partners on the basis of policy distances.

We use one-dimensional policy distances to predict which non-religious partner the predominant confessional party will choose. Table 10.4 shows the policy distances between KVP/CDA and PvdA and VVD. The last column in the table indicates whether the closest party is in government.

From the total of twelve coalition cases only eight are relevant for this analysis. In 1948 a coalition was formed that included both PvdA and VVD. In 1972 and 1981 CDA and VVD didn't have a majority of the seats in the Tweede Kamer, while in 1971 the PvdA and its progressive allies refused to form a coalition with other parties. The table shows us, that the PvdA is not closest, yet in government in 1946, 1952, 1956. It is closest, yet not in government in 1959 and a part of the period after 1963. The only times the closest party is in government is in the other part of the period after 1963 (PvdA), in 1967 (VVD) and in 1977 (VVD). Policy-distance theory predicts the correct coalition only in three out of eight relevant cases.

Table 10.4   Policy distances between predominant confessional party (KVP/CDA) and non-confessional parties (PvdA and VVD) on one dimension, Netherlands 1946–81

Election	PvdA	VVD	Party with smallest distance in coalition
1946	24	15	–
1948	both PvdA and VVD in coalition		
1952	43	13	–
1956	30	1	–
1959	19	26	–
1963	18	23	–\+
1967	32	3	+
1971	coalition determined by constraints		
1972	CDA and VVD together no majority		
1977	33	26	+
1981	CDA and VVD together no majority		

Policy payoffs

Table 10.5 also gives the policy positions of the governments that formed during the study period. It is immediately obvious that the policies of the Dutch government tend to be very middle of the road, with policy positions that fluctuate around the centre of the scale. Table 10.5 gives the distances between the policy positions of the main parties and the policy-positions of the governments on the one-dimensional scale.

A very interesting aspect of this table is that seven out of eleven government policy-positions are closest to the policy position of KVP/CDA (1946, 1948, 1963a, 1963b, 1972 and 1977), while one government position is very close to the KVP position, but not closest (1967). The mean distance between the government and the party policy position is however only slightly less than it is for three other parties (CHU, ARP, VVD). The VVD's policy position is in three out of eleven cases closest to the policy position of the government (1967, 1971, and 1981) and the mean distance between the government programme and the party position is comparatively small for the VVD. Although its bargaining position was almost as

Table 10.5 Distances between policy-positions of main parties and policy positions of governments on left–right dimension, Netherlands, 1946–81

Year	Government	PvdA	KVP/ CDA	ARP	CHU	VVD
1946	Beel	+30	+6	−11	−12	−9
1948	Drees I	+15	+7	−18	−21	−20
1952	Drees III	n/a	n/a	n/a	n/a	n/a
1956	Drees IV	+18	−12	−12	−30	−13
1959	De Quay	+35	+16	−10	−7	−10
1963a	Marijnen	+21	+3	−12	−8	−20
1963b	Cals	+22	+4	−11	−7	−19
1967	De Jong	+36	+4	+16	+1	+1
1971	Biesheuvel	+41	+27	+19	+23	+3
1972	Den Uyl	+26	−4			−39
1977	Van Agt I	+44	+11			+15
1981	Van Agt II	+30	+20			−7
Mean distance (md)		29	10	14	14	14
md in government		24	–	15	15	12
md not in government		35	–	13	10	17

+ Government position to the right of the party
− Government position to the left of the party

weak as that of the PvdA, the VVD managed to get a far better result. This probably reflects the less isolated position of the VVD. Note especially that the VVD did quite well even when it was out of office, as in 1946, 1956 and 1981. The mean distances between the positions of ARP and CHU and the government positions are comparatively small, but they are not smaller than for the VVD. This is probably because the two small religious parties took a relatively extreme stand on the religious dimension, while the position of the government programmes on this dimension always was relatively moderate. The mean distance between the government and party policy-position is by far the largest for the PvdA. This reflects both the rather isolated, left-wing policy-position of the PvdA and its rather weak bargaining position. The table also compares the mean policy distance between party and government, depending on whether the party concerned was in or out of office. For the three parties who were typically close to government policy participation in government made relatively little difference to policy payoffs. For the PvdA, however, participation in government made a big difference: government policy was closer to PvdA policy when the PvdA was in office.

TWENTY-DIMENSIONAL ANALYSIS: GOVERNMENT FORMATION

If we deal with the full set of twenty policy categories we can model coalition formation as a process of clustering. For the Netherlands it is most appropriate to use hierarchical clustering. The twenty-dimensional policy-distances between parties and the results of the cluster analysis are given in the appendix to the Chapter; Table 10.6 below, shows the most interesting conclusions of the twenty-dimensional analysis.

The first column of this table gives an answer to the question whether the twenty-dimensional analysis correctly predicts the direction of the coalition, in the sense of predicting which non-confessional party, the PvdA or the VVD, the predominant confessional party will take as a coalition partner. The second column shows whether the twenty-dimensional analysis correctly predicts the exact composition of the full coalition.

The table shows that, in six out of eight relevant cases, the twenty-dimensional analysis does correctly predict the direction of the coalition. Only in 1946, when the first regular post-war government was formed, and in 1963b, when the confessional parties exchanged the VVD for the PvdA without prior elections being held, was the coalition partner predicted by the twenty-dimensional analysis not taken by the KVP or CDA.

Table 10.6   Does 20-dimensional analysis predict correctly the direction and the
composition of Dutch governmental coalitions?

Year	Government	Direction (PvdA or VVD)	Composition (Total coalitions)
1946	Beel	wrong	wrong
1948	Drees I	†*	wrong
1952	Drees III	right	right
1956	Drees IV	right	right
1959	De Quay	right	right
1963a	Marijnen	right	right
1963b	Cals	wrong	wrong
1967	De Jong	right	right
1971	Biesheuvel	†	—
1972	Den Uyl	‡	—
1977	Van Agt I	right	right
1981	Van Agt II	‡	right

* : both PvdA and VVD in coalition
‡ : coalition determined by exclusions
† : CDA and VVD have together no majority

As far as the total composition of coalitions is concerned, the prediction of the twenty-dimensional analysis are less successful. They are correct in seven out of ten cases. Besides the two cases in which, according to the twenty-dimensional analysis the direction of the coalition was not predicted, there is an erroneous characterisation for 1948. In that year the ARP should have been in government: actually it was not in government because of its uncompromising stand on the decolonisation of Indonesia, a delicate matter on which there was some sort of consensus between the other parties. In general, however, the twenty-dimensional policy-distances provide a relatively accurate basis for prediction of both the direction and the exact composition of Dutch post-war coalitions.

DISAGGREGATED TWENTY-DIMENSIONAL ANALYSIS

Coalition formation

We look at each of the 20 policy dimensions individually. This allows us to see whether a particular party occupies a central position across the range of policy dimensions. The more dimensions on which a given party controls the median legislator, the stronger the bargaining position that it would appear to command. If a particular party controls a substantial part of the dimensions over a period of time, we might think of it as the predominant party.

Table 10.7 shows the number of policy dimensions on which each of the respective parties occupies a core-position. The figure in parenthesis is an estimate of the aggregate salience of these dimensions (operationalised as the mean proportion of party manifestos devoted to the dimensions in question).

It is immediately clear from the table that the KVP and, after 1972, the CDA, are the predominant parties in Dutch post-war politics. On average, they occupy a pivotal position on more than 50 per cent of the 20 dimensions; the mean salience of these dimensions in 48 per cent. If we look at the separate elections, we see that only in 1948 did the KVP not occupy the strongest position, while in 1971 it had to share this position with the CHU – its close ally. In the other six elections until 1972 the KVP had by far the strongest position. After 1972, the merger of the three former confessional parties into the CDA only strengthened the predominant position of the

Table 10.7 Numbers of times Dutch parties include the median legislator over 20 policy dimensions, with the relative saliency of dimensions

Election year	KVP/CDA	ARP	CHU	PvdA	D'66	PPR	VVD	DS'70
1946	12(59)	6(23)	3(7)	0(0)			4(10)	
1948	5(22)	6(24)	4(14)	7(29)			0(0)	
1952	9(49)	4(30)	4(15)	4(7)			3(8)	
1956	13(52)	5(21)	2(15)	5(17)			5(8)	
1959	7(35)	3(3)	1(5)	8(29)			2(2)	
1963	9(51)	2(16)	0(0)	4(18)			4(9)	
1967	10(41)	4(19)	5(29)	3(12)	2(9)		4(17)	
1971	11(41)	3(7)	8(42)	4(24)	5(12)	0(0)	7(28)	3(3)
1972	13(53)			8(40)	8(40)	8(40)	5(13)	1(1)
1977	15(63)			5(14)	2(8)		3(11)	
1981	14(67)			6(25)	3(6)		5(10)	
Mean	11(48)	4(18)	4(16)	5(19)	4(15)	4(20)	4(11)	2(2)

The first figure in each column refers to the number of dimensions on which the respective parties include the median legislator. As verTCy small differences have been counted as equivalent, many cases are tied so the number of cases adds to more than 20 in most years.

The figure in brackets refers to the saliency of these dimensions.

* Common manifesto for PvdA, D'66 and PPR (Progressive Three)

confessional element in Dutch politics. The number of dimensions on which the CDA has a median legislator as well as the salience of these dimensions, strongly increase in comparison with the period in which the confessional parties acted separately. All the other parties had a weak bargaining position. Only now and again did they occupy a relatively strong position, as is the case with the PvdA in 1948, the progressive three in 1972 and the CHU in 1971. The ARP and the VVD never disposed of a very strong bargaining position.

In short, the analysis of the disaggregated twenty dimensions confirms an earlier conclusion arrived at on the basis of the one-dimensional analysis: the KVP and, after 1972, the CDA are the predominant parties in Dutch politics. This explains why these parties are always strongly represented in Dutch post-war coalitions: their predominant position lends them so much bargaining power that they cannot be passed over in coalition-building processes.

Government policy

Table 10.8 shows the distances between the policy-positions of the five main parties and the policy-positions of the respective governments on the

Table 10.8   Distances between policy positions of main parties and policy positions of government on 20 dimensions (aggregate figures), Netherlands, 1946–81

Coalitions		KVP/ CDA	ARP	CHU	PvdA	D'66	PPR	VVD	DS'70
1946	Beel	50.1	52.6	33.8	63.4			56.6	
1948	Drees I	36.1	41.0	45.0	59.8			68.7	
1952	Drees III	?	?	?	?			?	
1956	Drees IV	29.1	27.1	54.0	45.0			46.0	
1959	De Quay	41.5	36.5	46.8	52.8			51.9	
1963a	Marijnen	46.0	30.5	52.9	47.5			49.2	
1963b	Cals	53.5	40.6	54.0	48.6			48.5	
1967	De Jong	20.1	39.9	20.1	71.7	74.7		27.7	
1971	Biesheuvel	39.2	43.6	38.8	68.2	52.0	85.3	25.3	48.4
1972	Den Uyl	40.8			45.2	45.2	45.2	56.8	48.2
1977	Van Agt I	30.7			66.7	45.9		30.1	
1981	Van Agt II	32.8			52.9	39.8		25.5	
Mean		38.2	39.0	43.2	56.5	51.5	65.3	44.2	48.3
In Government		38.2	36.4	41.6	52.5	42.5	85.3	42.1	
Not in Government		–	46.8	54.0	61.4	57.5	45.2	46.6	

20 dimensions. The patterns are quite clear. The confessional parties, including the predominant KVP/CDA, have the largest policy payoff overall, though it makes little difference whether they were in or out of office. The VVD did much better than the PvdA, in or out of office. The PvdA, as a result of its isolated position, did worst of the major parties, though government participation did made a noticeable difference to its payoffs.

CONCLUSIONS

Our analysis gives ample evidence for the existence of a strong predominant party in the Netherlands. In the period between 1946 and 1971 this was the Catholic party, the KVP; afterwards the predominant position was taken over by the new interconfessional party, the CDA. These parties dispose of a very advantageous bargaining position, and this explains why they have always been in government after 1945.

In order to summarise the main patterns that we have been discussing above we tested six different hypotheses that use policy-distances to predict the composition of Dutch governments (see Table 10.9). Three of these tests concern the direction, the other three the exact composition of the coalition.

The three direction tests relate to the question of whether the predominant parties KVP and CDA preferred co-operation with the PvdA or the VVD on the basis of policy-distances. The table shows that the direction of two of the eight relevant coalitions is predicted correctly by all three of the tests (De Jong and Van Agt I). The direction of three coalitions is predicted correctly by two out of the three tests (Drees III, Drees IV, Cals), while for the other coalitions direction is predicted correctly only by one (De Quay and Marijnen) or by none of the tests (Beel). As we saw in the above discussion, the 20-dimensional analyses were the more successful.

The table makes clear why after 1967, the VVD was more successful in forming a coalition with the predominant party than the PvdA. After that year, the direction of the coalition was either determined by the constraints (as was the case in 1971, 1972 and 1981), or by the much smaller policy-distances between KVP/CDA and VVD (in 1967 and 1977). The only times the PvdA was in government after 1967 was when CDA and VVD together did not have a majority of the seats in parliament (as in 1972 and 1981).

The other three tests relate to the exact composition of the coalition. We tested within the one-dimensional space whether a coalition would form with the minimum aggregate policy distance (MAP), or the one in which the distance between the policy centre of the coalition and the predominant

Table 10.9 Success rates of policy-based theories in the Netherlands

Coalitions		Possible coalitions	Feasible coalitions after constraints	Direction of coalitions			Exact composition of coalitions		
				A	B	C	D	E	F
1946	Beel	127	10	No	No	No	Yes(3)	No(6)	No(3)
1948	Drees I	255	10	–	–	–	No(3)	Yes(3)	No(3)
1952	Drees III	255	10	No	Yes	Yes	No(2)	No(2)	Yes(3)
1956	Drees IV	127	13	No	Yes	Yes	No(1)	No(1)	Yes(3)
1959	De Quay	255	6	No	Yes	No	No(1)	No(2)	Yes(2)
1963a	Marijnen	1023	7	No	No	Yes	No(1)	No(1)	Yes(3)
1963b	Cals			Yes	Yes	No	No(1)	Yes(1)	No(3)
1967	De Jong	2047	11	Yes	Yes	Yes	Yes(1)	Yes(1)	Yes(1)
1971	Biesheuvel	4095	1	–	–	–	–	–	–
1972	Den Uyl	4095	1	–	–	–	–	–	–
1977	Van Agt I	2047	3	Yes	Yes	Yes	Yes(1)	Yes(1)	Yes(2)
1981	Van Agt II	1023	2	–	–	Yes	Yes(1)	Yes(1)	Yes(2)
Predictive success				.37	.75	.62	.40	.50	.70
				(3/8)	(6/8)	(5/8)	(4/10)	(5/10)	(7/10)
Predictive efficiency				.37	.75	.62	.27	.26	.27
				(3/8)	(6/8)	(5/8)	(4/15)	(5/19)	(7/26)

A   Predominant party (KVP/CDA) in majority coalition with closest non-confessional party (one dimension)
B   Predominant party (KVP/CDA) in majority coalition with closest non-confessional party (twenty-dimensional clustering)
C   Predominant party (KVP/CDA) in majority coalition with closest non-confessional party (disaggregated 20 dimensions)
D   Majority coalition with smallest MAP (one dimension)
E   Majority coalition with smallest dcp (one dimension)
F   Majority coalition is at majority node on cluster tree (twenty-dimensional clustering)

The figures in brackets refer to the number of predicted coalitions. Base numbers of predictions and numbers in predictions sets refers to feasible coalitions party (DCP) was minimised. These theories in general were not very successful.

The 20-dimensional cluster analysis is more successful than the one-dimensional analysis: it predicts the composition of the coalitions correctly in seven out of ten cases. In general, all the 20-dimensional models (clustered or disaggregated) give better results than the one-dimensional models. As the measures of predictive success and predictive efficiency show, policy distance models are much better at explaining Dutch coalitions (at any rate, once the effects of constraints have been allowed for) than those of some other countries, notably Scandinavia.

In conclusion, we may say that policy-distances give a particularly robust explanation for the coalitions of 1967 and 1977. The twenty-dimensional tests are useful in explaining the composition of the Drees III and IV cabinets. As far as the other coalitions are concerned, policy-distance theory can be used to give insight into some aspects of the coalition-processes (such as the broadening of the cabinet in 1948 and the collapse of the Marijnen government). But it is hard to explain these coalitions solely in policy-distance terms. Especially in the formation of the De Quay (1959) and Marijnen governments (1963) other considerations than pure policy-distance must have played a decisive role. Moreover, in 1971 and 1972, and to a certain extent in 1981, the coalitions were solely determined by the constraints.

As far as the policy payoffs are concerned we may conclude, on the basis of the one-dimensional and the disaggregated 20-dimensional analysis, that the predominant parties used their strong bargaining position to drag government policy fairly close to their own policy-position. However, the differences with three other parties (ARP, CHU and VVD) are rather small. Only for the PvdA is the distance to the government programme relatively large, even when the socialists are in government. The PvdA, furthermore, is also the only party for which being in or out of the government really seems to matter in policy terms.

APPENDIX H

Table H.1 Seat distribution in Tweede Kamer, 1946–86

Party	1946	1948	1952	1956	1959	1963	1967	1971	1972	1977	1981	1982	1986
KVP	32	32	30	49	49	50	42	35	27	–	–	–	–
ARP	13	13	12	15	14	13	15	13	14	–	–	–	–
CHU	8	9	9	13	12	13	12	10	7	–	–	–	–
CDA	–	–	–	–	–	–	–	–	–	49	48	45	54
subtotal	53	54	51	77	75	76	69	58	48	49	48	45	54
PvdA	29	27	30	50	48	43	37	39	43	53	44	47	52
D'66	–	–	–	–	–	–	7	11	6	8	17	6	9
PPR	–	–	–	–	–	–	–	2	7	3	3	2	2
subtotal	29	27	30	50	48	43	44	52	56	64	64	55	63
VVD	6	8	9	13	19	16	17	16	22	28	26	36	27
DS'70	–	–	–	–	–	–	–	8	6	1	–	–	–
PSP	–	–	–	–	2	4	4	2	2	1	3	3	1
CPN	10	8	6	7	3	4	5	6	7	2	3	3	–
BP	–	–	–	–	–	3	7	1	3	1	–	–	–
SGP	2	2	2	3	3	3	3	3	3	3	3	3	3
GPV	–	–	–	–	–	1	1	2	2	1	1	1	1

Table H.1 (cont'd)

Party	1946	1948	1952	1956	1959	1963	1967	1971	1972	1977	1981	1982	1986
Others	–	1	2	–	–	–	–	2	1	–	2	4	1
No. of Seats	100	100	100	150	150	150	150	150	150	150	150	150	150
No. of Parties	7	8	8	7	8	10	11	14	14	11	10	12	9

KVP   Catholic People's Party
ARP   Anti Revolutionary Party (Calvinist)
CHU   Christian Historical Union (Dutch Reformed)
CDA   Christian Democratic Appeal (Interconfessional)
PvdA   Labour Party
VVD   Conservative Liberals
DS'70   Right-wing social democrats
PSP   Radical socialist and pacifist party
D'66   Radical democratic party
PPR   Political Party of Radicals (leftist party)
CPN   Communist Party
BP   Farmers Party (poujadist)
SGP   Extreme religious party
GPV   Extreme religious party

Table H.2 Dutch cabinets, 1946–86

Investiture	Name of Cabinet	Composition						Seats	%	Minority	Minimal	Oversized
										Numerical Basis		
07-46	Beel I	KVP			PvdA		Non-party	61	61		X	
08-48	Drees I	KVP	ARP	CHU	PvdA	VVD	Non-party	76	76			X
03-51	Drees II	KVP		CHU	PvdA	VVD	Non-party	76	76			X
09-52	Drees III	KVP	ARP	CHU	PvdA		Non-party	81	81			X
10-56	Drees IV	KVP	ARP	CHU	PvdA		Non-party	127	85			X
12-58	Beel II*	KVP	ARP	CHU				77	51		X	
05-59	De Quay	KVP	ARP	CHU		VVD		94	63		X	
07-63	Marijnen	KVP	ARP	CHU		VVD		92	61		X	
04-65	Cals	KVP	ARP		PvdA			106	71			X
11-66	Zijlstra*	KVP	ARP					63	42	X		
04-67	De Jong	KVP	ARP	CHU		VVD		86	57		X	
07-71	Biesheuvel I	KVP	ARP	CHU		VVD	DS'70	82	54		X	
07-72	Biesheuvel II*	KVP	ARP	CHU		VVD		74	49	X		
05-73	Den Uyl	KVP	ARP		PvdA		D'66, PPR	97	65	X		
12-77	Van Agt I		CDA			VVD		77	51		X	
11-82	Van Agt II		CDA		PvdA		D'66	109	73			X
05-82	Van Agt III		CDA				D'66	65	43	X		
11-82	Lubbers I		CDA			VVD		81	54		X	
07-86	Lubbers II		CDA			VVD		81	54		X	
Mean		38.2	39.0	43.2	56.5	51.5	65.3	44.2	48.3			
In Government		38.2	36.4	41.6	52.5	42.5	85.3	42.1				
Not in Government		–	46.8	54.0	71.7	57.5	45.2	46.6				

(*) Caretaker or interim government

Table H.3 Minimum aggregate policy distances (MAPs) and distances between coalition and predominant party position (DCPs), 1946–81 (Calculated on basis of scores of Dutch parties on the standard left–right scale)

Year	Ranking	Coalition	MAP	Ranking	Coalition	DCP
1946	1	ARP,KVP,VVD	21.6	1	CHU,KVP,PvdA	1.83
		KVP,PvdA(*)	23.7		ARP,KVP,PvdA,VVD	2.18
		ARP,CHU,KVP,VVD	25.3		ARP,KVP,PvdA	2.27
	2	KVP,PvdA,VVD	41.93		CHU,KVP,PvdA,VVD	2.5
		ARP,KVP,PvdA	42.87		KVP,PvdA,VVD	2.73
		CHU,KVP,PvdA	43.73		ARP,CHU,KVP,PvdA	2.85
	3	ARP,KVP,PvdA,VVD	56.1	2	ARP,CHU,PvdA,VVD	6.73
		CHU,KVP,PvdA,VVD	57.4	3	ARP,KVP,VVD	10.8
		ARP,CHU,KVP,PvdA	58.8		KVP,PvdA(*)	11.85
		ARP,CHU,PvdA,VVD	60.85		ARP,CHU,KVP,VVD	12.65
1948	1	ARP,KVP,VVD	17.33	1	ARP,KVP,PvdA,VVD	0.5
		ARP,CHU,KVP,VVD	20		ARP,CHU,KVP,PvdA	0.5
		KVP,PvdA	20		CHU,KVP,PvdA,VVD(*)	1
	2	ARP,KVP,PvdA	34.67	2	KVP,PvdA,VVD	3
		KVP,PvdA,VVD	36		CHU,KVP,PvdA	3
		CHU,KVP,PvdA	36		ARP,KVP,PvdA	3.67
	3	ARP,KVP,PvdA,VVD	46		ARP,CHU,PvdA,VVD	4
		ARP,CHU,PvdA,VVD	46	3	ARP,KVP,VVD	7.67
		CHU,KVP,PvdA,VVD(*)	48		ARP,CHU,KVP,VVD	9
		ARP,CHU,PvdA,VVD	50	4	KVP,PvdA	11

Table H.3 (cont'd)

Year	Ranking	Coalition	MAP	Ranking	Coalition	DCP
1952	1	ARP,KVP,VVD	20.2	1	KVP,ARP,CHU,VVD	2.5
		KVP,ARP,CHU,VVD	21		ARP,KVP,VVD	2.6
	2	KVP,PvdA	42.2	2	PvdA,ARP,CHU,VVD	8.25
	3	ARP,KVP,PvdA	53.53		ARP,KVP,PvdA,VVD	8.5
		ARP,CHU,PvdA	55.34	3	KVP,PvdA,VVD	10.1
		KVP,PvdA,ARP,VVD	56		ARP,PvdA,VVD	11.47
		KVP,PvdA,CHU	58		KVP,ARP,CHU,PvdA (*)	11.5
	4	ARP,PvdA,VVD	62.27	4	KVP,CHU,PvdA	14
		KVP,PvdA,ARP,CHU(*)	63		ARP,CHU,PvdA	15.34
		KVP,PvdA,VVD	65		ARP,KVP,PvdA	15.83
		PvdA,ARP,CHU,VVD	69.5	5	KVP,PvdA	21.5
1956	1	ARP,KVP,VVD	2.4	1	ARP,KVP,VVD	0.1
	2	ARP,CHU,KVP,VVD	26.55	2	ARP,CHU,PvdA,VVD	2.85
		KVP,PvdA	29.5		CHU,ARP,PvdA,VVD	2.85
	3	ARP,KVP,PvdA	39.33		ARP,CHU,KVP,PvdA(*)	3.3
		KVP,PvdA,VVD	40.53		CHU,PvdA,VVD	3.63

Table H.3 (cont'd)

Year	Ranking	Coalition	MAP	Ranking	Coalition	DCP
	4	ARP,PvdA,VVD	40.53	3	ARP,CHU,PvdA	4.23
		ARP,KVP,PvdA,VVD	45.15		CHU,KVP,PvdA	4.23
					ARP,CHU,KVP,VVD	4.53
		ARP,CHU,KVP	51.53	4	ARP,KVP,PvdA,VVD	7.43
		CHU,KVP,PvdA	51.53		KVP,PvdA,VVD	9.73
		CHU,PvdA,VVD	53.4		ARP,PvdA,VVD	9.73
		ARP,CHU,KVP,PvdA	53.4		ARP,KVP,PvdA	10.33
		ARP,CHU,PvdA,VVD	54.3			
		CHU,KVP,PvdA,VVD	54.3	5	KVP,PvdA	15.25
1959	1	KVP,PvdA	19.3	1	CHU,KVP,PvdA	1.2
					ARP,KVP,PvdA	2.13
	2	CHU,KVP,VVD	33.07	2	ARP,CHU,KVP,PvdA	7.38
		ARP,KVP,VVD	34.93		KVP,PvdA	9.75
		ARP,CHU,KVP,VVD(*)	37.8			
	3	CHU,KVP,PvdA	43.8	3	CHU,KVP,VVD	16.43
		ARP,KVP,PvdA	47.53		ARP,KVP,VVD	17.37
					ARP,CHU,KVP,VVD(*)	18.8
	4	ARP,CHU,KVP,PvdA	68.5			
1963	1	KVP,PvdA	17.7	1	ARP,KVP,PvdA(*)	0.9
	2	CHU,KVP,PvdA	23.53	2	ARP,CHU,KVP,PvdA	2.0

Table H.3 (cont'd)

Year	Ranking	Coalition	MAP	Ranking	Coalition	DCP
		ARP,KVP,VVD	25.8		CHU,KVP,PvdA	2.47
		ARP,CHU,KVP,VVD(*)	27.8			
	3	CHU,KVP,PvdA	30.87	3	KVP,PvdA	9.05
		ARP,KVP,PvdA(*)	34		CHU,KVP,PvdA	11.13
					ARP,CHU,KVP,VVD(*)	12.2
					ARP,KVP,VVD	12.7
	4	ARP,CHU,KVP,PvdA	44.2			
1967	1	ARP,CHU,KVP,VVD(*)	21.9	1	ARP,CHU,KVP,VVD(*)	1.35
	2	KVP,PvdA	31.7	2	CHU,KVP,VVD,D'66	4.62
		ARP,KVP,PvdA	34.0		ARP,CHU,KVP,VVD,D'66	6.16
	3	KVP,PvdA,D'66	38.13	3	ARP,KVP,CHU,D'66	8.55
					ARP,KVP,VVD,D'66	8.55
	4	ARP,KVP,CHU,D'66	41.2		CHU,KVP,PvdA	9.37
		ARP,KVP,VVD,D'66	41.2		ARP,CHU,KVP,PvdA	10.1
		CHU,KVP,D'66	41.55			
	5	CHU,KVP,PvdA	44.47	4	ARP,KVP,PvdA	16.6
		ARP,KVP,PvdA,D'66	44.8		PvdA,KVP	17.75
					ARP,KVP,PvdA,D'66	19.3
	6	ARP,CHU,KVP,PvdA	47.4		KVP,PvdA,D'66	20.97
		ARP,CHU,KVP,VVD,D'66	50.76			

305

Table H.3 (cont'd)

Year	Ranking	Coalition	MAP	Ranking	Coalition	DCP
1971		Coalition determined by constraints				
1972		Coalition determined by constraints				
1977	1	CDA,VVD(*)	25.0	1	CDA,VVD(*)	11.0
		CDA,PvdA	34.0	2	CDA,PvdA,D'66	15.83
		CDA,PvdA,D'66	35.53		CDA,PvdA	16.5
1981	1	CDA,PvdA	9.2	1	CDA,PvdA,D'66(*)	4.37
		CDA,PvdA,D'66(*)	10.47		CDA,PvdA	5.0

The MAPs with about the same value are combined in separate 'clusters', since small differences in this parameter almost certainly have no practical significance. The same goes for the DCPs.

Table H.4 Twenty-dimensional distance matrices for Dutch parties, 1946–81 (city-block matrix)

1946

ARP				
CHU	14			
KVP	11	17		
PvdA	19	23	14	
VVD	13	17	15	18
	ARP	CHU	KVP	PvdA

1948

ARP				
CHU	13			
KVP	13	15		
PvdA	15	20	18	
VVD	18	27	22	22
	ARP	CHU	KVP	PvdA

1956

ARP				
CHU	16			
KVP	8	15		
PvdA	17	27	17	
VVD	17	26	19	23
	ARP	CHU	KVP	PvdA

1963

ARP				
CHU	12			
KVP	16	19		
PvdA	16	20	18	
VVD	13	17	17	23
	ARP	CHU	KVP	PvdA

Table H.4 (cont'd)

1967

	ARP	CHU	KVP	PvdA	VVD
ARP					
CHU	11				
KVP	12	9			
PvdA	16	22	23		
VVD	14	13	7	23	
D'66	18	21	22	12	23

1971

	ARP	CHU	KVP	PvdA	VVD	D'66	PPR	DS'70	CDA
ARP									
CHU	9								
KVP	12	7							
PvdA	15	12	11						
VVD	13	12	12	18					
D66	15	12	14	15	15				
PPR	26	25	25	23	29	26			
DS'70	15	17	18	20	17	19	26		
CDA	6	8	10	14	14	16	20	14	
ProgIII	13	14	14	12	19	16	24	16	12

1977

	PvdA	VVD	D'66	PPR	DS'70
PvdA					
VVD	27				
D'66	15	23			
PPR	11	29	16		
DS'70	18	19	15	17	
CDA	17	16	15	19	10

1981

	PvdA	VVD
PvdA		
VVD	18	
D66	10	15

Figure H.1   Cluster diagrams for the Netherlands, 1946–81

1946

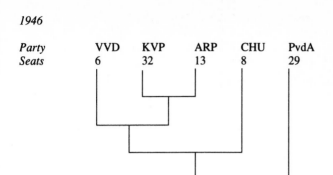

	VVD	KVP	ARP	CHU	PvdA
Party					
Seats	6	32	13	8	29

1948

	VVD	KVP	ARP	CHU	PvdA
Party					
Seats	8	32	13	9	27

1952

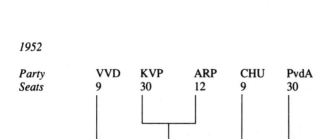

	VVD	KVP	ARP	CHU	PvdA
Party					
Seats	9	30	12	9	30

1956

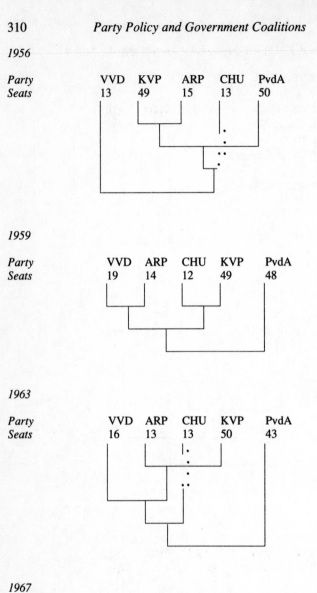

Party   VVD   KVP   ARP   CHU   PvdA
Seats   13   49   15   13   50

1959

Party   VVD   ARP   CHU   KVP   PvdA
Seats   19   14   12   49   48

1963

Party   VVD   ARP   CHU   KVP   PvdA
Seats   16   13   13   50   43

1967

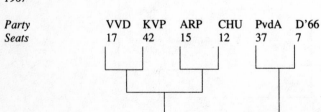

Party   VVD   KVP   ARP   CHU   PvdA   D'66
Seats   17   42   15   12   37   7

1971

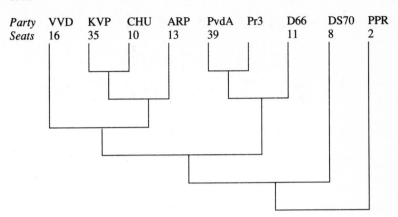

	VVD	KVP	CHU	ARP	PvdA	Pr3	D66	DS70	PPR
Party									
Seats	16	35	10	13	39		11	8	2

1977

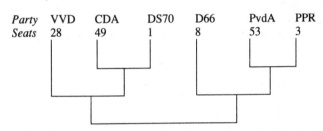

	VVD	CDA	DS70	D66	PvdA	PPR
Party						
Seats	28	49	1	8	53	3

1981

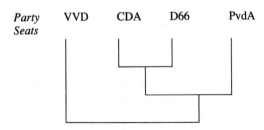

	VVD	CDA	D66	PvdA
Party				
Seats				

11 Party Policy and Coalition Bargaining in Italy, 1948–87: Is There Order Behind the Chaos?

Alfio Mastropaolo and Martin Slater

The central paradox of Italian politics contrasts governmental instability on the one hand with the unchanging role of the Christian Democrats on the other. While there have been over forty separate governments in the post-war period, averaging slightly less than a year in office apiece, the Christian Democratic Party (DC) has formed the bed-rock of all of them. The DC took the largest share of the ministries in each of the 40 governments analysed here, and held the Premiership in 37 of them. The dominance of the Christian Democrats is not in itself unusual; this situation is reproduced in the Low Countries. But the fact that a dominant party can be found in a system with such governmental instability is unexpected. Sartori (1976) has explained this paradox in terms of 'polarised pluralism'. According to this account, Italian parties are exceptionally fragmented and ideologically polarised. However, the presence of strong parties on the extremes – the Movimento Sociale Italiano (MSI) on the right, and the Partito Communista Italiano (PCI) on the left – has obliged the other parties to combine to form coalition governments despite the fact that they have relatively little in common. Italian governments are often 'negative' coalitions, (Di Palma, 1978, pp. 331–3), whose cohesion derives more from a desire to keep others out than from anything else.

To set against this interpretation, however, Mastropaolo and Slater, (1987) found a surprising level of agreement between the main parties on major policies. This agreement, moreover, has consistently increased in the later post-war period. Mastropaolo (1987) suggests that policy-based coalition bargaining goes through series of cycles. In the first phase a group of parties converges towards the centre on the basis of a common political programme. In the second phase, convergent parties suffer electoral defeats owing to the discontent provoked among some of their voters by the concessions made to their partners in government. The parties then become more and more intransigent and their policies more and more diverse, even though they stay in government. This leads to the final phase in the cycle, in which parties outside government indicate their willingness to enter, typically resulting in the reconstitution of a centrist government, with or without a new partner.

A BRIEF HISTORY OF COALITION FORMATION IN POST-WAR ITALY

Centrism 1948–63

The elections of 1948, held in a crisis atmosphere at the start of the Cold War and regarded as a significant victory for American diplomacy against international Communism, gave the Christian Democrats an absolute majority in Parliament. De Gasperi, however, who had emerged as the undisputed party leader, chose to govern in coalition with the minor parties with which the DC had previously been in partnership, above all the Liberals. The purpose of this was to reduce the influence both of the Church and the more conservative elements within the party. Some reforms were undertaken, which led to an erosion of votes to the right and the loss of the DC's absolute majority in 1953. This ushered in a series of precarious governments from 1953–8 with the minor parties alternating between government participation and grudging external support. The stance of the government parties during this period was rewarded by the return of some of their supporters in 1958.

Some reinforcement of the government majority seemed necessary, and an opportunity was offered by the break between the Socialist Party (PSI) and the Communist Party (PCI). These had formed an electoral coalition in 1948 and 1953, to the detriment of the Socialists. Many clerical elements within the Christian Democrats, and industrial employers within the Liberal Party, pushed instead for an alliance with the Monarchists and Neo-Fascists (MSI). The attempt of the Tambroni government in 1960 to rely on MSI support provoked such massive popular hostility, however, that the initiative was hastily abandoned, leaving an alliance with the Socialists as the only alternative.

In the experience of Christian Democratic governments up to 1963, therefore, we see a first cycle of coalition politics: the construction of a programmatic majority from 1948–53; its erosion from 1953–58, and the attraction of a new external party, the PSI, from 1958–63.

Centre–Left 1963–76

The entry of the Socialists into government was the first time that a party clearly based on the working class had managed to share power in Italy. Vast projects of reform and modernisation were aired. While elements among the Christian Democrats were receptive to these (partly because votes might in this way be taken from the Communists), others wanted simply to use the Socialists as support for their majority while giving little in return. Some reform projects were instituted but these were hampered by a combination of political opposition and an economic downturn. Governments were exceptionally stable (Moro was Prime Minister for four years and a half in three successive governments). However, both leading parties lost votes, the Christian Democrats to the right and the Socialists to the left.

The elections of 1968 coincided with the intense political mobilisation of that year, in Italy as well as in Europe in general. The Communists, sensing power at last, aligned themselves with these forces. A Socialist move to unite with the Social Democrats fell apart as the Socialists felt they, too, had to move leftwards. Right-wing elements sought to destabilise the political situation in order to provide conditions for a coup, and the extra-parliamentary left began to view direct action as the only possible response.

The Christian Democratic response was to rally its moderate and right-wing factions by replacing Moro and then distancing itself from the PSI. In the early stages of the legislature elected in 1972 the right-wing Liberals were called back into the coalition. This shift to the right was, however, electorally disastrous for the Christian Democrats, who lost votes not only in elections but in national referendums on divorce and abortion. Meanwhile the government had to face not only the oil crisis but also growing terrorism, social unrest and the seemingly irresistible advance of the PCI at the local level. During this period, we see once more how a programmatic centre–left majority was eroded under social and electoral pressures which led to the DC seeking to attract another external supporter into government.

National solidarity 1976–9

Good election results for both PCI and DC ushered in two minority Christian Democratic governments bolstered by Communist abstention in the first and actual voting support in the second. Given the complications which full PCI entry to the government would have produced, above all with Italy's chief ally and overseas customer the United States, a more active participation was not for the moment possible. The Communists, were, however, fully if informally consulted over all actions undertaken by the governments, which were reasonably stable.

Political difficulties multiplied rapidly, however. The Socialists, under new leadership, remained aloof and floated the idea of a united government of the left. The Communists had to abandon their reform programme almost totally after the assassination of Moro, the Christian Democrat most convinced of the need for collaboration. They saw no prospect of political concessions from the DCI, but only electoral losses. Their withdrawal from the Compromesso Storico did not, however, avert these losses in the General Election of 1979.

The Pentapartito 1979–89

The only alternative to Communist collaboration in government, given the gradual erosion of Christian Democratic seats to just over a third of the total legislature, was a grand coalition between the DC and the four other significant parties, including both Liberals and Socialists. The latter, however, were now in a position to extract substantially better terms for their collaboration. As no programmatic base existed for the collaboration of the five parties of this *pentapartito* collaboration, payoffs were almost exclusively of ministerial posts and political nominations to the *sottogoverno*. (With the extension of welfare services and of State boards and enterprises, the administrative substructure had become vast, and most of it was open to governmental intervention.) The DC were forced to accept first the Republican Spadolini, and then their chief rival Craxi as Prime Minister – the latter for almost four years, during which he managed to enforce some significant economic reforms and to push up the Socialist vote to almost 15 per cent in 1987, mainly at the expense of the Communists. The Christian Democrats, however, managed to hold their vote stable and to return to the Premiership, and the *pentapartito* formula looks set to continue for the foreseeable future.

CONSTRAINTS AND INFLUENCES ON ITALIAN COALITION BARGAINING

Table 11.1 summarises the main factors constraining or influencing coalition building in Italy. Probably the most important constraint is exogenous, and concerns the exclusion of the PCI from government, despite the fact that it was the second-largest party in the system, and came very close in size to the DC in the mid 1980s. This constraint originated and was initially sustained by a perceived American veto on Communist participation in the government of such a key NATO ally. However, PCI exclusion has probably owed more in recent years to the determination of the other parties to keep the spoils of office for themselves and to demonstrate to Communist electors that they are wasting their votes. By the same logic, the Socialist became eligible for government only after breaking with the Communists at the end of the 1950s.

As we have seen, elements in the centrist parties would certainly, left to themselves, have co-operated with the Neo-Fascists (MSI) but their attempt to do so in 1960 was aborted by massive street demonstrations. The prob-

Table 11.1   Constraints and structural influences on coalition-formation in Italy

	Period Operative	Effects
1. American veto on participation of Communists in Government	1948–85	Limits parties available for government and gives more importance to small parties.
2. American veto on Socialist participation in government.	1948–58	Same.
3. Exclusion of extreme Right (now MSI) from participation in governments for fear of popular reactions.	all years	Weakens Christian Democratic ability to play off Left against Right.
4. Extreme internal factionalisation of all parties except Communists.	all years	Parliamentary majority necessary.
5. Secret vote on Parliamentary legislation, which encourages party defection within majority.	1948–88	Renders necessary negotiations with Opposition to secure passage of legislation and often aborts it.
6. Constitutional provisions and procedures which give considerable independent power to Parliamentary Presidents and chairmen.	all years	Renders it necessary to get widest possible agreement on legislation and often blocks it.
7. Independent position of Party secretaries who do not usually participate in government.	all years	Dependence of government on support of party secretaries in the majority.

able involvement of MSI activists and leaders in the right-wing terrorism of the 1970s helped maintain their effective exclusion from office.

Several features of the Italian parliamentary system, notably the secret ballot for legislative votes and the independent power bases of parliamentary presidents and chairman, reinforce the factionalism that makes lax party discipline such an endemic feature of Italian politics. The lax party discipline in turn forces government coalitions to be larger than would otherwise be necessary.

GOVERNMENT FORMATION AND PARTY BARGAINING

It is probably fair to characterise Italian politicians as being more concerned with the rewards of office than with public policy. This is reflected in the detailed processes of government formation. These are initiated by the President after consultations with practically everyone who might have an interest in the matter: the Presidents of Lower House and Senate; leaders of the parliamentary groups of the parties; party secretaries; and many other notables. As a result of these consultations, the President usually has little leeway in designating a Prime Minister elect, just as he has little choice in who will occupy particular ministerial posts, once these have been shared out among the government parties. Bargaining among the parties settles which party will have which office but nominations of particular politicians to particular ministries are almost as important in negotiating the coalition. This has the long term effect that each minister assumes full control of his or her own ministry, and Prime Ministers are reduced to acting as mediators between ministers, party secretaries, leaders of parliamentary groups, chairmen of parliamentary commissions, party secretaries, civil servants and interest groups.

In this context, presenting an agreed policy programme to the two Houses of Parliament is only the final stage of coalition negotiations. More important is the share-out of the ministries. As Table 11.2 demonstrates, certain portfolios have been practically monopolised by the DC, partly on grounds of their intrinsic and symbolic importance (for example Foreign and Internal Affairs), partly because of the patronage value (for example Agriculture).

Clearly some ministries are also sought on policy-based grounds: the Labour portfolio has usually gone to Social Democrats, Socialists, or a 'Social Christian' within the DC. The overall distribution of portfolios, however, generally conforms to what we would expect on the basis of an

Table 11.2   Distribution of ministries among government parties, Italy, 1948–83

Premiership	Value (s=symbolic i=intrinsic c=clientalistic)	No. of times over all governments controlled by:					
		DC	PSI	PSDI	PRI	PLI	Independents
Premiership	si	30	2				
Vicepremiership	s	8	5	4	2		
Foreign Affairs	s	32		3	2	2	
Interior	si	39					
Justice	si	28			5		
Defence	sic	19	5	4	5		
Treasury	si	33		1	1		
Finance	sic	19	6	7	3		
Budget	si	21	7	3	5		
Public Works	c	19	5	8	3		
Labour & Social Security	ic	26	2	6			
Education	ic	31		1	2	2	
Industry	i	27		4		4	
Nationalized Industries	ic	23	5	1			
Agriculture	c	34					
Post	c	33		2			1
Health	i	14	6		6		
Transport	c	23	6	5		1	
Merchant Marine	c	29		4	3		
Foreign Trade	i	17	8	2	4		4
Tourism	c	17	5	3			1
South	c	19	5	2			
Culture	s	5		1	2		
Ministers without Portfolio		74	11	14	5	4	

office-based rather than a policy-pursuing interpretation of Italian coalition bargaining.

DOCUMENTS CODED

The estimates of party policy positions used in this analysis are those derived from party manifestos by Mastropaolo and Slater (1987). The 'Government programmes' analysed below are the programmatic declarations made by the Prime Minister designate to the Legislative Chambers as part of the investiture process. These are rather rhetorical and often very detailed and long, since they typically list the ideal preferences of parties making up the coalition. As such they are quite revealing, even if the coalitions usually succeed in putting into effect only a small part of the programme. As we have pointed out, however, programmatic majorities do on occasion form in Italy, usually in the first few governments after an election. Hopefully, therefore, the analysis of distances between party and government programmes is capable of revealing if the convergence of party platforms provides some form of policy basis for making a government.

DIMENSIONS OF PARTY COMPETITION

The common left–right scale fits the Italian case quite well. An earlier factor-analysis of party election programmes produced a clear-cut left–right contrast as the main policy dimension in Italian politics (Mastrapaolo and Slater, 1987). Defining the left–right policy dimension in terms of the scale used in the other chapters leaves out certain variables which are important in these terms in Italy (for example support for farmers, government efficiency, and opposition to the EC, all on the left). It is unlikely, however, that adding these variables in the Italian case would have contributed much to its discriminatory power. In the interests of comparability, the common scale was used, in the expectation that any idiosyncratic effects of particular variables in Italy should be captured by the 20-dimensional analysis to which we turn below. The face validity of the standard left–right scale can be seen, in Table 11.3, which also lists the governments we have included in the analysis, identifies the parties which belonged to them and shows the party controlling the median legislator.

The mean scores of parties over the whole post-war period, derived from those in Table 11.3, are: Communists (PCI) –12; Socialists (PSI) –14; Social Democrats (PSDI) –9; Republicans (PRI) –5; Christian Democrats (DC) –1; Liberals (PL) +4; Neo-Fascists (MSI) +7. Generally speaking this conforms to most conventional accounts, except that the Socialists are slightly to the left of the Communists. However, this is not entirely unreasonable, given their radical stances of the '50s and swing to the left in the early '70s. The fact that the Liberals sometimes appear to the left of the DC is less satisfactory, though it is true that they move rightwards on the common scale in the more recent part of the period and are most to the right for the period of their flirtation with the extreme right, 1958–63.

320

Table 11.3   Party and coalition policy in Italy, 1946–83, on common left–right dimension

Year	PCI	PSI	PSDI	PRI	PLI	DC	MSI	Coal ID	PM	Government Policy Scores
1946	-16	-17	-26	-13	-13	*40*	-12	1	De Gasperi V	4
1948	-6		-27	-28	-21	*10*	-12	2	De Gasperi VI	-20
	-6		-27	-28	21	*10*	-12	3	De Gasperi VII	19
	-6		-27	-28	21	*10*	-12	4	De Gasperi VIII	1
1953	-1	-9	0		-9	*-3*	-9	5	Pella	3
	-1	-9	0		-9	*-3*	-9	6	Fanfani I	-14
	-1	-9	0		-9	*-3*	-9	7	Scelba	-8
	-1	-9	0		-9	*-3*	-9	8	Segni I	-11
	-1	-9			-9	*-3*	-9	9	Zoll I	10
1958	-22	-17	-14	13	34	*-9*	7	10	Fanfani II	0
	-22	-17	-14	-13	34	*-9*	7	11	Segni II	2
	-22	-17	-14	-13	34	*-9*	7	12	Tambroni II	-2
	-22	-17	-14	-13	34	*-9*	7	13	Fanfani III	4
	-22	-17	-14	-13	34	*-9*	7	14	Fanfani IV	0
1963	-26	-17	-29	-16	-4	*-5*	8	15	Leone I	4
	-26	-17	-29	-16	-4	*-5*	8	16	Moro I	-2
	-26	-17	-29	-16	-4	*-5*	8	17	Moro II	0
	-26	-17	-29	-16	-4	*-5*	8	18	Moro III	-8
1968	-31	-28	@	-7	*-5*	-4	-3	19	Leone II	-7
	-31	-28	@	-7	*-5*	-4	-3	20	Rumor I	-1
	-31	-28	@	-7	*-5*	-4	-3	21	Rumor II	-9
	-31	-28	@	-7	*-5*	-4	-3	22	Rumor III	-4
	-31	-28	@	-7	*-5*	-4	-3	23	Colombo I	5

Table 11.3 (cont'd)

| Year | \multicolumn{7}{c}{Party Score} | | \multicolumn{2}{c}{Coalition} | Government |
	PCI	PSI	PSDI	PRI	PLI	DC	MSI	Coal ID	PM	Policy Scores
1972	−3	−27	−3	1	−8	0*	2	24	Andreotti I	17
	−3	−27	−3	1	−8	0*	2	25	Andreotti II	−3
	−3	−27	−3	*1*	−8	*0**	2	26	Rumor IV	1
	−3	−27	−3	1	−8	0*	2	27	Rumor V	−3
	−3	−27	−3	1	−8	0*	2	28	Moro IV	−9
1976	−2	−3	−4	3*	4	*4*	27	29	Moro V	−3
	−2	−3	−4	3*	4	*4*	27	30	Andreotti III	−18
	−2	−3	−4	3*	4	*4*	27	31	Andreotti IV	−11
1979	−7	0	4	0	7	3*	7	32	Andreotti V	−3
	−7	0	4	0	7	3*	7	33	Cossiga I	0
	−7	0	4	0	7	3*	7	34	Cossiga II	0
	−7	0	4	0	7	3*	7	35	Forlani I	−5
	−7	0	4	0	7	3*	7	36	Spadolini I	10
	−7	0	4	0	7	3*	7	37	Spadolini II	4
1983	−5	−4	−9	0*	2	2	3	38	Craxi	−3

Missing programmes marked with @
Party with median legislator marked with *
Government parties italicised.

ONE-DIMENSIONAL ANALYSIS

Government membership

Table 11.3 shows the party controlling the median legislator on the left–right scale. The predominant position of the Christian Democrats, especially up to 1963, can be seen quite clearly since the DC typically controlled the median position. When it did not, control passes to one or other of the DC's habitual allies, the Liberals or Republicans, which are generally very close to it on the left–right scale. (Indeed the difference when they have the median legislator is never more than two points on a two hundred point scale – if we allow for potential measurement error the DC was quite probably in control of the median legislator following each election.) The Christian Democrats have of course also been members of all post-war governments. Thus the central feature of the politics of coalition in Italy, the predominance of the DC, is clearly captured by our one-dimensional policy-based representation.

What remains to be explained are the differences between governments. Sometimes the Christian Democrats govern alone, sometimes in coalition with others, while certain 'formule di governo' have tended to hold over relatively long periods, the most recent being the pentapartito.

As noted above, the great electoral turning point of the post-war era was in 1963, when the four parties clearly to the left won more seats than DC and Liberals combined (see Table I.2 in the Appendix to this Chapter). A centre–right alliance was precluded following the fall of the Tambroni government, Communist participation was unacceptable, the only possibility of maintaining a parliamentary majority was an alliance with the Socialists – who, with the exception of 1976–9, were usually in government thereafter.

Table 11.3 shows, however, that formal policy positions on the common left–right scale are not much use in predicting the precise membership of government, though one or two trends do emerge. The Historic Compromise is clearly presaged in policy movements by the PCI, which moves in rapidly from its most extreme left–wing position in 1968 to more or less its most centrist position in 1976 – the start of its collaboration with the DC. It is difficult to reconcile PSI policy with government membership, however. It most and least extreme policy positions have both been associated with government membership – and the same pattern holds for the PSDI and PRI. The policy positions of the smaller Italian parties, therefore, appear to bear little relationship to the details of their government participation.

'Outside' support for governments

Given the weak position of government *vis-á-vis* Parliament in Italy and the constant effort that goes into creating and maintaining a legislative as well as a purely Governmental majority, it may at times have made little difference to policy outputs whether or not particular parties were formally included in the current administration. The frequent need of the DC for outside Parliamentary support may have enabled parties to extract policy concessions while staying out of office. In the Italian context, therefore, patterns of 'outside' legislative support for executive coalitions are particularly important. For this reason, it is conventional to distinguish the different levels of commitment in political support that a party can offer a government from outside. The various kinds of support are: (1) a positive vote in confidence motions; (2) abstention in confidence motions; (3) co-ordinated abstention by a group of parties sympathetic to the government, used particularly by Communists and other parties from 1976–9 ('non-sfiducia'). Table 11.4 notes the different kinds of external support, as well as governmental participation, though it does not distinguish co-ordinated abstention from ordinary abstention.

The patterns reported in Table 11.4 cause us to reassess some of the apparent non-relationships between party policy and government membership, certainly in regard to minor parties. Thus, from 1948–53, the DC clearly acted with the support of the Liberals, even if they were in only one government. The cohesive centrist alliance continues to 1957; it makes much more sense of policy proximities to look at patterns of support in the legislature than to concentrate exclusively on government participation.

Patterns of legislative support do not help much, however in interpreting either the abortive move to the Right in the 1960s, or the subsequent opening to the Left. During this period the Liberals were clearly in total opposition while being the party closest to the DC (and possibly controlling the median legislator from 1968–72). The strategy of the PRI in the 1970s is much more explicable once we consider legislative support patterns, however, given their consistent support for the government, as is that of the Social Democrats. Table 11.4 also indicates that, by the 1980s, practically all support for the government was accompanied by participation, perhaps indicating a growing concern for office rather than policy payoffs.

Table 11.4   Participation in government and external support for the government, Italy, 1948–83

		PCI	PSI	PSDI	PRI	PLI	DC	MON	MSI
De Gasperi	(23/5/48–27/1/50)	o	o	g/s	g	g	g	o	o
De Gasperi	(27/1/50–26/7/51)	o	o	g/s	g	a	g	o	o
De Gasperi	(26/7/51–16/7/53)	o	o	a/s	g	s	g	o	o
De Gasperi	(16/7/53–16/8/53)	o	o	a/s	s	s	g	o	o
Pella	(1/8/53–18/1/54)	o	o	a	s	s	g	s	a
Fanfani	(19/11/54–8/2/54)	o	o	o	o	a	g	o	o
Scelba	(10/2/54–6/7/55)	o	o	g	s	g	g	o	o
Segni	(6/7/55–19/5/57)	o	o	g	s/a	g	g	o/a	o
Zoli	(19/5/57–1/7/58)	o	o	o	o	o	g	s	s
Fanfani	(1/7/58–15/2/59)	o	o	g	a	o	g	o	o
Segni	(15/2/59–25/3/60)	o	o	o	o	s	g	s	s
Tambroni	(25/3/60–26/7/60)	o	o	o	o	o	g	o	s
Fanfani	(26/7/60–22/2/62)	o	a	s	s	s	g	a	o
Fanfani	(22/2/62–16/5/63)	o	a	g	g	o	g	o	o
Leone	(16/5/63–4/12/63)	o	a	a	a	o	g	o	o
Moro	(4/12/63–23/7/64)	o	g	g	g	o	g	o	o
Moro	(23/7/64–23/2/66)	o	g	g	g	o	g	o	o
Moro	(23/2/66–24/6/68)	o	g	g	g	o	g	o	o
Leone*	(24/6/68–12/12/68)	o	a*		a	o	g	o	o
Rumor*	(12/12/68–5/8/69)	o	g*		g	o	g	o	o
Rumor	(5/8/69–23/3/70)	o	g	g	a	o	g	o	o
Rumor	(23/3/70–6/7/70)	o	g	g	g	o	g	o	o
Colombo	(6/7/70–15/2/72)	o	g	g	g	o	g	o	o
Andreotti	(15/2/72–24/6/72)	o	o	a	a	a	g	o	o
Andreotti	(24/6/72–7/7/73)	o	o	g	g	g	g	o	
Rumor*	(7/7/73–15/3/74)	o	g	g	g	o	g	o	
Rumor*	(15/3/74–20/11/74)	o	g	g	s	o	g	o	
Moro	(20/11/74–11/2/76)	o	s	g	s	a	g	o	
Moro	(11/2/76–29/7/76)	o	a	s	a	a	g	o	
Andreotti	(29/7/76–13/3/78)	a	a	a	a	a	g	o	
Andreotti	(13/3/78–21/3/79)	s	s	s	s	o	g	o	
Andreotti	(21/3/79–3/8/79)	o	o	s	s	o	g	o	
Cossiga	(3/8/79–4/4/80)	o	a	g	a	g	g	o	
Cossiga	(4/4/80–18/10/80)	o	s	g	s	g	g	o	
Forlani	(18/10/80–18/6/81)	o	g	g	g	s	g	o	
Spadolini	(18/6/81–23/8/82)	o	g	g	g	g	g	o	
Spadolini	(23/8/82–1/12/82)	o	g	g	g	g	g	o	
Fanfani	(1/12/82–4/8/83)	o	g	g	s	g	g	o	
Craxi	(4/8/83–30/7/86)	o	g	g	g	g	g	o	

*PSU (Partito Socialista Unificato)
g = indicates participation in the Government
s = indicates external support
a = abstention from voting against the Government
o = in opposition

Government policy

Table 11.5 shows the distances between party and government policy on the common left–right scale.

Table 11.5   Distance between Italian parties and coalition policy on the left–right dimension, 1948–83

Year	PCI	PSI	PSDI	PRI	PLI	DC	MSI	Coal	PM
1948	10	4	31	32	−17	−6	16	1	De Gasperi V
	−14	−20	(7)	(8)	(−41)	(−30)	−8	2	De Gasperi VI
	25	19	(46)	(47)	−2	(9)	31	3	De Gasperi VII
	7	1	28	(29)	−20	(−9)	13	4	De Gasperi VIII
1953	4	12	3	3	12	(6)	12	5	Pella
	−13	−5	−14	−14	−5	(−11)	−5	6	Fanfani I
	−7	1	(−8)	−8	(1)	(−5)	1	7	Scelba
	−10	−2	(−11)	−11	(−2)	(−8)	−2	8	Segni I
	11	19	10	10	19	13	19	9	Zoll I
1958	22	17	(14)	13	−34	(9)	−7	10	Fanfani II
	24	19	16	15	−32	(11)	−5	11	Segni II
	20	15	12	11	−36	(7)	−9	12	Tambroni II
	18	13	10	9	−38	(5)	−11	13	Fanfani III
	22	17	(14)	(13)	−34	(9)	−7	14	Fanfani IV
1963	30	21	33	20	8	(9)	−4	15	Leone I
	24	(15)	(27)	(14)	2	(3)	−10	16	Moro I
	26	(17)	(29)	(16)	4	(5)	−8	17	Moro II
	18	(9)	(21)	(8)	−4	(−3)	−16	18	Moro III
1968	24	21	−7	0	−2	(−3)	−4	19	Leone II
	30	(27)	−1	(6)	4	(3)	2	20	Rumor I
	22	19	−9	−2	−4	(−5)	−6	21	Rumor II
	27	(24)	(−4)	(3)	1	(0)	−1	22	Rumor III
	36	(33)	(5)	(12)	10	(9)	8	23	Colombo I
1972	20	44	20	16	25	(17)	15	24	Andreotti I
	0	24	(0)	−4	(5)	(−3)	−5	25	Andreotti II
	4	(28)	(4)	(0)	9	(1)	−1	26	Rumor IV
	0	(24)	(0)	−4	5	(−3)	−5	27	Rumor V
	−6	18	−6	(−10)	−1	(−9)	−11	28	Moro IV
1976	−1	0	1	−6	−7	(−7)	−30	29	Moro V
	−16	−15	−14	−21	−22	(−22)	−45	30	Andreotti III
	−9	−8	−7	−14	−15	(−15)	−38	31	Andreotti IV

1979	4	–3	(–7)	(–3)	–10	(–6)	–10	32	Andreotti V
	7	0	(–4)	0	(–7)	(–3)	–7	33	Cossiga I
	7	(0)	–4	0	(–7)	(–3)	–7	34	Cossiga II
	2	(–5)	(–9)	(–5)	–12	(–8)	–12	35	Forlani I
	17	(10)	(6)	(10)	(3)	(7)	3	36	Spadolini I
	11	(4)	(0)	(4)	(–3)	(1)	–3	37	Spadolini II
1983	2	(1)	(6)	(–3)	(–5)	(–5)	–6	38	Craxi

Mean Absolute difference:

14.5	14.0	11.8	10.6	12.3	7.6	10.6		Overall
14.5	13.5	12.6	10.1	13.6	–	10.6		Out of office
15.2	11.1	11.2	8.2	7.6	–	–		In office
7.1	3.3	5.1	3.4	6.7	4.7	6.8		After 1979

Note: Parties in parentheses are in government

The table also presents some summary indicators of this relationship. The mean absolute difference between each party's policy and that of the coalition shows that the DC received the highest policy payoff of any party in the system. There is markedly less policy distance between the Christian Democrats and government policy than there is for any other party. Given the Christian Democrats' domination of most governments, this result is reassuring and supports the idea that policy pay-offs do enter into the political scheme of things in Italy.

Looking at the other parties, the traditional allies of the DC do not appear to benefit any more than the excluded MSI. The major pattern is that parties of the right and centre are much closer to government policy than the parties of the left – the Communists and Socialists – despite the latter's government participation after 1963.

Table 11.5 also compares average payoffs when a party is in office compared with those it gets when out of office. Save for the Liberals, and to a lesser extent for Social Democrats, government participation seems to make little difference to policy payoffs. Overall, the picture painted by Table 11.5 is quite clear. The predominant party, the DC, gets the highest policy payoffs. The bargaining position of other parties seems to have been too weak to have had an impact on government policy. These parties, therefore, receive policy payoffs according to how close their own policies are to those of the DC.

The predominant position of the DC may have eroded somewhat after 1979, on the evidence of the emergence of the pentapartito coalition and the choice of non-DC politicians as Prime Minister for the first time in the post–war period. The bottom line of Table 11.5 shows policy payoffs after 1979 and suggests that this is indeed the case. Inside government the DC are no longer the main beneficiaries – these become the Socialists and Republicans, both of whom supplied Prime Ministers. The government party least benefited is the PLI. Both excluded parties get marginally less than those of the government but the gap is not great, indicating perhaps the tendency to ever-growing parliamentary co-operation which we emphasised above.

THE TWENTY-DIMENSIONAL ANALYSIS

Government formation

Given the complexities of Italian politics, the impact of policy on government formation may well be better captured in a 20-dimensional rather than a one-dimensional space. A multi-dimensional representation allows us to consider themes, such as social justice and modernisation, which are important in Italy but were not incorporated in the common left–right scale. The distance matrices and cluster diagrams take the same form as in the other chapters, so we do not need to discuss their technicalities here. They are presented in full in the Appendix to this chapter (Figure I.1).

The simple clustering models presented there do not take account of the constraints which operated in Italy, in particular, those operating against government participation by Communists, Socialists (in the 1950s) and the MSI. The unconstrained cluster models, therefore, give a much more central role to the communists than a constrained model would allow. If, as seems more realistic, we centre the coalition-building process on the DC, by forcing it into the analysis as the first node on the cluster tree and adding coalition partners to it on the basis of 20-dimensional city block policy distances, a very different pattern emerges. Also applying the constraints on excluded parties, the interesting question becomes which combination of coalitionable parties will join the DC in office. In 1948 the constrained cluster prediction is that the other parties would join the DC in the following order: Liberals, Social Democrats and Republicans. This is the first coalition that actually formed, though since all non-excluded parties joined, it owes it success more the operation of the overall constraints than to the policy distances between parties. The PLI, the party closest to the DC in the

20-dimensional space, was the first to leave the government though, as Table 11.4 demonstrates, they continued to offer varying degrees of support from outside.

In 1953 the constrained cluster prediction is that the other parties would join the DC in the order: PSDI and PLI (information on the Republicans is missing). In fact, when the DC did not govern alone, these parties did indeed join it. In 1958 it seems reasonable to count the Socialists as still being effectively excluded so that the cluster prediction is: PSDI, PRI, with the Liberals very far away. In fact, this was the period of Christian Democratic flirtation with the Right, so it was only after the collapse of the Tambroni government that the predicted combination really emerged.

In 1963 the 'apertura a sinistra' was anticipated by the closeness of the Socialist electoral stance to that of the DC. On the other hand the Liberals were also close to the DC but were excluded from all governments of the later 1960s (and indeed, opposed them actively). This also contradicts the prediction for 1968, which again puts Liberals closest to the DC. The other parties predicted to join (Socialists, Republicans and Social Democrats) did indeed do so. In 1972, on the other hand, parties are predicted by the constrained clustering model to join the DC in the order: Social Democrats, Republicans, Socialists and Liberals. This is borne out in the sense that the PSDI was most often in government with the DC, followed by Republicans, Socialists and then Liberals. Owing to the series of minority 'monocolore' DC governments from 1976–9, with the external support of all the other parties, including Communists, the cluster prediction is superfluous. However in 1979 with the development of the pentapartito formula, the PSI, PSDI, PRI and PLI are predicted to join (in that order), which seems a fair approximation. The same can be said for 1983, when the ordering was Social Democrats, Liberals, Socialists and Republicans.

Overall, the very heavy set of constraints that must be applied to the Italian case mean that the standard 20-dimensional analysis of coalition formation is of limited usefulness. Generally, all the non-excluded parties join governments at some points during a given legislature, since so many governments form! The fact that we do not have information on party policy movements during interelection periods means, however, that it is difficult to see how the analysis can be substantially improved.

Government Policy

As in the one-dimensional analysis, and as might be generally expected from its predominant position, the DC gained the highest policy payoffs from Italian governments, in the sense of having the lowest distances between party and coalition positions in the full 20-dimensional policy space. Distances between each party programme and that of relevant governments are given in Table 11.6, in which government parties are distinguished from others.

Table 11.6   Distance between Italian parties and coalition policy on the left–right dimension, 1948–83

Election year	Party							Coalition	Prime minister
	PCI	PSI	PSDI	PRI	PLI	DC	MSI		
1948		65	(66)	(86)	(60)	(75)	(82)	1	De Gasperi V
		49	(54)	(76)	72	(69)	86	2	De Gasperi VI
		73	82	(84)	58	(91)	106	3	De Gasperi VII
		72	71	75	73	(92)	113	4	De Gasperi VIII
1953	54	52	37	na	59	(44)	36	5	Pella
	70	56	53	na	61	(46)	36	6	Fanfani I
	69	63	(48)	na	(50)	(47)	47	7	Scelba
	76	76	(59)	na	(45)	(70)	66	8	Segni I
	71	61	48	na	(46)	(39)	43	9	Zoli I
1958	58	61	(46)	49	112	(48)	45	10	Fanfani II
	56	59	40	41	96	(50)	49	11	Segni I
	40	39	24	29	100	(32)	33	12	Tambroni II
	49	54	43	42	103	(49)	36	13	Fanfani III
	64	57	(46)	(53)	106	(46)	59	14	Fanfani IV
1963	48	46	42	51	30	(38)	53	15	Leone I
	58	(36)	(44)	(25)	50	(36)	75	16	Moro I
	65	(49)	(59)	(48)	47	(37)	80	17	Moro II
	55	(39)	(45)	(34)	55	(35)	78	18	Moro III
1968	61	57	na	53	43	(56)	52	19	Leone II
	72	64	na	(60)	54	(53)	63	20	Rumor I
	57	53	na	57	45	(34)	52	21	Rumor II
	64	(56)	na	(50)	44	(37)	39	22	Rumor III
	67	(53)	na	(57)	47	(34)	54	23	Colombo I
1972	55	72	66	60	78	(40)	50	24	Andreotti I
	52	65	(63)	59	(71)	(43)	61	25	Andreotti II
	59	(62)	(64)	(60)	64	(38)	56	26	Rumor IV
	52	(53)	(59)	53	71	(37)	53	27	Rumor V
	47	58	62	(48)	52	(44)	50	28	Moro IV
1976	41	52	41	39	38	(35)	68	29	Moro V
	56	55	62	54	57	(48)	89	30	Andreotti III
	56	53	50	46	49	(40)	75	31	Andreotti IV
1979	54	46	(57)	(39)	65	(48)	52	32	Andreotti V
	54	46	(55)	53	(59)	(50)	42	33	Cossiga I
	62	(48)	53	45	(63)	(52)	48	34	Cossiga II
	52	(44)	(57)	(51)	63	(46)	54	35	Forlani I
	56	(40)	(51)	(37)	(53)	(48)	30	36	Spadolini I
	46	(36)	(47)	(27)	(57)	(42)	36	37	Spadolini II

1983	53	(43)	(35)	(43)	(48)	(44)	47	38	Craxi

Average distance:

58	56	46	50	66	–	58	Out of Office
–	48	53	52	60	48	–	In Office
55	43	51	42	58	47	44	After 1979

Note: Parties in parentheses are in government

As in the one-dimensional analysis, the range of mean differences between parties is relatively small. The Socialists do as well as the DC when they are in office (this result might be seen as more satisfactory than that of the one-dimensional analysis). The Liberals again benefit from being in office, but their payoff in the 20-dimensional policy space is less than that of the MSI and PCI.

It is again instructive to see how the dependence of the Christian Democrats on their coalition partners and indeed on the parliamentary opposition, has affected policy payoffs since 1979. In the 20-dimensional space the more recent periods is associated with increased policy payoffs to all parties though, for the DC and Liberals, the increase is very small.

DISAGGREGATED TWENTY-DIMENSIONAL ANALYSIS

The party controlling the median legislator on each of the individual policy dimensions is identified in Table 11.7. The results testify to the predominant position of the Christian Democrats. They always control the median legislator on a plurality of policy dimensions (and up to 1963 and in 1983, on a majority of dimensions).

What is particularly interesting, however, is that the disaggregated 20-dimensional analysis demonstrates the breakdown, after 1963, in the absolutely central position of the DC. Before 1963, it controlled the median legislator on virtually every dimension. In 1963 the PSI emerged as controlling on an unprecedented four dimensions. After this date the left (generally the PCI) controlled the median legislator on several issue dimensions in each Parliament. In particular the dimensions of capitalist economics, productivity, freedom and human rights, and decentralisation tended to be under left-wing control after 1963. There is no doubt, then, that in general the policy-positions of the DC make it the predominant party in Italian politics. Nevertheless it was much less predominant in 1979 than it was in 1948 or 1953. What is not explained by that analysis, however, is why DC's

Table 11.7   Party controlling the median legislator on each of 20 dimensions, Italy, 1948–83

Dimension	Year								
	1948	1953	1958	1963	1968	1972	1976	1979	1983
State intervention	DC	DC	*	PSDI	DC	DC	DC	DC	DC
Quality of life	DC	DC	DC	DC	PCI	*	PCI	DC	DC
Peace and co-operation	DC	DC	DC	DC	DC	DC	DC	DC	MSI
Anti-establishment	DC	*	*	*	*	*	DC	PLI	DC
Capitalist economics	DC	DC	DC	PSI	DC	PCI	PCI	DC	MSI
Social conservatism	DC	DC	DC	PSI	DC	MSI	PLI	PSI	DC
Productivity/ infrastructure	DC	PSDI	PCI	PSI	DC	PCI	DC	DC	PCI
Military (positive)	DC	*	DC	*	*	*	PCI	*	PCI
EEC (positive)	DC	*	DC	DC	MSI	DC	DC	PSDI	DC
EEC (negative)	DC	*	*	*	*	*	*	*	PCI
Freedom & domestic human rights	DC	DC	DC	DC	PCI	DC	PCI	PCI	PLI
Democracy	DC	DC	DC	PCI	DC	DC	DC	PSI	DC
Decentralisation	DC	*	DC	DC	PSI	PCI	PCI	PSI	DC
Government efficiency	DC	*	PSDI	DC	PLI	*	PSI	PCI	DC
Social justice	DC	DC	*	*	*	*	DC	*	*
Social service expansion	DC	PLI	DC	DC	MSI	DC	DC	DC	DC
Education services (+)	DC	*	*	*	*	*	*	*	*
Labour groups (+)	DC	*	DC	PSI	*	DC	PLI	*	PSI
Agriculture and farmers	DC	DC	PSI	DSC	PCI	DC	DC	PCI	DC
Minorities	DC	*	*	DC	*	*	*	*	DC

No. of dimensions on which party controls median legislator

PCI	0	0	1	1	3	3	5	3	3
PSI	0	0	1	4	1	0	1	3	1
PSDI	0	1	1	1	0	0	0	1	0
PRI	0	0	0	0	0	0	0	0	0
DC	20	9	11	9	6	8	9	6	11
PLI	0	1	0	0	1	0	2	1	1
MSI	0	0	0	0	2	1	0	0	2
No Party	0	9	6	5	7	8	3	6	2

* No party controlling median position.

enhanced bargaining position in 1983 was associated with such notable loss of political control within the pentapartito arrangement.

SUCCESS RATES OF POLICY-BASED COALITION MODELS IN ITALY

After the detailed discussion in previous sections of what the various policy-based models and interpretations can, and cannot, tell us about the twists and turns of coalition making in Italy, we present here a final overall evaluation of the success of the models. Our evaluation can be found in Table 11.8, which incorporates many of the policy-based theories tested in other chapters. The first column lists the number of theoretically possible coalitions, though it ignores the further combinations made possible by the rise of the small fringe parties, such as the Radicals, Proletarian Unity, and the minority Nationalist parties, in the late 1970s and 1980s. These are treated as non-coalitionable, though whether they are included or not, the number of feasible coalitions would have remained severely constrained in Italy, especially after 1979 when only the *pentapartito* was possible if the Communists were to be excluded.

The other columns in Table 11.8 report the success or failure of theories already tested elsewhere. The first three, A, B and C, as in the Netherlands, concern themselves with the direction of the DC's choice of coalition partners, based on ideological closeness as measured in terms of the left–right scale (Hypothesis A); measured in terms of the 20-dimensional space (Hypothesis B); measured in terms of the disaggregated 20 dimensions (Hypothesis C). We have regarded the crucial distinction as being between on the one hand an exclusively centre–right combination (whether this includes all of Liberals, Republicans or Social Democrats or only one or two) and, on the other hand, a more left-wing coalition that includes the PSI. 'Closeness' to the parties of the centre–right is measured in terms of the mean position of all centre–right parties. Naturally, where the bargaining constraints mean that only one combination of parties is possible, more refined policy-based criteria are irrelevant. These cases are marked with a small 'c' in the appropriate cell. Models D, E, F concern themselves with the more detailed composition of the coalition. Model D predicts that the coalition which forms will be the most policy-compact. (The most policy compact coalition is taken as the one with the minimum aggregate policy distance (MAP) between each coalition member's position and the mean position of all members). Model E predicts the coalition with least distance

Table 11.8 Success rates of policy-based theories in Italy

		Possible coalitions	Feasible coalitions after constraints	Direction of coalitions			Composition of coalitions			Connectedness of coalitions	
				A	B	C	D	E	F	G	H
1	De Gasperi V	127	8	c	c	c	no	no	yes	no	yes
2	De Gasperi VI	127	8	c	c	c	no	no	yes	no	yes
3	De Gasperi VII	127	8	c	c	c	no	no	yes	no	yes
4	De Gasperi VIII	127	8	c	c	c	(yes)	(yes)	(yes)	(yes)	(yes)
5	Pells	127	1	c	c	c	c	c	c	no	(yes)
6	Fanfani I	127	1	c	c	c	c	c	c	no	(yes)
7	Scelba	127	1	c	c	c	c	c	c	yes	yes
8	Segni	127	1	c	c	c	c	c	c	yes	yes
9	Zoli I	127	1	c	c	c	c	c	c	(yes)	(yes)
10	Fanfani II	127	1	c	c	c	c	c	c	no	yes
11	Segni II	127	1	c	c	c	c	c	c	no	(yes)
12	Tambroni II	127	1	c	c	c	c	c	c	no	(yes)
13	Fanfani III	127	1	c	c	c	c	c	c	no	(yes)
14	Fanfani IV	127	1	c	c	c	c	c	c	yes	yes
15	Leone I	127	8	no	no		no	no	no	no	yes
16	Moro I	127	8	no	no		no	no	no	no	(yes)
17	Moro II	127	8	yes	yes		no	no	yes	yes	yes
18	Moro III	127	8	yes	yes		no	no	yes	yes	yes
19	Leone II	127	1	c	c	c	c	c	c	no	no
20	Rumor I	127	1	c	c	c	c	c	c	no	no
21	Rumor II	127	8	no	no		no	no	no	no	(yes)
22	Rumor III	127	8	no	yes		no	no	no	no	no
23	Colombo I	127	8	no	yes		no	no	no	no	no
24	Andreotti I	127	9	no	no		no	no	no	no	(yes)
25	Andreotti II	127	9	yes	yes		no	no	no	no	yes
26	Rumor IV	127	9	no	no		no	no	no	no	no
27	Rumor V	127	9	no	no		no	no	no	no	no

Table 11.8 (cont'd)

	Possible coalitions	Feasible coalitions after constraints	Direction of coalitions			Composition of coalitions			Connectedness of coalitions	
			A	B	C	D	E	F	G	H
28 Moro IV	127	9	no	no		no	no	no	no	yes
29 Moro V	127	9	no	no		no	no	no	no	(yes)
30 Andreotti III	127	8	no	no		no	no	no	no	(yes)
31 Andreotti IV	127	8	no	no		no	no	no	no	(yes)
32 Andreotti V	127	1	c	c	c	c	c	c	no	yes
33 Cossiga I	127	1	c	c	c	c	c	c	no	yes
34 Cossiga II	127	1	c	c	c	c	c	c	no	no
35 Foriani I	127	1	c	c	c	c	c	c	yes	yes
36 Spadolini I	127	1	c	c	c	c	c	c	yes	yes
37 Spadolini II	127	1	c	c	c	c	c	c	yes	yes
38 Craxi I	127	1	c	c	c	c	c	c	yes	yes
Predictive success			.20	.33	**	0.0	0.0	.30	.40	.81
			(3/15)	(5/15)	**	(0.0)	(0.0)	(6/19)	(11/38)	(31/38)
Predictive efficiency			.20	.33	**	0.0	0.0	.09	.10	.16
			(3/15)	(5/15)	**	(0.0)	(0.0)	(6/66)	(11/110)	(31/181)

Notes: Small c in table indicates only one outcome possible given constraints. If (yes) or (no) bracketed indicates single party government.
**No alternative outcomes possible.

A Predominant party (DC) in majority coalition with closest lay bloc (Centre–Right or Socialists).
B DC in majority coalition with closest of Centre–Right or Socialists (20-dimensional clustering).
C DC in majority coalition with closest of Centre–Right or Socialists (disaggregated 20-dimensions).
D Majority coalition with smallest MAP (one dimension).
E Majority coalition with smallest DCP (one dimension).
F Coalition is at majority node on cluster tree (20-dimensional cluster).
G Coalition is minimum connected winning on one dimension.
H Coalition is connected around predominant party on one dimension.

between the Christian Democratic position and the mean policy positions of all government parties. Model F involves the familiar prediction that the coalition which forms will be at a majority node of the cluster tree. Again all these theories are irrelevant where the constraints render only one coalition possible; these cases are indicated by a small 'c' in the cell. Axelrod's proposal that coalitions should not only be minimal winning but also ideologically connected to minimise internal conflict, seemed to find its strongest empirical support in Italy (Axelrod 1970; Taylor and Laver, 1973). This may have been an artifact of the very judgemental and possibly tautological representations of party positions on the left–right continuum then available. We thus retest this theory as Model G, which predicts that coalitions will be minimal connected winning. Model H adapts this theory to the specific Italian case, predicting that coalitions will be connected but will also include the DC (taking this as the predominant party).

What is immediately clear from Table 11.8 is the overwhelming role of bargaining constraints in designating one particular coalition. Sometimes, of course, the sole coalition designated by the constraints failed to form, with the usual result of a minority Christian Democratic government. However, as we have seen (Table 11.4) this was generally supported from the outside by the parties which were predicted to have joined and was generally a stage on the way to the formation of a broader coalition. A second point which emerges from Table 11.8, and which does not need detailed review, is the generally poor performance of all policy-based models in Italy. This is particularly true for Models D and E, which worked well in the Netherlands. Though the prediction that the coalition will be found somewhere on a majority node of the clustering produces a non-negligible .30 success rate, its prediction set is quite large and its efficiency is therefore low. The same can be said for the connectedness hypotheses, which work relatively well but only because they are compatible with a lot of different outcomes. The directional models, A, B and C, attain fairly low success rates, especially since the requirements are less onerous in their cases.

All in all therefore it cannot be said that policy works well as a basis for predicting coalition formation in Italy. The impression that overwhelmingly emerges from our analysis is of the pervasive effects of party fragmentation and the exclusion of certain pariah parties. These put overwhelming pressure on politicians to patch together any arrangement that would work, even if only temporarily. As we pointed out above, the constraints on coalition bargaining in Italy are so strong as to make the basic business of putting together a legislative majority for government investiture so difficult as almost always to predominate over policy. This may well force politicians to concern themselves primarily with office, because this is the only certain payoff they can secure.

APPENDIX I

Table I.1   Legislative seat distribution in Italy, 1948–83

Year	Party seats										
------	-----	-----	------	-----	-----	-----	-----	-------	PCI+PSI+PSDI+PRI+PLI	PCI+PSI+PSDI+PRI	DC+PLI
	PCI	PSI	PSDI	PRI	PLI	DC	MSI	Total	PCI+PSI+ PSDI+ PRI+PLI	PCI+PSI+ PSDI+ PRI	DC+ PLI
1948	133	50	33	9	19	305	6	574	244	225	324
1953	143	75	19	5	13	263	29	590	255	242	276
1958	140	84	22	6	17	273	24	596	269	252	290
1963	166	87	33	6	39	250	27	630	331	292	289
1968	177	91		9	31	266	24	630	308	277	297
1972	179	61	29	15	20	267	56	630	304	284	287
1976	227	57	15	14	5	263	35	630	318	313	268
1979	201	62	20	16	9	262	30	629	308	299	271
1983	198	73	23	29	16	225	42	630	339	323	241

Table I.2 Twenty-dimension distance matrices of Italian parties, 1946–83 (City-block matrix)

1946

	PCI	SOC	SD	REP	LIB
PCI					
SOC	52				
SD	47	27			
REP	73	63	76		
LIB	69	87	94	76	
CD	88	96	99	81	123

1948

	PCI	LIB	SD	CD	REP
PCI					
SD	57				
REP	67	70			
LIB	57	64	90		
CD	84	73	95	63	
MSI	77	86	96	86	115

1953

	PCI	SOC	SD	LIB	CD
PCI					
SOC	42	57			
SD	43	69	60		
LIB	67	62	37	49	
CD	62	40	51	57	46
MSI	52				

1958

	PCI	SOC	SD	REP	LIB	CD
PCI						
SOC	27					
SD	32	29				
REP	39	44	33			
LIB	104	89	88	87		
CD	34	19	26	37	90	
MSI	43	46	33	38	85	43

1963

	PCI	SOC	SD
PCI			
SOC	42		
SD	46	42	
REP	41	27	41

1968

	PCI	SOC	REP
PCI			
SOC	26		
REP	48	42	
LIB	54	56	36

Table I.2 (cont'd)

	PCI	SOC	SD	REP	LIB	CD
LIB	40	36	48	35	36	73
CD	44	28	40	41	63	
MSI	85	81	77	80		

1972

	PCI	SOC	SD	REP	LIB	CD
PCI						
SOC	41					
SD	21	44				
REP	29	48	34			
LIB	57	64	60	42		
CD	33	50	36	38	60	
MSI	35	60	34	40	52	30

1976

	PDEM	PCI	SOC	SD	REP	LIB	CD	MSI
PDEM								
PCI	46							
SOC	55	39						
SD	42	28	39					
REP	50	40	39	38				
LIB	51	29	40	25	19			
CD	50	32	29	30	46	51		
MSI	77	47	56	59	65	72	57	
RAD	78	64	79	62	80			

1979

	PCI	SOC	SD	REP	LIB	CD
PCI						
SOC	32					
SD	39	27				
REP	43	31	38			
LIB	49	49	34	36		
CD	38	20	23	41	49	
MSI	54	40	43	37	37	44

1983

	PDEM	PCI	SOC	SD	PDUP	REP	LIB	CD
PDEM								
PCI	38							
SOC	50	32						
SD	60	52	30					
PDUP	29	33	35	43				
REP	44	34	34	28	35			
LIB	45	33	25	31	32	21		
CD	59	37	27	23	42	35	26	
MSI	38	42	42	40	31	26	23	31

Figure I.1   Cluster diagrams for 20-dimensional representations of Italian parties, 1946–83

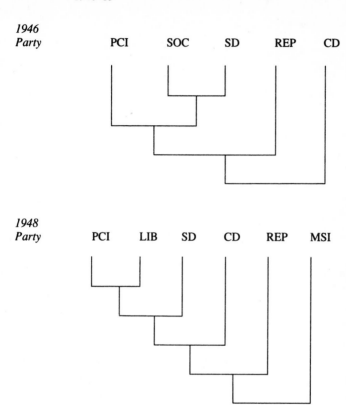

1946 Party   PCI   SOC   SD   REP   CD

1948 Party   PCI   LIB   SD   CD   REP   MSI

1953
Party   PCI   MSI   SOC   SD   CD   LIB

Centroid, average linkage

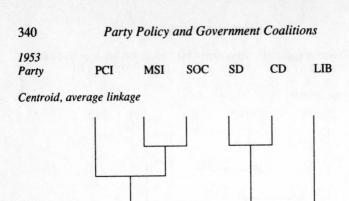

K-means

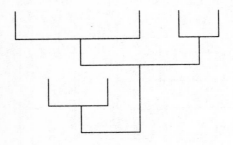

1958

PCI   SOC   CD   SD   REP   MSI   LIB

Centroid, average linkage

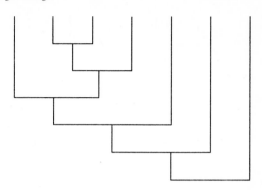

K-means

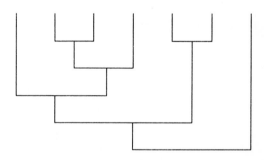

1963

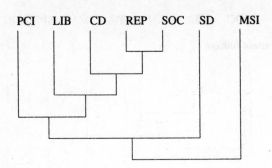

1968

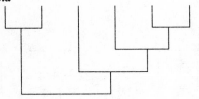

Average, centroid

K-means

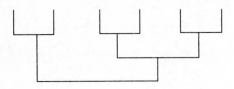

1972

SOC PCI SD REP CD MSI LIB

Average, centroid linkage

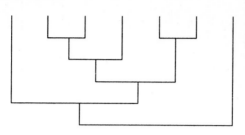

K-means

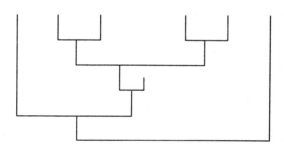

1979

1979

Centroid

Average

K-means

1983

PDUP   Prol   PCI   SOC   SD   CD   REP   LIB   MSI

Centroid, average linkage

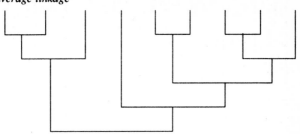

K-means

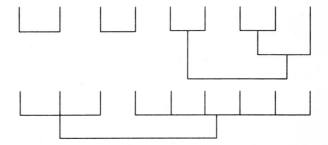

12 Party Policy and Coalition Bargaining in Israel

Judith Bara

Israel has an extremely fragmented party system. As a result, every government formed since independence in 1948 has been a coalition. Academic observers of the Israeli political scene have made many attempts to explain the coalition system. Most views derive, at least in part, from Duverger's notions on the relationship between proportional electoral systems and multipartism. (Duverger, 1964) The particular circumstances of Israel, however, require other factors to be taken into account, notably the nature of the political culture, the evolution of the party system during the period of the British Mandate for Palestine (1920–48) and the development of Zionism as a political movement in the early twentieth century (Arian, 1985; Bara, 1987; Luebbert, 1986; Nachmias, 1975; Paltiel, 1975; Seliktar, 1982).

Israel does not fit easily into conventional models of coalition behaviour. Separate studies by Nachmias (1975) and Seliktar (1982) have shown that conventional models were unable to account adequately for why Israeli governments are consistently larger than minimal winning coalitions. Nachmias, who deals only with the period of Labour dominance in government (1947–77) claims that we must look beyond cabinet office to explain why Labour operated as if it were a party with an absolute majority. Paltiel (1975) and Seliktar (1982) each suggest that Israeli parties have sought traditionally to provide an image of consensus, especially during the period of Labour dominance. It is not, therefore surprising that governments in Israel have generally been conceived as needing not only a clear majority of support in the Knesset but also a broad base which will allow for flexibility in carrying out and modifying policy whilst in office. It was thought inappropriate for the dominant coalition member to rely on a single small partner to keep the government in office. Rather the dominant party normally takes several partners who might be played off against each other so that the loss of one small party would not bring down the government.

Almost all who have analysed the Israeli coalition system have agreed upon one thing, however. This is that coalition formation has a lot to do with finding a legislative mandate for a joint programme of government action. This chapter, is, therefore, concerned with the relationship between party positions and the content of this joint programme

THE FORMAL PROCESS OF COALITION BUILDING

Despite the complexity of the party system, formal procedures for coalition formation are quite straightforward. The constitutional and legal provisions were set out in the Transition Law of February 1948 and later codified in the Basic Law of Government of August 1968.

After the result of a general election is declared – or after a government has fallen between elections – the President of the State formally designates a member of the Knesset to form a government. It is crucial that this government should receive a mandate to carry a programme of legislation through parliament. Normally the member designated is the leader of the party with a relative majority of seats and is often prime minister of the outgoing government, which serves as a caretaker until a successor is found or a general election takes place. Negotiations among potential coalition partners then take place both formally and informally. In the first instance, negotiators are specified officially by the parties concerned. These then meet in formal session to work out the basis of an agreement. Policy rather than office distribution is the main focus of bargaining at this stage since discussions centre on the leading party's ideas concerning the programme of government that it envisages. The disposition of ministerial offices is recognised as being governed by constraints concerning the role of religion and other conventions which will be discussed later.

At the same time as these official discussions take place, informal contacts take place among parties and these involve a much wider spectrum of potential allies. The major party may have no serious intention of including these other parties but simply engages in discussion with them to render its desired partners more flexible. It is important, however, that the implicit 'threat' involved in these informal discussions be carried out if necessary. This is clearly illustrated by the formation of the first Rabin administration in 1974. In order to woo the National Religious Party (NRP), the Labour Alignment opened discussions with the Citizens Right Movement (CRM) which normally it would have been unlikely to wish to include (see section on constraints below). Indeed Labour went so far as to form a coalition without the NRP, although this was based on a majority of only two seats. Four months later, the NRP entered the coalition and the CRM left.

The formal and informal processes of negotiation eventually result in a written coalition agreement upon which the government bases its intended policy across a broad spectrum of issues. In addition informal, often unwritten and certainly secret agreements between party leaders are often made. These might concern, for example, the appointment of conveners of influential Knesset legislative committees. The written agreement is presented to the Knesset by the leader of the major party in the potential coalition, or Prime Minister designate, in the form of a statement of intended government policy, and a vote is then taken. Normally an agreement would not be presented to the Knesset until it was clear that it would pass, and the government would receive a mandate to govern on the basis of the principles outlined. Theoretically this mandate would last until the next election is due, or until the government loses the confidence of the Knesset. The approved programme is binding on all individual members of the government and their party members in parliament are expected to support it. A viable government is one which can command a majority of Knesset votes and thereby ensure that its agreed programme is supported and it can withstand a vote of no confidence. It appears that the Israeli political system does not tolerate minority governments. On only one occasion has a minority government been approved – Rabin's third government in 1976, but it was clearly understood that this was only a caretaker government until elections could be held in 1977.

The legal provisions concerning coalition formation are quite vague, apart from setting a time limit of 119 days for discussions, after which the President can call a general election. Seliktar (1982) argues that this time limit has helped in practice to protract deliberations, although the limit is not usually reached. Although the Knesset has always had 120 members despite substantial population growth since 1948, there is no legal limit to the number of portfolios which the Prime Minister designate may offer.

THE DISTRIBUTION OF PORTFOLIOS AS A FORM OF POLICY BARGAINING

This study is mainly concerned with the role of policy in the building of coalition governments. In the case of Israel, however, it is difficult to discuss policy in isolation from the distribution of cabinet portfolios. In addition, posts other than cabinet ministries are included in the 'spoils of victory'. These include chairs of Knesset standing committees and the Speakership, besides a host of less prominent positions. The allocation of these portfolios is an important aspect of policy bargaining in Israel, since each party's programmatic concerns are reflected in preferences for particular cabinet ministries. It is normal for parties to devote much of the bargaining process to ensuring that these preferences are catered for, and different policy priorities mean that a tradeoff can take place. For example, if the Labour Party seeks ministries concerned with defence and foreign affairs it may have the basis of an agreement with the NRP, wanting the religious or internal affairs portfolios. When more than one party has had designs on the same portfolios, the solution has generally been to agree both a pecking order and a convention that important posts such as the Premiership, Defence and Foreign Affairs accrue to the major partner. After the more prestigious posts have been distributed, the rest are shared out, bearing in mind conventions associated with particular party interests. (For a detailed specification of the processes involved see Budge and Keman, 1990).

As a result of these conventions, major partners dominate cabinets in Israel. In every case their percentage of cabinet seats outweighs (often grossly) their percentage of parliamentary seats. Conversely, very small parties who come into cabinet often have a greater voice there than their share of parliamentary seats might be thought to merit.

Occasionally, and in a departure from what is conventionally taken as the formal definition of government membership in other coalition systems, a party which signs a coalition agreement and is a full member of an Israeli government might forego the right to hold cabinet office. This was particularly true of the Agudah parties in the 1960s and of the CRM in Rabin's first administration of 1974.

STRUCTURAL INFLUENCES AND CONSTRAINTS ON COALITION BUILDING

A number of conventional practices have set limits to the number and types of allies that a potential major coalition partner might select. It is often difficult to identify such factors precisely in documentation relating to coalition agreements, government programmes or party platforms, but they clearly do influence behaviour. Four are of particular importance.

In the Knesset, as in other countries, certain parties are in practice excluded from coalitions on ideological or tactical grounds. Throughout the period of Labour dominance, the Labour Party (MAPAI) precluded any agreement with the Communist Party/ies (MAKI and RAKAH). It is still the case that neither the Labour Alignment nor the Likud would be willing to serve alongside communists. The ideological standpoints of these parties are regarded as being essentially anti-system since they challenge the fundamental tenets of Zionism.

For most of the same period MAPAI precluded any alliance with Herut/GAHAL. This could be related to the near civil war between their armed forces in the 1940s and to the intense personal animosity between their leaders – David Ben-Gurion and Menahem Begin. The situation was eased after Ben-Gurion led the break-away Rafi faction out of MAPAI in 1965 and was succeeded as Prime Minister by Levi Eshkol. Indeed, GAHAL was invited to join the national government which was established on the eve of the 1967 Six Day War and remained within the governing coalition until the fall of Golda Meir's second administration in 1970. More recently it could be said that a similar proscriptive constraint operates *vis-á-vis* the extreme right wing Kach movement of Rabbi Meir Kahane, which was first elected to the Knesset in 1984.

Another constraint relates to the fact that Israeli parties are perpetually subject to fragmentation. It is unlikely that a splinter party of recent formation, even if quite close ideologically to the parent party, would be invited to join a coalition. A clear example is the exclusion of RAFI from the government after the 1965 election. This ostracism often leads to reconstituted alliances under different labels – such as the formation of the Ma'arach in 1969, which a major part of RAFI did enter. However, it is the case that these splinter parties may be used by major parties as a form of bait to entice other parties emanating from different political families into the coalition. We have already discussed one such case – the first Rabin administration's playing-off of the NRP and CRM in 1974.

The whole area of religion is an important factor which constrains the process of coalition building in Israel. We should firstly note that coalition agreements and other documentation often refer to maintaining the 'status quo' in religious affairs, implicitly referring to the agreement forged in 1948 between Ben-Gurion and the religious partners. Ben-Gurion needed the co-operation of orthodox sections of the Jewish community during the War of Independence and this agreement has given the religious bloc in general, and the NRP in particular, a considerable degree of legitimate influence over a wide range of policy areas. In effect, Ben-Gurion's settlement led to the NRP effectively cornering for itself a position in virtually every Cabinet with control of what it considered a number of key ministries, such as religious affairs, the interior and education. Throughout the history of the modern State of Israel, these positions have been filled by members of religious parties, apart from short periods amounting to ten months or so

Table 12.1   Constraints on coalition formation in Israel

1. Exclusion of Communist parties from Government.
2. Exclusion of Kach movement from Government.
3. Refusal of Mapai (mainstream Labour) to form coalition with Herut/GAHAL 1948–1963.
4. Refusal of parent party to form coalition with breakaway parties immediately after a split (eg Mapai–Rafi 1963–68).
5. Tradition of religious communities administering themselves in matters concerning religion, leading to general expectation that religious parties will be in government with control of relevant ministries.

between 1974 and 1977 when they were not members of a coalition. Clearly background and practice give religious standard bearers both a semi-prescriptive right and also an obligation to be in government, independently of current policy positions. Their claim on office and availability to serve with any other party must clearly affect the application of policy-based characterisations of coalition government to the Israeli case.

DIMENSIONS OF POLICY COMPETITION

The common left–right dimension used elsewhere in this book does reflect the major lines of cleavage between the major parties in Israel which relate to economic policy. Likud favours deregulation, monetarism and general economic modernisation and Labour defends welfare programmes and the collectivist status quo. Further divisions are also reflected in the common left–right dimension, with its emphasis on state intervention, peace and co-operation on the left and capitalist economics and social conservatism on the right. The left–right dimension also reflects something of the contemporary religious division in Israeli politics though this was not always the case; Likud is now clearly a more traditional and orthodox party than Labour.

The positions of the main Israel parties on this left–right dimension are reported in Table 12.2 and are unsurprising, suggesting that we accept the face validity of the scale. Perhaps the clearest positioning to emerge from the Table is the strongly rightist location taken by the religious parties, Agudah and particularly the NRP. Labour takes up its expected centrist position as does its small ally, the Progressives or Independent Liberals, with MAPAM, until absorbed by the Alignment, relatively far to the left. While generally fairly far to the right, Likud and its predecessors – Herut and the General Zionists (GZ) – do make surprising leftward lurches at times, at the crucial re-aligning election of 1977, and again in 1981, they were left of Labour. This may be due to the element of populism in their appeal. By 1984, however, they had again reverted to a very right-wing position.

The extreme right-wing position of the religious parties is, at least to some extent, probably an artifact of the use of a one-dimensional representation of Israeli politics. The religious parties are not notable upholders of capitalist economics or strongly opposed to state intervention. On the other hand, they certainly do not emphasize a soft line with Arabs and they are clearly socially conservative. It is these aspects of their programmes which push them towards the right of the left–right dimension.

However, there is clearly an argument in the Israel case for considering party politics in terms of a religious dimension that is unrelated to the left–right continuum. We accordingly developed a two-dimensional representation of the Israeli party system and report the results of this analysis. Naturally this demonstrated that the religious parties were different from the others. However, exactly the same puzzles and problems cropped up with the two-dimensional as with the one-dimensional representation, which may in part be because the common left–right scale already incorporates important elements of the 'religious effect' in the shape of right-wing emphases on social conservatism and traditional morality.

THE DOCUMENTS CODED

Since many changes in Israeli governments resulted from the maverick actions of small parties or even groups of people within parties, it was necessary to broaden the database used in our previous analysis of party policy, by extending the number of election manifestos analysed from 30 to 94. The sources of the additional party policy documents are similar to those used in the original analysis (Bara 1987). More of the programmes for the 1981 and 1984 elections were derived from Hebrew sources than was previously the case, and these were translated with the author's active participation.

Despite all efforts, a few remained elusive and regrettably this means that individual platforms are missing for some elections. These are the election programmes for MAPAM, 1951, Achdut Ha'avodah, 1955, MAKI, 1955, 1965, RAKAH, 1969, Agudah parties, 1951, 1955, 1969. The platforms for the Agudah parties are combined throughout. There was no separate platform for 1949, as all religious parties combined to form one list. Some parties, especially in the early years of statehood, did not produce statements of policy intention, the main example being the Sephardi Independents, 1949–51. One or two platforms were omitted for other reasons, for example TELEM, a list headed by Moshe Dayan in 1981, winning two seats. Dayan died shortly after the election and the other member formed the Ometz list in the 1984 election, which is included. The proliferation of lists for 1984 made it impossible to cover all. Lists effectively pertaining to individual independents were omitted, for example Lova Eliav's 'list'. Lists which previously put forward candidates and won seats, or which developed directly from existing parties were all included. In the event, the data accounts for lists which captured 119 of the 120 seats in the 1984 Knesset. The one exception is Meir Kahan's extreme right-wing Kach, not at all crucial to the coalition analysis, although with a small impact on the ideological range of the party system.

Information on coalition policy was derived from reports of the speeches of the Prime Minister Designate to the Knesset outlining the proposed government programme or, where possible, the actual written coalition agreement. Where it proved difficult to acquire the latter, media reports of the programme are usually very full, and often reproduce the speech to the Knesset outlining the agreement. As in the case of party platforms, the main source of information was the Jerusalem Post. Thus the coalition materials were almost exclusively in English and similar coding procedures were employed for the coalition programmes as for the party manifestos (Bara, 1987). It should be noted again that the coding categories are not always ideally adapted to the Israeli case, and we must be aware that references which have implications for one category often have to be coded in another; for example, 'peace' statements may be very similar to those concerned with security, yet would need to be coded as military negative. Also, the categories concerning national way of life and traditional morality, reflecting in the Israeli cases Zionism and religion respectively, cannot be distinguished precisely.

Although 26 governments took office during the study period, only eighteen are included in this study (see Table J.2 in Appendix). Eight of the governments appear to lack a coalition agreement or programme, almost certainly because they involve very minor changes in the executive. In such cases the incoming government simply states that it will carry out the programme of its predecessor, which has already been approved by the Knesset. It is worth noting that even among the 18 governments which did present programmes, differences with the outgoing government are often small.

THE ONE-DIMENSIONAL ANALYSIS

Government formation

Table 12.2 reports party and government positions on the common left–right dimension and identifies the party controlling the median legislator. It is clear that, if we judge policy proximity on the basis of this dimension alone, the religious parties should have been out of most governments in the post-war era. As we have already argued, however, circumstances associated with the turbulent formation of the Israeli state have meant that the presence of religious parties in government is the product of a constraint which we do not need to explain in terms of policy proximities. In assessing the role of policy, therefore, we shall consider only the non-religious parties in the government coalition.

In 14 out of the 18 cases analysed, the party controlling the median legislator is also in the government. The pivotal party is almost always Labour, which both controls the median legislator and dominates the government. On the face of it, this convincingly upholds the hypothesis that control of the median legislator gives a key role in coalition formation. However, Labour also controlled the median legislator when it was calamitously ousted from government in 1977; and this pivotal position passed to Likud at precisely the time that Likud was forced to admit Labour to a National Unity government in 1984! In other words the party controlling the median legislator lost out at the two key turning-points in recent Israeli political history!

Only in four out of 18 cases are non-religious government parties ideologically connected. Thus minimal connected winning theory fares rather poorly in a one-dimensional representation of Israeli politics. This is mainly because of a combination of the exclusion of the Communists and the refusal of Labour and Likud to share office for much of the period. As a consequence, Labour has often been forced to look for partners among small parties to the right of Likud.

In summary, it is clearly the case that governments tend to form round the party with the largest seat share in the Knesset. Clearly, the religious parties accept whichever of Labour or Likud have the electoral advantage. Beyond this, however, it remains rather unclear from the one-dimensional analysis which, if any, of the lay parties the dominant partner will choose as partners in government.

Table 12.2 Party and coalition policy in Israel, 1949–84

Year	Party 1	2	3	4	5	6	7	8	9	10	11	12	13	14	15	16	17	18	19	20	21	22	Coal	PM	Policy
1949	-33	4	-1*						-15	6	32										na		1	Ben Gurion I	-20
1950	-33	4	-1*						-15	6	32										na		2	Ben Gurion II	-14
1951	na*	1	0*						24	15		17	na								na		3	Ben Gurion III	3*
1952	na*	1	0*						24	15		17	na										4	Ben Gurion IV	1
1954	na*	1	0*						24	15		17	na										5	Sharrett I	6
1955	-10	16	21*		na				10	11	41		na										6	Ben Gurion V	20
1959	-1	1	0*		0				32	34	64	70											7	Ben Gurion VII	20
1961	-1	1*	0		21					70	67	43											8	Ben Gurion VIII	20
1965	-59	-7	-7*			1				2	55	15											9	Eshkol III	-15
1969	-59	-7	-7*			1				2	55	15											10	Meir I	15
1969	14	14*	4*							28	58	na				55	69						11	Meir II	12
1974	18*	5	5							47	70	71											12	Meir IV	13
1974	18*	5	5							47	70	71											13	Rabin I	14
1976	18*	5	5							47	70	71											14	Rabin III	15
1977	-13	0*	0*	-19				16		-6	46	65	55										15	Begin I	45
1977	-13	0*	0*	-19				16		-6	46	65	55										16	Begin II	41
1981	8		27*	36		-3				-2	51	51	-9									52	17	Begin III	39
1984		0	2			10				47*	75	19	61	76					32	68		48	18	National Unity	11

* MAPAM position not ascertained but assumed at extreme left for the calculation of party with median legislator.

Table 12.2 (cont'd)

Key to Parties

1	MAPAM	12	NRP
2	LP	13	AG
3	LAB	14	TAM
4	CRM	15	SHS
5	AA	16	MOR
6	SHM	17	SL
7	RAR	18	FC
8	GZ	19	YH
9	DMC	20	DMZ
10	LIKUD	21	SPR
11	SHL	22	THA

Median legislator marked with an asterisk.
Government party is italicised.

Government policy

Table 12.3 reports the distance between each party's policy position, expressed on the common left–right dimension, and the position of the government. To make the main patterns clearer, the table also reports rank-orderings of the closeness between party and government policy positions.

From the rank-orderings it appears that Labour, the party most often in a position of legislative and governmental dominance, does moderately well in policy terms. It is generally closer to government policy than Likud and its predecessors. Labour is rarely the party whose position is closest to that of the government, however. The party that often does best is Labour's small governmental partner, the Progressives–Independent Liberals. Paradoxically, however, this party does less well under the governments (Ben Gurion 8, Rabin 1 and 3) where it controls the median legislator. Likud does less well under the governments it controls than it does when sharing with Labour, or when in opposition.

The pattern of policy payoffs confirms the other evidence we have for asserting that religious parties enter governments for other reasons than policy. The National Religious Party consistently does worse than Labour or Likud in terms of the coincidence between its policies and those of the coalition (except under Begin where there was no separate agreement on the "status quo" and hence where religious matters played a more central role in bargaining and in government policy). Presumably, the general lack of coincidence between the NRP's position and that of the government mat-

Table 12.3 Percentage difference between party scores and coalition scores along the left–right dimension, Israel

Party	\-\-	\-\-	\-\-	\-\-	Coalition government													
	BG1	BG2	BG3	BG4	SH1	BG5	BG7	BG8	EK3	ME1	ME2	ME4	RB1	RB3	BN1	BN2	BN3	NU
LAB	19	−13	−3	−1	−6	1	−20	−20	8	−22	−8	−8	−9	−10	−45	−41	−9	11
LIK	26	20	12	14	9	−9	14	50	17	−13	16	34	33	32	−51	−47	−37	36
NRP	52	46	14	16	11	21	44	47	70	40	16	57	56	55	20	24	16	64
MPM	−13	−19	n/a	n/a	n/a	−30	−21	−21	−44	−74								
AA						n/a		1										
RAF							−20		16									
CRM										−14								
GZ	−5	1	21	23	18	−10	12	−8	8		2	2	1	0	−68	−60	−71	−9
ILP	24	18	−2	0	−5	−4	−19	−19		−22	2	5	4	3	−62	−54	−27	
DMC															−33	−25		
SHN																	−38	−1
YH																		21
OMZ																		57
SL											43							
FC											57							
SHL															−3			
THA																5		
AG			n/a	n/a	n/a	n/a	50	23	33	30	n/a	48	47	46	6	14	17	37
TAM																	16	8
SHS																	−44	50
MOR																		68

Rank ordering in terms of party closeness to government position of:

Party	BG1	BG2	BG3	BG4	SH1	BG5	BG7	BG8	EK3	ME1	ME2	ME4	RB1	RB3	BN1	BN2	BN3	NU
LAB	3	2	2	2	2	1	4	3	1=	2=	2	3	3	3	5	5	6	1
LIK	5	5	3	3	3	3	2	7	4	1	3	4	4	4	6	6	7	6
NRP	6	6	4	4	4	5	7	6	7	5	5	6	6	6	8	3	3	2= 10

n/a: Data unavailable despite the fact that the party took part in the election.
Key: See glossary in the appendix to this chapter.

357

tered little if its main objective in coalition bargaining was to gain control of certain ministries.

Overall, while the one-dimensional representation is sufficiently plausible not to be dismissed as a gross over-simplification of Israeli politics, these clearly contain many nuances which may be better represented in the multi-dimensional analysis.

TWENTY-DIMENSIONAL ANALYSIS

Government formation

It must be remembered that we could not get information on the policy positions of certain parties which entered coalitions or which might be reasonably considered as potential allies – especially in the earliest ways of statehood. In particular the Sephardi independents participated in five co-alitions covered by this period, though they were by no means crucial to government survival. The same might be said for Achdut Ha'Avodah in 1955. Although the Agudah parties also lack data for 1951, 1955, and 1969, the coalitions they entered would have probably survived without them. The absence of MAPAM programmes for the coalitions of the early 1950s are also less important than on other occasions, since the party was not involved in government.

These data problems take their toll on the multidimensional analysis for the 1949–1959 period. What the results do show overwhelmingly is that, in the Israeli case at least, it is crucial to take account of the constraints on bargaining. Consider the 1949 election results, which were responsible for producing two coalitions.

The closest pair of parties is represented by Herut and the Progressives, followed by Progressives and NRP and then by MAPAI and Herut. MAPAI

Table 12.4   Twenty-dimensional city-block party distances, Israel, 1949

	MAKI	MAPAI	MAPAM	HERUT	GZ	PROG	NRP
MAPAI	106						
MAPAM	126	92					
HERUT	106	72	82				
GZ	84	96	96	76			
PROG	106	100	76	60	68		
NRP	108	114	104	96	94	64	
Seats	4	48	19	14	7	5	16

is clearly the largest single party, with 48 seats; 61 seats are needed for a bare majority. Technically a MAPAI–Herut coalition could survive with 62 seats. We should not be too surprised that, in 1949, MAPAI and Herut appeared close in policy terms, given recent history, their stress on Zionism and the gathering of the exiles, security issues, and so on. In reality, however, such a MAPAI–Herut coalition would have been unthinkable at this stage. Alone, MAPAI could have been outvoted by a technically possible coalition of most of the other parties, but this again was most unlikely to form. Many of the parties would certainly not have entered alliances with each other, for example. MAKI or MAPAM would have been unthinkable as allies to Herut or NRP, and vice versa. Indeed we can ignore MAKI as an anti-system party, together with its related offshoots, descendants and 'fellow-travellers' (RAKAH, MOKED, PLP, Ha'olam, Hazeh). Taking all of this into account MAPAI, in both numerical and cultural terms, is the obvious centre of a coalition in 1949. Given the constraints, perhaps the most logical government would have been a MAPAI–MAPAM coalition controlling 67 seats. However, we also have to take account of the 'status quo' agreements on religious policy, to which MAPAM would have been hostile. Given the status quo factor, the nucleus of a government has to be MAPAI–NRP. These two, taken together, are closest to the Progressives and this group of three parties was indeed the basis of the two governments formed after the 1949 election, together with the Sephardi independents.

Similar problems confront us in milder form when we move to a period when the Israeli party system seemed more settled. Consider the 20-dimensional city-block distance matrix relating to the 1969 election, ignoring MAKI as an anti-system party. At this election Labour won 60 seats, its highest number to date, rendering it capable of at least attempting to form a minority government. Instead, we find a coalition which accounts for over 80 per cent of the Knesset.

The party distances suggest that a basic coalition should consist of Labour and the Independent Liberals, with 64 seats between them, but this is close to a minimal winning coalition, which would be unusual for Israel for the reasons discussed above. The next closest party appears to be GAHAL, giving 90 seats in all. (The constraint against GAHAL, as a Herut-based entity, had now vanished. Ben Gurion had retired from active politics and GAHAL had served in the 'national' government brought about by the security situation in 1967 and had continued to serve after the immediate danger was removed). Should an even large coalition be required, the most likely addition would be the NRP since this is the next closest party to Labour. This is essentially the coalition which formed, together with two of the Agudah members.

Table 12.5   Twenty-dimensional city-block party distances, Israel, 1969

ILP	94					
GHL	104	68				
FC	47	101	75			
SL	101	99	63	78		
LAB	89	55	61	92	104	
	NRP	ILP	GHL	FC	SL	LAB
Seats	12	4	26	2	4	60

A more systematic analysis of the complex Israeli 20-dimensional city block distance matrices can be achieved using the cluster models applied in the other country chapters in this book. The non-hierarchical clustering algorithm seems to be the more plausible in the case of Israel. As might be expected from the preceding discussion, the cluster analyses must be interpreted carefully, with due regard to the operative bargaining constraints. Consider the coalition formation process predicted by the cluster model after the 1951 General Election, and reported in Figure J.1.

The analysis predicts something that is quite close to what actually happened in this case. The predicted minimal winning coalition involves MAPAI, NRP and PROG, and this grouping formed the nucleus of two of the three coalitions that formed in this interelection period. If Herut is excluded on the grounds of the constraints operating, then the model predicts the actual coalition exactly. It is also interesting to note that the cluster model shows the close relationship between Herut and the General Zionists, and continues to do so for cases throughout the 1950s. This relationship was the basis of GAHAL, which came into being in 1965.

The situation after 1965 is shown in Figure J.1. In the case of Meir1, the cluster model produces what is ironically one of the closest fits between projection and reality. The coalition actually contained Moshe Dayan, one of the leaders of the RAFI which had broken away from MAPAI in 1965. Dayan joined Eshkol's 'national' government as Defence Minister in June 1967. In 1968, elements of RAFI formally joined the Labour alignment, henceforth Ma'arach, and the rest gravitated to the Likud via the State List. The irony refers to the fact that these coalitions, because they existed in the prelude to and aftermath of the 1967 June War, were to be freed from the constraint of not being able to include the Herut-based GAHAL.

The main problem in applying the cluster models in a systematic way is that constraints change over time and affect interpretations based solely on the logic of closeness of policy positions. However, there are some close approximations to the nuclei of the coalitions which formed, and it is

Table 12.6 Actual Israeli coalitions compared with majority coalitions predicted, within constraints, on the basis of the 20-dimensional analysis

Previous election date	Government	Actual coalition formed (parties+seats)	Majority coalition predicted
1949	Ben-Gurion1	MAP+NRP+PROG+SPR 48 16 5 4	MAP+NRP+GZ+PROG
	Ben-Gurion2	MAP+NRP+PROG+SPR 48 16 5 4	MAP+NRP+GZ+PROG
1951	Ben-Gurion3	MAP+NRP+SPR+AG 50 10 2 5	MAP+NRP+PROG
	Ben-Gurion4	MAP+NRP+PROG+GZ 50 10 4 20	MAP+NRP+PROG
	SH1	MAP+NRP+PROG+GZ 50 10 4 2	MAP+NRP+PROG
1955	Ben-Gurion5	MAP+NRP+PROG+AA+MPM 45 11 5 10 9	MAP+GZ+PROG+MPM+NRP
1959	Ben-Gurion7	MAP+NRP+PROG+AA+MPM 52 12 6 7 9	MAP+PROG+AA+GZ+MPM+NRP
1961	Ben-Gurion8	MAP+NRP+AA+AG 46 12 8 2	MAP+LIB+AA+NRP+AG
1965	Eshkol3	LAB+NRP+ILP+MPM+AG 49 11 5 8 2	LAB+GHL+ILP+NRP+AG+MPM
	Meir1	LAB+NRP+ILP+MPM+AG+GHL 49 11 5 8 2 26	LAB+GHL+ILP+NRP+AG+MPM

Table 12.6 (cont'd)

Previous election date	Government	Actual coalition formed (parties+seats)	Majority coalition predicted
1969	Meir2	ALI+NRP+ILP+GHL+AG 57 11 4 26 2	ALI+ILP+GHL+NRP+AG
1973	Meir4	ALI+NRP+ILP 54 10 4	ALI+ILP+CRM+LIK+NRP+AG
	Rabin1	ALI+ILP+CRM 54 4 3	ALI+ILP+CRM+LIK+NRP+AG
	Rabin3	ALI+ILP 53 4	ALI+ILP+CRM+LIK+NRP+AG
1977	Begin1	LIK+NRP+AG+SHA+FS 44 12 4 2 1	LIK+DMC+ALI+NRP+AL
	Begin2	LIK+NRP+AG+SHA+FS+DMC 44 12 4 2 1 15	LIK+DMC+ALI+NRP+AG
1981	Begin3	LIK+NRP+AG+TAMI+THA 48 6 4 3 3	LIK+ALI+SHN+TAMI+NRP
1984	National Unity	ALI+LIK+NRP+AG+SHI+MOR+SHAS+DMZ+YA	YA+ALI+LIK+AG+MOR+SHAS+TAMI+NRP

particularly striking that the technique suggested the 1965 merger between the Herut and General Zionist wing of the Liberal party as early as 1951, given the consistent pattern of the relationship between the two parties.

We can take a more systematic overview of the results by comparing the majority coalitions predicted by the cluster models with the coalitions which actually formed. The results of the comparison are in Table 12.6. We made a unique prediction of the expected coalitions by applying the following procedure to the cluster trees. First, we take majority coalitions, but not barely winning ones – given the tendency of Israeli governments to base themselves on surplus majorities. Second, we decide which surplus majority coalition to predict by taking the position of the National Religious Party (often associated with other religious parties) as a marker. As the NRP is almost always included in coalitions for the reasons we have already gone into, its policy position in a way constitutes an ideological 'boundary' for the parties which can be included. Thus, in making our postdictions, we took all parties clustering between and around the major partner and the NRP. This was the major influence of the bargaining constraints on our coalition predictions. Other parties were excluded when this is indicated by the constraints, though the Communist parties were usually too far away in policy terms for this to make any difference anyway.

The major impression from the table is that the multi-dimensional analysis, operating within the specified constraints, gets coalitions almost but not quite right most of the time. Only two coalitions (Meir 1 and 2) are exactly characterised, out of eighteen in all. But in the other cases, the major components of the coalition are typically identified, while the adhesion or non-adhesion of minor elements seems to be a much more haphazard affair. Often the characterisation misses the actual coalition formation by just one minor party, included or omitted.

Given the complexity of the Israeli party system and the consequently vast number of arithmetically possible coalitions (typically over 1000), the task of predicting the exact membership of particular governments is a particularly onerous one for coalition theories. Note that a model would be doing very much better than a random selection in the Israeli context if it were exactly right for only one government in a hundred. It may thus be fairer to judge the analysis, not on the basis of holistic characterisations of the entire coalition, but rather in terms of parties correctly predicted to be either in government or in opposition. Table 12.7 shows the cluster models rarely placed less than three quarters of the parties accurately. This indicates that the policy-based models do add markedly to our ability to interpret government formation in Israel.

Table 12.7　Success of multi-dimensional analysis in locating parties inside or outside Israeli government coalitions

Coalition	Parties correctly placed	Parties incorrectly placed	Proportion successes
BG1	6	2	.75
BG2	6	2	.75
BG3	8	1	.88
BG4	8	1	.88
SH1	8	1	.88
BG5	7	2	.77
BG7	8	1	.88
BG8	6	1	.85
ESH3	9	1	.90
ME1	10	0	1.00
ME2	9	0	1.00
ME4	5	3	.62
R1	5	3	.62
R3	4	4	.50
B1	6	4	.60
B2	7	3	.70
B3	9	2	.82
NU	12	2	.89

Government policy

Policy distances between parties and governments in the multi-dimensional space are reported in Table 12.8 The table also rank orders parties in terms of their closeness to government policy. The main pattern evident in Table 12.8 concerns the higher policy payoffs accruing to the dominant parties, particularly to the Labour Alignment and its predecessor Mapai. The exception is Likud, which does no better than Labour under Begin. The great beneficiary from the Begin governments are in fact the religious parties – after trailing at the end of the rank-ordering the NRP suddenly advances to first rank in the Begin period, while Labour and Likud share very similar, rather adverse, payoffs. Both Labour and Likud benefit from the National Unity coalition. The other government parties, apart from the ILP, show no clear pattern of gains compared to those outside.

DISAGGREGATED TWENTY-DIMENSIONAL ANALYSIS

Each of the 20 policy dimensions can be examined separately in order to discover whether any party has occupied a predominant position in the full

Table 12.8 Twenty-dimensional analysis: distances between parties and coalitions, Israel

Government	Party																							Rank ordering in terms of closeness to govt position of:			
	LAB	MPM	ADT	CRM	LKD	SHL	FC	SL	RFI	NRP	AG	TMI	SHS	MOR	THA	ILP	GZ	SPR	DMC	SHN	VHD	OMZ	LAB	LAB	LIK	NRP	Lay parties
BG1	92	62		92						96						60	66	n/a						4=	4=	6	1,4
BG2	91	63		85						91						53	65	n/a						5=	4	5=	1,5
BG3	52	n/a		93						72	n/a					76	83	n/a						1	5	2	1
BG4	75	n/a		96						75	n/a					87	86	n/a						1=	5	1=	3,4
SHT1	52	n/a		83						58	n/a					68	71	n/a						1	5	2	1,3,4
BG5	53	91	n/a	49						123	n/a					90	55							2	1	6	2,3,4,5
BG7	49	100	72	65						95	112					73	67							1	2	6	1,3,4,5
BG8	72	149	81	126						82	75					61								2	6	5	2,4
ESH3	72	81		65					65	116	96					66								4	7	7	3,4,5
ME1	80	97		93					75	98	82					90								2	5	7	2,4,5,6
ME2	70			73			96	114		93	n/a					65								2	3	4	1,2,3
ME4	80			70						108	89					94								2	1	6	2,4
RAB1	38		100	40						98	67					50								1	2	6	1,3,5
RAB3	80		86	68						104	85					96								2	1	6	2,4
BEG1	86		128	87		78				42	42					113			81					5	6	6	6
BEG2	86		124	81		74				42	36					109			79	88				6	5	1=	4.5
BEG3	73		152	73						32	51	108			38	103								4=	4=	1	4.5
NU	66		102	67						87	83	71	75	84	80	103				72	42	81		2	3	8	2,3

n/a Not available because of missing data

Table 12.9 Parties controlling the median legislator on 20-dimensions, Israel, 1949–84

Policy Dimension	1949	1951	1955	1959	1961	1965	1969	1973	1977	1981	1984
State intervention	NRP	LAB	LAB	LAB	LAB	*	LAB	*	*	*	*
Peace & Co-operation	LAB	NRP	LAB	LAB	LAB	LAB	LAB	LAB	LIK	LAB	LIK
Anti-establishment	LAB	NRP	NRP	LAB	NRP	LAB	ILP	LIK	LIK	LASB	*
Capitalist economics	LAB	NRP	LAB	LAB	*	LAB	LAB	LAB	LIK	LAB	NRP
Social conservation	LAB	LAB	LAB	LAB	LAB	LAB	LAB	LAB	LAB	LAB	LAB
Productivity	MPM	LAB	LAB	LAB	LAB	LAB	LAB	LAB	*	LIK	LAB
Military (+)	MPM	LAB	LAB	LAB	LAB	LAB	LAB	LAB	LIK	LIK	*
Freedom & Human Rights	NRP	NRP	LAB	LAB	LAB	LAB	LAB	LAB	*	LAB	*
Democracy	HER	NRP	LAB	LAB	LAB	LAB	LAB	ILP	DMC	LIK	*
Government efficiency	*	NRP	*	*	*	LAB	LAB	LIK	*	LAB	*
Social justice	LAB	GZ	GZ	LAB	AH	LAB	LAB	*	*	LAB	*
Social services(+)	*	LAB	LAB	AH	LIB	GHL	LAB	LAB	*	AG	*
Education (+)	*	LAB	LAB	LAB	NRP	NRP	*	*	*	LIK	*
Labour Groups (+)	*	LAB	LAB	MPM	LIB	LAB	*	*	*	LIK	*
Agriculture	*	LAB	LAB	LAB	*	MPM	*	*	*	*	*

No of dimensions where median legislator controlled by:

	1949	1951	1955	1959	1961	1965	1969	1973	1977	1981	1984
LAB	5	8	12	12	7	11	11	7	1	6	2
LIKUD	1	0	0	0	0	1	0	2	4	5	1
NRP	2	6	1	0	2	1	0	0	0	0	1
MPM	2	0	0	1	0	1	—	—	—	—	—
GZ	0	1	1	0	0	0	—	—	—	—	—
ILP-LIB	0	0	0	0	2	0	1	1	0	0	0

* Represents an inconclusive result

20-dimensional policy space. The underlying assumption in this is that the more dimensions on which a single party controls the median legislators, the more the policy space is dominated by that party, and the stronger its bargaining position in the coalition building process. In the case of Israel, several of the dimensions discussed elsewhere in this volume are excluded since they either have no relevance to Israeli politics – for example, EEC positive and EEC negative – or they were not reflected in party platforms – for example, quality of life, decentralisation and minorities. The results are reported in Table 12.9, from which it will be apparent that Labour occupied a predominant position across most dimensions during the period 1949 to 1973, which corresponds to the era of Labour hegemony within government. Even on those dimensions for which Labour was not the dominant party, the pivotal position seems to have been occupied by one of its main coalition allies, usually the NRP or Independent Liberal Party.

From 1973 two changes are apparent. First, the Likud takes over the dominant position on a number of dimensions, certainly in the case of 1977 which represents the party's first electoral victory. Second, the number of dimensions which appear salient overall diminishes. Traditional areas of policy disappear, and the situation becomes much more volatile. The platforms of the major parties – and indeed their relative electoral strengths – are very close to each other in 1981 and 1984. The chaotic nature of the 1984 election and its ensuing, novel, 'grand' coalition government mean that it is not surprising that results for that case are inconclusive. What is interesting is that the analysis generates only four dimensions of any salience – peace, capitalist economics, social conservatism (which encompasses the religious dimension) and military positive (which relates to security). These were indeed the major issues of debate in Israeli politics in the 1980s.

Overall, the disaggregated analysis shows that control of the median legislator over a number of policy dimensions seems clearly associated with dominance of the government, since the balance of control clearly alters in 1977 and 1984, the crucial turning-points in Israeli politics.

CONCLUSIONS: THE SUCCESS OF POLICY BASED MODELS

A general evaluation of the coalition models tested in previous chapters can be found in Table 12.10. This evaluates the success rates of the clustering models (Theory A): the prediction that coalitions will include the party with the median legislator over most dimensions (Theory B): and the prediction that coalitions will include the party with the median legislator on the

Table 12.10 Success rates of policy based coalition models in Israel, 1949–84

Election year	Government	Number of Governments Arithmetically possible	Number of Governments Feasible under constraints	Theory A Predictions Set	Theory A Predictions Correct	Theory B Predictions Set	Theory B Predictions Correct	Theory C Predictions Set	Theory C Predictions Correct
1949	BG1	517	11	1	NO	11	YES	11	YES
	BG2	517	11	1	NO	11	YES	11	YES
1951	BG3	1023	19	1	NO	19	YES	19	YES
	BG4	1023	19	1	NO	19	YES	19	YES
	SH1	1023	19	1	NO	19	YES	19	YES
1955	BG5	511	11	1	NO	11	YES	11	YES
1959	BG7	511	11	1	NO	11	YES	11	YES
1961	BG8	511	11	1	NO	11	YES	16	NO
1965	ESH3	1023	19	1	NO	19	YES	19	YES
	Meir1	1023	19	1	NO	19	YES	19	YES
1969	Meir2	1023	27	1	YES	27	YES	27	YES
1973	Meir4	255	11	1	YES	11	YES	11	YES
	Rabin1	255	11	1	NO	11	YES	11	YES
	Rabin3	255	11	1	NO	11	YES	11	YES
1977	Begin1	2047	19	1	NO	19	YES	19	NO
	Begin2	2047	19	1	NO	19	YES	19	NO
1981	Begin3	1023	19	1	NO	19	NO	19	NO
1984	NAT UN	32767	10	1	NO	10	YES	10	YES
Predictive Accuracy (No correct/No cases)					.11(2/18)		.94(17/18)		.77(14/18)
Predictive Efficiency (No correct/No predictions)					.11(2/18)		.06(17/277)		.05(14/272)

Theory A: Government will comprise range of parties around and between party with plurality of seats and NRP and be policy-viable on at least one dimension

Theory B: Government will include party with control of median legislator over most of 20 dimensions common left–right scale (Theory C). We do not check the success of connected policy based theories since these are so clearly inapplicable in the Israeli case, given the role of the religious parties.

The predictions of the cluster models, as we have already seen, rarely characterise coalitions exactly. Only two out of 18 are predicted precisely. While their success rate is low, the fact that they make unique predictions in an environment where sometimes thousands of coalitions could have formed means that their predictive efficiency is high; the cluster models do very much better than chance at predicting Israeli coalitions. The prediction that the coalition will include the party with the median legislator on the left–right scale is, on the other hand, very successful but compatible with practically all feasible coalitions, given constraints; thus its predictive efficiency is low. The prediction that the coalition will contain the party with control of the median legislator on a plurality of the twenty dimensions fares better than the prediction based on the left–right dimension, and has the same predictive efficiency.

The most successful aspect of the Israeli part of this analysis remains the ability of the cluster models to identify most of the parties that go into coalitions and most of those that stay out: reported in Table 12.7. While this rests in part on the structural constraints identified in Table 12.1, it draws on policy distances between parties to identify those which will go into government with the NRP and the party winning a plurality at the preceding election.

Given the very strong constraints that affect coalition bargaining, and given the special role and the instrumental office-seeking approach of the religious parties, it is difficult to see how predictions based purely on policy proximity could ever work well in Israel.

NOTE

1   Data for the small parties relating to the period 1949–1977 was collected at the British Newspaper Library and in Israel, with the help of a Nuffield Foundation grant. The data for the 1981 and 1984 elections and for most of the coalitions was collected by Yael Enoch-Levy, and she and Chana Sladowsky helped with the translation of Hebrew materials. The author would like to thank all involved in this exercise for their help and patience.

APPENDIX J

Table J.1 Seats gained by parties at Knesset elections, Israel, 1949–84

Party	1949	1951	1955	1959	1961	1965	1969	1973	1977	1981	1984
Achdut			10	7	8						2
Agudah		5	6	6	6	6	6	5	5	4	3
CRM								3	1	1	
DMC									15		
Free Centre							2				
GAHAL						26	26				
GZ/Liberal	7	20	13	8							
Herut	14	8	15	17	17						
Ind. Liberal/Progressive	5	4	5	6		5	4	4	1		
Liberal (GZ/Prog)					17						
Likud								39	43	48	41
Ma'arach							60	54	33	47	44
MAKI	4	5	6	3	5	1	1				
MAPAI	48	50	45	52	46	49					
MAPAM	19	15	9	9	9	8					
MOKED/Haolem Hazeh						1	2	1			
Morasha											2

Table J.1 (cont'd)

Party	1949	1951	1955	1959	1961	1965	1969	1973	1977	1981	1984
NRP	16	10	11	12	12	11	12	10	12	6	4
Ometz											1
PLP											2
RAFI						10					
RAKAH/HADAS H						3	3	4	5	4	4
SHAS											4
SHELLI									2		
Shinui										2	3
Shlomzion									2		
SPR	4	2									
State List							4				
TAMI											1
Tehiya										3	5
Yahad											3
Other	3	1							1	2	1

Table J.2   Coalition governments in Israel included in analysis

Government and date	Members and seats						% Knesset
Ben Gurion I	MAP	NRP	PROG	SPR			60.8
10 March 1949	48	16	5	5			
Ben Gurion II	MAP	NRP	PROG	SPR			60.8
30 October 1950	48	16	5	4			
Ben Gurion III	MAP	NRP	SPR	AG			55.8
9 October 1951	50	10	2	5			
Ben Gurion IV	MAP	NRP	PROG	GZ			68.9
23 December 1952	50	10	4	20			
Sharrett I	MAP	NRP	PROG	GZ			68.9
7 January 1954	50	10	4	20			
Ben Gurion V	MAP	NRP	PROG	AA	MPM		66.7
3 November 1955	45	11	5	10	9		
Ben Gurion VII	MAP	NRP	PROG	AA	MPM		71.7
12 December 1959	52	12	6	7	9		
Ben Gurion VIII	MAP	NRP	AA	AG			56.7
2 November 1961	46	12	8	2			
Eshkol III	LAB	NRP	ILP	MPM	AG		60.8
12 January 1966	49	11	5	8	2		
Meir I	LAB	NRP	ILP	MPM	AG	GHL	84.2
17 March 1969	49	11	5	8	2	26	
Meir II	ALI	NRP	ILP	GHL	AG		83.3
15 December 1969	57	11	4	26	2		
Meir IV	ALI	NRP	ILP				56.7
10 March 1974	54	10	4				
Rabin I	ALI	ILP	CRM				50.8
3 June 1974	54	4	3				
Rabin III	ALI	ILP					47.5
20 December 1976	53	4					
Begin I	LIK	NRP	AG	SHA	FS		52.5
20 June 1977	44	12	4	2	1		
Begin II	LIK	NRP	AG	SHA	FS	DMC	65.0
24 October 1977	44	12	4	2	1	15	
Begin III	LIK	NRP	AG	TAMI	THA		53.3
5 August 1981	48	6	4	3	3		
National Unity/(Peres /Shamir)	ALI	LIK	NRP	AG	SHI	MOR	86.7
13 September 1984	44	41	4	2	3	2	
	SHAS	OMETZ	YAHAD				
	4	1	3				

Table J.3   Coalition governments in Israel not included in analysis

Government and date	Reason for Non-inclusion
Sharrett II 29 June 1955	Same agreement as Sharrett I
Ben Gurion VI 7 January 1958	Same agreement as Ben Gurion V
Eshkol I 26 June 1963	Same agreement as Ben Gurion VIII
Eshkol II 22 December 1964	Same agreement as Ben Gurion VIII
Eshkol IV 1 June 1967	No agreement or programme owing to security emergency
Meir III 30 July 1970	Same agreement as Meir II
Rabin 2 30 October 1974	Same agreement as Meir IV
Shamir I 10 October 1983	Same agreement as Begin III

Table J.4   Twenty-dimensional distance matrices, Israel, 1951–84

1951

	MAKI	MAPAI	HERUT	NRP	GZ	PROG
MAPAI	91					
HERUT	136	89				
NRP	113	50	71			
GZ	132	83	50	75		
PROG	109	50	49	57	57	
Seats	5	50	8	19	20	4

1955

	MAKI	MAPAI	HERUT	NRP	GZ	PROG
MAPAI	72					
HERUT	70	90				
NRP	88	66	116			
GZ	56	94	52	102		
PROG	67	99	79	99	65	
Seats	6	45	15	11	13	5

1959

	MAPAI	MAPAM	HERUT	NRP	GZ	PROG	AA	AG
MAPAM	99							
HERUT	68	129						
NRP	110	135	78					
GZ	74	109	72	104				
PROG	66	121	92	130	70			
AA	125	106	79	119	87	107		
AG	83	156	87	39	129	143	128	
Seats	52	9	17	12	8	6	7	6

1961

	MAKI	MAPAI	MAPAM	HERUT	NRP	AA	AG	LIB
MAPAI	127							
MAPAM	116	123						
HERUT	169	124	171					
NRP	159	110	171	142				
AA	166	81	130	117	93			
AG	138	79	156	139	57	82		
LIB	142	77	150	137	75	86	116	
Seats	5	46	9	17	12	8	6	

1965

	MAKI	MAPAM	NRP	ILP	AG	RAK	MAPAI	RAF	GHL
OAPAM	108								
NRP	163	161							
ILP	111	87	132						
AG	149	133	42	110					
RAK	50	126	177	151	161				
MAPAI	141	125	112	102	90	161			
RAF	126	102	101	69	93	148	57		
GHL	118	96	109	51	87	154	83	60	
Seats	1	8	11	5	6	3	49	10	26

1973

	NRP	ILP	AG	RAK	LAB	LIK	CRM	MOK/S
ILP	134							
AG	43	99						
RAK	128	58	107					
LAB	116	48	85	68				
LIK	88	58	57	94	60			
CRM	120	94	113	102	92	102		
MOK/S	122	78	109	62	64	104	100	
Seats	10	4	5	4	54	39	3	1

1977

	NRP	ILP	AG	RAK	LAB	LIK	CRM	SHL	DMC	MOK/S
ILP	143									
AG	26	123								
RAK	144	107	130							
LAB	110	105	90	106						
LIK	106	71	100	116	66					
CRM	148	79	122	110	120	116				
SHL	82	117	70	134	76	72	146			
DMC	95	78	77	101	67	59	111	65		
MOK/S	135	90	109	89	89	109	75	115	74	
Seats	12	1	5	5	33	43	1	2	15	2

1981

	NRP	ILP	AG	RAK	LAB	MOK/S	THA	TAM	SHN	LIK
ILP	109									
AG	57	116								
RAK	133	118	162							
LAB	77	76	100	110						
MOK/S	124	95	153	89	101					
THA	10	113	59	133	73	120				
TAM	124	57	99	121	91	94	124			
SHN	76	59	105	89	63	56	66	66		
LIK	83	68	100	90	38	85	83	77		
Seats	6	0	4	4	47	0	3	3	1	48

1984

	MOR	SHAS	PLP	NRP	AG	RAK	LAB	LIK	THA	TAM	SHN	YAH	OMT
SHAS	27												
PLP	163	154											
NRP	41	38	144										
AG	95	82	106	88									
RAK	147	152	66	150	104								
LAB	86	79	111	87	87	101							
LIK	71	58	134	76	50	124	59						
THA	56	51	133	49	67	123	80	71					
TAM	31	44	144	58	98	128	79	80	57				
SHN	94	107	79	105	77	61	64	79	108	99			
YAH	86	75	115	79	85	105	68	61	78	77	70		
OMT	55	50	154	70	56	144	85	56	47	60	109	85	
Seats	2	4	2	4	2	4	44	41	5	1	3	3	1

GLOSSARY OF ABBREVIATIONS

MAP Mapai
LAB Labour
MPM MAPAM
AA Achdut Ha'avodah
CRM Citizens Rights Movement
ALI Labour Alignment (Labour, MAPAM, RAFI)

Note: All entries relating to the Labour Party include associated Arab Minority Lists.

PROG Progressive Party which became ILP, Independent Liberal Party.
GZ General Zionists which became Liberal Party and joined Herut to form GAHAL (the Herut-Liberal Bloc). This formed the basis of:
LIK LIKUD
SHA Shlomzion (Ariel Sharon's party) which later joined LIKUD
DMC Democratic Movement for Change
SHI Shinui
THA Tehiya
FS Flatto–Sharon list
NRP National Religious Party

TAMI   Israel Tradition Movement
AG   Agudah parties (also called Torah Front)
MOR   Morasha
SHAS   (Association of Sephardi Observants of the Torah)
SPR   Sephardi Independents

Sources: Seliktar (1982)
        Keesings Contemporary Archives
        Statistical Abstract of Israel (1983, 1984)

Figure J.1   Cluster diagrams for 20-dimensional representations of Israeli political
           parties, 1949–84

1949

Party	HERUT	PAG	GZ	MPM	MAP	NRP	MAKI
Seats	14	5	7	19	48	16	4

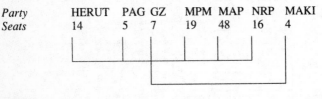

1951

Party	HERUT	PAG	GZ	MAP	NRP	MAKI
Seats	8	4	20	50	10	5

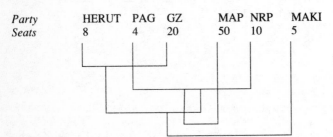

1955

Party   HERUT GZ   MAP   PRG   MPM   NRP
Seats   15   13   45   5   9   11

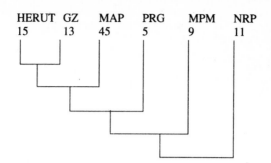

1959

Party   AA   HERUT GZ   MAP   PRG   MPM   NRP
Seats   7   17   8   52   6   9   12

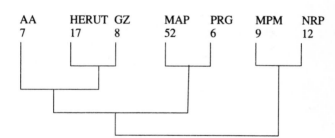

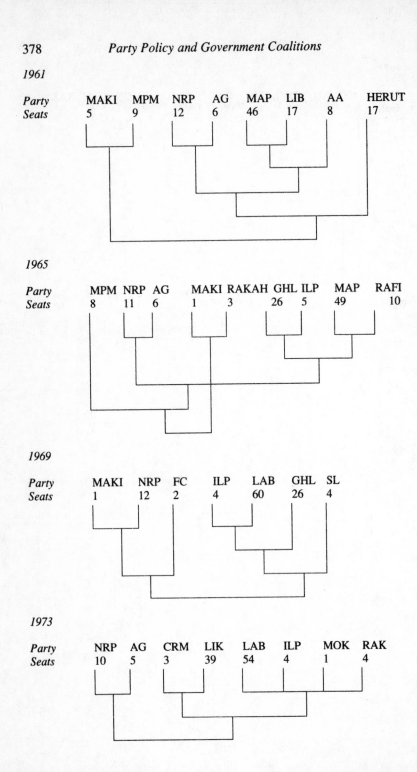

1977

Party	NRP	AG	DML	LIK	LAB	SHL	ILP	MOK	CRM	RAK
Seats	12	5	15	43	33	3	1	2	1	5

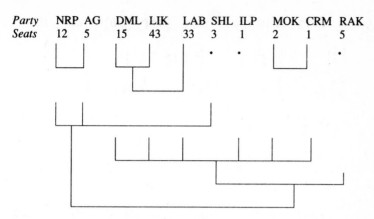

1981

Party	THA	NRP	AG	LIK	LAB	SHN	TAM	RAK
Seats	3	6	4	48	47	2	3	4

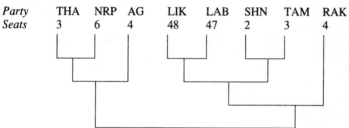

1984

Party	YD	LAB	MOR	SHAS	TAM	NRP	THA	OMT	AG	LIK	SHN	RAK	PLP
Seats	3	44	2	4	1	4	5	1	2	41	3	4	2

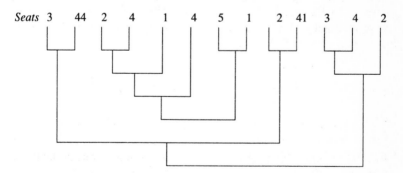

13 Coalition Bargaining in the French Fourth Republic 1946–58

François Petry

Party politics in the Fourth Republic were characterised by extreme instability. Two different explanations have been advanced for the political environment which led to the formations of 28 governments in the space of twelve years. The first concentrates upon the machinations of party leaders and other senior politicians eligible for office (*ministrables*). It is argued that these office-seeking actors constantly sought to undermine the existing government in the hope of entering its replacement or at least of improving their bargaining position (Leites, 1958). The second explanation of instability concentrates upon the extreme ideological polarisation of the Fourth Republic's fragmented party system, which created a large fringe of parties opposed to the existing regime, compounded by deep incompatibilities between the regime's supporters. Government coalitions were, on this account, based on agreements over narrow sets of policies. In the absence of party discipline, these alliances tended to collapse when new issues emerged (Fauvet, 1957). The contrast between these two accounts, one based on office motivations, the other on policy, echoes the themes discussed in Chapter 1. Thus the case of the French Fourth Republic provides a good environment for elaborating some of the basic distinctions that lie at the heart of coalition theory.

THE PARTY SYSTEM OF THE FOURTH REPUBLIC

Formed in the aftermath of a traumatic military defeat and a foreign occupation which proved internally divisive, functioning at the height of the Cold War and forced to face the need for major readjustments in France's world role, it was no wonder that French parties were exceptionally fragmented and divided. The degree of polarisation and ideological hostility to the regime on the part of some of the largest and most cohesive groupings is not encountered in the other countries we have examined. Some of these features were inherited from the Third Republic (1875–1940). Chief among

380

these was the fact that most parties of the centre and right were loose groupings of notables – cadre parties in the fullest sense (Duverger, 1953) – with only limited internal cohesion and national party organisation. This had two effects. First, parties often split on the matter of entering or leaving the government, so that the 'unitary actor' assumption that parties act as a cohesive bloc is more suspect here than in the other cases we have examined. Second, electoral coalitions (*apparentements*) were purely tactical manoeuvres which imposed no obligations on the partners to act together in the subsequent legislature.

We can distinguish seven broad political 'families' in the party system of the Fourth Republic. Sometimes the 'family' corresponded to a single reasonably cohesive party grouping; more often it comprehended several small groupings divided among themselves on grounds of personality or ideology.

The Communists

The Parti Communiste Français (PCF) enjoyed the largest parliamentary representation. After their departure from the Ramadier government in May, 1947, they went into permanent opposition. They did support governments on two subsequent occasions (Mendès-France in 1954 and Mollet in 1956) but this support was limited in both cases to the premier's investiture only.

The Socialists

The Section Française de l'Internationale Ouvriere (SFIO) had a stable parliamentary representation (at around 16 per cent) and formed the second largest group in two legislatures out of three. They were in power during most of the first and third legislatures but chose to remain outside all government coalitions (although offering conditional support to some) during the second legislature.

The Communist and Socialist parties were internally unified and had mass followings and organisations which they could use to influence public policy outside the parliamentary arena. In contrast, most remaining parties had little or no structure outside the Assembly. Their only chance to influence policy was, therefore, to participate in office.

The Radicals

The size of the Radical family (Radical Party, Union Democrate et Socialiste de la Resistance – UDSR, Rassemblement de la Gauche Republicaine – RGR and Neo-Radicals) was stable overall at about 12 per cent. The Radical party and the UDSR were systematically over-represented both in terms of cabinet portfolios and the premiership. They were the only parties in power for all 28 governments of the Fourth Republic.

The Christian Democrats

The Christian democratic family (Mouvement Republicain Populaire – MRP) steadily lost electoral ground, from 28 per cent in the first legislature to 12 per cent in the third legislature. The MRP was a member of all but three cabinets (Mendès-France in the second legislature, Mollet and Bourges-Maunoury in the third legislature).

The moderate right

The moderate right (Independents, Paysans and various small splinter groups) increased its parliamentary representation from 8 per cent in 1946 to 17 per cent in 1956. The group of Independents was the most stable and important in the moderate family. Though there were Independent ministers in all cabinets except those of Mollet and Bourges-Manoury, the moderate right was excluded from the premiership before 1952.

The Gaullists

The Rassemblement du Peuple Français (RPF), later Republicains Socials (ARS) voted against all cabinets until de Gaulle's withdrawal from politics and their contemporaneous split into separate left-leaning and right-leaning entities. The Gaullists, who had fulfilled the role of rightist anti-system opposition during the first and part of the second legislatures were succeeded in that role by the Poujadists (Union de la Fraternité Française – UFF) after the 1956 election. Gaullist representation in the third legislature was drastically reduced, principally to the benefit of the UFF.

Others

A few remaining parliamentary groups are difficult to classify into well defined families. The Poujadists are one of these as is also the Parti Republicain de la Liberté (PRL), a small right wing party which lasted for the length of the first legislature only. The PRL differed from the other parties of the right in its recruitment and organisation. Its ideology was similar in many points to that of the Gaullists. In fact, several PRL deputies were notoriously Gaullists. Another group that is difficult to classify are the deputies from France's overseas colonies, who had only peripheral interests in metropolitan issues but sought to obtain concessions on colonial matters through support of and participation in cabinets.

FORMING A GOVERNMENT IN THE FRENCH FOURTH REPUBLIC: THE RULES OF THE GAME

When a premier was overthrown, the selection of a successor followed a sequence of well defined steps. After initial consultations with party leaders and officials, the President of the Republic asked a politician to stand for the premiership. At this stage the candidate for the succession, called *president du conseil pressenti* could either refuse the mandate given him by the President or, after a trial run of consultations called a *tour de piste*, accept the mandate and become *president du conseil designe*. A designated premier was required by the constitution to win absolute majority support for a proposed government programme in Parliament so as to be invested and become *president du conseil investi*. Once invested, the premier still had to select a ministerial team and receive majority approval for the composition of a proposed cabinet. After the 1954 constitutional modification, however, it was only required that the designated premier announce the composition of his cabinet before being invested by a simple majority vote. In other words, the investiture and cabinet votes were no longer distinct.

President Auriol approached 59 *sollicites*, of which 24 accepted to become *designes*. Of these, 14 achieved success at investiture but two (Schuman, 1948 and Queuille, 1950) failed to secure majority support for their cabinet. There were 23 *sollicites* under President Coty. Of these ten confronted a vote in the Assembly and only seven succeeded in forming a government.[1]

A candidate for the premiership thus first faced the challenge of being asked by the President to form a government. At this initial stage, the ultimate outcome (whether or not majority support for the candidate's proposed government could be found in the legislature) was still quite uncertain and the candidate's programme and ministerial team were still unknown. The second challenge that a candidate faced, at least until 1954, was to get majority investiture support for a proposed government programme. At this stage the parties judged the designated-but-not-yet-invested premier on the basis of this programme so that the candidate's success or failure at investiture should be predictable on the basis of the expected policy payoffs accruing from the programme to each party. In the final stage, the parties had to approve or oppose the composition of the cabinet proposed by the invested premier.

STRUCTURAL CONSTRAINTS AND INFLUENCES

Constraints

While, in theory, French parties were free to join any other in coalition, several strong constraints removed certain coalition possibilities. The most important of these was exogenous and resulted from party system polarisation. It involved the systematic exclusion of anti-system parties, including the Communists throughout the period, the Gaullists until 1953, and the Poujadists in the third legislature. These parties were typically quite large, and their exclusion made parliamentary seats a scarce resource for any designated premier. The proportion of all legislative seats available from pro-system parties varied from around .70 in the First Legislature, down to .64 at the outset of the Second. The availability of Gaullist seats after the General withdrew from the movement and 'Gaullist' Deputies signified their willingness to play the Parliamentary game raised the proportion briefly to .84 in the second half of the second legislature. With the entry of the Poujadistes in 1956, however, it returned to .69. On average, therefore, little more than two-thirds of total parliamentary seats could be considered as even potentially available to any designated premier who sought investiture. The effects of this constraint on coalition formation are, quite naturally, crucial.

First, in a situation where there are few seats to spare, all, or almost all, pro-system parties were indispensable for coalition formation and maintenance. Systematic exclusion of the largest parties dramatically reduced the number of coalition possibilities among the remaining pro-system parties. This made it much more likely that more than one party would be at the intersection of every feasible coalition and should therefore have been in power without interruption during the course of a legislature.

Second, as a corollary of this, it is less likely that a single centre party would occupy a pivotal position in coalition bargaining. This is because, given the need for almost all pro-system parties, centre parties have much less latitude in deciding whether to ally with coalition partners of the left or the right. They cannot use threats to deal with alternative coalition partners as leverage when bargaining for a larger share of policy or portfolio payoffs.

Influences

The proportional representation electoral system was an important structural influence on the party system of the Fourth Republic. It accounts for the singular absence of those binding commitments by parties to govern together which became the norm under the single constituency two ballot electoral system of the Fifth Republic. Electoral alliances were also formed in the proportional representation elections of the Fourth Republic, in 1951 and 1956 in particular. This followed a reform which instituted a list ballot at the department (multi-candidate) level with a majority take all provision. The pro-system parties sought to take advantage of this by adding together their votes so as to win all the seats in particular departments. These *apparentements*, as they were called, were however purely tactical arrangements aimed at isolating anti-system parties so as to reduce their overall representation in the Assembly. They did not reflect electoral agreements between national party headquarters, let alone programmatic alliances which would commit parties to govern together.

Various other institutional features of the Fourth Republic clearly did not make it any easier for prospective coalitions to survive. As we have seen, the existence of the two different votes of confidence obviously increased opportunities for defection, while the requirement for an absolute majority of votes (over 50 per cent of seats in the legislature) meant that abstentions counted against the government rather than for it. The fact that the legislature could not be dissolved by the outgoing government had the effect that the parties did not have to concern themselves with the possibility of losing votes if they brought down the government. Each of these features, summarised in Table 13.1, made it harder to form governments, as well as easier to bring down those governments that did form.

Table 13.1 Constraints and influences upon coalition bargaining under the French Fourth Republic

---

1. Exclusion of Communists from government after 1947.
2. Exclusion of Gaullists from government up to 1953.
3. Exclusion of Poujadistes (UFF) from government after 1956.
4. Coalition must be explicitly approved by Legislature.
5. Coalition requires an absolute majority of legislature votes up to 1954.
6. Two separate votes of confidence in coalition make coalition formation and survival less likely.
7. No power of dissolution so parties able to bring down a government without worrying about electoral effects.
8. PR electoral system does not reward electoral coalitions

DOCUMENTS CODED

Policy distances between the parties in each legislature were measured on the basis of coded policy statements by the parliamentary groups represented in the National Assembly (declarations politiques des groupes). These statements were reprinted in the *Journal Officiel* (sittings) at the beginning of each legislature. Since party policy statements for the first legislature are not reprinted in the *Journal Officiel*, party documents and press releases for the 1946 elections were used instead.

The content of the party statements were coded into 18 policy categories which are listed in the left-hand column in Table K.5 in the Appendix. The French coding scheme was adapted from the common coding scheme, and differences are not great. Several categories in the common scheme were either excluded (Internationalism negative, Decentralisation and Underprivileged minorities) or combined with others (Labour, Farmers and Education). In addition, five categories not found in the common scheme were included so as to accommodate specific aspects of the ideological debate in the French Fourth Republic. They are: Pro- and Anti-regime, Anti-right, Laicity and pro-Church references.

ONE-DIMENSIONAL ANALYSIS

These coded policy statements were used to generate two measures of policy distances between the parties, one uni-dimensional, the other multi-dimensional. The positions of each party on the left–right scale after each election can be seen in Table 13.2, and are consistent with the party positions that have been proposed by previous authors (see in particular MacRae, 1967). Specific party movements between elections are particularly well captured. Notably we can see the Radical party shifting toward the right while the Independents move towards the Left.

As noted above, the systematic exclusion of large anti-system parties makes it more than likely that more than one party will be at the common intersection of all feasible coalitions. In other words it makes much less sense in the case of the Fourth Republic to identify a single party (the party controlling the median legislator) as being in a distinctively pivotal 'core' position. It makes more sense to identify a group of centre parties as being collectively indispensable for the policy viability of a government. We say that these parties comprise the 'plural' core of the coalition formation game. The parties forming the plural core in each legislature are identified in bold

Table 13.2   Party positions on the French left–right scale

Party	1946	Year 1951	1956
PCF	–40	–53	–43
SFIO	–30	–22	–17
UDSR	–18	–4	–7
Radicals	–1	+16	+31
MRP	+4	0	+11
Independent (from 1951)	+33	+23	+18
Gaullist	—	+47	+42
Paysans	+45	+51	+62
PRL	+24	—	—

Note: Italicised parties constitute 'plural core'.

italic in Table 13.2. Typically, the MRP, UDSR and Radicals are all in the core, being joined from 1951 by the Independents. The parties in the plural core are predicted to be part of all majority winning coalitions, since none can be excluded while keeping the coalition policy-viable.

Government formation

The plural core predicts coalitions rather well in the first legislature in the sense that no premier won investiture without the support of all core parties. However, this is also true of the SFIO which was not in the plural core. This model makes several wrong predictions in the second legislature since Mendès-France won investiture without MRP and Independent support despite the fact that these two parties were in the plural core. The predictive power of the plural core is considerably less in the third legislature, mainly because the Independents, in the core, were rarely in government. Overall, three of the parties typically in the 'plural core', the MRP, UDSR and radicals, did form the basis of most governments in the French Fourth Republic. The fourth party added to the core after 1951, the Independents, was a much less regular member. While the one-dimensional analysis goes quite a long way towards interpreting government formation in the French Fourth Republic, it does not explain the behaviour of the Independents very convincingly.

Government policy

During the Fourth Republic, there were 37 premiers; politicians who accepted the mandate to form a government given to them by the President. They accepted because they expected that they could gather sufficient support for their investiture in the Assembly. However, 16 (40 per cent) of these *designes* failed in their bid to be invested. At the investiture stage, the policy programme of the prime minister designate, but not his cabinet, became known to the legislature. We therefore hypothesize that parties decide to support or oppose a proposed government at this stage primarily on the basis of the policy payoffs they expect to receive.

The one-dimensional distances between party and coalition policy in France are given in Table 13.3, which also gives mean party-government policy distances depending on whether or not the party concerned was in office. It is indeed generally true in the Fourth Republic that parties in government did better in policy terms than parties out of office, quite

Table 13.3   Party policy payoffs in one dimension, France, Fourth Republic

Designated Premier 1946	COM	SOC	UDSR	RAD	MRP	IND	PAYS	GAUL
Thorez	8	*19*	38	45	51	80	92	
Bidault	44	33	23	6	*1*	28	*40*	
Blum	*10*	*17*	*36*	43	49	78	90	
Ramadier	*44*	*33*	*23*	6	*1*	28	*40*	
Blum	13	*14*	33	40	46	74	87	
Schuman	54	43	*33*	16	*11*	18	30	
Marie	58	47	37	20	15	14	26	
Schuman	32	*21*	*11*	6	*11*	40	52	
Queuille	19	*8*	2	21	24	53	65	
Moch	26	*15*	*5*	12	*17*	46	58	
Mayer	59	48	*38*	21	16	13	25	
Bidault	39	28	18	*1*	*4*	33	45	
Queuille	49	38	28	*11*	6	23	35	
Pleven	39	28	18	*1*	*4*	33	45	
Mollet	14	*3*	7	24	29	58	70	
Queuille	47	37	26	9	*4*	23	37	
In	21	25	22	13	16	25	50	
Out	35	41	27	27	51	47	57	

1951	COM	SOC	UDSR	RAD	MRP	IND	PAYS	GAUL
Meyer	46	*15*	*3*	23	7	30	58	54
Petsche	64	33	*15*	*5*	*11*	12	40	36

	COM	SOC	UDSR	RAD	MRP	IND	PAYS	GAUL
Pleven	39	*8*	*10*	30	14	9	*37*	33
Faure	51	20	2	14	2	25	*53*	49
Pinay	61	30	*12*	8	8	*15*	43	39
Mayer	64	33	*15*	5	*11*	12	40	*36*
Reynaud	73	42	24	4	20	*3*	*31*	27
Mendes-France	28	*3*	21	41	25	48	76	72
Bidault	64	33	15	5	*11*	12	*40*	36
Marie	71	40	22	2	18	*5*	*33*	29
Laniel	76	45	27	7	*23*	*0*	28	*24*
Mendes-France	29	*2*	20	8	24	47	75	*71*
Pineau	*36*	5	13	*33*	*17*	40	68	64
Faure	50	19	*1*	19	32	26	*54*	*50*
In	–	9	13	15	11	12	40	45
Out	54	34	18	14	19	41	63	44

1956	COM	SOC	UDSR	RAD	MRP	IND	PAYS	GAUL
Mollet	*47*	*13*	*11*	27	7	14	58	38
Bourges-Mon	51	25	15	23	*3*	10	54	34
Pinay	91	65	55	17	37	*30*	*14*	6
Mollet	43	*17*	7	31	*11*	42	62	42
Gaillard	48	22	*12*	26	*6*	*13*	57	*37*
Pfimlin	69	*43*	*33*	5	*15*	8	36	16
De Gaulle	47	13	*11*	27	7	*14*	58	*38*
In	47	24	17	16	8	19	36	38
Out	58	39	26	25	38	19	23	27

Italicised figures represent parties in government.

possibly because of the very explicit investiture process in which party support for the government depended on its proposed policy programme.

Note that the median party, the Radicals, do very well in the first and second legislatures, in terms of closeness to government policy. All parties of the 'plural core' do better than others in the first legislature, but in the second the Socialists, though in general in opposition, make comparable gains. In the third legislature it is the Socialists, the main government party, who clearly do better than the core parties. Overall, therefore, government policy in the Fourth Republic does respond to coalition bargaining, but it is the government parties rather than those in the one-dimensional plural core, who receive the highest policy payoffs. The main reason for this has to do with the role of the SFIO, which received high policy payoffs when it was in government, despite the fact that it was not in the plural core.

THE MULTI-DIMENSIONAL ANALYSIS

Government formation

The matrices of interparty city block distances in the full 18-dimensional French policy space are given in Table K.2 in the Appendix to this chapter. Given the processes of coalition formation we have described, in which the President of the Republic first choses the *pressenti* who then goes to the Assembly as the *designe*, we modify the cluster-analytic models of coalition formation in the French case. For each legislature, we estimated a series of cluster models, each putting a different party in the initial node. This way we can predict, on the basis of policy distance minimisation, which parties are likely to be included in a coalition, depending on the identity of the initial prime ministerial candidate. Otherwise, the clustering techniques are the ones familiar from preceding chapters, based on hierarchical clustering using the average linkage algorithm. The actual clustering sequences are reported in Table K.3 in the Appendix to this chapter, together with each party's percentage of seats in the Assembly.

On the basis of the clustering sequences of the first legislature it appears that four parties – Socialists, UDSR, Radicals and MRP – were equally likely to form the same minimum winning connected coalition, regardless of which party leader was selected to initiate the process. On the other hand, the coalitions predicted to result from making the parties of the moderate right prime minister designate lead to non-connected coalitions spanning almost the entire political spectrum. Thus, on the basis of policy distance alone, conservative (Independent and Paysan) party leaders appear relatively less likely to be selected as potential premiers.[2] The policy distance interpretation is quite consistent with empirical observation. President Auriol's choice of *pressentis* during the first legislature was limited to the four predicted parties. As noted earlier, the possibility of Conservative support for a Socialist-led coalition – as well as that of Socialist support for a Conservative majority – was excluded at all times as a matter of principle. This mutual exclusion did not apply in coalitions that were led by third parties. Most Radical premiers, and others as well, successfully managed to get Socialist and Conservative support for their coalitions. In the first legislature, the balance of pro-regime parliamentary seats was such that a Conservative-led coalition could not win a majority without Socialist support. This effectively prevented President Auriol from inviting a Conservative leader to form a government. In contrast, a Socialist leader was theoretically eligible because a Socialist-led coalition could achieve winning status with the support of the Radicals, MRP and UDSR only.[3] The relative party strength in the Assembly changed substantially after the 1951 elections. The MRP's share of legislative seats was reduced from 25 per cent to 14 per cent, mostly to the benefit of the Conservative and Gaullist parties whose joint seat share jumped to 34 per cent as compared with 15 per cent in the first legislature. In the first months of the second legislature, with the Gaullists still in anti-regime opposition, any majority coalition of pro-system parties had to include the Socialists in conjunction with the moderate right. Neither Socialist nor moderate leaders could hope to lead a winning coalition. The choice of possible *pressentis* was consequently reduced to the three centre parties (Radicals, UDSR and MRP). Even after the Gaullist reversal, the Socialists could not hope to form a majority winning coalition since the combined forces of the anti-regime Communists, the Conservatives and the Gaullists amounted to one half of the total seats in the assembly. To survive, a Socialist-led coalition would have required unfailing support from all the other parties, a condition that could not be realistically achieved, given the tendency for most parties to divide into factions. Rather than abandon their principles and compromise with the Conservatives or the Gaullists, the Socialist leadership decided to retreat into lasting opposition. This did not deter the President from calling upon Socialist leaders to form a government on several occasions.[4]

In the early months of the second legislature, there was no chance of a moderate premier forming a majority government as was demonstrated by the failure of Maurice Petsche to receive investiture.[5] A few months after the elections, however, the leaders of the RPF decided to abandon their anti-regime posture, thus becoming eligible for the premiership. As a result of the Gaullist move, Socialist support was no longer essential for a moderate premier to succeed at investiture and the President of the Republic felt free to call upon Conservative personalities to form a government. Two of them, (Pinay in 1953 and Laniel in 1954) were invested and eventually formed a cabinet.

There is a new clustering sequence in the second legislature which begins with the Gaullist party. Because the RPF was the largest party, it was normal for the President of the Republic to call upon its leaders to attempt to form a government. But the Gaullist *pressentis* all refused to face the challenge of investiture. One main reason for their refusal was that they knew they could not hope for Socialist support. Socialist support was not arithmetically necessary for a Gaullist to win investiture. However, the RPF did not wish to govern in a purely rightist coalition and consequently required Socialist support as a condition for accepting a mandate to govern. The cluster models thus lead to predictions which are consistent with observations for the second legislature. With the exception of the Socialists, the leaders of all relevant pro-regime parties could theoretically obtain the support of a connected minimum winning coalition.

After the 1956 elections the balance was not changed fundamentally. Theoretically, the same range of choice of *pressentis* or *designes* should have been observed as in the second legislature. In particular the Socialists were still prevented from forming a majority winning connected coalition. However, in practice, things had changed quite a lot. Absolute majority support in the legislature was no longer required to form a government; the Algerian War prompted government actions that were often at variance with party commitments;[6] several parties in the third legislature, moreover, were split right down the middle, with one half supporting a particular premier at investiture while the other opposed. All of these factors render predictions based on the standard cluster models rather less appropriate.

Government policy

The distances between party and coalition policy in the full 18-dimensional policy space are given in Table 13.4., which also shows the mean policy distance between party and government, depending on whether or not the party supported the government. The pattern is quite striking. The centre parties achieved markedly higher policy payoffs than the others (measured as lower policy distances). In addition, however, parties were noticeably more likely to support governments if these offered them a higher policy payoff. For more or less every party in every legislature, the policy distance between a given party and the government declaration was less when the party offered support. This applied not only to the parties of the centre, such as the MRP, but also to the Socialists and even to parties at the extremes, such as the Communists.

Overall, while centre parties got higher payoffs than others, government parties got higher payoffs than others, regardless of ideological position, in a result very similar to that of the one-dimensional analysis described above.

CONCLUSION: A COMPARATIVE EVALUATION OF POLICY-BASED COALITION MODELS FOR THE FRENCH FOURTH REPUBLIC

We now sum up our discussion of how the concept of policy distance can help us to interpret the formation and policy outputs of coalition govern-

Table 13.4 Distances between party electoral programmes and programmes of candidates for premiership in 18-dimensional policy space, (city-block metric) France, 1946–58

Designated Premier								
1946	COM	SOC	UDSR	RAD	MRP	IND	PAYS	GAUL
Thorez	*38*	75	96	81	83	116	118	
Bidault	96	92	72	48	*56*	*48*	*68*	
Blum	*59*	*66*	82	70	74	109	*121*	
Ramadier	*111*	82	*57*	73	64	70	85	
Blum	80	*93*	87	100	75	96	*126*	
Schuman	105	87	70	*81*	65	72	66	
Marie	88	75	*57*	*60*	53	76	*91*	
Schuman	101	*86*	*92*	69	66	80	93	
Queuille	92	74	86	80	58	83	*83*	
Moch	72	*59*	*83*	52	53	60	78	*73*
Mayer	109	*86*	72	47	55	*48*	51	87
Bidault	108	*89*	62	49	52	73	82	93
Queuille	110	*89*	67	52	*64*	69	69	106
Pleven	101	80	75	52	57	66	*83*	94
Mollet	74	*61*	*63*	50	62	104	113	90
Queuille	125	*90*	*66*	*63*	73	86	*100*	127
In	69	79	72	63	62	68	89	–
Out	97	89	80	66	83	83	89	96
1951	COM	SOC	UDSR	RAD	MRP	IND	PAYS	GAUL
Meyer	96	*63*	*76*	*57*	67	73	93	99
Petsche	119	76	*84*	59	68	*57*	70	88
Pleven	94	*47*	75	68	55	58	*81*	89
Faure	103	*53*	*57*	*41*	54	48	73	83
Pinay	117	67	*79*	52	57	*41*	*58*	78
Meyer	114	67	75	*38*	75	54	67	74
Reynaud	130	85	87	68	93	67	78	82
Mendes-France	78	*56*	51	75	64	86	97	98
Bidault	126	72	*79*	*50*	70	*39*	*60*	79
Marie	122	89	*68*	53	82	67	*63*	81
Laniel	136	94	*109*	*73*	87	72	*84*	94
Mendes-France	*66*	*65*	*56*	74	73	85	90	*96*
Pineau	86	*55*	*73*	72	*55*	75	94	95
Faure	115	55	*66*	59	47	52	*96*	86
In	–	57	75	57	63	55	74	88
Out	107	76	73	68	76	78	88	87

1956	COM	SOC	UDSR	RAD	MRP	IND	PAYS	GAUL
Mollet	95	43	59	55	74	67	74	82
Bourges-Mon	112	66	80	83	79	87	92	107
Pinay	151	103	110	83	111	87	92	109
Mollet	81	55	85	82	77	91	89	96
Gaillard	102	48	77	74	67	67	95	92
Pfimlin	124	99	100	96	98	102	107	106
De Gaulle	119	121	117	106	131	115	88	86
In	95	62	88	76	88	90	90	89
Out	115	112	92	86	111	87	91	100

ments in the French Fourth Republic. We do this by comparing the success and efficiency of various policy-based models in postdicting the coalitions that actually formed. The results are presented in Table 13.5

As Table 13.5 shows, the policy-based theories are generally very successful. The median party on the left–right dimension was nearly always in government – there were only three exceptions to this rule. It was rather more common in the later part of the period for the coalition to exclude at least one member of what we have called the 'plural' core. Usually the excluded party was the Independents. Thus the success rate of this model is lower. Particularly in the early part of the period, the multi-dimensional models were effective in identifying coalition partners, given the selection of a particular prime minister designate. A striking feature of the reported results is the extent to which the constraints on coalition-formation reduce an extremely wide range of arithmetically possible coalitions to only two or three feasible possibilities. The constraints are so severe that they not only ensure that the median party and the 'plural core' must be generally represented in government, but make it practically inevitable that the coalition will be connected and minimal winning.

Note, however, that very few coalitions were minimum winning in the sense of being the majority coalition with the smallest seat total. This is because the very low levels of party discipline meant that prime ministers could not expect the support of all legislators who were nominally members of the parties in their support coalition. They therefore had to make sure that the parties in the support coalition between them controlled more than a bare majority of seats.

Table 13.5 Success rates of policy-based theories in the French Fourth Republic

Coalition	Possible coalitions	Feasible coalitions after operation of constraints	Coalition includes median party in one dimension	Coalition includes all parties of plural core	Coalition is minimum connected winning around plural core	Coalition is as indicated by multi-dimensional clustering around party of designated premier
Ramadier I	1023	2	yes	yes	no	yes
Ramadier II	1023	2	yes	yes	no	yes
Schuman I	1023	2	yes	yes	yes	yes
Marie	1023	2	yes	yes	yes	yes
Schuman II	1023	2	yes	yes	yes	yes
Queuille I	1023	2	yes	yes	yes	yes
Bidault I	2047	2	yes	yes	yes	yes
Bidault II	2047	2	yes	yes	yes	yes
Queuille II	2047	2	yes	yes	yes	yes
Pleven I	2047	2	yes	yes	yes	yes
Queuille III	2047	2	yes	yes	yes	yes
Pleven II	512	2	yes	yes	yes	yes
Faure	512	2	yes	yes	yes	yes
Pinay	512	2	yes	yes	yes	no
Mayer	512	3	yes	yes	yes	yes
Laniel	1023	3	yes	yes	yes	yes

Table 13.5 (cont'd)

Coalition	Possible coalitions	Feasible coalitions after operation of constraints	Coalition includes median party in one dimension	Coalition includes all parties of plural core	Coalition is minimum connected winning around plural core	Coalition is as indicated by multidimensional clustering around party of designated premier
Mendes-France I	1023	3	yes	no	no	no
Mendes-France II	1023	3	yes	no	no	no
Mendes-France III	1023	3	yes	no	no	no
Faure I	2047	3	yes	yes	yes	yes
Faure II	2047	3	yes	yes	yes	yes
Mollet I	2047	3	no	no	no	no
Mollet II	2047	3	no	no	no	no
Bourges-Mon	4095	3	yes	yes	yes	yes
Gaillard	4095	3	yes	yes	yes	no
Deimlin I	4095	3	yes	no	no	no
Deimlin II	4095	3	yes	no	no	no
De Gaulle	4095	3	yes	yes	yes	yes
Predictive Success			.90(25/28)	.71(20/28)	.64(18/28)	.71(20/28)
Predictive Efficiency			.36(25/70)	.30(20/70)	.26(18/70)	.71(20/28)

METHODOLOGICAL NOTE

Derivation of French policy spaces

The proportions of party manifestos coded into the eighteen policy categories were first used as input to a principal components analysis, similar to the kinds of factor analysis described in Chapter 2. Three factors accounted for over half of the total variance. Table K.5, in the Appendix to the chapter, reports the loadings of the original categories on these.

The first factor, which accounts for 26 per cent contrasts right-wing with left-wing attitudes. Tradition, freedom, order and the Army are contrasted with emphases on intervention social services and international peace and co-operation. The second factor (18 per cent of variance) uncovers a pro- versus anti-regime cleavage, also with left versus right overtones. The third factor contrasts strong positive loadings in the Productivity, Social Justice and Laicity categories with negative loadings in the Freedom and Anti-establishment categories, seemingly reflecting the socio-economic constraints of a modern mixed economy. There is a remarkable similarity between the results of this analysis and an equivalent analysis previously performed for the French Fifth Republic (Petry 1987). It appears that the policy dimensions of French party politics changed very little between regimes.

The results of the principal component analysis were used as a guide to constructing a single left–right scale combining the categories 'Capitalist economics', 'Social conservatism', 'Military', 'Government Efficiency' and 'Freedom' at the right end, and the categories 'State Intervention', 'Cooperation', 'Laicity' and 'Labour' at the left end. Party positions on this scale, after each election, are those reported in Table 13.2. Interparty distances in the full 18-dimensional policy space are reported in Table K.3.

NOTES

1   The constitutional rules of the game were not always followed to the letter by designated premiers. Before the 1954 modification, a few premiers chose to give in to parliamentarians' demands to know the team before choosing the captain and announced the composition of their cabinet at investiture time. But some premiers in the post-1954 period also ignored the new rule and appointed their cabinet only after they had been securely invested.

2   Conservative led coalitions appear non-connected because they include the PRL and RPF (Gaullist). The PRL and RPF were anti-regime parties and consequently their respective seat shares are not represented in the Table.

3   The clustering sequence beginning with the Communist party was included in the first legislature to account for the fact that Maurice Thorez, the Communist

leader, was called upon to form a government in 1946. Thorez failed at investiture. But this was during the period of Tripartism, when the Communists had not yet gone into anti-regime opposition.

4 All these invitations were declined with one exception toward the end of the legislature, when Christian Pineau attempted – and failed – to form a Socialist-led government. This episode marked the first attempt at coalition formation under the new relatively majority constitutional rule.

5 Petsche was the first moderate *designe* of the Fourth Republic. His candidacy at the start of the second legislature was not intended to succeed but rather to 'lift' the mortgage (*lever l'hypotheque*) in order to reveal the range of coalition possibilities.

6 The best example is that of the Mollet government which carried out military operations in Algeria that were in direct contradiction with the Socialist campaign rhetoric. The initial Socialist government's military involvement in Algeria set the pace for subsequent governments which continued the same policy with the backing of the SFIO.

APPENDIX K

Table K.1 Seat distribution in the National Assembly, France, 1946–58

	PCF	SFIO	RAD	UDSR	MRP	IND	PAYS	AR/UDI	PRL	GAUL	IDM	
First Legislature												
Start	181	101	43	26	166	29	7		38			
Middle	181	100	45	26	152	24	11	18	34			
End	177	99	46	13	144	25	23	7	27	22	7	
Second Legislature								ARS	PUS			
Start	103	107	75	16	86	53	43			121	9	
Middle	100	105	75	23	89	55	46	32		83	12	
End	98	104	75	23	85	53	27	32	21	70	16	
Third Legislature								RGR	NED			POUJ
Start	150	96	58	19	73	83	12	14		22	10	52
End	148	97	42	16	74	97	11	14	13	20	10	30

Table K.1 (cont'd)

Abbreviations:

PCF	Communist Party
SFI0	Socialist Party
RAD	Radical Party
UDSR	Union Democratique et Socialiste de la Resistance
MRP	Christian Democratic Party
IND(RI)	Republican Independent
PAYS	Farmers
IOM	Overseas Nationalists
AR	Action Republicaine
UDI	Independent Democratic Union
PRL	Freedom Republican Parti
GAUL	Gaullist Party
ARS	dissident Gaullists
PUS	dissident Moderates
RGR	dissident Radicals
NEO	dissident Radicals
POUJ(UFF)	Poujadist Party

Table **K.2**   18-Dimensional city-block party distances, France, 1946–58

1946

	COM	SOC	UDSR	RAD	MRP	IND	PAYS	GAUL	PARL
SOC	75								
UDSR	103	82							
RAD	82	68	52						
MRP	93	71	64	59					
IND	122	90	93	75	66				
PAYS	123	103	102	87	89	48			
GAUL	68	88	122	91	83	102	104		
PRL	87	97	104	75	68	60	67	98	
% Seats	29	16	3	7	25	5	5	5	5

1951

	COM	SOC	UDSR	RAD	MRP	IND	PAYS	GAUL	IOM
SOC	65								
UDSR	91	47							
RAD	124	78	71						
MRP	97	44	51	81					
IND	132	79	73	35	67				
PAYS	129	102	96	60	90	63			
GAUL	117	98	89	87	84	85	63		
IOM	102	114	96	132	112	115	138	140	
% Seats	15	17	3	12	14	9	7	19	2

Table K.2 (cont'd)

1956

	COM	SOC	UDSR	RAD	MRP	IND	PAYS	GAUL	UFF	IOM	RGR
SOC	77										
UDSR	93	52									
RAD	99	54	49								
MRP	94	57	58	77							
IND	130	70	73	45	88						
PAYS	120	98	99	85	101	75					
GAUL	113	108	120	86	113	84	88				
UFF	103	107	115	104	110	104	71	86			
IOM	80	90	81	90	78	112	131	120	101		
RGR	108	73	65	65	78	49	62	109		100	
% Seats	25	16	4	10	12	14	2	4	7	1	2

Table K.5 Clustering sequences for the coalitions likely to result from choice of a premier from selected parties, France, 1946–58

First Legislature

Clustering sequence starts								Clustering sequence ends
SOC 16	RAD 7	MRP 25	UDSR 3	IND 4	PRL 5	GAUL	PAYS 5	COM
UDSR 3	RAD 7	MRP 25	SOC 16	IND 4	PRL 5	GAUL	PAYS 5	COM
RAD 7	UDSR 3	MRP 25	SOC 16	IND 4	PRL 5	GAUL	PAYS 5	COM
MRP 25	RAD 7	UDSR 3	SOC 16	IND 4	PRL 5	GAUL	PAYS 5	COM
IND 4	PAYS 5	PRL 5	GAUL	MRP 25	RAD 7	UDSR 3	SOC 16	COM
PAYS 5	IND 4	PRL 5	GAUL	MRP 25	RAD 7	UDSR 3	SOC 16	COM
COM	GAUL	SOC 16	RAD 7	UDSR 3	MRP 25	PRL 5	IND 4	PAYS 5

Second Legislature

Clustering sequence starts								Clustering sequence ends
SOC 17	MRP 14	UDSR 3	IND 9	RAD 12	GAUL 19	PAYS 7	COM	IOM 2
UDSR 3	SOC 17	MRP 14	IND 9	RAD 12	GAUL 19	PAYS 7	COM	IOM 2

Table K.3 (cont'd)

RAD 12	IND 9	PAYS 7	GAUL 19	MRP 14	UDSR 5	SOC 17	COM	IOM 2
MRP 25	SOC 17	UDSR 3	IND 9	RAD 12	GAUL 19	PAYS 7	COM	IOM 2
IND 4	RAD 12	PAYS 7	GAUL 19	MRP 14	UDSR 3	SOC 17	COM	IOM 2
PAYS 7	RAD 12	IND 9	GAUL 19	MRP 14	UDSR 3	SOC 17	COM	IOM 2
GAUL 19	PAYS 7	IND 9	RAD 12	MRP 14	UDSR 3	SOC 17	IOM	COM 2

Third Legislature

Clustering sequence starts									Clustering sequence ends	
SOC 16	UDSR 4	RAD 10	MRP 12	RGR 2	IND 14	IOM 1	PAYS 2	GAUL 4	UFF	COM
UDSR 4	RAD 10	SOC 16	MRP 12	RGR 2	IND 14	IOM 1	PAYS 2	GAUL 4	UFF	COM
RAD 10	IND 14	UDSR 16	RGR 2	SOC 16	MRP 12	PAYS 2	IOM 1	GAUL 4	UFF	COM
MRP 12	SOC 16	UDSR 4	RAD 10	RGR 2	IND 14	IOM 1	PAYS 2	GAUL 4	UFF	COM
IND 14	RAD 10	UDSR 4	RGR 2	SOC 16	MRP 12	PAYS 2	IOM 1	GAUL 4	UFF	COM
PAYS 2	RGR 2	IND 14	GAUL 10	UFF 10	RAD 4	UDSR 12	MRP 16	SOC 1	IOM	COM
GAUL	IND	RAD	RGR	PAYS	MRP	UDSR	SOC	IOM	UFF	COM

Table K.4 Fourth Republic governments and investiture support, 1946–58

First legislature			Parties										Support from:		
													Governing	Cabinet	Investiture Coalition
Premiers	Tenure		COM	SOC	UDSR	RAD	MRP	IOM	IND	PAYS	GAUL	PRL	(%)	(%)	(%)
Thorez			Y	Y	N	N	N		N	N		N	–	–	42
Bidault			N	N	N	N	Y		Y	Y		Y	–	–	39
Blum	12.46–1.47		Y	Y	Y	Y	Y		P	Y		P	16	93	93
Ramadier	1.47–5.47		Y	Y	Y	Y	Y		N	Y		N	84	83	89
Ramadier	5.47–11.47		N	Y	Y	Y	Y		P	Y		N	57	53	*
Blum			N	Y	N	P	Y		N	N		N	–	–	48
Schuman	11.47–7.48		N	Y	Y	Y	Y		Y	Y		Y	53	52	67
Marie	7.48–8.48		N	Y	P	Y	Y		P	Y		P	59	53	59
Schuman	9.48		N	Y	Y	Y	Y		P	N		N	53	51	53
Queuille	9.48–10.49		N	Y	P	Y	Y	P	P	Y		N	60	56	56
Moch			N	Y	Y	P	Y	Y	N	N	N	N	–	–	49
Mayer			N	Y	Y	Y	Y	Y	P	P	N	N	–	–	55
Bidault	10.49–2.50		N	Y	Y	Y	Y	Y	P	N	N	P	55	59	59
Bidault	2.50–6.50		N	N	Y	P	Y	Y	N	N	N	N	39	37	37
Queuille	7.50		N	Y	Y	Y	Y	Y	Y	Y	N	N	39	37	58
Pleven	7.50–2.51		N	Y	Y	Y	Y	Y	Y	Y	N	N	55	52	55
Mollet			N	Y	Y	P	Y	Y	N	N	N	N	–	–	46
Queuille	3.51–6.51		N	Y	Y	Y	Y	P	Y	Y	N	N	55	52	56

Table K.4 (cont'd)

Second legislature

Premier	Tenure	Parties COM	SOC	UDSR	RAD	MRP	IOM	IND PAYS	GAUL	PRL (%)	(%)	(%)
Meyer		N	Y	Y	Y	N	Y	P	N	N	–	–	38
Petsche		N	N	Y	Y	Y	Y	Y	Y	N	–	–	45
Pleven	8.51–2.52	N	Y	Y	Y	Y	Y	Y	Y	N	47	60	62
Faure	2.52	N	Y	Y	Y	Y	Y	Y	Y	N	47	63	64
Pinay	3.52–12.52	N	N	Y	Y	Y	Y	Y	Y	N	47	50	52
Mayer	1.53–5.53	N	N	Y	P	Y	Y	P	P	Y	51	–	62
Reynaud		N	N	P	P	P	Y	N	N	P	–	–	44
Mendes-France		N	Y	P	Y	P	Y	Y	N	P	–	–	48
Bidault		N	N	N	N	Y	Y	Y	Y	P	–	–	49
Marie		N	N	Y	Y	N	Y	Y	Y	P	–	–	43
Laniel	6.53–6.54	N	N	Y	Y	Y	Y	Y	Y	Y	59	61	63
Mendes-France	6.54–8.54	N	Y	Y	Y	N	Y	N	N	Y	35	67	67
Mendes-France	8.54–9.54	N	Y	Y	Y	N	Y	P	N	Y	32	–	–
Mendes-France	9.54–2.55	N	Y	Y	Y	N	Y	P	N	Y	50	–	–
Pineau		N	Y	P	P	N	Y	N	N	N	–	–	43
Faure	2.55–10.55	N	N	Y	P	Y	Y	Y	Y	Y	62	–	59
Faure	10.55–2.56	N	N	Y	Y	Y	Y	Y	Y	Y	51	–	–

Table K.4 (cont'd)

Third legislature

Premier	Tenure	Parties										Coalition	
		COM	SOC	UDSR	RAD	MRP	IOM	IND	PAYS	GAUL	POU	Governing (%)	Supporting (%)
Mollet	2.56	Y	Y	Y	Y	Y	Y	N	N	N	N	30	73
Mollet	2.56–5.57	N	Y	Y	Y	Y	Y	N	N	N	N	35	–
Bourges-Mon	6.57–9.57	N	Y	P	P	Y	Y	P	P	P	N	28	40
Pinay		N	N	N	N	P	N	Y	Y	N	N	–	–
Mollet		N	Y	N	P	Y	P	N	N	N	N	–	–
Gaillard	10.57–4.58	N	Y	Y	Y	Y	P	Y	Y	Y	N	59	56
Pfimlin	5.58	N	Y	Y	Y	Y	P	N	N	N	N	38	46
Pfimlin	5.58	N	Y	Y	Y	Y	P	N	N	N	N	54	–
De Gaulle	6.58–1.59	N	P	Y	P	Y	P	Y	Y	Y	N	55	55

Key:

Y = Full investiture support (75% or more)
P = Partial support
N = Opposition or abstention (less than 255 support)

Notes:

Starting with the Pineau cabinet, only relative majorities were required.
Moderate and Gaullist dissidents were included in the groups in which they had been originally.

Table K.5   The three main dimensions emerging from principal components analysis of party election programmes under the Fourth Republic and the relationship of the original categories to them

Original codings	First Dimension	Second Dimension	Third Dimension
	Left–right	*Pro-anti regime*	*Social justice vs Freedom*
	Factor loadings	*Factor loadings*	*Factor loadings*
State intervention	−.29	−.25	0.25
Peace and co-operation	−.33	0.08	−.19
Anti establishment	−.17	−.25	−.26
Capitalist economy	0.29	0.11	0.13
Social conservatism	0.30	−.10	−.16
Productivity	0.16	0.05	0.40
Military	0.37	−.17	0.17
Europe	−.01	0.40	−.03
Freedom	0.22	0.21	−.43
Democracy	−.13	−.15	−.13
Government efficiency	0.30	0.07	−.14
Social Justice	0.21	0.03	0.46
Social Services	−.18	−.24	−.09
Pro-regime	−.11	0.48	−.09
Anti-regime	0.01	−.47	0.01
Laicity	−.26	0.17	0.37
Church	0.13	−.13	−.07
Anti Right	−.33	0.15	0.15
Eigen value	4.74	3.28	2.04
% of variance	0.26	0.18	0.11

14 The Relationship Between Party and Coalition Policy in Europe: An Empirical Synthesis

Ian Budge and M. J. Laver

The idea that government policy is affected by the policies of government members is at the heart of the theory of representative democracy. If government policy does not respond to the policies of elected government members, after all, then the purpose of having elections is obscure.

From the specific perspective of the theory of government coalitions, moreover, the link between coalition policy and party policy is central because it makes sense of the process of coalition bargaining. Much of this book has been concerned with the consequences of bargaining between actors who are motivated by the desire to influence government policy. If it transpires that the membership of government coalitions cannot be predicted from the policies of the various parties in the system, and that the parties which actually succeed in getting into office cannot influence government policy, then 'policy-motivated' political actors are unaware of the futility of their endeavours, are deluding themselves or are dissembling. Most policy driven coalition theories do of course operate on the basis that the party membership and policy position of any given coalition is in some senses predictable from the policies of the parties in the system. If coalitional behaviour cannot be predicted in this way, then one of the key linkages in policy-driven coalition theories is broken.

These relationship have been explored on a country by country basis in the previous chapters. In this chapter, we set out to synthesise the findings comparatively. We begin by evaluating the general validity of our measures of party and government policy positions, and of our spatial representations of these, in the light of our experience of applying them. We move on to synthesise the judgements made by each country authors about the role of policy in coalition bargaining. We conclude by evaluating the one and the twenty-dimensional accounts of government formation and government policy outputs, as well as the impact of bargaining constraints upon these.

THE VALIDITY OF INDICATORS AND ASSUMPTIONS

Party programmes as indicators of policy preferences

We have argued previously (Budge, Robertson and Hearl, 1987, Chapter 2) that election programmes do have an important impact on politics, not through being generally read by voters, but through shaping the comments and discussion that reach them through the media. Given this, we have assumed that policy programmes should be taken seriously as statements of party policy positions. None of the country-based analyses of coalition bargaining that we have considered give any reason to believe that this is not true. The positions assigned to parties on the basis of the programmatic evidence and the policy distances separating different parties have rarely been queried as being implausible or misleading in the country discussions. On the contrary, the representations (with the partial exception of Israel) have conformed to conventional wisdom about the positioning of the parties.

Parallel research has also suggested that manifesto emphases should be taken seriously for different reasons. In a large number of countries, policy emphases in the election programmes show high correlations with government expenditures in corresponding policy areas (Hofferbert and Klingemann, 1990; Budge and Hofferbert, 1990). This linkage suggests either that parties take election programmes seriously as pledges endorsed by the electorate or at least that they strategically retain electoral policy positions once they enter government. Either way, party policy programmes do seem to be related to systematic regularities in party politics.

Government programmes as indicators of coalition policy

Published government policy programmes are susceptible on three counts to the criticism that they do not reflect 'real' government policy positions. First, these programmes may be patched up hastily between party leaders more as a public relations exercise to justify them going into coalition together, rather than as a carefully negotiated compromise on the main points at issue between the parties (Luebbert, 1986). Parties wanting to form a coalition simply to get into office, for example, may cast around for peripheral questions on which they can agree, and insert these into the government programme. Second, a number of country authors have commented upon the lack of relationship between party and coalition policy, documented more systematically below. Election programmes and government programmes correlate reasonably closely in five countries but hardly at all in another five. This could be an interesting substantive finding, but equally it could indicate that the role of general declarations of government policy is strategically obscure in at least half the countries we study. Third, there is a general 'rightward' tendency of government programmes relative to election programmes, summarised in Table 14.1. It is obvious from this that, with the exception of Norway, Denmark and Ireland, government programmes tend to have more right-wing scores on the common left–right dimension than party programmes.

We might interpret this as reflecting a preoccupation of the framers of government programmes with administrative concerns and on-going matters of government (for example defence and foreign policy) which have not necessarily entered into the election campaign. However, these factors in themselves cast some doubt upon the validity of using published policy declaration as indicators of 'real' government policy.

Given these potential problems, it is encouraging that there is a remarkable consistency in the policy payoffs, operationalised in terms of the distance between party and government policy as defined above. This is discussed in the country chapters and summarised more systematically below. Parties in government (with only idiosyncratic exceptions) are consistently closer to the government programme than parties out of government. This reinforces

Table 14.1   'Rightwardness' of government programmes

	Election Programme Mean	Government Programme Mean
Ireland	+ 4.9	+ 3.2
Norway	−15.0	−17.0
Sweden	−19.0	− 9.8
Denmark	+ 1.4	+ 0.8
Germany	+ 3.0	+11.4
Luxembourg	−21.4	+ 6.4
Belgium	− 4.5	+ 6.4
Netherlands	− 6.1	− 1.0
Italy	− 4.6	− 1.0
Israel	+ 3.3*	+12.3
Mean of means	− 5.88	+ 3.93

* Excludes religious parties

Note: Fourth Republic omitted from this table owing to difficulties of comparison.

our contention that the government programme does say something important about politics, since it produces marked and interpretable differences between parties in a position to have an impact on policy and those less able to do so.

To sum up this consideration of the validity of our measures of party and government policy, we cannot ignore the possibility that election and government programmes have serious failings as indicators of policy positions. Nonetheless, the face validity of the results they generate is good and they have the additional massive benefit, when compared with any alternative data currently available, that they allow us to track movements of party and coalition policy over time, allowing us to predict and/or interpret policy responses to developments in party politics.

Spatial representations of party and government policy

Having described party and government policy in terms of the content analysis of key policy documents, we portrayed the relative positions of these in terms of two alternative spatial representations. One, the 20-dimensional representation, used as much of the data as possible for each party system. The other, the one dimensional representation, described policy positions in terms of a familiar construct, the left–right dimension; this allowed easy interpretation of the results and straightforward checks on their face validity. Table 14.2 summarises the broad judgements made in the country chapters about whether the 20-dimensional representation of policy emphases gave 'better results', in terms of predictive success and efficiency, than the one-dimensional representation.

From the table it is clear that the 20-dimensional representation works best, as we might have expected, in countries with complex cleavage structures – for example Belgium, the Netherlands, Italy, Israel, the French Fourth Republic. The single left–right dimension seems to describe politics better in Scandinavia, Germany and Luxembourg, where coalition formation depends on a limited number of actors or coherent blocs, who may well create a more restricted policy space.

In addition to the 'common' policy spaces used in all chapters, a number of country authors experimented with two-dimensional representation, (for example in Norway, Netherlands, Israel and Belgium). Except in the case of Belgium, these were not found to be an improvement over the other representations. In Belgium, however, the country specific two-dimensional representation gave better results, so it seems clear that any future analysis of the politics of coalition in Belgium should start from a two-dimensional 'picture' that changes dramatically in 1960.

Table 14.2 Performance of unidimensional versus multi-dimensional representations

	Unidimensional better	Both give similar results	Multidimensional better	Is two dimensional clearly as good/better
Ireland	No	Yes	No	No
Norway	Yes	No	No	No
Sweden	Yes	No	No	No
Denmark	No	Yes	No	No
Germany	Yes	No	No	No
Luxembourg	Yes	In some cases	No	No
Belgium	No	No	Yes	Yes
Netherlands	No	No	Yes	No
Italy	No	No	Yes	No
Israel	No	No	Yes	No
Fourth Republic	No	No	Yes	No

Note: 'Performance' is judged on basis of which type of representation gives policy models better success and efficiency rates.

Policy versus office as a motivation in coalition bargaining

Each country author made an evaluation of the basic motivations of politicians who engaged in coalition bargaining. These are summarised in Table 14.3.

Ireland, Germany and Italy are characterised as having politicians who tend to pursue office for its own sake, for a diversity of reasons and with exceptions in each country, such as the Irish Labour Party or the Italian Communists. Policy seems to predominate over office as a motivation in most other countries. Sweden, Denmark, Belgium, France and the Netherlands emerge as countries where pure policy motivations appear to prevail in the making of coalitions. In Norway, Luxembourg and Israel office seems to be sought as a means to advance policy.

Table 14.3 compares the judgements of our country authors with the results of a comprehensive expert survey of country specialists on the same matter (Laver and Hunt, 1992). Respondents were asked to rate each system according to whether cabinet portfolios were valued more as rewards in themselves, or as means to influence policy outputs. The mean score for each system is listed in Table 14.3, on a scale that runs from 1, when portfolios are sought only to influence policy, to 9, when they are sought only as rewards in themselves. While the Laver and Hunt study does find a

Table 14.3   Predominant type of party motivation

	Pure office seeking	Instrumental office seeking	Instrumental policy pursuing	Pure Policy pursuing	Cabinet Portfolios as office (9) or Policy (1) payoffs
Ireland	Yes				6.6
Norway		Yes			2.8
Sweden				Yes	2.8
Denmark				Yes	3.7
Germany		Yes			4.5
Luxembourg		Yes			5.0
Belgium				Yes	6.0
Netherlands				Yes	3.2
Italy	Yes				7.8
Israel		Yes			–
Fourth Republic			Yes	Yes	6.0

greater concern for policy in Germany, and a greater concern for office in France and Belgium, than our country authors suggest the results otherwise confirm the judgements of the country chapters above. Ireland and Italy are the most office-oriented systems and the Scandinavian system plus the Netherlands are the most policy-oriented.

The place of policy in the sequence of coalition negotiations

Table 14.4 synthesises the judgements of our country authors on the sequence in which coalition negotiations take place in each of the party systems we deal with. Rational political actors will obviously anticipate deals that may be done at later stages in the coalition negotiations. Thus it clearly does not make sense to assume that, if the membership of a coalition is settled before its agreed policy package, then policy plays no part in the business of deciding coalition membership. However, politicians may well anticipate that policy negotiations between a set of parties which have publicly committed themselves to going into government together will differ from policy negotiations between parties which are still trying to decide whether such a commitment should be made. Given the costs of abandoning nego-tiations when public commitments have been made, the possibility that one of the partners might try to 'hijack' policy negotiations is clearly greater in the former case.

Table 14.4 suggests that the final stage in coalition negotiations typically has to do with the distribution of offices. Not surprisingly decisions about

Table 14.4   Sequence of coalition negotiations

	Composition of coalition	Policy programme	Distribution of offices
Ireland	1	2	3
Norway	1	2	3
Sweden	2	1	3
Denmark	2	1	3
Germany	1	2	3
Luxembourg	1	2	3
Belgium	2	1	3
Netherlands	1	2	3
Italy	1	3	2
Israel	2	1	3
Fourth Republic	2	1	3

which parties to include in the coalition come first in those systems where electoral pacts are so important; thus in Ireland, Germany and Norway, for example, the party composition of the government is decided before detailed policy negotiations take place. Policy negotiations tend to come first in Sweden, Denmark, Belgium, Israel and the Fourth Republic.

A COMPARATIVE EVALUATION OF POLICY-BASED THEORIES OF COALITION FORMATION

We are now in a position to evaluate the relative success of the policy-based theories of government formation that have been discussed in the various country chapters. Relevant findings are reported in Table 14.5, which gives, for each theory, both a success rate (the proportion of governments correctly characterised out of all that actually formed) and an efficiency level (the proportion of governments correctly characterised out of all that the theory predicts could have formed). Generally speaking there is a trade-off between exclusiveness and predictive success: the more governments that the theory predicts, the greater its success rate but the lower its efficiency. Models which make a unique prediction (such as a coalition forming at the first majority node on the cluster tree) have of course the same efficiency and success rate.

Two further cautions need to be given about the interpretation of Table 14.5. In some countries, many single party governments, sometimes majority administrations, emerge between coalitions. These can produce many 'successes' for the models, as well as high efficiency rates, which are not

Table 14.5 Performance of main policy-based models over 10 countries

Model / Country	1 Coalition at node on cluster tree with median legislator on at least one dimension		2 Coalition at first majority node on cluster tree		3 Government includes median party with median legislator on plurality of 20 dimensions		4 Government includes median legislator on one-dimensional continuum		5 Government is one-dimensional minimum connected winning	
	Success	Efficiency	Success	Efficiency	Success	Efficiency	Success	Efficiency	Success	Efficiency
Ireland	1.0:11/11	.17/11/66	1.0:11/11	1.0:11/11	.91:10/11	.91:10/11	.82:9/11	.19:9/46	.54:6/11	.54:6/11
Norway	.64:9/14	.07/9/130	.07:1/14	.07:1/14	.71:10/14	.01:10:664	.60:8/13	.14:8/56	.15:2/13	.08:2/26
Sweden	.75:12/16	.13:12/93	.33:7/21	.33/7/21	.81:13/16	.06:13/222	.54:7/13	.11:7/63	.19:3/16	.10:3/30
Denmark	.80:16/20	.06:16/255	.00:0/20	.00:0/20	.60:10/16	.03:10/376	.40:7/18	.07:7/96	.06:1/18	.04:1/36
Germany	.25:4/15	.04:4/100	.20:3/15	.20:3/15	.67:10/15	.06:10/162	.93:14/15	.08:14/162	.73:11/15	.07:11/173
Luxembourg	.62:5/8	.13:5/40	.62:5/8	.62:5/8	1.0:8/8	.33:8/24	.87:7/8	.12:7/56	.75:6/8	.37:6/16
Belgium	.49:14/29	.14:14/102	.49:14/29	.49:14/29	.86:26/30	.10:26/264	.85:26/30	.10:26/299	.28:7/25	.08:7/82
Netherlands	.7:7/10	.70:7/10	.40:4/10	.40:4/10	.91:10/11	.13:10/74	1.0:11/11	.15:11/74	.31:4/13	.14:4/30
Italy	.42:8/19	.05:8/170	.30:6/19	.08:6/66[1]	1.0:38/38	.17:38/228	1.0:38/38	.17:38/228	.40:11/38	.10:11/110
Israel	.11:2/18	.11:2/18	.11:2/18	.11:2/18[2]	.94:17/18	.06:17/277	.77:14/18	.05:14/272	.27:5/18	.12:5/40
Fourth Republic	–	–	.71:20/28	.71:20/28	–	–	.90:25/28	.36:25/70	.64:18/28	.26:18/70
Overall Performance:										
Country-based mean:	.50	.16	.35	.33	.84	.18	.77	.14	.38	.17
Case-based mean:	.55	.08	.32	.25	.89	.06	.80	.10	.35	.10

Note: Fourth Republic not included in overall totals owing to different basis of calculation.
[1] Any majority node, not just first.

Table 14.5 (cont'd)

Model / Country	6 Government is one-dimensional connected		7 Government has smallest MAP on one dimension		8 Government has smallest DCP on one dimension		9 Government consists of 'swing' party plus party(ies) closest to it in one dimension		10 Government consists of 'swing' party with party(ies) closest to it on 20 dimensions	
	Success	Efficiency	Success	Efficiency	Success	Efficiency	Success	Efficiency	Success	Efficiency
Ireland	1.0:11/11	.17:11/66	.82:9/11	.82:9/11	–	–	–	–	–	–
Norway	1.0:13/13	.06:13/195	.70:9/13	.14:9/65	–	–	–	–	–	–
Sweden	.90:19/21	.09:19/210	.80:16/21	.19:16/87	–	–	–	–	–	–
Denmark	.80:14/18	.04:14/312	.66:12/18	.14:12/84	.60:11/18	.60:11/18	.66:12/18	.66:12/18	.60:11/18	.60:11/18
Germany	.90:13/15	.13:13/100	.55:8/15	.53:8/16	–	–	.53:8/15	.53:8/15	.49:7/15	.49:7/15
Luxembourg	.75:6/8	.12:6/48	.37:3/8	.37:3/8	.25:2/8	.25:2/8	.37:3/8	.37:3/8	.25:2/8	.25:2/8
Belgium	.28:7/25	.02:7/466	.40:13/30	.40:13/30	.33:10/30	.33:10/30	.33:10/30	.33:10/30	.41:12/29	.41:12/29
Netherlands	.69:9/13	.13:9/69	.40:4/10	.27:4/15	.50:5/10	.26:5/19	.37:3/8	.37:3/8	.75:6/8	.75:6/8
Italy	.81:31/38	.16:31/181	.00:0/19	.00:0/19	.00:0/19	.00:0/19	.20:3/15	.20:3/15	.33:5/15	.33:5/15
Israel	.27:5/18	.12:5/40	.11:2/18	.11:2/18	–	–	–	–	–	–
Fourth Republic	–	–	–	–	–	–	–	–	–	–
Overall Performance:										
Country-based mean:	.71	.10	.49	.30	.30	.34	.27	.41	.47	.47
Case-based mean:	.69	.07	.46	.22	.22	.33	.30	.40	.46	.46

really justified in terms of their prediction of coalitions. Ireland is a particular case in point, where out of eleven governments eight were single party administrations, sometimes with majority status. More often than not, however, European single party governments form in situations in which one party does not control a majority of seats, so that legislative coalitions are needed in order to maintain them in office and the government cannot be 'read off' directly from the election result. The frequency of surplus majority coalitions, furthermore, demonstrates that even a legislative majority does not necessarily settle the composition of the government. For these reasons, and for the sake of cross-national comparability, we therefore evaluate the success of predictions in each country on the same basis, though the potential for inflated success rates in systems in which one party government is common must be continually kept in mind.

The second caveat concerns the identification of the set of coalitions which could theoretically have formed after any given election, which obviously affects the evaluation of the models. Given the important role which bargaining constraints play in many systems in limiting and sometimes even determining the coalition possibilities, certain theoretical possibilities have been eliminated from consideration in the country studies reported in previous chapters. Table 14.5 follows the practice of the country authors with regard to bargaining constraints.

The models reviewed in Table 14.5 fall into pairs. The first two are based on the cluster models operationalised in 20 dimensions. Model 1 predicts that the coalition that forms will both be at a node on the cluster tree and contain the party with the median legislator on at least one of the 20 policy dimensions. Model 2 predicts that the coalition will be the one at the first node on the cluster tree for which the parties control a legislative majority. Models 3 and 4 are based on the idea of the median legislator. Model 3 predicts that the government will include the party controlling the median legislator on a plurality of the 20 policy dimensions. Model 4 predicts that the government will include the party controlling the median legislator on the common left–right policy dimension. Model 5 tests Axelrod's prediction that coalitions will be minimal connected winning on one dimension; Model 6 predicts simply that the coalition will be connected on one dimension. Models 7 and 8 generate predictions based on minimising policy distances on one dimension between government parties. Models 9 and 10 predict that particular parties identified by the country authors as 'predominant' or 'swing' parties will join in government with the parties closest to them in either the one or the 20-dimensional policy space.

Table 14.5 summarises the performance of these models in two ways. The first averages success and efficiency rates treating each country as a single case, so as to give each national experience equal weighting. The second averages success and efficiency rates treating each coalition as a single case, in which case the countries with larger numbers of coalitions dominate the evaluation (these tend to be countries with larger numbers of governments, hence ones where coalitions are less stable). Generally, however, we can arrive at the same evaluation using either summary measure.

Table 14.5 shows us that the general cluster model (Model 1) is inefficient, since it admits so many cases into its prediction sets (there are many nodes of each cluster tree, including all single party governments and the grand coalition of all parties). The cluster model based on the first majority node (Model 2), in spite of its lack of realism when applied to Norway and Denmark, turns in a respectable performance overall, the result of a relatively good performance in countries where a majority is required. The two median legislator models (Models 3 and 4) have very high success rates. Nearly all coalitions that form do include the party with the median legislator on the left–right dimension, and the party with the median legislator on a plurality of the 20 dimensions. This predictive success, however, is undermined by the fact that the models are very inclusive, making many different predictions and therefore showing low overall efficiency rates. The same pattern holds for the two models based on ideological connectedness. Both predict quite well, especially Model 6 which predicts merely that coalitions will be connected, but this model is also very inclusive, so its efficiency is low. Characterisations based on the idea of minimising aggregate policy distances (Models 7 and 8), on the other hand, perform well except in Israel and Italy. And the fact that they tend to give unique predictions increases their efficiency levels considerably. The last two models (Models 9 and 10) are based on the idea that particular parties are in a position to take the initiative and choose the closest coalition partners, either in one or 20 dimensions. These models have quite high success rates and, because they identify a single set of parties as the predicted coalition, tend also to be efficient. Were it not for the fact that they can only be applied in a limited number of national settings, these 'swing' models would probably be judged most effective overall.

Given the importance and centrality of policy to coalition theory the performance of the operational models listed in Table 14.5 is disappointing. At the very best (but over half the countries only) policy attains success and efficiency levels of around .50; and this is with the more difficult cases taken out (where external constraints effectively determine outcomes). Had these been included, success and efficiency would have been markedly lower. This applies also to the other figures in the Table.

No policy based theory of coalitions can remain impervious to these results, even if their exact assumptions are not directly represented in the Table. It seems that policy on its own just cannot bear the weight put on it by coalition theory.

A general evaluation of the results in Table 14.5, taken together with the analyses in each of the country chapters, suggests that no single model performs well enough to provide an acceptable general account of coalition formation over all the countries studied. Nonetheless, their usefulness in characterising the governments that form is indisputable.

They perform well enough to imply that policy is a major influence on the formation of government coalitions.

A COMPARATIVE EVALUATION OF THE RELATIONSHIP BETWEEN PARTY AND COALITION POLICY

We can supplement our checks on the operational models of coalition-formation by a direct examination of the links between party policy (as specified by the election programme) and coalition policy (as specified by relevant agreements or government declarations). Clearly, if policy is important in coalition-formation, it is because parties expect to get some kind of policy payoff from being in government. This can be examined most directly by checking the distances between party and government positions in some kind of policy-space.

The actual space we use is our one-dimensional left–right continuum. This is because party and government positions on it, and the distances between them, can each be summarised by a single figure which fits into the regression analysis we employ below. The representation of locations and distances in our 20-dimensional space would require much more and we have been unable to think of some summary mode of presentation (other than locations on the left–right continuum) which would get around this difficulty. As emphasised in Chapter Two, our one-dimensional continuum *is* in any case the best reduced representation of positions in the 20-dimensions, so it is unlikely that findings would be substantially different were we able to base ourselves on the 20-dimensions directly.

Our investigation of the general relationship between party and coalition policy proceeds in three stages. First, for each party that has been in government, we assess the extent to which the policies of governments which include the party differ from those which exclude it. Second, defining the 'policy payoff' going to a party to be the difference between party policy and government policy, we assess the extent to which policy payoffs are greater when parties are in government rather than out. Finally, in a much more severe test, we set out to discover whether it is possible to make precise predictions about the location of substantive coalition policy, on the basis of the policies of parties in the system.

We omit Ireland and Israel from the analysis for two reasons. In the first case the evaluation of distances between party and government positions is too strongly affected by the many single party, and in some cases majority, governments which emerge. Israel is the country where our left–right representation fits least well, and where there is most risk of distortion from the reduced representation. Had it been included in the following tables this would have artificially depressed the relationship between party and government policy. So, we have chosen to omit it. Figures for the French Fourth Republic were calculated on a different basis from those of our other studies so we have chosen to omit these also.

Does the party membership of a government affect government policy?

For each party that had been in government during the period under study, we compared the left–right scores of governments that included the party with the left–right scores of governments that excluded it. Table 14.6 gives the mean left–right scores of governments including and excluding each relevant party.

Table 14.6 The impact of party participation on government policy on the left–right dimension

Party	Mean government left–right score: party out	Mean government left–right score: party in
BELGIUM		
Socialists	12.7	10.5
Social Christians	5.4	12.5
Liberals	13.4	8.6
Volksunie	7.0	50.8
Front des Francophones	1.5	39.9
DENMARK		
Social Democrats	8.6	−5.3
Radical Liberals	1.3	−8.4
Liberals	−5.3	8.6
Conservatives	−3.7	10.5

GERMANY

Social Democrats	14.4	7.8
Free Democrats	20.0	10.5
Christian Democrats	3.3	16.0

ITALY

Socialists	−2.5	−0.5
Social Democrats	−0.7	−3.3
Republicans	−2.5	−1.0
Liberals	−1.5	−3.8
Christian Democrats	*	*

LUXEMBOURG

Socialists	1.7	−9.0
Liberals	−12.7	12.4
Christian Democrats	*	*

NETHERLANDS

Socialists	6.8	1.6
Liberals	2.2	6.3
CHU	4.1	5.1
ARP	13.0	1.6
KVP/CDA	*	*

NORWAY

Socialists	4.2	−14.3
Liberals	−11.6	4.8
Center Party	−12.6	3.8
Conservatives	−13.9	7.0
Christian Peoples Party	−12.6	3.8

SWEDEN

Social Democrats	2.8	−14.3
Liberals	−14.3	2.8
Centre Party	−17.4	2.7
Conservatives	−1.4	−2.0

* party always, or almost always, in government: statistics meaningless. Parties never, or almost never, in government have been omitted, for the same reason.

Table 14.6 shows that, while government policy does tend to vary with the inclusion or exclusion of particular parties, this pattern is much stronger in some systems than in others. In Norway, Denmark, Luxembourg and Sweden, for example, the pattern is quite clear. Governments which included the main left–wing party had markedly more left–wing policies than those that did not; governments which included the main right–wing parties had markedly more right-wing policies than those that did not.

Mean government policy positions, in Luxembourg and Sweden, also appear to differ on the basis of which parties are in, or out, of the coalition. In Belgium, Germany, Italy and the Netherlands, however, there are less clean-cut patterns. (The only exception is the strong tendency of the language parties in Belgium to be associated with right-wing governments.) It is much less systematically the case that the inclusion of left-wing parties in the government is associated with more left-wing government declarations and the inclusion of right-wing parties in the government is associated with more right-wing government declarations. Still, there are only three un-ambiguous cases overall, out of the 31 comparisons possible from the table, where government policy changes in an unanticipated direction with the participation of the party in government.

Note that, in those systems in which we observe the strongest link between party membership and government policy, there tends to be a clear-cut alternation of government between one bloc of parties and an alternative bloc with little or no overlapping membership. This is most obviously the case in Norway, where we observe the strongest party effects on government policy and note that the Norwegian Labour Party has never gone into a government containing any bourgeois party. In Denmark, in contrast, the Radical Liberals have gone into coalition with both Social Democrats and bourgeois parties, softening an otherwise strong pattern of 'two bloc' politics, a pattern which also characterises the Swedish system. At the opposite extreme are countries such as Italy and the Netherlands, in which the Christian Democrats are always in office, the alternation effects are therefore much weaker, and the impact of party membership on gov-ernment policy harder to discern.

Does membership of a government coalition affect policy payoffs?

In the previous section we considered whether party membership of a coalition affected government policy, regardless of the professed policies of the party in question. In this section, we look at the problem from the point of view of the party. The theories that we deal with in this book are based on the assumption that politicians participate in government in order to affect government policy. As we have noted, however, policy payoffs go to all parties, whether they are in or out of office. It is possible, therefore, to receive high policy payoffs while remaining outside the government. Table 14.7 reports the impact of government membership on policy payoffs for those parties covered in Table 14.6. It compares the mean distance between party and coalition policy for those situations in which the party is in government with the mean distance when the party is out of government.

Once more, we see some clear patterns. Again, Norway shows the most marked results with government policy moving strongly between the Labour Party and the Conservatives as these alternate in government. (Note, however, that the Liberals' preferred policies are closer to those of Labour, but that if they go into coalition they join with Labour's opponents. This creates a situation in which the Liberals consistently do worse under the government in which they participate than they do when they are in opposition and Labour is in government.) Similar, but weaker, patterns can be seen in Denmark, the Netherlands and Belgium, (excepting the 'perverse' payoffs of the language parties who clearly do not go into coalitions on the basis of their policies on the left–right dimension). In Germany, Italy, Luxembourg and Sweden in contrast, all systems dominated by a single party, the policy payoffs of going into government are not at all clear. In each case, the distance between party and government policy seems to be unaffected by whether or not the party is in government.

Table 14.7 The impact of coalition membership on party policy payoffs on the left–right dimension

Party	Mean policy distance: party out	Mean policy distance: party in
BELGIUM		
Socialists	38.8	32.3
Social Christians	26.8	18.2
Liberals	17.4	14.7
Volksunie	15.5	46.4
Front des Francophones	16.2	41.0
DENMARK		
Social Democrats	17.8	11.2
Radical Liberals	12.7	4.4
Liberals	24.1	14.3
Conservatives	33.2	23.6
GERMANY		
Social Democrats	9.2	11.8
Free Democrats	22.1	14.7
Christian Democrats	11.2	24.2
ITALY		
Socialists	14.9	15.3
Social Democrats	11.1	13.4
Republicans	9.6	11.9

Liberals	13.9	6.6
Christian Democrats	*	*
LUXEMBOURG		
Socialists	35.3	36.5
Liberals	15.9	11.0
Christian Democrats	*	*
NETHERLANDS		
Socialists	38.9	29.4
Liberals	17.6	10.3
CHU	18.0	13.7
ARP	13.3	15.7
KVP/CDA	*	*
NORWAY		
Socialists	34.4	19.3
Liberals	12.7	33.1
Center Party	18.4	18.0
Conservatives	18.1	7.8
Christian Peoples Party	20.7	11.8
SWEDEN		
Social Democrats	16.1	25.9
Liberals	18.4	14.3
Centre Party	18.5	19.1
Conservatives	47.7	14.5

* party always, or almost always, in government; statistics meaningless. Parties never, or almost never, in government have been omitted, for the same reason.

Overall, therefore, while parties do seem to be able to have some impact on the policy of the governments in which they participate, these effects are rather modest. While policy payoffs in a number of systems seem to be as great when a party is in opposition as they are when it is in government, in others, government participation does make a difference. This pattern seems to be related to the extent to which there is an alternation in the membership of different government coalitions.

Predicting substantive government policy positions

Perhaps the sternest test of any policy-based coalition theory is whether it can predict the actual substantive location of coalition policy. Below, we test six hypotheses about the relationship between party and coalition policy on the common left–right scale. In each case we tested hypothesis H_i by calculating a predicted position for coalition policy (X_i) and then comparing this, using a simple regression, with the actual coalition policy position (Y). Hypothesis H_i is supported if $Y = a_i + b_iX_i$ such that $a_i = 0$ and $b_i = i$. This procedure is necessitated by the limited number of cases available in many countries which preclude a straight regression of party positions on government policy.

The hypotheses tested were as follows:

H_1 Coalition policy is located at the mean of the policy positions of all parties in the system

H_2 Coalition policy is located at the weighted mean of the policy positions of all parties in the system; each party's position being weighted by the share that it controls of the total number of legislative seats.

These hypotheses are derived from the argument that policy outputs go to all parties in the system whether they are in or out of government. This argument suggests that government membership is not directly relevant to the content of the government policy package either because policy-making is highly consensual or the threats that can be used in attempts to influence government policy outputs, threats to defeat the government in confidence votes, depend upon legislative voting strategies that are available to all parties. The weighting of policy positions that distinguishes H_2 from H_1 takes account of the legislative impact available to each party, though legislative bargaining power is related to legislative seat share in only a very general way.

H_3 Coalition policy is located at the mean of the policy positions of government members.

H_4 Coalition policy is located at the weighted mean of the policy positions of government members; each member's policy position being weighted by the share that it controls of the total number of legislative seats controlled by all government members taken together.

These hypotheses are derived from the argument that, while policy outputs go to all parties, the cabinet has much greater control over policy (because of the ineffectiveness of legislative control over the executive). The hypotheses are also related to the status of the precise document we use to measure the policy position of a coalition. Since this is a document directly resulting from coalition negotiations between government members, it might be expected to reflect the policy concerns of government members only. On this account, the policy impact of the opposition is more likely to have an effect once the legislature goes into session (after which, of course, provisions in the coalition policy document may well be abandoned). These hypotheses are more specific versions of the general idea that it is the party composition of the coalition that somehow determines coalition policy. Once more, we take the share of the legislative seats controlled by the governments as having some crude relationship with bargaining power, other things being equal.

H_5 Coalition policy is located at the position of the party containing the median legislator on the left–right scale.

H_6 Coalition policy is located at the position of the predominant party

These hypotheses derive from arguments about the key role of pivotal parties. In a one-dimensional system, the core party is the party controlling the median legislator (H_5). The difficulty with this is that the party controlling the mean legislator may change from election to election, but parties may assess the bargaining system from a longer-term perspective. If a particular party is normally at the median, but leaves this position for a single election, then this may or may not be reflected in coalition bargaining. The change may be taken by the parties as a new bargaining reality; or they may anticipate a return to 'normality' and bargain as if nothing had happened. Thus H_6 emphasises the influence of the dominant party in each system – one that will usually be found at the median position – and, regardless of whether it was estimated to control the median legislator at a particular election, predicts that government policy will be the policy of that party.

The detailed evaluations of these hypotheses for the left–right scale can be found in Table 14.8. As might be expected from our earlier results, the strongest policy effects can be seen in Denmark, Norway, Sweden and Luxembourg. Some effects from the position of the median party (H_5) also appear in Germany. In Denmark and Luxembourg, a dominant party seems to have a strong impact on government policy. In Denmark, it is the Social Democrats that have this effect; in Luxembourg, it is the Christian Socials. In each case, the dominant parties seem to have an effect on government policy, whether they are in or out of office, a finding that reinforces their portrayal as 'core' parties. We also note that government policy in these systems can be predicted from the policies of all coalitionable parties, whether these are in or out of office. It is possible that this is because the policies of the other parties vary with those of the core party. Exploration of this possibility using multiple regressions, however, shows that the impact of Social Democratic Party policy on government policy in Denmark remains statistically significant once the policies of all other parties have been

Table 14.8 Percentage of variance in coalition policy over the left–right dimension explained by H_1–H_6

Country	Hypothesis						Dominant party
	H_1	H_2	H_3	H_4	H_5	H_6	
Belgium	.03	.03	.01	.00	.01	.00	PSC
Denmark	.46	.47	.44	.46	.00	.32	SD
Germany	.11	.00	.01	.05	.21	.09	FDP
Italy	.02	.00	.00	.01	.01	.03	DCI
Luxembourg	.03	.36	.20	.36	.55	.43	CSV
Netherlands	.04	.05	.00	.02	.03	.00	KVP/CDA
Norway	.00	.00	.27	.29	.05	.00	Lab or Lib
Sweden	.39	.38	.13	.12	.06.	00	SD

controlled. (The number of valid cases in Luxembourg is too small to allow meaningful multiple regressions of this sort to be run). In short, we can think of government policy in these systems as being 'dominated' by the predominant party, whether it is in or out of office.

This pattern is not repeated in Sweden (which on the face of it seems to have a clearly predominant party in the Social Democrats) or in Norway (where no party has dominated since the decline of the Labour Party in the mid-1960s). Government policy in Norway is best predicted as the mean policy of government members, as opposed to the mean policy of all parties in the system. In Sweden in contrast, government policy is best predicted using the mean policy of all parties in the system. Multiple regressions in the Swedish case suggest that government policy is best characterised by the cumulative effect of all party policies, taken together, rather than from the independent effect of any one party. In Belgium, Italy and the Netherlands, there is no immediately obvious relationship between the policies of parties and the policies of governments. Note that, while Italy and the Netherlands can be viewed as systems dominated by Christian Democratic parties that are never out of office, government policy cannot be predicted from the policies of these dominant parties. It seems simply to be the case that the link between party and coalition policy is attenuated in these systems.

CONCLUSIONS

Our analysis confirms that policy is an important factor in the formation of European coalition governments. This, notwithstanding, the patterns that emerge are not as clear cut as we might have expected. In particular no single model fits all political systems.

There are many possible reasons for this. Policy seems less important in some countries (notably Israel and Italy) than in others, (notably Scandinavia). Models adapted to one-dimensional policy spaces work better in some areas (notably Scandinavia) while models adapted to multi-dimensional policy spaces work better in others (notably in Italy, Belgium and the Netherlands). Significant system-specific bargaining constraints dramatically modify the prediction sets of the models, sometimes even rendering them empty and thus leaving them incapable of making predictions.

Nonetheless, as both the specific country studies and our general syntheses show, policy does help us interpret the politics of coalition in Europe. As often as not, a simple policy-space based on the left–right dimension is the best indicator, suggesting that policy has a relatively simple impact on coalition bargaining. Perhaps the most striking consequence is that, if a single party regularly controls the median legislator in the left–right dimension, it can become an almost permanent fixture in office and receive consistently higher policy payoffs than other parties. The most striking examples can be found in Italy and the Netherlands, where Christian Democratic parties play a pivotal role in government formation. In such cases, not surprisingly, government membership makes little difference to policy outputs. In the Scandinavian two-bloc politics, in contrast, control over the median legislator can shift regularly from bloc to bloc. As a consequence alternate coalitions tend to comprise groups of parties from rival blocs. In such circumstances, the partisan composition of the cabinet does make a difference to government policy programmes.

No doubt considerable improvements can be made both in the accuracy of our data and in the refinement of the theoretical models available. In this sense, our investigation represents a first stage in the systematic exploration of policy impacts on coalitions. One major conclusion is unlikely to be reversed, however. That is, that party policy, influential though it obviously is in coalition-bargaining, still has less consistent and strong effects than those assumed by policy-based spatial models.

This finding points in two directions so far as new developments in the field of coalition theory are concerned. One is to devote mere attention to developing and fitting theory on a country-specific basis. In order to prevent such theories reverting into more *ad hoc* descriptions based on the special circumstances of each case, it will be necessary to develop policy-based models that are general enough to cover a wide range of cases, yet flexible enough to be adapted to the vagaries of each party system. Budge and

Keman's non-spatial, but policy based, theory of democratic governments (1990) represents one type of approach to this problem.

Another possibility, stemming from Budge and Keman's work on sectoral policy influences (1990, Chapter 5) and from other findings made by the Research Group on links between programmatic emphases and government expenditures (Hofferbert and Klingemann, 1990) suggests that a crucial intervening link between party policy and government action is control of relevant ministries in the coalition. This points to abandoning the idea of ministries as interchangeable coin in coalition transactions and substituting party concerns with particular ministries as a means of forwarding policy goals. This is also an idea incorporated in Budge and Keman's non-spatial approach (1990, Chapter 4) and formalised spatially by Laver and Shepsle (1990).

However, it makes its influence felt, policy is clearly important for government coalitions. This comparative study has made a start in specifically investigating some of the processes involved. We hope that future developments of both theory and data will be able to build on the foundations which have been laid here.

Bibliography

Aarebrot, F. (1982) 'Norway: Centre and Periphery in a Peripheral State', in S. Rokkan and D. W. Urwin (eds), *The Politics of Territorial Identity* (London: Sage Publications) pp. 75–111.

Allum, P. (1973) *Republic Without Government?* (London: Weidenfeld & Nicolson).

Amato, G. (1976) *Economia, politica e istituzioni in Italia* (Bologna: Il Mulino).

Andeweg, R. B., Tak, van der, Th. and Dittrich K. (1980) 'Government Formation in the Netherlands', In R. T. Griffiths (ed.), *The Economy and Politics of the Netherlands since 1945* (s-Gravenhage: North Holland Publishing Co.).

Arain, A. (1985) *Politics in Israel: The Second Generation* (Chatham, NJ: Chatham House).

Arian, A. (1973) *The Choosing People: Voting Behaviour in Israel* (Cleveland, Ohio: Case Western Press).

Arter, D. (1984) *The Nordic Parliaments* (New York: St. Martin's Press).

Arter, D. (1985) 'The Nordic Parliaments: Patterns of Legislative Influence', *West European Politics*, vol. 8, no. (1), pp. 55–70.

Austen-Smith, D., and Banks, J. (1988) 'Elections, Coalitions and Legislative Outcomes', *American Political Science Review*, vol. 82, pp. 405–22.

Austen-Smith, D., and Banks, J. (1990) 'Stable Portfolio Allocations', *American Political Science Review*, vol. 84, no. 3, pp. 891–906.

Axelrod, R. (1970) *Conflict of Interest* (Chicago: Markham).

Azmon, Y. (1981) 'The 1981 Elections and the Changing Fortunes of the Israeli Labour Party', *Government and Opposition*, vol. 16, no. 41.

Bara, J. (1987), 'Israel 1949–1981', in I. Budge, D. Robertson and D. Hearl (eds), *Ideology, Strategy and Party Change: Spatial Analyses of Post-War Election Programmes in 19 Democracies* (Cambridge: Cambridge University Press).

Baron, D. and Ferejohn, J. (1987). *Bargaining in legislatures*, mimeo, Stanford University.

Battegazzorre, F. (1987) 'L' instabilita di governo in Italia', *Rivista italiana di scienza politica*, vol. 17, no. 2, pp. 285–317.

Beilin, Y. (1985) 'The Israeli General Election of 1984', *Electoral Studies*, vol. 4, pp. 79–83.

Berg, J. Th. J. van den, (1986) 'Democatische hervormingen, politieke machtsverhoudingen en coalitievorming in Nederland', *Acta Politica*, vol. 3, pp. 265–90.

Berglund, S., and Lindstrom, U. (1978) *The Scandinavian Party System(s)* (Lund: Studentlitteratur).

Berglund, S., and Pesonen, P. with Gylfi P. Gislason (1981) 'Political Party Systems', in Erik Allardt *et al.* (eds) *Nordic Democracy* (New York: St. Martin's Press).

Bergstrom, H. (1987) *Rivstart?* (Stockholm: Tidens Forlag).

Beyme, K. V. (1985) *Political Parties in Western Democracies* (New York: St. Martin's Press).

Bilstad, Karl-Anders (1986) 'Konfliktstruktur og Partiavstand', unpublished graduate thesis, Department of Comparative Politics, University of Bergen.

Birgersson, B. O., Hadenius, S., Molin. B. and Wieslander, H. (1984) *Sverige efter 1900: En modern politisk historia* (Stockholm: BonnierFakta).

Bjorklund, T., and Hagtvet, B. (eds.) (1981). *Hoyrebolgen – Epokeskifte i norsk politikk?* (Oslo: Aschehoug).

Bjornberg, A (1939). *Parlamentarismens Utveckling i Norge Efter 1905* (Stockholm: Almqvist & Wiksell).

Bogdanor, V. (1983) 'Introduction', in V. Bogdanor (ed.) *Coalition Government in Western Europe* (London: Heinemann).

Browne, E. (1973) *Coalition Theories: A Logical and Empirical Critique* (London: Sage Professional Papers in Comparative Government).

Browne, E. C. and Dreijmanis, J. (1982) *Government Coalitions in Western Democracies* (New York: Longman).

Browne, E. C. and Franklin, M. N. (1973) 'Aspects of Coalition Payoffs in European Parliamentary Democracies'. *American Political Science Review*, vol. 67, no. 2, pp. 453–69.

Browne, E. C. and Franklin, M. N. (1986) 'Editors' Introduction: New Directions in Coalition Research', *Legislative Studies Quarterly*, vol. 11, no. 4, pp. 469–83.

Budge, I. (1984) 'Parties and Democratic Government. A Framework for Comparative Explanation', *West European Politics*, vol. 7, pp. 95–118.

Budge, I. and Herman, V. (1978) 'Coalition and Government Formation: An Empirically Relevant Theory', *British Journal of Political Science*, vol. 8 no. 4, pp. 459–77.

Budge, I. and Laver M. (1986) 'Office Seeking and Policy Pursuit in Coalition Theory', *Legislative Studies Quarterly*, vol. 11 no. 4, pp. 485–506.

Budge, I., and Keman. H. (1990) *Parties and Democracy Coalition Formation and Government Functioning in 20 Democracies* (Oxford: Oxford University Press).

Budge, I., Robertson, D., and Hearl, D. (1987) *Ideology Strategy and Party Change* (Cambridge: Cambridge University Press).

Bueno de Mesquita, B. (1979) 'Coalition Payoffs and Electoral Performance in European Democracies', *Comparative Political Studies*, vol. 12, no. 1, pp. 61–81.

Calise, M. and Mannheimer R. (1982). *Governanti in Italia. Un trentennio republicano 1946–1976* (Bologna: Il Mulino).

Calvert, R. (1985) 'Robustness of the Multi-dimensional Voting Model: Candidate Motivations, Uncertainty and Convergence', *American Journal of Political Science*, vol. 29, no. 1, pp. 69–95.

Calzolaio, V. (1982) 'Governi, crisi di governo e storia costituzionale', *Democrazia e diritto*, vol. 5, pp. 29–49.

Carstairs, A. M. (1980) *A Short History of Electoral Systems in Western Europe* (London: George Allen & Unwin).

Casey, J. (1987) *Constitutional Law in Ireland* (London: Sweet and Maxwell).

Cassese, S. (1980) 'Is There a Government in Italy? Politics and Administration at the Top', in R. Rose and E. Suleiman (eds), *Presidents and Prime Ministers* (Washington: American Enterprise Institute).

Castles, F. G. and Mair, P. (1984) 'Left–Right Political Scales: Some Expert Judgements', *European Journal of Political Research*, vol. 12, no. 1, pp. 73–88.

Coakley, J. (1987) 'The Election in Context: Historical and European Perspectives', in M. Laver, P. Mair, and R. Sinnott (eds) *How Ireland Voted: the Irish General*

Election 1987 (Swords, Co. Dublin: Poolbeg Press, in association with PSAI Press).

Cohen, L. (1979) 'Cyclic Sets in Multi-dimensional Voting Models', *Journal of Economic Theory*, vol. 20, no. 1, pp. 1–12.

Cohen, L., and Matthews, S. A. (1980) 'Constrained Plott Equilibria, Directional Equilibria and Global Cycling Sets', *Review of Economic Studies*, vol. 47, pp. 975–86.

Cotta, M. (1987) 'Il sotto-sistema governo-parlamento', *Rivista italiana di scienza politica*, vol. 17, no. 2. pp. 241–84.

Daalder, H. (1986) 'Changing Procedures and Changing Strategies in Dutch Co-alition Building', *Legislative Studies Quarterly*, vol. 4, pp. 507–31.

Dagens Nyheter, Resultatet av riksdagsvalet 1988, September 27, 1988.

Di Palma, G. (1977, trans. 1978). *Surviving without Governing: Italian Parties in Parliament* (Berkeley: University of California Press).

Diskin, A. (1984) 'The Jewish Ethnic Vote: An Aggregative Perspective', in D. Caspi, E. Guttman and A. Diskin (eds.) *The Roots of Begin's Success*, (Croom Helm: London)

Dittrich, K. (1987) 'The Netherlands 1946–1981', in I. Budge, D. Robertson and D. Hearle (eds), *Ideology, Strategy and Party Change: Spatial Analyses of Post-War Election Programmes in 19 democracies* (Cambridge: Cambridge University Press) pp. 206–30.

Dodd, L. C. (1976) *Coalitions in Parliamentary Government* (Princeton: Princeton University Press).

Downs, A. (1957) *An Economic Theory of Democracy* (New York: Harper & Row).

Duverger, M. (1974) *Political Parties* (3rd Edition) (Methuen: London).

Duynstee, F. J. F. M. (1966) *De kabinetsformaties 1946–1965*, (Berlin: Deventer).

Elia, L. (1969) 'Forme di governo', *Enciclopedia del diritto*, XIX (Milan: Giuffre).

Eliassen, K. A. and Pedersen, M. N. (1985) *Nordiske Politiske Fakta* (Bergen: Tiden Norsk Forlag).

Farneti, P. (1985) *The Italian Party System (1945–1980)* (Francis Pinter: London).

Farrell, B. (1989) 'The Road from 1987: Government Formation and Institutional Inertia', in M. Gallagher and R. Sinnott (eds) *How Ireland Voted*, 1989 (Galway: Centre for the Study of Irish Elections).

Franklin, M., and Mackie, T. (1984) 'Reassessing the Importance of Size and Ideology for the Formation of Governing Coalitions in Parliamentary Democracies', *American Journal of Political Science*, vol. 28, no. 4, 671–92.

Friedmann, M. (1984) 'The NRP in Transition: Behind the Party's decline', in D. Caspi, E. Guttman and A. Diskin (eds), *The Roots of Begin's Success* (London: Croom Helm).

Furre, B. (1976) *Norsk Historie 1905–1940* (Oslo: Det Norske Samlaget).

Gallagher, M. (1982) *The Irish Labour Party in Transition 1957–81* (Dublin: Gill & Macmillan).

Gallagher, M. (1985) *Political Parties in the Republic of Ireland*, (Dublin: Gill & Macmillan).

Galli, G. (1974). *I partiti politici*, (Turin: UTET).

Gamson, W. A. (1961) 'A Theory of Coalition Formation' *American Sociological Review*, vol. 26, no. 3, pp. 373–82.

Groennings, S. (1961). 'Cooperation among Norway's Non-Socialist Political Parties', unpublished PhD dissertation, Stanford University.

Grofman, B. (1982) 'A Dynamic Model of Protocoalition Formation in Ideological N-Space', *Behavioural Science*, vol. 27, pp. 77–90.

Grofman, B. (1987) 'Extending a Dynamic Model of Protocoalition Formation, with Special Application to Denmark and Italy, mimeo, University of California, Irvine.

Gronmo, S. (1975a) 'Politiske skillelinjer i norske partiprogrammer: En analyse av utviklingen fra 1936 till 1973', paper presented for the Nordic Political Science Association Conference, Arhus, Denmark.

Gronmo, S. (1975b). 'Skillelinjer i partipolitikken 1969–1973: Noen virkninger av EF-striden', *Tidsskrift for Samfunnsforskning* vol. 16, pp. 119–153.

Guidorossi, G. (1984) *Gli italiani e la politica* , (Milan: Angeli).

Hadenius, A. (1981) *Spetlet om Skatten* (Lund: Norstedts).

Hadenius, S. (1985). *Swedish Politics During the 20th Century* (Stockholm: The Swedish Institute).

Halevi, N. and Klinov-Malul, R. (1968). *The Economic Development of Israel* (Praeger: New York).

Halvarson, A. (1980) *Sveriges Statskick: En Faktasamling*, 5th edn (Stockholm: Esselte Studium).

Hearl, D. (1987) 'Luxembourg 1945–82: Dimensions and Strategies', in Budge, I., Robertson, D., and Hearl, D. (eds) *Ideology, Strategy and Party Change* (Cambridge: Cambridge University Press).

Herman, V., and Pope, J. (1973) 'Minority governments in Western Democracies' *British Journal of Political Science*, vol. 3, no. 2, pp. 191–212.

Holmberg, E. and Stjernquist, N. (1983) *Var Forfattning* (Stockholm: P. A. Norstedt & Soners forlag).

Holmberg, S. (1981). *Svenska Valjare* (Stockholm: Liber).

Holmberg, S. and Gilljam, M. (1987) *Valjare och cal i Sverige* (Stockholm: BonnierFakta).

Holmstedt, M. and Schou, T.L., (1987) 'Sweden and Denmark, 1945–1982: Election Programmes in the Scandinavian Setting', in I. Budge, D. Robertson and D. Hearle (eds), *Ideology, Strategy and Party Change: Spatial analyses of Post-War Election Programmes in 19 Democracies* (Cambridge: Cambridge University Press), 177–206.

Inglehart, R. and Klingemann, H.D. (1976) 'Party Identification, Ideological Preferences and Left–Right Dimension among Western Mass Publics', in I. Budge, I. Crewe and D. Farlie (eds), *Party Identification and Beyond* (London and New York: Wiley) pp. 243–73.

Jong, J. de and Pijnenburg, B. (1986) 'The Dutch Christian Democratic Party and Coalition Behaviour in the Netherlands: a Pivotal Party in the Face of Depillarisation', in G. Pridham (ed) *Coalitional Behaviour in Theory and Practice: An Inductive Model for Western Europe* (London: Cambridge University Press) pp. 145–70.

Keesing's Contemporary Archives (after January 1987: Keesing's record of World Events), various editions (Harlow: Longman).

Kramer, G. H. (1973) 'On a class of equilibrium conditions for majority rule', *Econometrica*, 41, pp. 285–97.

Krehbiel, K. (1988) 'Spatial models of legislative choice', *Legislative Studies Quarterly*, vol. 13, no. 3, pp. 259–319.

Lanke, J. and Bjurulf, B. (1986) 'En gransking av den svenska vallagen i ljuset av riksagsvalen 1970–1985', *Statsvetenskaplig Tideskrift*, vol. 89, no. 2, 123–9.

LaPalombara, J. (1987) *Democracy Italian Style* (New Haven: Yale University Press).

Laver, M. (1985) 'The Relationship Between Coalition Policy and Party Policy', *European Journal of Political Economy*, vol. 1 no. 2, pp. 243–69.

Laver, M. (1986) 'Between Theoretical Elegance and Political Reality: Deductive Models and Cabinet Coalitions in Europe', in G. Pridham (ed), *Coalitional Behaviour in Theory and Practice: An Inductive Model for Western Europe* (London: Cambridge University Press) p.. 32–44.

Laver, M. (1989) 'Party Competition and Party System Change: The Interaction of Coalition Bargaining and Electoral Competition', *Journal of Theoretical Politics*, vol. 1, no. 2, pp. 183–201.

Laver, M. (1991) 'Using Cluster Analysis to Model Coalition Formation in Policy Spaces of High Dimensionality', in N. Schofield (ed) *Coalition Theory and Coalition Government* (Dordrecht: Kluwer).

Laver, M., and Arkins, A. (1990) 'Coalition and Fianna Fail', in M. Gallagher and R. Sinnott (eds) *How Ireland Voted, 1989* (Galway: Centre for the Study of Irish Elections).

Laver, M., and Higgins, M. D. (1986) 'Coalition or Fianna Fail? The Politics of Inter-Party Government in Ireland', in G. Pridham (ed.), *Coalitional Behaviour in Theory and Practice* (Cambridge: Cambridge University Press).

Laver, M., and Hunt, W. B. (1992) *Policy and Party Competition* (New York: Routledge).

Laver, M., and Schofield, N. (1990) *Multiparty Government: the Politics of Co-alition in Europe* (Oxford: Oxford University Press).

Laver, M., and Shepsle, K. (1990) 'Coalitions and cabinet government', *American Political Science Review*, vol. 84, no. 3, pp. 837–90.

Leiserson, M. (1966) *Coalitions in Politics*, PhD, Yale University.

Leites, N. (1958) *House Without Windows* (New Haven : Yale University Press).

Lewin, L. (1984) *Ideological och Strategi* (Lund: Norstedts).

Lindstrom, U. (1985). *Fascism in Scandinavia 1920–40* (Stockholm: Almqvist & Wiksell).

Lindstrom, U. (1986) 'The Swedish Elections of 1985', *Electoral Studies*, vol. 5 no. 1, pp. 76–8.

Lindstrom, U. and Worlund, I. (1988) 'The Swedish Liberal Party', in E. Kirchner (ed.), *Liberal Parties in Western Europe* (Cambridge: Cambridge University Press).

Lipset, S. M. (1981) *Political Man: The Social Bases of Politics* (Expanded edition) (Baltimore, MD: Johns Hopkins University Press).

Lucas, N. (1974) *The Modern History of Israel* (Weidenfeld & Nicolson: London).

Luebbert, G. (1986) *Comparative Democracy: Policy-making and Governing Co-alitions in Europe and Israel* (Columbia University Press: New York).

Lyne, T. (1987) 'The Progressive Democrats, 1985–87', *Irish Political Studies*, vol. 2, pp. 107–124.

Mackie, T. T. and Rose, R. (1982) *The International Almanac of Electoral History* (London: Macmillan).

MacRae, D. (1963) 'Intraparty Division and Cabinet Coalitions in the Fourth French Republic', *Comparative Studies in Society and History*, 5, pp. 164–211.

MacRae, D. (1967) *Parliament, Parties and Society in France* (New York: St. Martin's Press)

Mair, P. (1987a) *The Changing Irish Party System* (Frances Pinter: London).

Mair, P. (1987b) 'Ireland', in I. Budge, D. Robertson, and D. Hearl (eds) *Ideology, Strategy and Party Changes* (Cambridge University Press: Cambridge)

Mair, P. (1987c) 'Policy competition' in M. Laver, P. Mair, and R. Sinnott (eds) *How Ireland Voted the Irish General Election, 1987* (Poolbeg Press: Dublin).

Mair, P. (1990) 'The Irish Party System into the 1990s', in M. Gallagher and R. Sinnott (eds) *How Ireland Voted, 1989* (Galway: Centre for the Study of Irish Elections).

Manzella, A. (1977). *Il parlamento* (Bologna: Il Mulino).

Marradi, A. (1982) 'Italy: From 'Centrism' to Crisis of Center-Left Coalitions', in E. C. Browne and J. Dreijmanis (eds) *Government Coalitions in Western Democracies*, (Longman: London).

Mass, P. F. (1982) *Kabinetsformaties 1959–1973* ('s-Gravenhage: North Holland Publishing Co.).

Mastropaolo, A. (1987) 'Ancora sul sistema dei partiti in Italia: tra spinte centrifughe e compensazioni centripete', *Teoria politica*, vol. 3, no. 1.

Mastropaolo, A. and Slater, M. (1987) 'Italy 1946–1979: Ideological Distances and Party Movements', in I. Budge, D. Robertson and D. Hearl (eds), *Ideology, Strategy and Party Change: Spatial Analyses of Post-War Election Programmes in 19 Democracies* (Cambridge University Press: Cambridge).

McKelvey, R. D. (1976) 'Intransitives in Multidimensional Voting Models and some Implications for Agenda Control. *Journal of Economic Theory*, 12, 472–82.

McKelvey, R. D., (1979) 'General Conditions for Global Intransitives in Formal Voting Models', *Econometrica*, 47, pp. 1085–1111.

McKelvey, R. D., and Schofield, N. (1987) 'Generalised Symmetry Conditions at a Core point', *Econometrica*, vol. 55, pp. 923–33.

Miller, N. R., Grofman, B., and Feld, S. L. (1989) 'The Geometry of Majority Rule', *Journal of Theoretical Politics*. vol. no. 4, pp. 406.

Moller, T. (1986) *Borgerlig Samverkan* (Uppsala: Diskurs).

Morgan, M-J. (1976). *The Modelling of Governmental Coalition Formation: A policy-based approach with interval measurement*, PhD, University of Michigan.

Nachmias, D. (1975). Coalition Politics in Israel, *Comparative Political Studies*, vol. 7, no. 3, pp. 316–33.

Nyman, O. (1982) 'The New Swedish Constitution', *Scandinavian Studies in Law*, vol. 26, 173–179.

Paltiel, K. Z. (1975) 'The Israel Coalition System', *Government and Opposition*, vol. 10, no. 4, pp. 397–414.

Peres, Y. and Shemer, S. (1984) 'The Ethnic Factor in Elections', in D. Caspi, E. Guttman and A. Diskin (eds) *The Roots of Begin's Success* (London: Croom Helm).

Peri, Y. (1984) 'Coexistence or Hegemony? Shifts in the Israeli Security Concept', in D. Caspi, E. Guttman and A. Diskin (eds) *The Roots of Begin's Success* (London: Croom Helm).

Pesonen, P. and Thomas, A. H. (1983) 'Coalition Formation in Scandinavia', in V. Bogdanor (ed.) *Coalition Government in Western Europe* (London: Heinemann) pp. 59–96.

Petersson, O. (1977) *Valjarna och valet 1976, Valundersokningar: Rapport 2* (Stockholm: Liber).

Petersson, O. (1979). *Regeringsbildningen 1978* (Stockholm: Raben & Sjogren).

Plott, C. R. (1967) 'A Potion of Equilibrium and it Possibility under Majority Rule', *American Economic Review*, vol. 57, pp. 787–806.

Predieri, A. (1975) *Il parlamento nel sistema politico italiano* (Comunita: Milano).

Pridham, G. (1986) *Coalitional Behaviour in Theory and Practice: an Inductive Model for Western Europe* (Cambridge: Cambridge University Press).

Pridham, G. (1986) 'Italy's Party Democracy and Coalitional Behaviour: A Case Study in Multidimensionality', in G. Pridham (ed.) *Coalitional Behaviour in Theory and Practice: An Inductive Model for Western Europe*, (Cambridge: Cambridge University Press).

Riker. W. (1962) *The Theory of Political Coalitions* (New Haven: Yale University Press).

Riksdagens Protokoll (The Protocols of the Riksdag) (Stockholm: Riksdagen, 1946–1986).

Ruin, O. (1968) *Melllan samlingsregering och tvapartisystem* (Stockholm: Bonniers).

Ruin, O. (1986) *I valfardsstatens tjanst* (Stockholm: Tidens Forlag).

Sarlvik, B. (1983) 'Scandinavia', In V. Bogdanor and D. Butler (eds). *Democracy and Elections: Electoral Systems and Their Political Consequences* (Cambridge: Cambridge University Press) pp. 122–148.

Sartori, G. (1976) *Parties and Party System* (Cambridge University Press: New York).

Schofield, N. (1983) Generic instability of majority rule', *Review of Economic Studies*, vol. 50, pp. 696–705.

Schofield, N. (1986) 'Existence of a Structurally Stable Equilibrium for a Non-Collegial Voting Rule', *Public Choice*, vol. 51, pp. 267–84.

Schofield, N. and Laver, M. (1985) 'Bargaining Theory and Portfolio Payoffs in European Coalition Governments 1945–83', *British Journal of Political Science*, vol. 15, pp. 143–164.

Seliktar, O. (1980), 'Electoral Cleavage in a Nation in the Making', in R. Rose (ed.) *Electoral Participation* (Sage: New Haven).

Seliktar, O. (1982) 'Israel: Fragile Coalitions in a New Nation', in E. C. Browne and J. Dreijmanis (eds) *Government Coalitions in Western Democracies* (Longman: London).

Shepsle, K. and Weingast, B. (1981) 'Structure Induced Equilibrium and Legislative Choice', *Public Choice* vol. 37, 503–19.

Strom, K. (1984) 'Minority Governments in Parliamentary Democracies: The Rationality of Non-winning Cabinet Solutions', *Comparative Political Studies*, 17, pp. 199–227.

Strom, K. (1990) *Minority Government and Majority Rule* (Cambridge: Cambridge University Press).

Strom, K. and Leipart, J. Y. (1989) 'Ideology, Strategy and Party Competition in Postwar Norway', *European Journal of Political Research*, vol. 17, pp. 263–88.

Swaan, A. de (1973) *Coalition Theories and Cabinet Formations: A Study of Formal Theories of Coalition Formation Applied to Nine European Parliaments After 1918* (Amsterdam: Elsevier).

Swaan, A. de (1982) 'The Netherlands: Coalitions in a Segmented Polity', in E. C. Browne and J. Dreijmanis (eds), *Government Coalitions in Western Democracies*, (New York: Longman) pp. 217–236.

Sykes, C. (1965) *Crossroads to Israel* (Collins: London).

Swaan, A. de and Mokken, R. (1980) 'Testing Coalition Theories: The Combined

Evidence', in L. Lewin, and E. Vedung (ed.) *Politics and Rational Action* (Dordrecht: Reidel).

Taylor, M., and Laver, M. (1973) 'Government Coalitions in Western Europe', *European Journal of Political Research*, vol. 1, 205–248.

The New York Times, 'Socialists Retain Power in Sweden: Greens in a Breakthrough', September 19, 1988.

Visser, A. (1986) *Alleen bij uiterste noodzaak? De rooms-rode samenwerking en hat einde van de brede basis 1948–1958* (Amsterdam: Elsevier).

Williams, P. M. (1964) *1964, Crisis and Compromise: Politics in the Fourth Republic* (Archon Books: Hamden, Conn.).

Wood, D. M. (1973) 'Responsibility for the Fall of Cabinets in the French Fourth Republic, 1951–1955', *American Journal of Political Science*, vol. 17, pp. 767–80.

Yishai, Y. (1968) 'Israel's Right Wing Proletariat', *Jewish Journal of Sociology*, vol. 24 no. 2, pp. 125–33.

Zuckermann, A. (1976) *Political Clienteles in Power: Party Factions and Cabinet Coalitions in Italy* (Sage: New York).

Zuckermann, A. (1979) *The Politics of Faction: Christian Democratic Rule in Italy* (New Haven: Yale University Press).

Index